"*Book Design Made Simp*   d online, and took me
book. It stood head and
every step of the way t   ook *Design Made Simple*
to every new book designer, whether they are familiar with InDesign or not. It's the ulti-
mate resource on creating a book using InDesign."

—LYLE LITZENBERGER, author of *Burke and Widgeon: A Hiker's Guide*, Coquitlam, BC

"Whether you are dreaming of publishing your first book or whether you are accomplished at book design, this promises to become the bible on book design. *Book Design Made Simple* covers so much more than the basics. From setting up the required software to practical advice and visuals of design and typography, how to obtain an ISBN and create a bar code to sending rock-solid press-ready files to the printer, this 500-page volume is truly a 'must have.'"

—ERNST VEGT, Coast Imaging Arts, prepress and color management professional, Comox, BC

"*Book Design Made Simple* is a golden goose for designers, authors, and anyone who wants to create a book. The instructions for InDesign are a revelation; Glenna and Fiona publish coveted secrets for saving time and adding magic to projects. Even experienced design-ers will profit from Glenna's and Fiona's wealth of intelligence and knowledge. I highly recommend *Book Design Made Simple*. It will make beginners look professional and pro-fessionals look even better."

—RAFAEL PEREZ, book cover designer, Colonus Publishing, Sandy, OR

"I recommend *Book Design Made Simple*. It is an excellent investment."

—KEVIN M. JOHNSON, MD, designer of *My Father, in Snow*, Madison, CT

"*Book Design Made Simple* presents a two-fold course in book design and production—the practical and the sublime. In a clear use of text and images the function and application of the power of InDesign is presented. Within this context the basics of good design and visual style—from page composition to typography—are offered in a manner that allows the reader to view options. This is not a recipe book, but a flexible process the reader may use to lay out the framework of a book. A perfect addition to the bookshelf of anyone who does multiple page layouts."

—KAREN SHEA, Karen Shea Design, Beverly, Massachusetts

book
design
made simple

A step-by-step guide to designing and typesetting
your own book using Adobe® InDesign®

FIONA RAVEN ✦ GLENNA COLLETT

12 PINES PRESS

VANCOUVER, CANADA ✦ BOSTON, MASSACHUSETTS

Published by 12 Pines Press
Vancouver, Canada
Boston, Massachusetts

E-mail: info@BookDesignMadeSimple.com

www.BookDesignMadeSimple.com

Library and Archives Canada Cataloguing in Publication Data

Fiona Raven, author
  Book design made simple / Fiona Raven, Glenna Collett.

Includes bibliographical references and index.
ISBN 978-0-9940969-0-6 (pbk.)

  1. Book design—Handbooks, manuals, etc. 2. Book design. I. Collett, Glenna, 1950–, author. II. Title.

Z246.R28 2015   686.2'252   C2015-902289-4

Library of Congress Control Number 2015904106

Editing by Joanna Eng
Book design by Fiona Raven
Proofreading by Dania Sheldon
Indexing by Katherine Stimson
Cover photograph by kertlis / iStock
Fiona's photo by Karen Massier Photography

Printed and bound by Friesens in Canada
First Printing January 2016
V. 1.0

MIX
Paper from responsible sources
FSC
www.fsc.org   FSC® C016245

The text in otherwise uncredited sample page designs is from either the first draft of this book or *Alice in Wonderland* by Lewis Carroll.

To my mentor, Richard Bartlett ~

the first person to have faith in me as a designer.

~ Glenna

◆　◆　◆

To my mum ~

the first self-publisher I ever knew,
who took a flyer on an inexperienced book designer
and launched my passion for book design.

Thanks, Mum! This one's for you.

~ Fiona

◆　◆　◆

And to YOU, our readers,
for inspiring us to write this book!

We hope you'll be equally inspired
to make your own book look its best.

~ Glenna & Fiona

Acknowledgments

We owe a lot to many people for their help, encouragement, and advice.

We are especially indebted to our first tester, Kevin Johnson, a doctor with no book production experience who wanted to design his sister's book, *Our Father, in Snow*. He used our first draft to design the pages and cover of the book, with outstanding results. We learned from his questions and appreciated his insightful comments. The result is a book that is twice as long, with many, many more examples and more precise directions.

Many thanks to Laurie Griffin and Erin Scullion for their thorough reading of the first draft. Renee and Mark D'Antoni of eBook DesignWorks graciously answered our questions and set us straight about some of the details of ebook conversion. Isobel Logan of EditFast generously explained the differences in usage of em dashes between North America and Australia. Brad Schmidt at Friesens offered technical expertise on prepress issues, and because of it we are confident that our directions are correct and up to date. And Wesley Raven was our hero in checking all of the hundreds of page references. Thank you!

A huge thanks to our copy editor, Joanna Eng, who not only made over 1,200 corrections to our manuscript, but also meticulously tested our instructions. Your work made this book so much better. Our proofreader, Dania Sheldon, corrected even more tiny inconsistencies throughout, and as a result, we are confident in presenting our words to the world. And finally, Katherine Stimson gave us a truly excellent index. For all of this work, we thank our outstanding production team.

We are so grateful to those of you who helped us with different aspects of self-publishing: writing reviews, advising us on media kits, taking head shots, referring us to distributors, liking and sharing our social media posts, and, most importantly, recommending us and our book to all your peeps in the biz. (You know who you are!) Thank you.

And finally, Glenna would like to thank her husband, George, for his patience as her work hours doubled during the writing of this book. And Fiona would like to thank her husband, Wes, her dad, Jack, and her sister-in-publishing, Jewelle, for their support and encouragement throughout.

We couldn't have done it without all of you!

Contents

Introduction

You've found your way to this book, so chances are good that you're a self-publishing author wanting to design and typeset your own book. This book is written specifically for *you*! Welcome!

Self-publishing a book involves a huge learning curve. So do designing and typesetting a book, but now you have *Book Design Made Simple* to guide you through every step of the production process. Think of this book as having two experienced book designers looking over your shoulder, offering suggestions and tips throughout the process. We've got your back!

We're assuming you've never used InDesign before, nor any other page layout software. Most likely you've written your book in Word and now want it to look professional and to compete with other books in the marketplace.

We'll explain how to lease InDesign and how you can expect it to differ from Word in **Part I: Getting Started**. You'll also get a guided tour of InDesign, and step-by-step instructions on how to set up your pages.

In **Part II: Creating Your Styles**, we'll explain what styles are for and why you need them, and lead you step by step through creating them for your book.

In **Part III: Formatting Your Pages**, you'll apply the styles you've created to all the text in your book. And by the end of this section, you'll have created a professional page design. If you're satisfied with the look of your pages, then you can skip the next part and head straight into adding images and/or typesetting your text.

At this stage, however, you may want to customize the design of your pages to suit your material. Perhaps you'd prefer a modern rather than traditional look for your pages, or a funky chapter opening page to suit your genre. In **Part IV: Designing Your Pages**, you'll find lots of design ideas and suggestions for your chapter opening pages, headings, page numbers, and every other element in your text. Have fun adding your own special touches! You'll also learn what to put in your book's front matter and back matter, and how to organize and design it, from title page to index.

Please don't think you'll need to read this entire book. Simply use the sections that'll help you design *your* book and feel free to skip the rest.

Adobe is constantly updating InDesign. So from time to time you may discover a new feature or find a process that works a little differently from what is described in this book. Every time you open InDesign, you'll see the Welcome screen (see page 12) which tells you about any updates or changes to InDesign.

In **Part V: Adding Shapes and Colors**, you'll learn how to create shapes and add colors to them. You might find that you need a shape to place in the background behind your sidebars or chapter numbers. And perhaps you'll decide to use color in your print book or, if not, in your ebook edition.

In **Part VI: Adding Images**, you'll learn how to add images to your pages, vary their size and placement, add captions, and optimize the images so they print looking their best. You'll also learn an easy way to keep your images organized on the computer. And if you don't have images inside your book, just skip this part.

Part VII: Typesetting is a chapter you won't want to skip. Here we explain how to polish your text so that it looks professionally typeset and flawless from start to finish.

Part VIII: Designing Your Cover guides you through the process of making your cover work in the marketplace to sell your book. You'll learn about using a cover image, choosing colors, finding a good arrangement for your title type, and combining all of that into a coherent unit. You'll also find out how to best use the space on your back cover and the flaps of your dust jacket—what elements to put there and how to arrange them for the greatest impact.

And, finally, in **Part IX: Preparing to Publish**, you'll obtain ISBNs and a barcode, and create a high-resolution PDF of your pages and cover to upload to your printer. In this part you'll learn about converting to ebooks, too.

Be sure to use the **Glossary** and **Index** at the back of this book to find what you're looking for. And note the list of InDesign **Keyboard Short-cuts** and the **Self-Publishing Process** chart. Please feel free to contact us at info@BookDesignMadeSimple.com if something in this book isn't clear. We're always looking for ways to make *Book Design Made Simple* the best it can possibly be for our readers.

And when you've finished designing your book using *Book Design Made Simple*, please send us a note. We'd love to hear from you! If you like, we'll also create a page in the Readers' Books section of www.BookDesign MadeSimple.com to show off your work.

All the best in designing success, and have fun!

Fiona and Glenna

 For the most part, ebooks can accommodate anything that goes into a print book, but there are exceptions, and they are noted with this symbol.

Part I: Getting Started

1

From Word to InDesign

You will soon discover that designing a book is nothing like writing a book, for you'll be more concerned with the way the words look than what they say. In general, InDesign cannot be thought of as any kind of word processing program. It is more like a drawing program in which you make shapes and then pour text into the shapes. And once you've done that, you can control every little thing about the type: the size, the amount of space between lines and between letters, the number of lines on a page, and so on.

If you wrote your book in a program other than Word, don't worry. See instructions on page 44.

Most likely you've written your book in Microsoft Word, and are familiar with how Word works. In Word, you begin at the top of your document and work downward in a linear fashion. Pre-made styles are available for titles and paragraphs, and are applied simply by selecting them.

InDesign allows you much more control over the different elements in your book, both on a large scale (for example, the overall size of your pages), right down to a very small scale (such as the amount of space surrounding a single letter).

How are the decisions you make carried out globally in your book? Well, that's where InDesign really shines!

Any large-scale changes (such as changes to your trim size or margins) are made on a master page that controls all other pages. When you make a large-scale change on a master page, all other pages in your book will change too.

For smaller-level changes, InDesign has a system of styles, including paragraph styles, character styles, object styles, table of contents styles, and so on. Each style includes detailed specifications for the appearance of one element.

Paragraph styles, for example, control the way your paragraphs look, similar to the way styles in Word work. You'll create a unique paragraph style for each different type of paragraph (main narrative, quotes, extracts, and so on), and apply one of those styles to every paragraph in your book. Then, if you subsequently make a change to a paragraph style, it'll globally change every paragraph with that style applied to it.

So *everything* in InDesign is explicitly controlled, not just the visible elements, but even the white space between paragraphs, words, and characters. InDesign works on several levels simultaneously, from the grand to the miniscule.

InDesign also allows you to place photos or drawings anywhere you like at any size—not just inside the margins, as in Word. You can tell the program to run type around the images, too, as you've seen in many print publications. You can run type vertically, at any other angle, or even on a curve if you want to, because InDesign incorporates many features that a drawing program would have. Using this great, comprehensive program, you can make an infinite variety of shapes and fill them with colors or images.

Don't worry; it's not difficult, it's just different! As you progress through *Book Design Made Simple*, you'll be guided through setting up the styles you need for *your* book—from the title page through the index—and applying them to the appropriate text or shapes. Then you'll be sure that everything in your book is consistent and can be changed quickly and easily if needed.

We truly hope that you find enjoyment and satisfaction in making the transition from writer to designer. By the time you finish the next two chapters of this book, you will have Adobe InDesign, Adobe Photoshop, and Adobe Acrobat on your computer. InDesign is the most popular design software in the graphics and publishing fields. Combining InDesign with the other two programs, you will have everything you'll need to complete your book project and get it off to the printer and your ebook conversion provider. And then when you're finished, you can remove the programs from your computer and end your lease agreement.

Let's get started!

Windows vs. Mac

InDesign works exactly the same way whether you are using Windows or a Mac operating system. The only difference is in the names of a few of the keyboard keys:

Windows uses **Control (Ctrl)**, **Alt (Alt)**, **Shift**, and **Enter**

Mac uses **Command (Cmd)**, **Option (Opt)**, **Shift**, and **Return**

In this book, the Windows and Mac abbreviations are combined for brevity. So rather than saying:

Press Control+Shift+S in Windows and
press Command+Shift+S on a Mac to "save as"

you'll see:

Press Ctrl/Cmd+Shift+S to "save as"

The numerous screenshots in this book were taken from both PC and Macintosh computers. They look so similar that most of the time we don't mention it, but when there is a difference, we show both.

Leasing InDesign

InDesign is created by Adobe and is available on their website at www.adobe.com. All Adobe software is available to lease by the month, and you can either lease individual programs (say, InDesign, Photoshop, and/or Acrobat), or simply lease their Creative Cloud package, which includes all their programs (recommended, as it also includes typefaces and off-site storage).

Although it costs a bit more per month to lease the Creative Cloud package, you'll probably find that Creative Cloud provides everything you need without your having to go out and find other programs, typefaces, or storage on your own.

Make sure your computer has the minimum requirements to run Creative Cloud!

You'll definitely need InDesign (for page layout), Photoshop (for images), and Acrobat (for creating PDFs for printing). You'll also use the typefaces that come with Creative Cloud (the service is called Typekit), and you may want to use their site for off-site backup of your working files.

Be aware that leasing the programs means that you will not own them, and you'll need to connect to the Internet in order to download the programs and try different fonts. When you're ready to lease InDesign or the Creative Cloud package, go to the Creative Cloud page of adobe.com and click on "Choose a plan," then look in the Individuals category and find the plan that is right for you.

Another option is a free one-month trial of InDesign, but it's not recommended for book design as it doesn't include the fonts you will need.

Here are the steps for setting up Creative Cloud on your computer:

1 Approve the license agreement.
2 Provide credit card or other payment information.
3 Download the desktop application (app), which you'll use to install Creative Cloud (CC).
4 Run the CC setup application. In the CC window that opens (see page 6), click the first button to install apps. Then choose InDesign, Photoshop, and Acrobat. Wait while the programs are synced to your computer. The installations take a while, but do not click anywhere

else on the screen while you're waiting. If you lose the screen you are on, click on the CC icon at the top of your screen (Mac) or at the bottom in your status bar (Windows) and then click Home (see below).

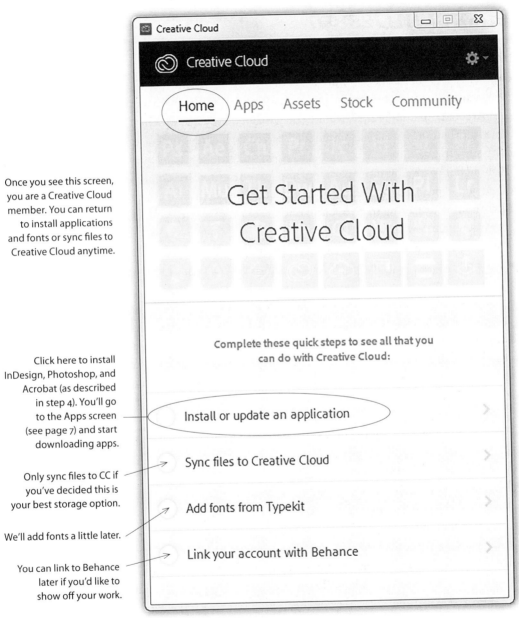

Once you see this screen, you are a Creative Cloud member. You can return to install applications and fonts or sync files to Creative Cloud anytime.

Click here to install InDesign, Photoshop, and Acrobat (as described in step 4). You'll go to the Apps screen (see page 7) and start downloading apps.

Only sync files to CC if you've decided this is your best storage option.

We'll add fonts a little later.

You can link to Behance later if you'd like to show off your work.

5 Once your applications are downloaded, your Apps screen will look similar to the one below. Next explore the CC pages:

- **Home**: You can install an app, sync files to CC, add fonts from Type-kit, and link your account with Behance. The Home screen also shows your activity stream (downloads, updates, and so on).
- **Apps** (see below) lists all the Adobe apps you've installed at the top, and the ones available to you below.

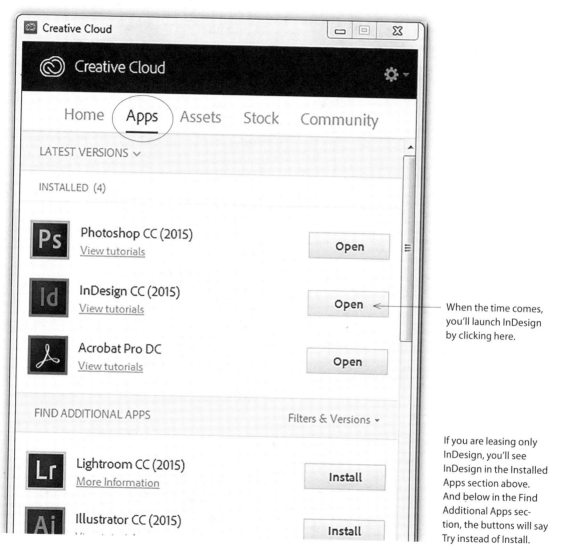

When the time comes, you'll launch InDesign by clicking here.

If you are leasing only InDesign, you'll see InDesign in the Installed Apps section above. And below in the Find Additional Apps section, the buttons will say Try instead of Install.

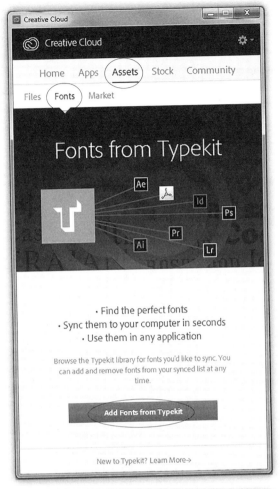

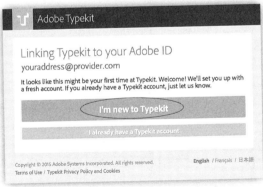

- **Assets:** Under Files you can sync your files to the Cloud and have access to them anywhere. Under Fonts, you'll find Typekit (see step 6). And Market includes content usable by paid CC members, including vectors, icons, patterns, brushes, and more.
- **Stock:** You can purchase images online through Adobe Stock.
- **Community** is the Behance site, an online gallery of work by designers and artists using Adobe products.

6 Under Assets>Fonts (see left), click Add Fonts from Typekit. This will take you to Adobe Typekit on the Internet. Typekit is a service that provides a huge number of fonts for CC members. The fonts are not actually *on* your computer, however; they are only synced to it. So any fonts you get from Typekit will no longer be available to you once you uninstall Creative Cloud; if you want to use them later, you'll need to buy them.

   The fonts you get from Typekit can be used in any Adobe application, plus in Microsoft Office and iWork. For your book design, you need only Sync fonts. Web fonts require an additional license. You'll find more information on buying, leasing, and the legal use of fonts on page 132.

7 Click on "I'm new to Typekit." Your email address is shown on the screen, and you'll have to provide the Adobe ID you created when you began the installation process. Your Typekit account will be set up and look similar to the one at the top of page 9.

8 Type "Minion" in the Search field, then click the Search icon to the right. Find the box with the Minion Pro font and click on it.

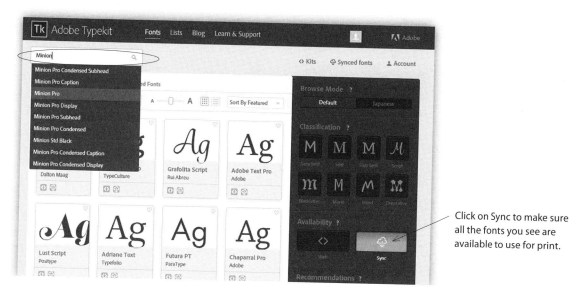

Click on Sync to make sure all the fonts you see are available to use for print.

9 Click on the Weights & Styles tab to get a feel for some of the terms used to describe type styles (italic, condensed, display, etc.) and weights (regular, bold, semibold, etc.) that are part of any type family. At the bottom of this screen you can also read more about Minion Pro, what it's commonly used for, its properties, and more.

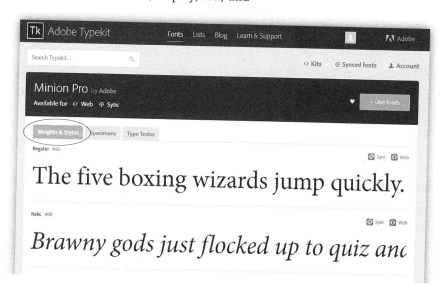

10 Click on the Specimens tab to see the same font shown at many differ-ent sizes. Notice that the units for the sizes are called *points*.

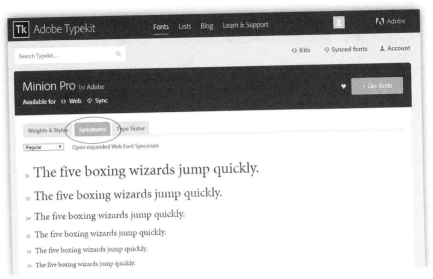

11 Now click on the Type Tester. Type the title of your book in the box. Use the slider to see it at different sizes and the drop-down list to try it with different type styles.

Click "+ Use fonts" in step 12

Style drop-down list and size slider

12 You'll be using the Minion Pro font throughout *Book Design Made Simple.* So click on the "+ Use fonts" button at the upper right.

13 On the next screen, select all the boxes that are available. Each of these has a note saying "Ready to sync" to the right, while others say "For web use only" or are grayed out. Now click "Sync selected fonts." Return to your Assets> Fonts tab (see page 8), and you'll see Minion on your list of synced fonts. (If for some reason the fonts didn't sync, follow the desktop sync troubleshooting guide.)

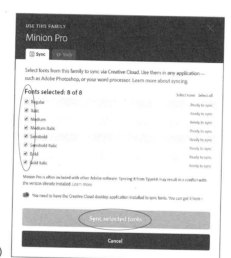

The Typekit fonts will be added to the fonts menu in each Adobe application, alongside all of your already-installed fonts. They will be immediately available in most other programs, but some (Microsoft Office, for instance) will need to be restarted to add the synced fonts to the menu.

Later on, you can return to Typekit (go to Assets> Fonts and click Manage Fonts) to look for other fonts. You'll see a screen similar to the one in step 8, with the classifications and properties to choose from on the right side of your screen (as shown to the right). You'll soon understand the classifications and choices, and be able to find what you're looking for quite efficiently.

Some of these type classifications and properties are defined in the glossary of this book.

A quick tour of InDesign

Now that you've leased and downloaded InDesign, this chapter will help you get familiar with it and learn the basics:

1. Starting a new document
2. Navigating through your document
3. Learning to use the tools in the Toolbox
4. Using panels
5. Watching the Control panel

Launch InDesign for the first time by double-clicking the program in Creative Cloud under Apps (see page 7). Once it's open, you'll see a screen that looks something like this:

opening screen

On a Macintosh, the background will be your desktop.

Throughout this book, you may see images of screens and dialog boxes that don't look quite like what you're seeing on your own computer, as there are many visual differences between Macintosh OS and Windows. You will find the same information on your screen, but perhaps in a different spot.

Click Done at the bottom of the box in the middle of the screen to close the box. At the top right of your screen it should say Essentials. This setting provides you with some of the panels you'll need, at the right edge of the screen. We will be adding several more panels there very soon.

1 Starting a new document

Start a new document by choosing File>New>Document. When the New Document dialog box appears, it will look similar to the one below.

Your measurements might be in millimeters or picas rather than inches. You'll change that later.

In chapter 7 you'll start a new document specifically for *your* book, but for now just make two changes to the dialog box: change the Number of Pages to 3, and check the box next to Facing Pages. This way you'll have a few pages to navigate through in the next example. Then click OK.

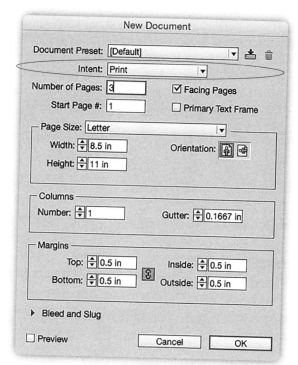

Don't worry if your New Document box doesn't look exactly like this one. It might be darker or have different values in the boxes. Just set the Number of Pages to 3, check the Facing Pages box, click OK, and turn the page to take a tour of InDesign.

InDesign provides different ways of completing most tasks. You can use the Control panel across the top, keyboard shortcuts, menus, or various other methods to accomplish the same task. After using the program for a while, you'll find which method works best for you.

For example, to view something larger, you can:
- use the Zoom Tool and click on the page a few times
- drag diagonally over an area with the Zoom Tool
- hold Ctrl/Cmd and press = a few times

Now your screen will look something like this:

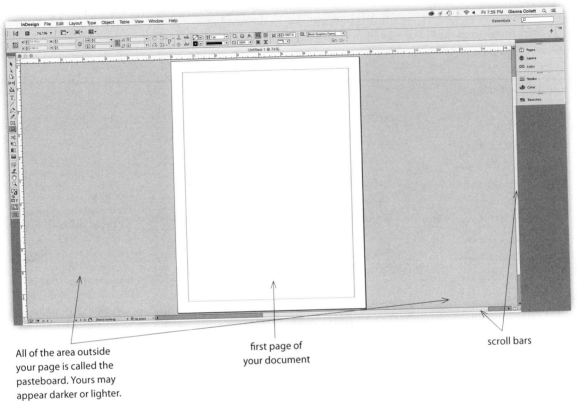

All of the area outside your page is called the pasteboard. Yours may appear darker or lighter.

first page of your document

scroll bars

2 Navigating through your document

The first page of your document is displayed on the screen. When you started this document, you checked Facing Pages in the New Document dialog box, and therefore your pages will be displayed in two-page spreads, or 2-*up* (except the first page, of course).

There are a few ways of viewing the pages in your document:

When you see a new or puzzling term, look in the glossary that begins on page 470 of this book.

• You can scroll up and down through the pages using the scroll bar on the right side of your document window, by rolling your mouse wheel back and forth, or by using the touchpad on your laptop.

- At the bottom left of your screen, you'll see the number 1. Click the downward-facing arrow just to the right and a pop-up menu will show you all the page numbers in your document. Choose any number to go directly to that page. Alternately, you can type Ctrl/Cmd+J and type in the page number you want to jump to, then hit Enter/Return.

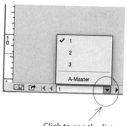

Click to see the list of all your pages.

- Click on the arrows immediately to the left and right of that pop-up menu and you'll proceed to the page before or after the current page, or the first or last page of your document.

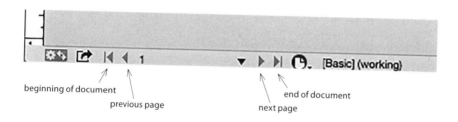

beginning of document

previous page

end of document

next page

- Also in your top menu bar is a drop-down menu that lets you display your pages at different sizes. You may want to see whole pages at a time or zoom in up to 4000% for fine-tuning your text.

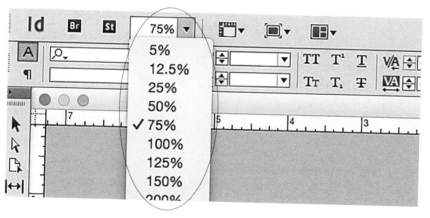

So the top and bottom of your screen have some great tools for navigating through your document.

Selection Tool

Type Tool

Hand Tool

Zoom Tool

View Tool

Type W
to toggle
between
Normal and
Preview.

3 Learning to use the tools in the Toolbox

The Toolbox is displayed on the left side of your screen. Each tool in the Toolbox has a different function. Hover over a tool and its function is displayed. When a tool is in use, there's a square behind it. In the Toolbox shown to the left, the Type Tool is currently in use.

For now, you'll only be using a few tools:

- **Type Tool** allows you to add text, select text, and make corrections or changes to it. Choose the Type Tool now, and create a text frame by holding down the left mouse button and dragging diagonally down and to the right anywhere on the page. When you release the mouse button, you'll see a cursor flashing. Type something, and you'll have created a text frame with text in it.

- **Selection Tool** allows you to select frames that contain text or images and make adjustments to them. Choose the Selection Tool now, then click on your text frame to select it. Press your up, down, left, and right arrow keys to move it a tiny bit at a time. Press the Delete key to delete it.

- **Hand Tool** allows you to move the page around on your screen. Choose the Hand Tool now, and your mouse pointer will change into a small hand icon. Click anywhere on the page to "grab" the page, then drag the page into any position you choose.

- **Zoom Tool** allows you to zoom in and out. Choose the Zoom Tool now, and hold down the left mouse button while dragging diagonally over a specific area to magnify it. Or, you can simply click anywhere on the page to zoom in a bit. To zoom out, press Alt/Opt while you click. The keyboard shortcut for zooming in is Ctrl/Cmd+ = and for zooming out is Ctrl/Cmd+ -.

- **View Tool** allows you to view your pages in different ways. **Normal** shows all your non-printing guides, such as margins. **Preview** shows your pages without non-printing guides, the way they'll appear in your printed book. Click and hold the View Tool to see the choices.

4 Using panels

Panels provide a quick and easy way to do things in InDesign. Each panel is for a specific group of functions. For example, the Pages panel is for navigating around the pages, the Character panel is for adjusting type characters, and the Paragraph panel is for adjusting paragraphs.

Panels are "docked," or parked, on the right side of your screen, with a few choices on how to display them. Find the drop-down menu for panels at the top right of your screen:

The drop-down menu to the left shows Essentials, but there are several other choices there that display a selection of panels.

Try several of the menus and see that they each include a different set of default panels. Start with the Typography menu, as it includes all the panels you'll need to get started. You can add other panels later as you need them by clicking the Window menu at the top of your screen, then choosing a panel to open. Once open, simply drag it into the docking area to attach it to the existing dock.

Because panels take up valuable space on your screen, you'll only want to display the panels you're actively using. The panels in your dock just show the name and icon of the panel, to save space. Click on one of the panel icons, and the panel will fly out to the left. Click on a different icon and watch its panel fly out while the first one disappears back into the dock. Notice that the panels are docked in groups of two or three.

Select the double-arrows at the top right of the dock, and the panels will expand to their normal size. However, you'll only see one panel from each group. The others are behind it and are accessed by selecting the tabs along the top of each group or by selecting the appropriate icon.

You may prefer to select the double-arrows again to reduce the panels to just the docked icons. This gives you the maximum screen area to view your document, and you can fly out the panels as you need them.

For designing your book, you'll be using five panels the most: the **Pages**, **Paragraph**, **Paragraph Styles**, **Character**, and **Character Styles** panels.

docked Typography panels

fly-out panel

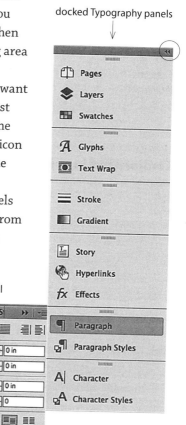

5 Watching the Control panel

The Control panel across the top of your workspace is loaded with information. Whenever you use the Type Tool, the Control panel displays text mode (top below), and whenever you use the Selection Tool, it displays object mode (bottom below). All of this information is also displayed in your docked panels, so you can choose where to make changes or find information.

Control panel in text mode

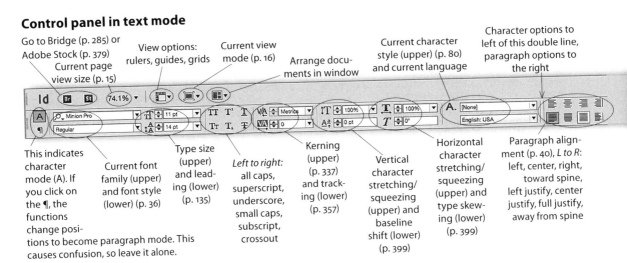

Go to Bridge (p. 285) or Adobe Stock (p. 379)

Current page view size (p. 15)

View options: rulers, guides, grids

Current view mode (p. 16)

Arrange documents in window

Current character style (upper) (p. 80) and current language

Character options to left of this double line, paragraph options to the right

This indicates character mode (A). If you click on the ¶, the functions change positions to become paragraph mode. This causes confusion, so leave it alone.

Current font family (upper) and font style (lower) (p. 36)

Type size (upper) and leading (lower) (p. 135)

Left to right: all caps, superscript, underscore, small caps, subscript, crossout

Kerning (upper) (p. 337) and tracking (lower) (p. 357)

Vertical character stretching/ squeezing (upper) and baseline shift (lower) (p. 399)

Horizontal character stretching/ squeezing (upper) and type skewing (lower) (p. 399)

Paragraph alignment (p. 40), L to R: left, center, right, toward spine, left justify, center justify, full justify, away from spine

Control panel in object mode

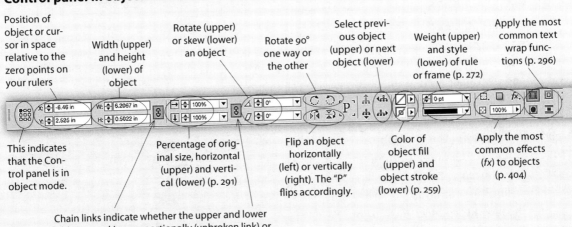

Position of object or cursor in space relative to the zero points on your rulers

Width (upper) and height (lower) of object

Rotate (upper) or skew (lower) an object

Rotate 90° one way or the other

Select previous object (upper) or next object (lower)

Weight (upper) and style (lower) of rule or frame (p. 272)

Apply the most common text wrap functions (p. 296)

This indicates that the Control panel is in object mode.

Percentage of original size, horizontal (upper) and vertical (lower) (p. 291)

Flip an object horizontally (left) or vertically (right). The "P" flips accordingly.

Color of object fill (upper) and object stroke (lower) (p. 259)

Apply the most common effects (fx) to objects (p. 404)

Chain links indicate whether the upper and lower fields are working proportionally (unbroken link) or independently (broken link) (p. 289).

In this book, you'll use the panels in your dock for most functions, so don't worry about learning about all the uses for the Control panel. Just be aware that it displays a lot of information, and sometimes you'll find it very handy either to use as a reference or to make a quick change.

Once you're more familiar with the panels in the dock, you'll start to recognize their counterparts in the Control panel.

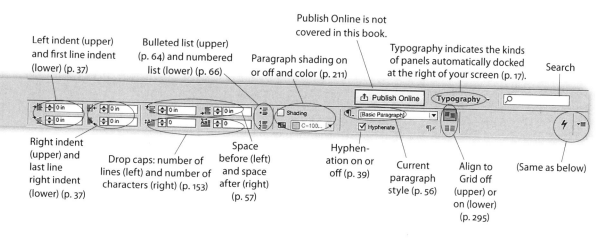

Publish Online is not covered in this book.

Left indent (upper) and first line indent (lower) (p. 37)

Bulleted list (upper) (p. 64) and numbered list (lower) (p. 66)

Paragraph shading on or off and color (p. 211)

Typography indicates the kinds of panels automatically docked at the right of your screen (p. 17).

Search

Right indent (upper) and last line right indent (lower) (p. 37)

Drop caps: number of lines (left) and number of characters (right) (p. 153)

Space before (left) and space after (right) (p. 57)

Hyphenation on or off (p. 39)

Current paragraph style (p. 56)

Align to Grid off (upper) or on (lower) (p. 295)

(Same as below)

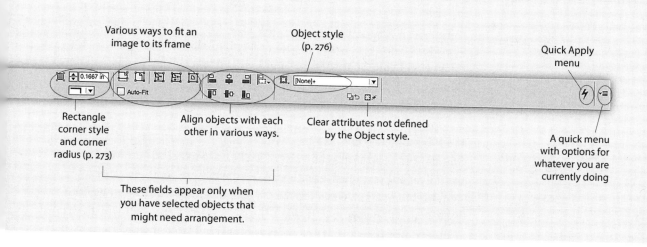

Various ways to fit an image to its frame

Object style (p. 276)

Quick Apply menu

Rectangle corner style and corner radius (p. 273)

Align objects with each other in various ways.

Clear attributes not defined by the Object style.

A quick menu with options for whatever you are currently doing

These fields appear only when you have selected objects that might need arrangement.

Choosing your trim size

Trim size is the size of the *pages* of a book, regardless of the type of book cover. A hardcover book will appear larger than a softcover book with the same trim size because the hardcover itself is larger than the pages.

What size should your book be? You'll want to consider three things when choosing your book's trim size:

- What sizes are other books in the same genre?
- Do you want a thinner or thicker book?
- Where will your book be printed?

What sizes are other books in the same genre?

Your book should fit in perfectly with other books in the same genre. Browse your bookstore or library and see what sizes the other books are.

Do you want a thinner or thicker book?

If you have a lot of text and want to keep your printing costs down, moving to a slightly larger trim size can lower your page count and save printing costs. Increasing your trim size from 5″ × 8″ to 6″ × 9″ will make a thick book slightly thinner. Or, if your book promises to be a slim volume because of a low word count, choose a smaller trim size to maximize the thickness of your book. A 5″ × 8″ book will appear thicker and less "floppy" than a 6″ × 9″ book with the same word count and give more perceived value to your potential reader.

Where will your book be printed?

Standard trim sizes are the most cost-effective to print, and some printers only print certain sizes of books. To the left are some examples of standard trim sizes. Often, at the design stage, you won't know where your book will be printed. If that's the case, select a size that will give you choices down the road. If you change your mind later, it won't be a disaster. Chapter 19 offers instructions on how to change your trim size.

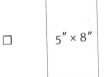

5″ × 8″

5.5″ × 8.5″

6″ × 9″

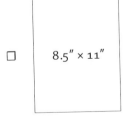

8.5″ × 11″

the most common
standard trim sizes

Printers' specifications for trim sizes

Printers offer standard trim sizes for cost-effective printing. Below are standard trim sizes from a sampling of printers, just to get you started. This is only a small sampling, so if you have a printer in mind, don't hesitate to contact them directly and ask for their standard book sizes. Also, keep in mind that printers' specifications change from time to time, so be sure to double-check these specs when you're ready to begin your book design. See page 22 for an explanation of the different printing methods.

	5"×8"	5.5"×8.5"	6"×9"	7"×10"	8.5"×11"
Digital printers (for short-run printing)					
Adibooks adibooks.com		•	•	•	•
Blitzprint blitzprint.com	•	•	•		•
Bookmasters bookmasters.com	•	•	•		•
Bookmobile bookmobile.com	•	•	•		•
DeHART's deharts.com	•	•	•		
Printorium printoriumbookworks.islandblue.com	•	•	•		
Print-on-demand printers					
CreateSpace createspace.com	•	•	•	•	•
IngramSpark ingramspark.com	•	•	•	•	•
Lightning Source lightningsource.com	•	•	•	•	•
Traditional printers (offset press)					
Friesens friesens.com	•	•	•	•	•
Puritan Capital puritanpress.com	•	•	•	•	•
Replika replikapress.com	•	•	•	•	•
Sheridan sheridanbooks.com		•	•	•	•
Transcontinental tcprinting.tc	•	•	•	•	•

Two methods of printing

	Offset printing on a press	Digital printing
Method	Books have traditionally been printed on a printing press using ink. A full-color book cover is printed with four ink colors (cyan, magenta, yellow, and black, or CMYK). The pages are usually printed with black ink on large sheets of paper, which are then folded into signatures (see page 321). Sheet-fed presses use 32-page signatures and are better for printing photographs and color; web presses use 48-page signatures and are more cost-effective for printing text and line art (black line drawings with no grays).	Laser printer technology allows books to be printed on high-quality laser printers using toner. The full-color cover is printed on cardstock and the pages on paper. The term **short-run printing** refers to digitally printing a small volume of books (say 20 or 200). Print-on-demand (POD) refers to POD printers that use digital printing to print and ship books after they are ordered (often one at a time).
Cost comparison	Offset printing is very cost-effective in larger quantities: the more copies printed at a time, the less it costs per book. However, you need to print at least 1,000 copies to make your offset printing cost-effective because of the cost of setting up the press.	It is less expensive to print books using digital printing if you want to print only a small number of books. However, digitally printed books are more expensive to produce per book than books printed on a press, as there is no cost saving for printing in quantity. Each book costs the same, no matter how many or few are printed.
Quality comparison	Offset printing allows you to control the quality of your book and gives you lots of flexibility. You can work with your printer to choose your book size, type of paper, binding, and many other options, to create a quality book exactly the way you want it. Offset printers offer several choices of paper, including environmentally friendly papers with recycled content.	Digital printing offers limited choices of trim size (usually standard sizes like 5.5" × 8.5" or 8.5" × 11") and usually two choices of paper (thinner and thicker). Book pages are printed with black ink only, and book covers are printed in color that can vary up to 10% on any given day (e.g., it might be slightly pinker or greener one day). However, many books look just fine within these limitations, and most readers would not know the difference.
Which is better?	Offset printing is better if you're printing in quantity or if you want to choose a certain trim size or paper for your book. Some publishers use digital printing initially for advance review copies to test their market and, if the book does well, switch to a larger print run on a press later.	Digital printing is better if you want smaller quantities and if your book is a standard size. Some publishers have already sold a large print run of books and now just want to print small quantities digitally as needed to keep their book in stock.

Planning your pages

6

Before setting up your pages in InDesign, take a few minutes to figure out what you'll need to include in your book pages. Use this chapter to make two checklists: one of the types of pages you'll include in the front and back matter of your book, and the other of the typographic elements you'll need to use throughout your book.

1 Choosing your front and back matter pages

Books can have several pages before and after the main text. As readers, we expect to find at least some of these pages in every book. A simple book, such as a novel, may only include a title page, copyright page, and dedication page at the front of the book. A nonfiction book may include a title page, copyright page, dedication page, table of contents, foreword, preface, and introduction in the front, and perhaps a glossary and index in the back. The material at the front of the book is called front matter, and the material at the back is called back matter.

On pages 24 and 25 you'll see the typical order of pages. All of the pages in the front and back matter are optional except the title page and copyright page. Odd-numbered pages are on the right-hand side of the book (called recto pages), and even-numbered pages are on the left (called verso pages).

Which types of pages will you need for your front and back matter? And is your book divided into parts or sections? Review the next two pages and make a note of which pages you might include in your book.

In a book, every single page is counted whether a page number is showing or not.

verso pages	recto pages
	half title
	i
blank	title
ii	iii
copyright ©	dedication
iv	v
blank	contents
vi	vii
contents 2 or blank	acknowledg- ments
viii	ix
blank	introduction
x	xi
introduction 2 or blank	
xii	

Front matter (includes some or all of these pages)

☐ **half title** includes just the book title

☑ **title page (mandatory)** includes the book title, subtitle, author's name, and (optional) publisher's company, city, and logo

☑ **copyright page (mandatory)**

☐ **dedication**

☐ **quote or epigraph**

☐ **contents** (table of contents)

☐ **list of illustrations**

☐ **foreword** written by someone other than the author

☐ **preface** written by the author

☐ **acknowledgments** (or they can go at the back of the book)

☐ **introduction**

There are only two pages you *must* include in your front matter: a title page and a copyright page. The title page must go on a recto page, and the copyright page must go on the verso page immediately following the title page (in other words, the copyright page is printed on the back of the title page).

All other pages in the front matter are optional. The usual order of the front matter is shown above. It's customary to begin each new item on a recto page (which may cause a few blank verso pages), or you may choose not to start each new item on a recto page, and that's fine too. You may decide that a Contents requiring two pages looks nicer on a spread. You'll see what suits *your* book when the time comes.

Front matter pages are usually numbered with lowercase roman numerals (i, ii, iii, and so on). It is less common, but still acceptable, to number a whole book consecutively starting with number 1. Page numbers are only added to pages following the Contents and never to blank pages. However, your final page count includes all blank pages.

Main text

☐ **page** 1 chapter 1 starts here, on a recto page

Or, if your main text is divided into parts:

☐ **page** 1 part 1 heading page
☐ **page** 2 blank
☐ **page** 3 chapter 1 starts here

verso pages	recto pages
	part one 1
blank 2	chapter one 3

Back matter (includes some or all of these pages)

☐ **acknowledgments** (if not included at the front of the book)

☐ **appendix(es)** usually listed as Appendix A, B, C, etc., or I, II, III, etc.

☐ **endnotes** numbered, sometimes divided into chapters

☐ **abbreviations**

☐ **glossary**

☐ **bibliography or references**

☐ **index(es)**

verso	recto
last page of text or blank #	appendix #
appendix 2 or blank #	endnotes #
endnotes 2 or blank #	index #
index 2 or blank #	

Including back matter in your book is optional. Most nonfiction books include some back matter, perhaps a glossary, bibliography, or index. The order of pages shown above is customary but not mandatory. It's recommended that the index go last.

Back matter pages are numbered continuously with the main text. If your main text ends on page 138, your back matter will start on page 139.

As a self-publisher, you may want to include a few extra pages at the back of your book, such as a page advertising other products and services you offer, and/or an "About the Author" page with a photo and bio.

2 Choosing which typographic elements to include

Every book is different, and before creating your page design you'll need to know which typographic elements to include in your book design. For example, look carefully at this page. It starts with a heading, followed by a few paragraphs of text. Below are bulleted lists with run-in subheads. A running foot and folio (page number) are at the bottom.

The treatment of these elements was planned in the design stage to make this book easy for readers to follow. Flip through the pages and you'll easily find where each new part begins, the start of each chapter, the main headings, and so on.

The goal of good book design is to guide readers through your book in an unobtrusive way. Do this by providing clear and consistent treatments for each element.

The two most common elements in a book, and ones you'll find in your manuscript, are:

- **chapter openings** can be as simple as starting a new page, or can include a number, title, and/or opening quote
- **main text** this is your book's narrative

Your manuscript may also include:

- **no indents** the first paragraph following any heading, including the chapter title, is not indented. This is traditional, and it does look nice and neat.
- **paragraph separators** extra space between paragraphs, sometimes including an ornament or asterisks (* * *), to denote the passage of time or a change of subject
- **bulleted lists** any list with bullets, like this one
- **numbered lists** same as bulleted lists except with numbers
- **extracts** lengthy quotations within the main text, usually indented or set in slightly smaller type to set them apart
- **sidebars** text expanding on the main text but set apart from it by a different type treatment or background, like the one opposite
- **run-in subheads** headings that are on the same line as the text they precede, like this one

Labels (margin annotations): heading 1, no indents, main text with indent, run-in subhead, bulleted list, running foot, folio

- **captions** explanatory notes for text or images
- **chapter numbers** can be spelled out (chapter one), a combination of words and digits (chapter 1), or simply digits (1)
- **chapter titles** can vary in length from one word to a phrase requiring multiple lines
- **opening quotes** a short quote at the beginning of each chapter
- **quote attributions** crediting the author of an opening quote
- **headings** if you have more than one level of heading, separate them into Heading 1, Heading 2, Heading 3, and so on. Heading 1 will be the most prominent heading, and each subsequent level will be less prominent so the reader can follow your hierarchy
- **running heads or feet** a repetitive heading above or below the main text. Often the book title goes on the verso page, and either the chapter title or the author's name goes on the recto page
- **folios** page numbers

Look through your manuscript now and make a note of all the typographic elements you'll need to include in your book design.

sidebar
↓

☑ **main text**

  ☑ text

  ☑ no indents

  ☐ paragraph separators

  ☐ bulleted lists

  ☐ numbered lists

  ☐ extracts

  ☐ sidebars

  ☐ run-in subheads

☐ **images**

  ☐ captions

☐ **chapter openings**

  ☐ chapter numbers

  ☐ chapter titles

  ☐ opening quotes

  ☐ quote attributions

☐ **headings**

  ☐ heading 1

  ☐ heading 2

  ☐ heading 3

☐ **page navigation**

  ☐ running heads or feet

  ☐ folios

7 *Creating your document*

Next you'll create a document for the pages of your book. All your book pages will be contained in one document, so it's important that this document is set up properly from the start.

This document will ensure that all your pages have consistent margins and spacing. You'll also create a paragraph style for your main text. This style will define the typeface and settings for your main text and, once applied to your paragraphs, they'll all be consistent.

Start by closing the document you experimented with in chapter 4 by clicking File>Close (there's no need to save this document). Next you'll set up a document for *your* book as described in this chapter, and chances are the settings will be just fine for your whole book. If you want to adjust a few things later on, you'll be able to do so easily. Once your document is set up, you'll be able to change your trim size, margins, or any of your paragraphs quickly, easily, and globally, simply by changing a few settings in your styles.

To create your document, the steps you'll take are:

1 Setting your Preferences
2 Starting a new document
3 Setting your Basic Paragraph style
4 Saving your document

1 Setting your Preferences

InDesign comes with a default set of Preferences. Not all of these are optimal for book design (because InDesign is used for many other kinds of design), so while no documents are open, make a few changes to your Preferences, and these will stay in effect for every document you open.

Choose Edit>Preferences>Interface (Windows) or InDesign>Preferences>Interface (Mac). This is one of the few menus in which Windows and Mac OS differ.

The Interface preferences affect the way the windows look on your screen. A light color theme is used for the screenshots in this book, but you may choose any color theme you like.

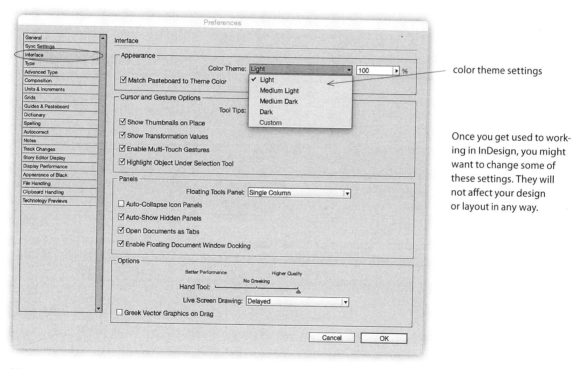

color theme settings

Once you get used to working in InDesign, you might want to change some of these settings. They will not affect your design or layout in any way.

You may see UI Scaling included among the Preferences categories on the left. It deals with scaling the size of the user interface (the size of the type in your panels, for example) on your monitor. In this book we're not concerned with these settings, but if you need to adjust the scaling, feel free to do that.

Now choose the Type tab on the list of Preferences. Fill in the check-boxes as shown below.

Notice this setting. It means that in order to select a single line of type and nothing else above or below it, you will put your cursor in the line of type and then click 3 times.

In order to select a single word, you'll click twice. To select an entire para-graph, you'll click 4 times.

Don't worry—we'll remind you of this again later.

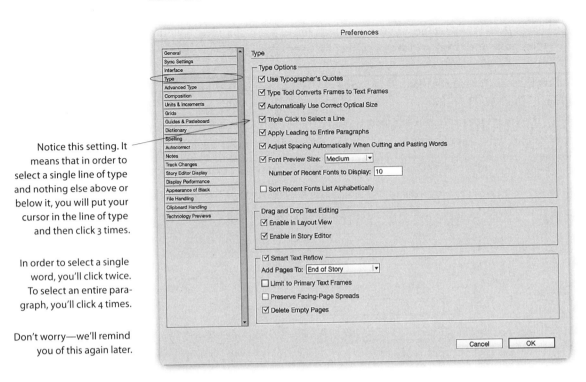

Next you'll check some settings on the Advanced Type tab. Type "67" in the Superscript and Subscript boxes if that is not the default setting, and leave the rest of the dialog box alone.

The Size settings for ^{superscript} and $_{subscript}$ characters determine the percentage of full-size characters that they will be. If they are any less than 60% of full size, they are usually too small to read. Sixty-seven percent is usually a good, readable size.

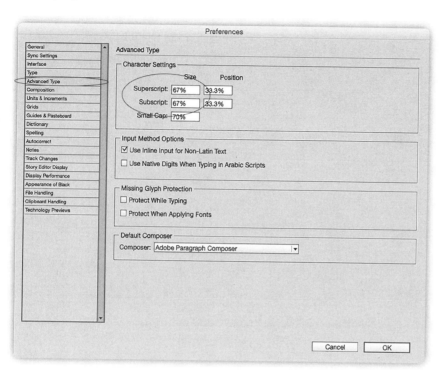

Next, select the Composition tab on the left and check the boxes as shown below. For now, don't try to understand the meanings of these settings. By the time you've finished with your book design, they will all be perfectly clear. If you're curious, though, the terms are all included in the glossary at the back of this book.

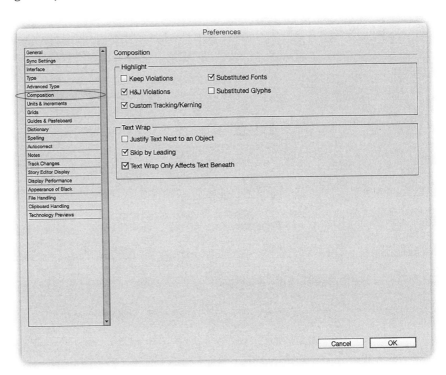

BOOK DESIGN MADE SIMPLE · PART I: GETTING STARTED

Finally, select the Units & Increments tab on the left, and under Ruler Units, change both Horizontal and Vertical to Inches.

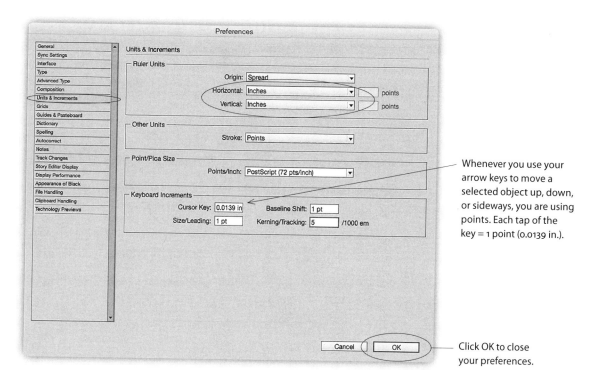

Whenever you use your arrow keys to move a selected object up, down, or sideways, you are using points. Each tap of the key = 1 point (0.0139 in.).

Click OK to close your preferences.

Inches, millimeters, points, or picas?

- Historically, typographers used points and picas (12 points = 1 pica; 72 points or 6 picas = 1 inch. Fonts are based on point sizes, such as 9-point Myriad, used in this sidebar).

- Printers outside North America use millimeters because their paper and book sizes are metric.

- Printers within North America use inches because their paper and book sizes are imperial.

- If your book is set up in inches and goes to a printer that uses metric measurements, it's no problem whatsoever, as long as the trim size is accurate in whatever measurement you've used.

2 Starting a new document

Start a new document by clicking File>New>Document. When the New Document dialog box appears, fill out the dialog box as shown below.

If you already know your book's trim size, feel free to add it into the width and height boxes now. If you're not sure yet, just use the trim size shown, and you can easily change it later on.

The margins shown work well for trim sizes 5″ × 8″, 5.5″ × 8.5″, and 6″ × 9″.

If your book will have a larger trim size, such as 7″ × 10″ or 8.5″ × 11″, use these margins for now. You'll adjust your margins for a larger trim size later on, in chapter 20.

This link should be "broken" to allow all the margins to have different sizes. If, by default, it's not broken, just click once to change it.

If you don't see the Bleed and Slug options at the bottom, click the little triangular button.

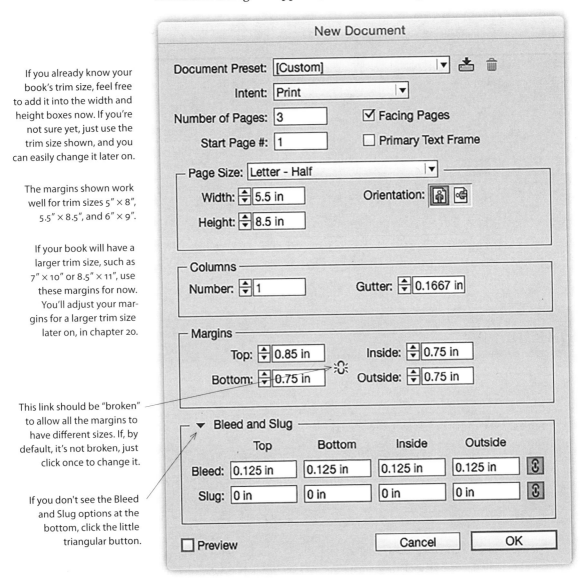

When you've completed the dialog box, click OK.

3 Setting your Basic Paragraph style

A paragraph style is a group of settings that can be applied to any number of paragraphs to make them all consistent. It specifies the typeface, type size, indents, and any other settings you choose.

The beauty of paragraph styles is that once you've applied them to your text, you can change all the text globally just by changing the paragraph style.

Every InDesign document comes with a default Basic Paragraph style. Open your Paragraph Styles panel and you'll see that your document already includes a paragraph style called Basic Paragraph. The style name is in square brackets because it's a default style and you don't have the option of deleting it. You'll use this style as a basis for all your text and adjust the settings so your type will look great.

Double-click the Basic Paragraph style in your Paragraph Styles panel, and you'll see the Paragraph Style Options dialog box:

Paragraph Styles panel

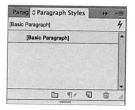

The Basic Paragraph style for *this* book specifies:

• Chaparral type, size 10.5 pt
• leading 14 pt
• left aligned

and so on.

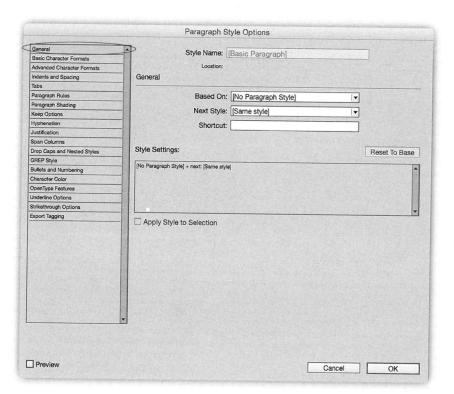

On the left side of the dialog box are several different categories.

The General category is selected in the example shown here. You needn't worry about all the categories and options. The ones you'll need are explained in this chapter.

General

No need to change any settings in the General category. You'll change these options in future paragraph styles, but the Basic Paragraph style is fine with the defaults.

Basic Character Formats

This is where you'll set the typeface and type size for the main narrative in your book. Select options from the drop-down menus to match what you see below.

The settings shown here are a good starting point for your book. This doesn't mean you're stuck with these settings. You may decide to change them later on, but for now they'll do just fine.

You synced Minion Pro to your computer in chapter 3. But if you do not see it in your list of available font families, go into the Creative Cloud application and click on Assets>Fonts> Add Fonts from Typekit. Type "Minion Pro" in the Search Typekit box. When you see the fonts displayed, click "+ Use fonts."

Minion is a typeface commonly used for all sorts of books, including fiction and nonfiction. It is easy to read and looks good at both small and large sizes. It includes bold, italics, and small caps, as well as condensed type and special ornaments and figures.

Leading is the space between lines of type. Tracking controls the amount of space between letters.

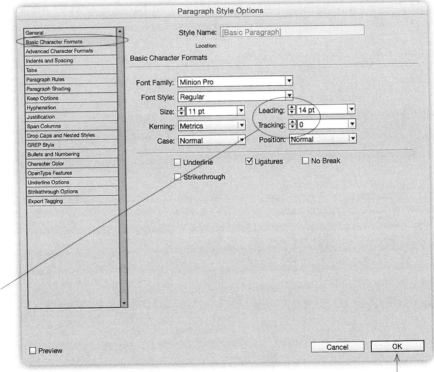

There's no need to click OK until you've made changes in all the tabs in the Paragraph Style Options in this chapter.

Advanced Character Formats

There's no need to change any settings in Advanced Character Formats unless your book is in another language or in a version of English other than U.S. English. If so, select the appropriate language from the drop-down menu.

Indents and Spacing

This category lets you set your indents, as well as spaces before and after paragraphs. The only setting you need to change is the Alignment. Make sure it's set to Left Justify. That way, your text will be left justified (aligned on the left and right, which is standard for books).

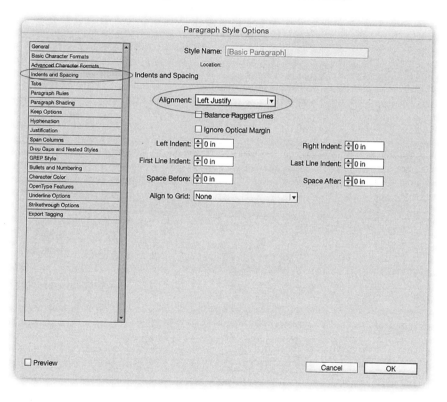

This book is set with unjustified, or ragged right, type. In InDesign, ragged right alignment is called "Left."

Tabs, Paragraph Rules, Paragraph Shading

No need to change any settings in the Tabs, Paragraph Rules, or Paragraph Shading categories.

Keep Options

In book typesetting, it's okay to have the first line of a paragraph be the last line on a page (an orphan) if it's unavoidable. However, it's never okay to have the last line of a paragraph be the first line on a page (a widow). The settings below will ensure that widows never happen.

Orphans are defined differently in various typography books. Some say an orphan is as described here, the first line of a paragraph at the bottom of a page.

Orphans are also defined as the last line of *any* paragraph containing only a very short word or phrase. This leaves a mostly empty linespace between paragraphs.

Generally, any word or line fragments stranded by themselves at the beginning or end of a paragraph are best avoided if possible.

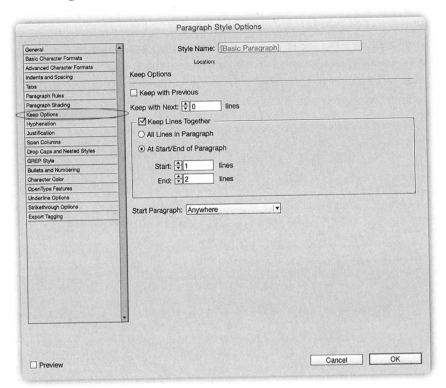

Widows are *never* okay.

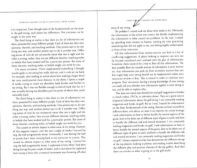

A few orphans are okay if kept to a minimum.

Hyphenation

These hyphenation settings are recommended for justified text. They ensure that:

- there aren't too many hyphens in a row
- words don't get broken with just two letters on a line, such as op-era or opi-um
- the last word in a paragraph isn't hyphenated, leaving part of a word alone on the last line

With these settings, you can be confident that most, if not all, of your paragraphs will have even spacing and not too many hyphens.

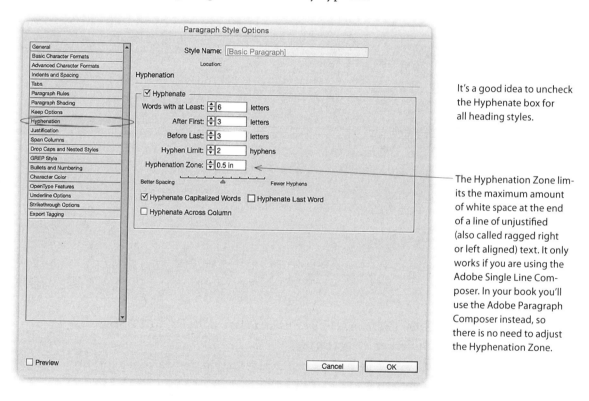

It's a good idea to uncheck the Hyphenate box for all heading styles.

The Hyphenation Zone limits the maximum amount of white space at the end of a line of unjustified (also called ragged right or left aligned) text. It only works if you are using the Adobe Single Line Composer. In your book you'll use the Adobe Paragraph Composer instead, so there is no need to adjust the Hyphenation Zone.

Justification

When text is justified, InDesign must do its best to make your type look as evenly spaced as possible, a difficult task as every line contains a different number of characters. These settings allow InDesign to add or remove space between words (word spacing) and between letters (letter spacing), and even to make the characters slightly wider or narrower (glyph scaling), in order to make your paragraphs look their best.

The Adobe Paragraph Composer adjusts letter spacing and word spacing to achieve the best look for the paragraph as a whole. The Adobe Single Line Composer adjusts spacing for the best look of each line separately.

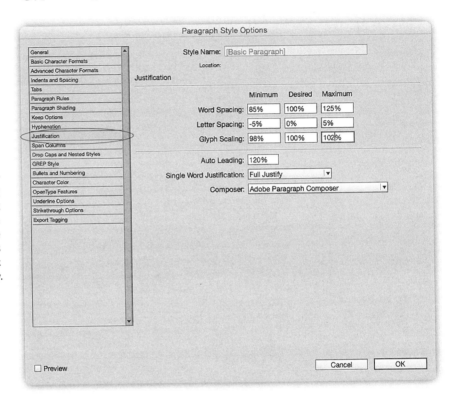

Span Columns, Drop Caps and Nested Styles, GREP Style, Bullets and Numbering

There's no need to change any settings in the Span Columns, Drop Caps and Nested Styles, GREP Style, or Bullets and Numbering categories.

Character Color

This is the color of your text, and it is always set to Black. This is the default color, hence the square brackets. Using the default color ensures that the black color of your text isn't made up of a combination of other colors, so it will print properly with one ink color.

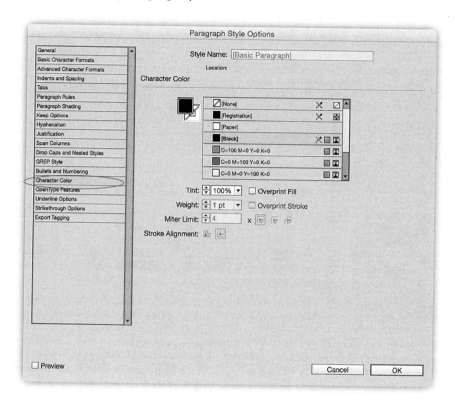

The solid black square (■) signifies the color of the type. The other square (□) behind it signifies the color of the outline around the type. Since we don't want any outlines around our letters, we make sure that the outline color is None.

You can switch between fill (■) and outline (□) by clicking on the symbol that's In back to bring it to the front.

You will encounter the fill and outline symbols often when you work with objects and design your cover (see chapter 31).

OpenType Features

You can choose the way numbers (called figures) are displayed in your book. Oldstyle figures look like this: 1234567890. They are the same size as the lowercase letters in your text. Lining figures look like this: 1234567890. They are the same size as the uppercase or capital letters.

Choose Proportional Oldstyle if your book is a novel or nonfiction book. However, if the numbers in your main text are very important (such as in a math, science, or history book), then choose Proportional Lining instead. The term "proportional" means that the numbers will be spaced so that they look their best visually. For example, the number 8 will get more space than the number 1 because 8 is wider.

Oldstyle figures look nicer than lining figures in regular text because they match in size and therefore aren't emphasized more than the surrounding text.

Proportional oldstyle:

a1b2c3d4e5f6g7h8i9j10

PROPORTIONAL LINING:

A1B2C3D4E5F6G7H8I9J10

Later you may choose to create a different style for charts or tables where it's important that the numbers line up in columns. You'll choose Tabular figures in that case (either oldstyle or lining), because Tabular figures are each allocated the same amount of space, so they'll line up properly in columns.

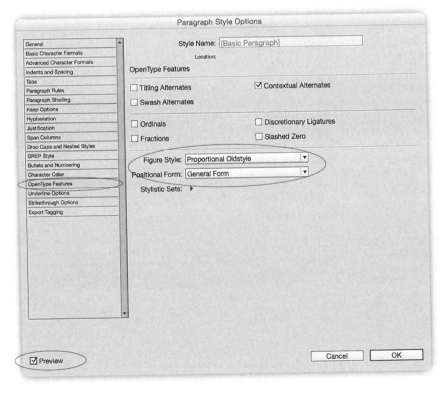

Check Preview.

Underline Options, Strikethrough Options, Export Tagging

No need to change any settings in the Underline Options, Strikethrough Options, or Export Tagging categories.

Once you've set all your options as shown, make sure the Preview box in the bottom left corner is checked, then click OK.

Open your Character panel and you'll see the new settings you created in the Basic Paragraph style. Then open your Paragraph panel and see the new settings there.

Character panel

Paragraph panel

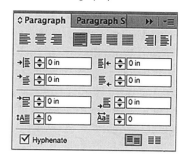

The Basic Paragraph style will be the master or parent style for all the paragraph styles you create for your book in subsequent chapters.

4 Saving your document

Before going any further, be sure to save your document by clicking File>Save As and navigating to an appropriate place to save your document. You may want to name your file with your book title and the date, to keep subsequent versions in order. Here is a sample file name for your document:

BookTitle_Pages_YY-MM-DD.indd

Now you've created an InDesign document for your pages, complete with a Basic Paragraph style for your book. You're ready to add your manuscript!

Placing your manuscript

Now you've set up your document with the appropriate trim size and margins for your book and created a Basic Paragraph style. Your next step is to place your manuscript into the document.

Text is always "placed" into your document in InDesign, rather than copied and pasted. If you copy and paste text from your Word document into InDesign, you risk losing some of the formatting, such as italics. So always *place* your text.

If your Word document includes embedded images, remove the images before placing your manuscript in InDesign. Save a copy of your Word document under a different name (InDesignCopy, for example) and then delete all the images from that copy. That way you'll still have your original manuscript to refer to later when you're placing your images.

The steps you'll take to place your manuscript are:

1 Placing your manuscript in your InDesign document
2 Autoflowing your text to create the pages of your book
3 Saving and backing up your file

InDesign can import files in .doc, .docx, .txt, and .rtf formats. If your book was not written in Word, you will need to convert it to one of these formats before you can proceed.

1 Placing your manuscript into your InDesign document

Open your InDesign document and navigate to page 1. With the Selection Tool, choose File>Place to open the Place dialog box. Browse to find the Word document containing your manuscript. Make sure Show Import Options at the lower left is checked, as shown here, then click Open.

You'll see the Import Options dialog box appear. Check the boxes as shown on page 45, and click OK.

The keyboard shortcut for Place is Ctrl/Cmd+D.

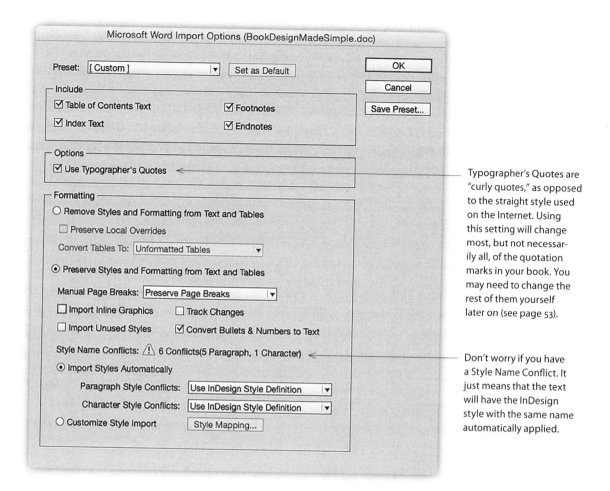

Typographer's Quotes are "curly quotes," as opposed to the straight style used on the Internet. Using this setting will change most, but not necessarily all, of the quotation marks in your book. You may need to change the rest of them yourself later on (see page 53).

Don't worry if you have a Style Name Conflict. It just means that the text will have the InDesign style with the same name automatically applied.

If your word-processing document includes any fonts that aren't available in InDesign, you'll see the Missing Fonts dialog box shown to the right. You'll fix any missing fonts later, so for now just click Close.

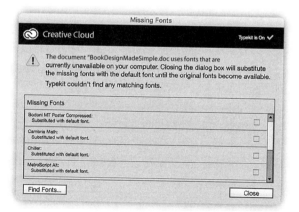

Now your pointer will be loaded with text, and you'll see the loaded text icon when you move your mouse around. You'll also see on page 1 a box showing you where your margins are. The area inside this box is where all your text will go, and it's called the text block.

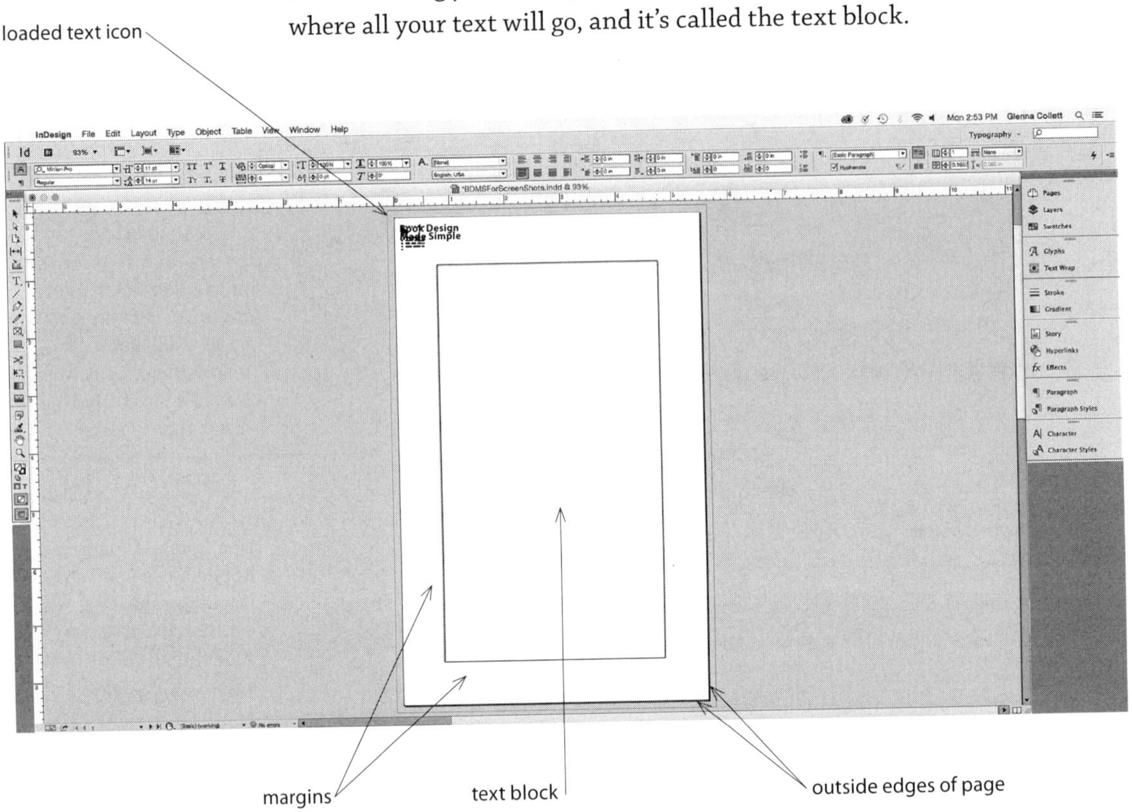

loaded text icon

margins

text block

outside edges of page

Move your mouse so the loaded text icon is poised at the top left corner of your text block, and then click your left mouse button once. The text will flow onto the page, staying within the margins.

Page 1 will now look something like this:

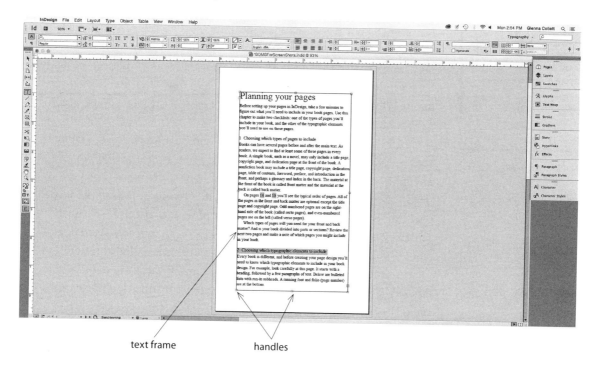

text frame   handles

You'll see the first page of your manuscript here. When you clicked the loaded text icon inside your margins, InDesign placed your manuscript into the text block. The text is enclosed in a text frame, which has a blue outline, as well as small boxes at each corner and in the center of each side, called handles. Take a moment to check this out. You still have the Selection Tool selected and can see a black arrow wherever you move your mouse. Move the Selection Tool over any of the handles and a small arrow will appear, showing the directions in which you can resize or change the shape of the text frame. Click and drag any of the handles to change the shape of your text frame. Then return the frame back to fit the margins.

You've now placed your manuscript into InDesign. You'll flow your text onto the pages next.

If your margins and text frame aren't visible, change to Normal view using the View Tool (see page 16), or simply press W.

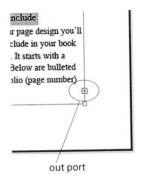

out port

2 Autoflowing your text to create the pages of your book

So far you only have three pages in your book. On the first page is a text frame with your whole manuscript in it.

There's a small red box with a plus sign at the lower right side of the text frame, called the out port. This means there is more text in this text frame than you can see. Your next step is to flow all of the text in your manuscript into your document and see how many pages there are in your book so far.

With the Selection Tool, click on the out port and once again you'll see the loaded text icon. While the loaded text icon is active, you can still navigate to different pages in your document or create new pages.

Go to page 2 of your document, and move your mouse so the loaded text icon is poised at the top left corner of your text frame. Press the Shift key, and notice that the loaded text icon changes. Instead of a text icon, you'll see a curved line with an arrow. This is called autoflow and means that InDesign will create however many pages are necessary to flow all of the text in your manuscript into your InDesign document. Press the Shift key, click the left mouse button, then release both.

Your whole manuscript will flow into your InDesign document. This may take a moment or two. Then open the Pages panel, and see how many pages your book has now.

Pages panel

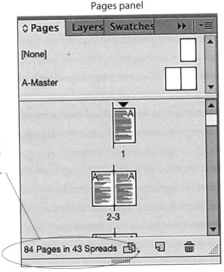

The Pages panel shows thumbnails of the actual text on each page. At the bottom is the total number of pages, followed by the number of 2-page spreads.

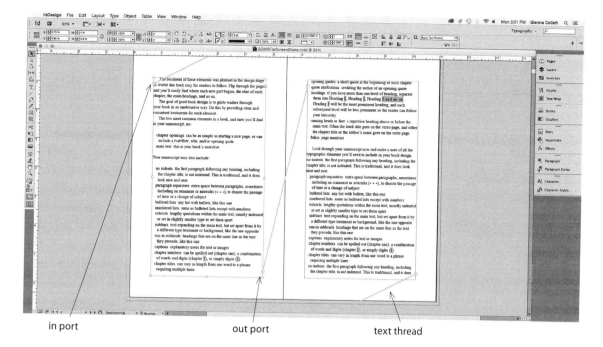

in port   out port   text thread

Notice that each page has a text frame containing text. Each text frame has handles for manipulating the frame, as well as an in port at the top left side and an out port at the bottom right side. If the ports have arrows in them, it means that the text is either continued from the previous page or continues on to the next page. The exceptions are that the very first page won't have an arrow in the in port, and the very last page won't have an arrow in the out port. Those ports will be empty.

Don't worry if your text comes into InDesign looking like a patchwork of typefaces, sizes, and alignments. You'll straighten everything out as you go.

To see how your text frames are linked together, choose View>Extras>Show Text Threads. You won't see these threads until you select a text frame with the Selection Tool. Then you'll see connecting threads between the out ports and in ports.

3 Saving and backing up your file

Now that your book is well underway, be sure to save it under today's date. Also consider saving a copy on a memory stick, external hard drive, or wherever it's convenient for you to keep a backup copy. You may also want to save a copy off site. Adobe Creative Cloud includes backup storage in the Cloud, so that is a good choice for free off-site storage.

Optimizing your text

Manuscripts tend to accumulate a lot of extra non-printing characters, such as tabs, spaces, and end-of-paragraph returns. In a perfect world, your manuscript would have one end-of-paragraph return at the end of each paragraph and one space between words, and paragraphs would be indented using paragraph styles rather than tabs or spaces. However, the odds are excellent that your manuscript isn't completely perfect, at least in the non-printing character department.

First take a look at the non-printing characters in your document by clicking Type>Show Hidden Characters. You must be in the Normal view (see page 16 for the View Tool), and you'll see the non-printing characters in blue.

You'll optimize your text by:

1 Removing extra spaces and end-of-paragraph returns
2 Removing spaces at the beginning and end of paragraphs
3 Removing extra tabs
4 Changing straight quotes to curly quotes
5 Saving your work

1 Removing extra spaces and end-of-paragraph returns

See those tiny blue dots between words? Each tiny dot represents a space. You should only see one dot at a time in your document, never two dots together. Repeat: never two dots together.

Chances are you have dots all over the place. If you're not a regular tab user, you probably used spaces to indent your paragraphs and center your headings. Or you may have used two spaces after periods and colons. There are lots of ways for extra spaces to creep in.

Extra spaces are easy to remove using the Find/Change feature in InDesign. Click Edit>Find/Change to display the Find/Change dialog box.

The keyboard shortcut for the Find/Change dialog box is Ctrl/Cmd+F.

In the Query drop-down menu, choose Multiple Space to Single Space. Click Change All, and all the extra spaces will be eliminated in one step.

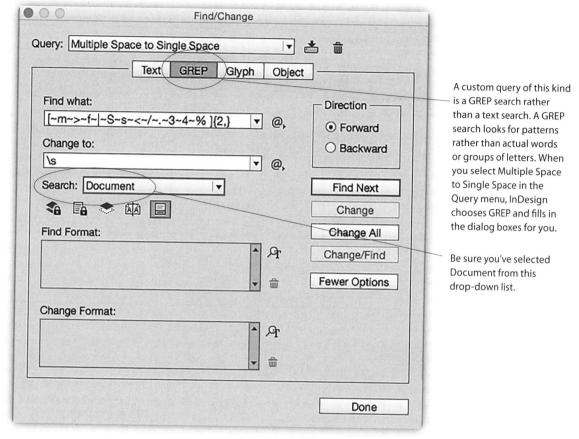

A custom query of this kind is a GREP search rather than a text search. A GREP search looks for patterns rather than actual words or groups of letters. When you select Multiple Space to Single Space in the Query menu, InDesign chooses GREP and fills in the dialog boxes for you.

Be sure you've selected Document from this drop-down list.

If you typed spaces to indent the paragraphs in your Word document, there will still be one space at the beginning of each paragraph. You'll remove these on page 52.

End-of-paragraph returns look like this: ¶. Manuscripts often have two end-of-paragraph returns after each paragraph to create extra space for editing and proofreading. In InDesign, you'll be controlling the amount of space between paragraphs using paragraph styles rather than extra end-of-paragraph returns, so any extras need to be removed.

In the Query drop-down menu, choose Multiple Return to Single Return. Click Change All to remove all extra end-of-paragraph returns.

2 Removing spaces at the beginning and end of paragraphs

Two more useful searches are for spaces stranded at the beginning and ends of a paragraph. If you used spaces to indent paragraphs in your manuscript or left extra spaces at the ends of paragraphs, your previous search will have removed all of the spaces except one.

To remove spaces at the end of paragraphs, choose Remove Trailing Whitespace in the Query drop-down box, and click Change All.

To remove spaces at the beginnings of paragraphs, first select the Text tab, then type ^p followed by one space in the "Find what" box, and type ^p in the "Change to" box. Make sure Document is selected in the Search drop-down menu, then click Change All.

The space that you typed after "^p" is invisible.

The ^p symbol represents the end-of-paragraph return. To type it, first type the caret symbol (^) by pressing Shift+6. Then type the letter P, which can be upper- or lowercase.

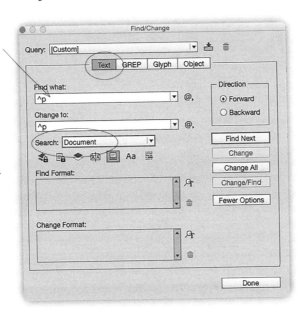

When you're finished with the Find/Change dialog box, click Done or the X (Windows) or button (Mac) at the top to close the box.

3 Removing extra tabs

If you've used tabs to indent the paragraphs in your manuscript, these tabs will need to be removed. But first be aware of whether or not you used tabs elsewhere in your manuscript. Lists and charts also use tabs, and you'll want to keep those tabs intact.

If you used tabs in your manuscript only to indent your paragraphs, first select the Text tab in the Find/Change dialog box, then type ^t in the Find what box, and make sure the Change to box is completely empty by selecting and deleting anything in there. That way, you'll be finding all the tabs and replacing them with nothing (in other words, deleting them). In the Search drop-down menu, choose Document. Then click Change All. InDesign will tell you when the search is completed and how many replacements were made.

If your manuscript includes a number of tabs that you want to keep (in lists and charts, for example), then you'll remove the tabs selectively. Fill in the Find/Change dialog box as described above, but instead of clicking Change All, click Find Next. You'll jump to the first tab and can either click Change to remove it (i.e., change it to nothing) or click Find Next to go to the next tab without making a change. When you've jumped to every tab in the document, a dialog box will appear saying "Search is Completed."

When you're finished, click Done to close the Find/Change dialog box, and save your file.

4 Changing straight quotes to curly quotes

If you notice any straight quotation marks (" or ') in your text, find and change them all to typographer's quotes ("" or ''). Select the Text tab, then look in the Query drop-down list and select Straight Double (or Straight Single) to Typographers Quote.

The Query drop-down list in Find/Change might be full of possibilities for you.

5 Saving your work

Always remember to save your document after making substantial changes. Here is a suggested workflow for saving:

1   The first time you save your document each day, click File>Save As (or Ctrl/Cmd+Shift+S) and save a new document with today's date.
2   Every time you complete a substantial change, click File>Save (or Ctrl/Cmd+S) to update your current work in the same file.
3   At the end of each day, save a copy of your latest file onto a memory stick or external hard drive, or upload it to an off-site storage space such as Creative Cloud.

Congratulations on learning how to navigate around InDesign, setting your Preferences and Basic Paragraph style, and placing and optimizing your text!

You're well underway now, and in Part II: Creating Your Styles you'll take another huge step and create all the styles you'll need for your book.

Part II:
Creating Your Styles

10

Creating your paragraph styles

Paragraph styles are an essential component of InDesign. They control every paragraph in your book, that is, every bit of text that finishes with an end-of-paragraph return, including titles, headings, page numbers, and so on. *All* the text in your book will ultimately have a paragraph style applied to it.

What is a paragraph style?

A paragraph style is a group of settings that make a paragraph appear a certain way.

For example, *this* paragraph has the Text style applied to it. The Text style specifies that the type is set in the typeface Chaparral Pro Regular at point size 10.5. It also specifies that the first line of the paragraph is indented 0.2″. The Text style is applied to all of the main narrative in this book, and therefore all the paragraphs with this style applied look the same.

Besides keeping paragraphs looking consistent, using paragraph styles makes it easy to implement global changes to paragraphs. You can change all the text in your main narrative to a different typeface, for example, just by changing that setting in your Text paragraph style. Or you can increase or decrease the type size. Any changes you make to a paragraph style will change *all* the paragraphs in your book with that style applied to them.

Using paragraph styles

There are two steps involved in using paragraph styles: 1) *creating* the styles and 2) *applying* the styles. In this chapter you'll *create* a standard set of paragraph styles for your book, and in chapter 14 you'll *apply* them to your text.

A set of paragraph styles for your book

On page 27 you completed a checklist of all the typographic elements you'll need to include in your book, such as chapter titles, headings, and so on. You'll create a separate paragraph style for each of these elements, using the design specifications provided in this chapter.

You may be satisfied with the way your pages look using these design specifications, or you may decide to make changes to some of your paragraph styles. When the time comes, you'll be able to make changes globally simply by changing the settings in a paragraph style rather than by changing each instance of that element individually. That's the beauty of paragraph styles!

Paragraph styles control more than just text

Besides controlling the way your text looks, paragraph styles also control:

- **white space** you can specify the amount of white space before and after a paragraph
- **rules** you can specify the size, weight, and type of a horizontal line (solid, dotted, dashed, and so on) above and below a paragraph

Creating new paragraph styles down the road

The paragraph styles you'll create in this chapter are for all the main typographic elements in your book. However, you'll need to add a few new styles later on.

Remember that *every* paragraph in your book needs to have a paragraph style applied to it. As you start applying paragraph styles to your text (in chapter 14), you'll find there are instances where you don't yet have a suitable paragraph style for that particular text. Perhaps you need a style with more white space after it, or a new style for, say, footnotes.

In chapter 14 you'll learn some easy ways to create new paragraph styles as needed.

Understanding the paragraph styles family tree

On page 59 you'll see the paragraph styles family tree that you'll be using for *your* book. At the top is the Basic Paragraph style. You've already set up your Basic Paragraph style (on page 35). All of the subsequent paragraph styles you create will be based on your Basic Paragraph style. It's the matriarch in your family of paragraph styles!

Creating subsequent paragraph styles *based on* the Basic Paragraph style sets up a parent-child relationship between the styles. The child inherits all the characteristics of the parent but also has unique characteristics of its own.

For example, look at the paragraph styles in Column A in the flowchart on page 59. The Text style is identical to Basic Paragraph, *except* it includes a first line indent (like this paragraph).

When a change is made to a parent style, that change will in turn be made to its children and to all subsequent generations. If you change the typeface in your Basic Paragraph style, for example, the typeface will change in all styles based on that style and in subsequent generations. The only exception is if that particular setting was modified earlier in one of those styles (say, you previously changed the typeface in the Captions style to Myriad), in which case InDesign will respect that prior change.

Your family of paragraph styles

Take a moment to refer back to page 27 and see the checklist you made of all the typographic elements you'll need for your book. Using that information, check all the paragraph styles you'll need in the paragraph styles family tree on page 59.

Now you can create your paragraph styles using the style settings provided in this chapter. You'll be guided step by step through setting up each style, and by the end of the chapter you'll have a set of styles ready to apply to your text.

Paragraph styles family tree

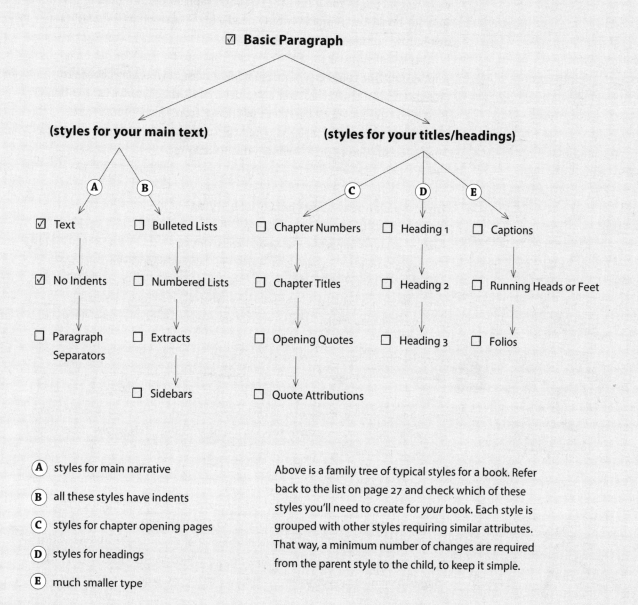

☑ **Basic Paragraph**

(styles for your main text)   **(styles for your titles/headings)**

Ⓐ   Ⓑ   Ⓒ   Ⓓ   Ⓔ

☑ Text   ☐ Bulleted Lists   ☐ Chapter Numbers   ☐ Heading 1   ☐ Captions

☑ No Indents   ☐ Numbered Lists   ☐ Chapter Titles   ☐ Heading 2   ☐ Running Heads or Feet

☐ Paragraph Separators   ☐ Extracts   ☐ Opening Quotes   ☐ Heading 3   ☐ Folios

☐ Sidebars   ☐ Quote Attributions

Ⓐ styles for main narrative

Ⓑ all these styles have indents

Ⓒ styles for chapter opening pages

Ⓓ styles for headings

Ⓔ much smaller type

Above is a family tree of typical styles for a book. Refer back to the list on page 27 and check which of these styles you'll need to create for *your* book. Each style is grouped with other styles requiring similar attributes. That way, a minimum number of changes are required from the parent style to the child, to keep it simple.

Creating the paragraph styles you need

Creating paragraph styles sounds complicated, but it really isn't. Over the next several pages you'll find a set of paragraph styles designed to use for your book. You'll probably only need a few, rather than the whole set, depending on the elements in your book.

This set of styles is for a book design that can be used for fiction or nonfiction. This could be your final book design, or you may choose to change some of the styles later on to better suit the material in *your* book. If so, there are lots of design ideas to choose from in chapters 17–29.

For now, create the styles you need by using the eight steps on page 61 and following the examples shown in this chapter.

Three quick notes about paragraph styles

Paragraph styles imported with your manuscript

You may notice a few paragraph styles already in your Paragraph Styles panel. These are styles that imported with your manuscript. Some will have a small download icon next to them. Just ignore these styles for now. When the time comes (in chapter 14), you'll transfer any paragraphs that use these styles over to your new paragraph styles.

Text = **tx**
Bulleted List = **bl**
Chapter Number = **cn**
Chapter Title = **ct**
Numbered List = **nl**

Why use abbreviated lowercase style names?

When you set up your styles, you'll use abbreviated lowercase style names. For example, your Text style will be named **tx** and your Paragraph Separator style named **sep**. Keeping the style names in lowercase, short, and with no spaces or commas aids in ebook conversion by keeping the file size down and complying with ebook specifications.

The new Creative Cloud Library feature

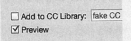

When you create your new styles following the steps in this chapter, you'll notice a checkbox with the option to save each style to a CC Library. If you plan to use more than one device to work on your book design, and/or if you are working on it with a group, then you'll find this dynamic new feature to be useful and should refer to a CC tutorial for information on using it. Otherwise, uncheck this box.

Create a new paragraph style in 8 steps

1 With the Selection Tool, click anywhere outside the text frames to make sure no text or frames are selected.

2 Open the Paragraph Styles panel.

3 Click once on the *parent style* of the style you are creating, to select it.

4 Open the Paragraph Styles fly-out menu by clicking the four horizontal lines at the top right of the panel (see example, above right), then click New Paragraph Style. This will open a New Paragraph Style dialog box with the General category selected on the left. It'll look familiar, as it has the same categories and options you went through in chapter 7.

5 In the General category, type the name of your new paragraph style in the Style Name box.

6 In the Based On box, use the drop-down menu to find the parent style.

7 Using the other tabs in the dialog box, make the appropriate changes to your new style (the things that make it different from its parent style).

8 Click OK, and your new style will appear in the Paragraph Styles panel.

Click here to open the Paragraph Styles fly-out menu.

Check or uncheck this box— it's up to you (see page 60).

If you happen to be *writing* your book in InDesign, as we did with this book, use the Next box in the General category to indicate which style will normally follow the one you're setting up. (For instance, all heading styles are always followed by the No Indent [**tx1**] style.) That way, when you're typing, the correct style will begin automatically when you start a new paragraph.

If you're not writing your book in InDesign, just ignore the Next box.

Creating the paragraph styles in Column A

Column A (see page 59) includes three styles: Text, No Indents, and Paragraph Separators. You'll definitely need the Text and No Indents styles. You'll use the Text style for your main narrative and the No Indents style for paragraphs following a chapter title or heading (such as this paragraph). Whether or not you need the Paragraph Separators style depends on whether there are breaks in the main narrative in your book.

Follow the eight steps listed on page 61 to create all the paragraph styles you need for *your* book. Use the settings shown for each paragraph style, and just skip the ones you don't need.

☑ **Text [tx]**

General:

Parent = [Basic Paragraph]
Style Name = **tx**
Based On = [Basic Paragraph]

Changes from the [Basic Paragraph] style:
Indents and Spacing:

First Line Indent = 0.2 in

☑ **No Indents [tx1]**

General:

Parent = [Basic Paragraph]
Style Name = **tx1**
Based On = [Basic Paragraph]

Changes from the [Basic Paragraph] style:
None

☐ **Paragraph Separators [sep]**

General:

Parent = **tx1**
Style Name = **sep**
Based On = **tx1**

Changes from the No Indent style:
Indents and Spacing:

Alignment = Center
Space Before = 14 pt *or* 0.1944 in
Space After = 14 pt *or* 0.1944 in

from a bottle marked 'poison,' it is almost certain to disagree with you, sooner or later.¶

However, this bottle was *not* marked 'poison,' so Alice ventured to taste it, and finding it very nice, (it had, in fact, a sort of mixed flavour of cherry-tart, custard, pine-apple, roast turkey, toffee, and hot buttered toast,) she very soon finished it off.¶

* — * — ¶

'What a curious feeling!' said Alice; 'I must be shutting up like a telescope.' And so it was indeed: she was now only ten inches high, and her face brightened up at the thought that she was now the right size for going through the little door into that lovely garden. First, however, she waited for a few minutes to see if she was going to shrink any further: she felt a little nervous about this; 'for it might end, you know,' said Alice to herself, 'in my going out altogether, like a candle. I wonder what I should be like then?' And she tried to fancy what the flame of a candle is like after the candle is blown out, for she could not remember ever having seen such a thing.¶

After a while, finding that nothing more happened, she decided on going into the garden at once; but, alas for poor Alice! when she got to the door, she found she had forgotten the little golden key, and when she went back to the table for it, she found she could not possibly reach it: she could see it quite plainly through the glass, and she tried her best to climb up one of the legs of the table, but it was too slippery; and when she had tired herself out with trying, the poor little thing sat down and cried.¶

'Come, there's no use in crying like that!' said Alice to herself, rather sharply; 'I advise you to leave off this minute!' She generally gave herself very good advice, (though she very seldom followed it), and sometimes she scolded herself so severely as to bring tears into her eyes; and once she remembered trying to box her own ears for having cheated herself in a game of croquet she was playing against herself, for this curious child was very fond of pretending to be two people. 'But it's no use now,' thought poor Alice, 'to pretend to be

tx Text style

sep Paragraph Separator style using three asterisks (Shift+8) with em spaces between them (Ctr/Cmd+Shift+M)

tx1 No Indents style

tx Text style

The Basic Paragraph style is never actually applied to any paragraph in your book. It is simply used as a base for all the other styles.

Creating the paragraph styles in Column B

Column B includes four paragraph styles: Bulleted Lists, Numbered Lists, Extracts, and Sidebars. All of these styles have indentations.

In order to typeset indented paragraphs nicely, it's easiest to create three different paragraph styles for each type of indented paragraph. This is because there is often an extra linespace before and after the indented paragraphs but not always *between* them.

If you have **bulleted lists** in your book, set up the three paragraph styles below for bulleted lists.

☐ **Bulleted Lists, First [bl1]**

General:

Parent = [Basic Paragraph]
Style Name = **bl1**
Based On = [Basic Paragraph]

Changes from the [Basic Paragraph] style:
Indents and Spacing:

Left Indent = 0.2 in
First Line Indent = −0.15 in
Space Before = 14 pt *or* 0.1944 in

Bullets and Numbering:

List Type = Bullets

☐ **Bulleted Lists, Middle [bl2]**

General:

Parent = **bl1**
Style Name = **bl2**
Based On = **bl1**

Changes from the Bulleted Lists, First style:
Indents and Spacing:

Space Before = 0

☐ **Bulleted Lists, Last [bl3]**

General:

Parent = **bl2**
Style Name = **bl3**
Based On = **bl2**

Changes from the Bulleted Lists, Middle style:
Indents and Spacing:

Space After = 14 pt *or* 0.1944 in

It may seem onerous to create three paragraph styles for each type of indented paragraph, but it will greatly simplify your typesetting later on. You'll apply the appropriate styles and everything will fall into place.

Geography. London is the capital of Paris, and Paris is the capital of Rome, and Rome—no, *that's* all wrong, I'm certain! I must have been changed for Mabel! I'll try and say "How doth the little—" and she crossed her hands on her lap as if she were saying lessons, and began to repeat it, but her voice sounded hoarse and strange, and the words did not come the same as they used to do.¶

- 'How doth the little crocodile¶
- Improve his shining tail,¶
- And pour the waters of the Nile¶
- On every golden scale!¶
- 'How cheerfully he seems to grin,¶
- How neatly spread his claws,¶
- And welcome little fishes in¶
- With gently smiling jaws!'¶

'I'm sure those are not the right words,' said poor Alice, and her eyes filled with tears again as she went on, 'I must be Mabel after all, and I shall have to go and live in that poky little house, and have next to no toys to play with, and oh! ever so many lessons to learn! No, I've made up my mind about it; if I'm Mabel, I'll stay down here! It'll be no use their putting their heads down and saying "Come up again, dear!" I shall only look up and say "Who am I then? Tell

bl1 This style sets the amount of space *before* the first item in the list (in this list there is one linespace before the first item).

bl2 This style sets the amount of space *between* the items (in this list there are no linespaces between the items).

bl3 This style sets the amount of space *after* the last item in the list (in this list, there is one linespace after the last item).

Hanging Indents

Bulleted and numbered lists have *hanging indents*. In other words, the whole paragraph is indented from the left, *except* the first line. This is done by giving the whole paragraph a left indent but then giving the first line a negative number for its indent.

Hanging first line indent is –0.2"
Left indent is 0.2"

1. Here is an example of a numbered list. You'll see that the whole paragraph is indented 0.2" on the left.
2. The first line, however, is indented –0.2", causing the whole first line to start flush at the left margin.

Numbered lists are the same as bulleted lists, with two exceptions. First, the hanging indent for the first line is slightly larger in numbered lists, as numbers need more space. Second, bullets can be generated automatically in InDesign, so the actual bullet is part of the paragraph style. You set up your bulleted lists styles this way on page 64.

If you have **numbered lists** in your book, set up the three paragraph styles below for numbered lists.

☐ **Numbered Lists, First [nl1]**
General:

Changes from the [Basic Paragraph] style:
Indents and Spacing:

Parent = [Basic Paragraph]
Style Name = **nl1**
Based On = [Basic Paragraph]

Left Indent = 0.2 in
First Line Indent = −0.2 in
Space Before = 14 pt *or* 0.1944 in

☐ **Numbered Lists, Middle [nl2]**
General:

Changes from the Numbered Lists, First style:
Indents and Spacing:

Parent = **nl1**
Style Name = **nl2**
Based On = **nl1**

Space Before = 0 in

☐ **Numbered Lists, Last [nl3]**
General:

Changes from the Numbered Lists, Middle style:
Indents and Spacing:

Parent = **nl2**
Style Name = **nl3**
Based On = **nl2**

Space After = 14 pt *or* 0.1944 in

of Rome, and Rome—no, *that's* all wrong, I'm certain! I must have been changed for Mabel! I'll try and say "How doth the little—" and she crossed her hands on her lap as if she were saying lessons, and began to repeat it, but her voice sounded hoarse and strange, and the words did not come the same as they used to do.¶

1. » 'How doth the little crocodile¶
2. » Improve his shining tail,¶
3. » And pour the waters of the Nile¶
4. » On every golden scale!¶
5. » 'How cheerfully he seems to grin,¶
6. » How neatly spread his claws,¶
7. » And welcome little fishes in¶
8. » With gently smiling jaws!'¶

 'I'm sure those are not the right words,' said poor Alice, and her eyes filled with tears again as she went on, 'I must be Mabel after all, and I shall have to go and live in that poky little house, and have next to no toys to play with, and oh! ever so many lessons to learn! No, I've made up my mind about it; if I'm Mabel, I'll stay down here!

nl1 This style sets the amount of space *before* the first item in the list (in this list there is one linespace before the first item).

nl2 This style sets the amount of space *between* the items (in this list there are no linespaces between the items).

nl3 This style sets the amount of space *after* the last item in the list (in this list, there is one line-space after the last item).

Keyboard shortcuts

You may have noticed the option to create a shortcut in the General section of the Paragraph Styles Options box. Shortcuts can be very handy, and some people prefer them to using the mouse or trackpad to apply styles when typesetting.

To create a shortcut, double-click a paragraph style name in the Paragraph Styles panel to open the Paragraph Styles Options box. In the General section, click your cursor in the Shortcut box, turn on Num Lock (or use your numeric keypad), and choose any combination of Control and

Shift (Windows), or Command, Option, and Shift (Mac), plus a number. For example, you might use Shift+1 for your Text style.

To use the shortcut to format your text (see chapter 14 of this book), place your cursor anywhere in a paragraph of text and type the shortcut. The paragraph style will be applied to the paragraph you've chosen.

Note that keyboard shortcuts are not available on computers without numeric keypads.

Extracts are longer indented quotations, separated from the main text by indenting and a smaller type size. If you have extracts in your book, set up the four paragraph styles below for extracts.

☐ **Extracts, First** [ext1]
General:

Changes from the [Basic Paragraph] style:
Basic Character Formats:
Indents and Spacing:

Parent = [Basic Paragraph]
Style Name = **ext1**
Based On = [Basic Paragraph]

Size = 10 pt
Left Indent = 0.2 in
Right Indent = 0.2 in
Space Before = 14 pt *or* 0.1944 in

☐ **Extracts, Middle** [ext2]
General:

Changes from the Extracts, First style:
Indents and Spacing:

Parent = **ext1**
Style Name = **ext2**
Based On = **ext1**

First Line Indent = 0.2 in
Space Before = 0

☐ **Extracts, Last** [ext3]
General:

Changes from the Extracts, Middle style:
Indents and Spacing:

Parent = **ext2**
Style Name = **ext3**
Based On = **ext2**

Space After = 14 pt *or* 0.1944 in

☐ **Extracts, Only** [ext0]
General:

Changes from the Extracts, First style:
Indents and Spacing:

Parent = **ext1**
Style Name = **ext0**
Based On = **ext1**

Space After = 14 pt *or* 0.1944 in

measure herself by it, and found that, as nearly as she could guess, she was now about two feet high, and was going on shrinking rapidly: she soon found out that the cause of this was the fan she was holding, and she dropped it hastily, just in time to avoid shrinking away altogether.¶

'That *was* a narrow escape!' said Alice, a good deal frightened at the sudden change, but very glad to find herself still in existence; 'and now for the garden!'¶

As she said these words her foot slipped, and in another moment, splash! she was up to her chin in salt water. Her first idea was that she had somehow fallen into the sea, 'and in that case I can go back by railway,' she said to herself.¶

(Alice had been to the seaside once in her life, and had come to the general conclusion, that wherever you go to on the English coast you find a number of bathing machines in the sea, some children digging in the sand with wooden spades, then a row of lodging houses, and behind them a railway station.)¶

However, she soon made out that she was in the pool of tears which she had wept when she was nine feet high.¶

'I wish I hadn't cried so much!' said Alice, as she swam about, trying to find her way out. 'I shall be punished for it now, I suppose, by being drowned in my own tears! That *will* be a queer thing, to be sure! However, everything is queer to-day.'¶

Just then she heard something splashing about in the pool a little way off, and she swam nearer to make out what it was: at first she thought it must be a walrus or hippopotamus, but then she remembered how small she was now, and she soon made out that it was only a mouse that had slipped in like herself.¶

'Would it be of any use, now,' thought Alice, 'to speak to this mouse? Everything is so out-of-the-way down here, that I should think very likely it can talk: at any rate, there's no harm in trying.'

ext1 This style sets the amount of space *before* the first paragraph in the extract (in this extract there is one linespace before the first paragraph).

ext2 This style sets the amount of space *between* the paragraphs (in this extract there are no linespaces between the paragraphs).

ext3 This style sets the amount of space *after* the last paragraph in the extract (in this extract, there is one linespace after the last paragraph).

ext0 This style sets the amount of space *before* and *after* this single-paragraph extract.

Sidebars are usually set in italics or a different typeface and separated from the main text by indents or by placing them in a separate box. If you have sidebars in your book, set up the four paragraph styles below.

☐ **Sidebars, First [sb1]**
General:

                                            Parent = [Basic Paragraph]
      Style Name = **sb1**
      Based On = [Basic Paragraph]

Changes from the [Basic Paragraph] style:
Basic Character Formats: Font Style = Italic
Indents and Spacing: Left Indent = 0.2 in
      Right Indent = 0.2 in
      Space Before = 14 pt *or* 0.1944 in

☐ **Sidebars, Middle [sb2]**
General: Parent = **sb1**
      Style Name = **sb2**
      Based On = **sb1**

Changes from the Sidebars, First style:
Indents and Spacing: First Line Indent = 0.2 in
      Space Before = 0

☐ **Sidebars, Last [sb3]**
General: Parent = **sb2**
      Style Name = **sb3**
      Based On = **sb2**

Changes from the Sidebars, Middle style:
Indents and Spacing: Space After = 14 pt *or* 0.1944 in

☐ **Sidebars, Title [sbt]**
General: Parent = **sb1**
      Style Name = **sbt**
      Based On = **sb1**

Changes from the Sidebars, Middle style:
Basic Character Formats: Font Style = Bold

So she began: 'O Mouse, do you know the way out of this pool? I am very tired of swimming about here, O Mouse!' (Alice thought this must be the right way of speaking to a mouse: she had never done such a thing before, but she remembered having seen in her brother's Latin Grammar, 'A mouse—of a mouse—to a mouse—a mouse—O mouse!') The Mouse looked at her rather inquisitively, and seemed to her to wink with one of its little eyes, but it said nothing.¶

Sidebar Example¶

'Perhaps it doesn't understand English,' thought Alice; 'I daresay it's a French mouse, come over with William the Conqueror.'¶

(For, with all her knowledge of history, Alice had no very clear notion how long ago anything had happened.) So she began again: 'Ou est ma chatte?' which was the first sentence in her French lesson-book.¶

The Mouse gave a sudden leap out of the water, and seemed to quiver all over with fright. 'Oh, I beg your pardon!' cried Alice hastily, afraid that she had hurt the poor animal's feelings. 'I quite forgot you didn't like cats.'¶

'Not like cats!' cried the Mouse, in a shrill, passionate voice. 'Would *you* like cats if you were me?'¶

'Well, perhaps not,' said Alice in a soothing tone: 'don't be angry about it. And yet I wish I could show you our cat Dinah: I think you'd take a fancy to cats if you could only see her. She is such a dear quiet thing,' Alice went on, half to herself, as she swam lazily about in the pool, 'and she sits purring so nicely by the fire, licking her paws and washing her face—and she is such a nice soft thing to nurse—and she's such a capital one for catching mice—oh, I beg your pardon!' cried Alice again, for this time the Mouse was bristling all over, and she felt certain it must be really offended. 'We won't talk about her any more if you'd rather not.'¶

sbt This style sets the amount of space *before* the sidebar title.

sb1 This style sets the amount of space *before* the first paragraph in the sidebar (in this sidebar there is one linespace before the first paragraph).

sb2 This style sets the amount of space *between* the paragraphs (in this sidebar there are no spaces between the paragraphs). It also gives the paragraphs a first line indent.

sb3 This style sets the amount of space *after* the last paragraph in the sidebar (in this sidebar, there is one linespace after the last paragraph).

Creating the paragraph styles in Column C

Column C includes all the paragraph styles needed for your chapter opening pages. You may only need **chapter numbers** for your novel, or you may need all four paragraph styles for the chapter opening pages in your nonfiction book. Set up the paragraphs styles you need as shown.

☐ **Chapter Numbers [cn]**

General:

Parent = [Basic Paragraph]
Style Name = **cn**
Based On = [Basic Paragraph]

Changes from the [Basic Paragraph] style:

Basic Character Formats:

Indents and Spacing:

Size = 14 pt
Alignment = Center
Space Before = 28 pt *or* 0.3889 in
Space After = 56 pt *or* 0.7778 in
(If your book includes Chapter Titles, set Space After at 28 pt or 0.3889 in instead)

OpenType Features:

Figure Style = Proportional Lining

☐ **Chapter Titles [ct]**

General:

Parent = [Basic Paragraph]
Style Name = **ct**
Based On = [Basic Paragraph]

Changes from the [Basic Paragraph] style:

Basic Character Formats:

Size = 14 pt
Leading = 28 pt

Indents and Spacing:

Alignment = Center
Space After = 56 pt *or* 0.7778 in
(If your book includes Opening Quotes, set Space After at 28 pt or 0.3889 in instead)

Hyphenation:

Hyphenate = Unchecked

¶

3¶ — **cn** Chapter Numbers style

A Caucus-Race and a Long Tale¶ — **ct** Chapter Titles style

¶ — **tx** Text (marker at top)

They were indeed a queer-looking party that assembled on the bank—the birds with draggled feathers, the animals with their fur clinging close to them, and all dripping wet, cross, and uncomfortable. ¶

The first question of course was, how to get dry again: they had a consultation about this, and after a few minutes it seemed quite natural to Alice to find herself talking familiarly with them, as if she had known them all her life. Indeed, she had quite a long argument with the Lory, who at last turned sulky, and would only say, 'I am older than you, and must know better'; and this Alice would not allow without knowing how old it was, and, as the Lory positively refused to tell its age, there was no more to be said.¶

At last the Mouse, who seemed to be a person of authority among them, called out, 'Sit down, all of you, and listen to me! I'LL soon make you dry enough!' They all sat down at once, in a large ring, with the Mouse in the middle. Alice kept her eyes anxiously fixed on it, for she felt sure she would catch a bad cold if she did not get dry very soon.¶

'Ahem!' said the Mouse with an important air, 'are you all ready? This is the driest thing I know. Silence all round, if you please! "William the Conqueror, whose cause was favoured by the pope, was soon submitted to by the English, who wanted leaders, and

Chapter titles are usually larger than headings, and it's important that the Chapter Titles style works equally well for different lengths of titles. For example, a short title like "Styles" should look just as good in the chapter opening as a longer title like "Impact of Paragraph Styles on Chapter Titles." Most books have a variety of title and heading lengths, some perhaps occupying two lines rather than one.

Chapter opening quotes require two paragraph styles: one for the opening quote itself and the other for the quote author's name (also called the attribution). If your book has opening quotes, then create these two styles. If not, just skip them.

☐ **Opening Quotes [quo]**
General:

Parent = [Basic Paragraph]
Style Name = **quo**
Based On = [Basic Paragraph]

Changes from the [Basic Paragraph] style:
Basic Character Formats:
Indents and Spacing:

Font Style = Italic
Alignment = Center
Left Indent = 0.5 in
Right Indent = 0.5 in

☐ **Quote Attributions [quoattr]**
General:

Parent = **quo**
Style Name = **quoattr**
Based On = **quo**

Changes from the Opening Quotes style:
Basic Character Formats:

Font Style = Regular
Size = 9 pt
Baseline Shift = −5 pt

Advanced Character Formats:
Indents and Spacing:

Space After = 56 pt *or* 0.7778 in

¶

3¶

A·Caucus-Race·and·a·Long·Tale¶

← quo Opening Quotes

A·book·can·look·good·using·almost·any·typeface;¬
it·just·depends·on·how·the·type·is·set.¶

—Fiona·Raven,·book·designer¶

← quoattr Quote Attributions

They·were·indeed·a·queer-looking·party·that·assembled·on·the·bank—the·birds·with·draggled·feathers,·the·animals·with·their·fur·clinging·close·to·them,·and·all·dripping·wet,·cross,·and·uncomfortable.¶

The·first·question·of·course·was,·how·to·get·dry·again:·they·had·a·consultation·about·this,·and·after·a·few·minutes·it·seemed·quite·natural·to·Alice·to·find·herself·talking·familiarly·with·them,·as·if·she·had·known·them·all·her·life.·Indeed,·she·had·quite·a·long·argument·with·the·Lory,·who·at·last·turned·sulky,·and·would·only·say,·'I·am·older·than·you,·and·must·know·better';·and·this·Alice·would·not·allow·without·knowing·how·old·it·was,·and,·as·the·Lory·positively·refused·to·tell·its·age,·there·was·no·more·to·be·said.¶

At·last·the·Mouse,·who·seemed·to·be·a·person·of·authority·among·them,·called·out,·'Sit·down,·all·of·you,·and·listen·to·me!·I'LL·soon·make·you·dry·enough!'·They·all·sat·down·at·once,·in·a·large·ring,·with·the·Mouse·in·the·middle.·Alice·kept·her·eyes·anxiously·fixed·on·it,·for·she·felt·sure·she·would·catch·a·bad·cold·if·she·did·not·get·dry·very·soon.·'Ahem!'·said·the·Mouse·with·an·important·air,·'are·you·all·ready?·This·is·the·driest·thing·I·know.·Silence·all·round,·if

These paragraph styles are for clean and simple chapter opening pages. If you'd like to embellish these styles, or add a feature to the first paragraph such as a drop cap or the first few words in small caps, see chapter 24.

Creating the paragraph styles in Column **D**

Create the levels of **headings** you need using the styles shown.

☐ **Heading 1** [h1]

General:

Parent = [Basic Paragraph]
Style Name = **h1**
Based On = [Basic Paragraph]

Changes from the [Basic Paragraph] style:
Basic Character Formats:
Indents and Spacing:

Size = 14.5 pt
Alignment = Center
Space Before = 28 pt *or* 0.3889 in
Space After = 14 pt *or* 0.1944 in

Keep Options:
Hyphenation:

Keep with next 2 lines
Hyphenate = Unchecked

☐ **Heading 2** [h2]

General:

Parent = **h1**
Style Name = **h2**
Based On = **h1**

Changes from the Heading 1 style:
Basic Character Formats:

Font Style = Semibold
Size = 12 pt
Case = OpenType All Small Caps
Tracking = 50

Advanced Character Formats:
Indents and Spacing:

Baseline Shift = 2 pt
Alignment = Left
Space Before = 14 pt *or* 0.1944 in
Space After = 0 in

☐ **Heading 3** [h3]

General:

Parent = **h2**
Style Name = **h3**
Based On = **h2**

Changes from the Heading 2 style:
Basic Character Formats:

Font Style = Semibold Italic
Size = 11 pt
Case = Normal
Tracking = 10

BOOK DESIGN MADE SIMPLE · PART II: CREATING STYLES

"Edwin and Morcar, the earls of Mercia and Northumbria, declared for him: and even Stigand, the patriotic archbishop of Canterbury, found it advisable—"¶

'Found *what*?' said the Duck.¶

'Found *it*,' the Mouse replied rather crossly: 'of course you know what "it" means.¶

Heading 1 Sample¶

'I know what "it" means well enough, when I find a thing,' said the Duck: 'it's generally a frog or a worm. The question is, what did the archbishop find?'¶

The Mouse did not notice this question, but hurriedly went on, '—found it advisable to go with Edgar Atheling to meet William and offer him the crown. William's conduct at first was moderate. But the insolence of his Normans—" How are you getting on now, my dear?' it continued, turning to Alice as it spoke.¶

HEADING 2 SAMPLE¶

'As wet as ever,' said Alice in a melancholy tone: 'it doesn't seem to dry me at all.'¶

'In that case,' said the Dodo solemnly, rising to its feet, 'I move that the meeting adjourn, for the immediate adoption of more energetic remedies—'¶

Heading 3 Sample¶

'Speak English!' said the Eaglet. 'I don't know the meaning of half those long words, and, what's more, I don't believe you do either!' And the Eaglet bent down its head to hide a smile: some of the other birds tittered audibly.¶

'What I was going to say,' said the Dodo in an offended tone, 'was, that the best thing to get us dry would be a Caucus-race.'¶

'What IS a Caucus-race?' said Alice; not that she wanted much to know, but the Dodo had paused as if it thought that somebody

---

In books where bolder headings are required, often the headings are set in a different typeface from the main text. You can experiment with alternate typefaces later (chapter 25).

h1 Heading 1 style

h2 Heading 2 style

h3 Heading 3 style

Most nonfiction books have three levels of headings at most, as any more tend to confuse the reader.

Creating the paragraph styles in Column E

The **Captions**, **Running Heads or Feet**, and **Folios** paragraph styles all use type in sizes quite a bit smaller than the main text. Create the styles you'll need for your book using the settings below.

☐ **Captions [cap]**

General:

> Parent = [Basic Paragraph]
> Style Name = **cap**
> Based On = [Basic Paragraph]

Changes from the [Basic Paragraph] style:

Basic Character Formats:

> Font Style = Italic
> Font Size = 10 pt

Indents and Spacing:

> Align to Grid: First Line Only

Running heads go at the top of pages and running feet go at the bottom. Choose **rh** or **rf**, whichever you prefer.

☐ **Running Heads or Feet [rh *or* rf]**

General:

> Parent = [Basic Paragraph]
> Style Name = **rh** *or* **rf**
> Based On = [Basic Paragraph]

Changes from the [Basic Paragraph] style:

Basic Character Formats:

> Size = 9 pt
> Case = OpenType All Small Caps
> Tracking = 50
> Alignment = Center

Indents and Spacing:

☐ **Folios [fol]**

General:

> Parent = **rh** *or* **rf**
> Style Name = **fol**
> Based On = **rh** *or* **rf**

Changes from the Running Heads or Feet style:

Indents and Spacing:

> Alignment = Away From Spine

Congratulations! You've finished creating all the paragraph styles you'll need for your book. Click on the fly-out menu at the top right of the Paragraph Styles panel, and select Sort By Name. This will put all your paragraph styles into alphabetical order. Then save your document.

rh Running Head style

fol Folio style

could not think of anything to say, she simply bowed, and took the thimble, looking as solemn as she could.¶

The next thing was to eat the comfits: this caused some noise and confusion, as the large birds complained that they could not taste theirs, and the small ones choked and had to be patted on the back. However, it was over at last, and they sat down again in a ring, and begged the Mouse to tell them something more.¶

'You promised to tell me your history, you know,' said Alice, 'and why it is you hate—C and D,' she added in a whisper, half afraid that it would be offended again.¶

'Mine is a long and a sad tale!' said the Mouse, turning to Alice, and sighing.¶

'It IS a long tail, certainly,' said Alice, looking down with wonder at the Mouse's tail; 'but why do you call it sad?' And she kept on puzzling about it while the Mouse was speaking, so that her idea of the tale was something like this:—¶

'Fury said to a mouse, That he met in the house, "Let us both go to law: I will prosecute *you*.—Come, I'll take no denial; We must

This is the caption that explains the image.¶

cap Caption style

11

Creating your character styles

Character styles are similar to paragraph styles in that they are applied to text. The difference is that paragraph styles are applied to entire paragraphs, whereas character styles are applied to individual characters or words within a paragraph.

When are character styles needed?

Character styles are needed when some characters in a paragraph need to be different from the rest of the paragraph. Here are some common reasons:

- **italics** Chances are your book includes a number of italicized words. Italics are used for emphasis, for specifying foreign words, for terms listed in a glossary, for book titles, and for many other reasons.

- **bold** If all the bold characters in your manuscript are in your titles and headings, then there's no need for a character style for bold, as bold is included in your headings paragraph styles. But if you've used bold for emphasis elsewhere in your manuscript, then you'll need a character style for bold.

- **digits** Digits look their best when they have extra spacing between them. It's a good typesetting practice to add more generous spacing to digits, using the Tracking feature in a character style.

- **run-in subheads** These are subheadings set into the beginning of a paragraph or list entry, such as this one.

- **small caps** Small caps are used for acronyms (e.g., CIA or UNHCR) and abbreviations (e.g., A.M. or B.C.). Depending on your book design, the first few words in each chapter or after a paragraph separator might be set in small caps, and sometimes running heads or feet are set in small caps as well (as in this book).

Using character styles

As with paragraph styles, there are two steps involved in using character styles: *creating* the styles and *applying* the styles. In this chapter you'll *create* a set of character styles for your book, and in chapter 13 you'll *apply* them to your text.

A set of character styles for your book

Take a moment now to look through your manuscript and see which character styles you'll need. Are there italicized words? Is bold used for emphasis? Does your text include lots of acronyms and/or numbers? Do you use run-in subheads? Check off the character styles below that you'll need to create for your book.

☐ Italics   ☐ Run-In Subheads

☐ Bold   ☐ Small Caps

☐ Digits   ☐ Reference numbers for notes

Now you can create your character styles using the style settings provided in this chapter. You'll be guided step by step through setting up each style, and by the end of the chapter you'll have a set of styles ready to apply to your text.

If you intend to create an ebook version of your print book, character styles are essential.

Click here to open the Character Styles fly-out menu.

Check or uncheck this box—it's up to you (see page 60).

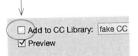

You may use keyboard shortcuts for character styles if you like. See page 67.

Create a new character style in 8 steps

1 With the Selection Tool, click anywhere outside the text frames to make sure no text or frames are selected.

2 Open the Character Styles panel.

3 Click once on the [None] style to select it.

4 Open the Character Styles fly-out menu by clicking the four horizontal lines at the top right of the panel, then click New Character Style. This will open a New Character Style dialog box with the General category selected on the left. It'll look familiar, as it has some of the categories and options you've seen when setting up your paragraph styles.

5 In the General category, type the name of your new character style in the Style Name box.

6 In the Based On box, the parent style will default to [None].

7 Using the other category tabs on the left, make the appropriate changes to your new style (the things that make it different from its parent style).

8 Click OK, and your new style will appear in the Character Styles panel.

Create a character style for italics

Create the **Italics** character style by following the eight steps shown on page 82 and using the settings below.

☐ **Italics [ital]**
General:

                                Parent = [None]
                                Style Name = **ital**
                                Based On = [None]

Changes from the [None] character style:
Basic Character Formats: Font Style = Italic

Create a character style for bold

Create the **Bold** character style by following the eight steps shown on page 82 and using the settings below.

☐ **Bold [bold]**
General:

                                Parent = [None]
                                Style Name = **bold**
                                Based On = [None]

Changes from the [None] character style:
Basic Character Formats: Font Style = Bold

Create a character style for digits

Create the **Digits** character style by following the eight steps shown on page 82 and using the settings below.

Tracking is a means of adding or subtracting space between characters. It is measured in thousandths of an em. So a tracking value of 50 is 5%. (An em is a value that is equal to the type size.)

☐ **Digits** [digits]
General:

Parent = [None]
Style Name = **digits**
Based On = [None]

Changes from the [None] character style:
Basic Character Formats:

Tracking = 50

Create a character style for run-in subheads

Create the **Run-In Subheads** character style by following the eight steps shown on page 82 and using the settings below.

☐ **Run-In Subheads** [ris]
General:

Parent = [None]
Style Name = **ris**
Based On = [None]

Changes from the [None] character style:
Basic Character Formats:

Font Style = Bold

You may wonder why the Run-In Subheads character style is exactly the same as the Bold character style. You're creating separate character styles for these elements because you may decide down the road to change your run-in subheads to, say, semibold. It'll be an easy change then, since your run-in subheads will have a separate character style applied to them.

Create a character style for small caps

Create the **Small Caps** character style by following the eight steps shown on page 82 and using the settings below.

☐ **Small Caps [smcap]**   Parent = [None]
    General: Style Name = **smcap**
                                           Based On = [None]

    Changes from the [None] character style:
    Basic Character Formats: Case = OpenType All Small Caps
                                           Tracking = 25

Create a character style for reference numbers for notes

Create the **References** character style for the superscript numbers that refer to footnotes or endnotes. Follow the eight steps shown on page 82 and use the settings below.

☐ **References [ref]**   Parent = [None]
    General: Style Name = **ref**
                                           Based On = [None]

    Changes from the [None] character style:
    Basic Character Formats: Tracking = 20
                                         Position = Superscript

When you're finished working with a character style, be sure to go back into your Character Styles panel and select [None] by clicking it once. Otherwise, you'll start typing something down the road and wonder why everything is showing up in the wrong style.

Great! You've finished creating all the character styles you'll need for your book. Click on the fly-out menu at the top right of the Character Styles panel, and select Sort By Name. This will put all your character styles into alphabetical order. Then save your document.

12 *Reversing or undoing mistakes*

It's never too early to learn how to reverse or undo mistakes. As soon as you begin typesetting your book, you'll find yourself in "oops" situations from time to time. Here are three ways to reverse or undo mistakes:

1 **Undo the last few things you did** You can undo something you just did by choosing Edit>Undo or simply pressing Ctrl/Cmd+Z. Undo once, and you'll undo the most recent step you took. Or, you can undo several times and go back several steps. If you undo too many steps by mistake, you can redo those steps by pressing Ctrl/Cmd+Shift+Z (or choosing Edit>Redo). This also comes in handy for seeing whether you prefer a change you made, or whether it was better the way it was.

2 **Reverting to your last save** Suppose you open your document, start working on it, and suddenly you've lost some text or things have gone horribly wrong. You can revert back to how your document was the last time you saved it, by choosing File>Revert. InDesign will ask you if you're sure you want to do that, as you'll lose any changes you've made since the last save. Usually you don't want to keep those changes, so click OK and start fresh from your last save.

3 **Going back to an earlier version** It's always useful to save your document under a different date each day you work on it. That way, earlier versions are always available to you. If your current document gets messed up for any reason, you can always close it and open an earlier version. Or, you may change your mind and decide to include a chapter you've deleted, and can then copy it from an earlier version and paste it into your current document.

It's inevitable that you'll make mistakes. Now you know how to fix them quickly and easily.

Part III:
Formatting Your Pages

13

Applying your character styles

Now that you've set up your document, placed your manuscript, and created paragraph and character styles for the different elements in your book, your next step is to format *all* your text.

In chapter 14, you'll apply paragraph styles to every paragraph in your whole book. But before doing that, it's important to apply your character styles first. Why? Because when you apply a paragraph style to a paragraph, it makes the whole paragraph comply to the settings you've specified in that style. So, for example, if you've specified Regular or Roman type in your Text paragraph style, it will convert the *whole* paragraph to Regular or Roman text, including any words or characters you may have italicized or bolded in the original manuscript. However, if you apply those character styles first, they will remain in place when your paragraph styles are applied.

You'll definitely want to apply the Italics character style to your text. Whether you choose to apply the Bold, Digits, and Small Caps character styles at this stage depends on whether you have those elements in your book. And sometimes it's simpler to apply them as you're formatting your pages (in chapter 14).

Start by applying the Italics character style, then read the explanations for the other character styles, and decide whether you need to apply them and, if so, now or later. Either way is fine.

Any character styles that imported with your Word document will show a download icon at the right (see below). If any of these styles are duplicating ones you've created (e.g., emphasis is the same as **ital**), drag them onto the trash can at the bottom right. A Delete Style dialog box will appear, and you can replace that style with the one you created in chapter 11.

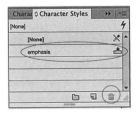

Character styles imported with your Word document

Look in your Character Styles panel to see whether any character styles were imported with your Word document. Delete these files one at a time, as explained to the left, and replace them with the styles you created in chapter 11. If you can't tell what a style is for by its description, double-click it to open it and see what settings are specified. Many imported Word styles have no settings specified, and these can be deleted outright.

You may find some character styles created by Word for footnotes. If so, just leave these for the time being, and you'll adjust those on pages 348–349.

Applying the Italics character style

You'll apply the Italics character style using the Find/Change feature in InDesign. Open Find/Change by clicking Edit>Find/Change or using the keyboard shortcut Ctrl/Cmd+F, then take the following steps:

The keyboard shortcut for Find/Change is Ctrl/Cmd+F.

1 Select the Text tab, then select and delete anything appearing in the Find What and Change To boxes. In the Search drop-down menu, choose Document.

2 Click once inside the empty Find Format box to open the Find Format Settings dialog box. Select Basic Character Formats from the list on the left, and in the Font Style drop-down box, select Italic and click OK.

3 Click once inside the empty Change Format box to open the Change Format Settings dialog box. Select Style Options from the list on the left, and in the Character Styles drop-down box, select Italics [**ital**] and click OK.

4 Now you'll see that the Find Format and Change Format boxes are filled in as shown to the right. Now click the Change All button and InDesign will give all your italic type the Italics [**ital**] character style.

Click your Type Tool in any italicized word, and you'll see that the Italics [**ital**] character style is applied to it. Now save your document.

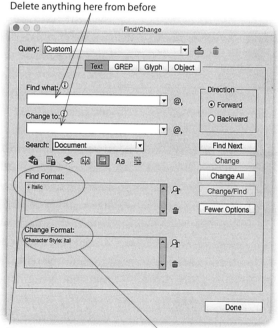

Delete anything here from before

Find italics applied in your Word document . . .

and change them to your InDesign Italics [**ital**] character style.

Applying the Bold character style

If all the bold characters in your manuscript are in your headings, then there's no need to use a Bold character style, as bold is included in your paragraph styles for headings. But if you've used bold for emphasis elsewhere in your manuscript, then you'll want to apply the Bold character style to any bolded text that is not a heading. To apply the Bold character style to your bolded text, follow these steps:

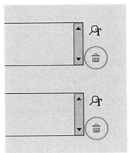

Click the trash cans to clear the Find Format and Change Format boxes.

1   In the Find/Change dialog box, click on the little trash cans next to the Find Format box and the Change Format box to delete the styles you added earlier. This deletes the styles so you can start fresh.

2   While still in Find/Change, select the Text tab, and click once inside the empty Find Format box to open the Find Format Settings dialog box. Select Basic Character Formats from the list on the left, and in the Font Style drop-down box, select Bold and click OK.

3   Click once inside the empty Change Format box to open the Change Format Settings dialog box. Select Style Options from the list on the left, and in the Character Styles drop-down box, select Bold [**bold**] and click OK.

4   If you used styles in Word when typing your headings, you may now click the Change All button and InDesign will give all your non-heading bold type the Bold [**bold**] character style. If, however, you used bold type in your headings in Word by applying the Bold attribute each time, it will be best to click the Find button and then Change each instance individually, skipping the headings as you go through the text and only applying the Bold [**bold**] character style to text that is not in headings.

If you click your Type Tool in any bold word, you'll see that the Bold [**bold**] character style is applied to it. Now save your document.

Applying the Digits character style

Digits look their best when they have extra spacing between them. It's a good typesetting practice to add more generous spacing to digits using the Tracking feature.

Applying the Digits character style uses a similar method to what you did for italics and bold type, but it involves a GREP search. Here's what you do:

A GREP search looks for patterns or attributes rather than actual characters or digits.

1   Open Find/Change and clear the Find Format and Change Format boxes if necessary by clicking on the little trash cans next to the boxes (see step 1 on page 90).

2   Select the GREP tab. To the right of the Find what box, click the little @ symbol, scroll down to Wildcards, then select Any Digit. Or you can type \d in the box.

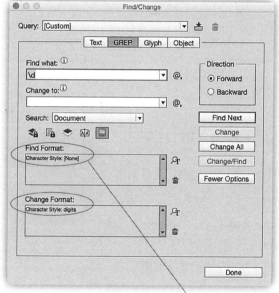

3   Click once in the Find Format box to open the Find Format Settings dialog box. Select Style Options from the list on the left, and in the Character Styles drop-down box, select [None] and click OK. Then click once in the Change Format box to open the Change Format Settings dialog box. Select Style Options from the list on the left, and in the Character Styles drop-down box, select Digits [**digits**] and click OK.

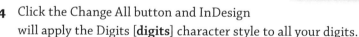

4   Click the Change All button and InDesign will apply the Digits [**digits**] character style to all your digits.

The character style [None] is included here so that your Digits [**digits**] character style doesn't get applied to digits that are already set in italics.

Now select any digit with your Type Tool, and you'll see that the Digits [**digits**] character style has been applied.

Change to Normal view (see page 16, or switch to your Selection Tool and press W), and you'll see that your digits are now highlighted with light blue. This is because they have a tracking value applied to them.

Applying the Small Caps character style

Small caps are used for acronyms (e.g., NASA or UNHCR) and abbreviatons (e.g., A.M. or B.C.). Depending on the book design, the first few words in each chapter or after a paragraph separator might be set in small caps, and sometimes running heads or feet are set in small caps as well.

You may decide that it's simpler to change the appropriate type to small caps as you format your pages (chapter 14), and that is perfectly fine. But if you want to change them all at once, follow the steps below. It is often simplest to apply the Small Caps character style to your acronyms and abbreviations while you're formatting your pages and applying your paragraph styles (in chapter 14). Then, when you come across an acronym or abbreviation (say, NASA), follow these steps:

1 In the Find/Change dialog box, under the Text tab, first clear out any old searches. Click on the little trash cans next to the Find Format and Change Format boxes to start fresh.

2 In the Find What box, type the specific acronym in uppercase letters (in this example, NASA).

If you notice your acronyms aren't changing to small caps using these methods, then it's likely the typeface you're using doesn't support the Open-Type All Small Caps feature. Once you apply your paragraph styles that use Minion, they'll change. If you choose to use a typeface that doesn't support small caps, in addition to the directions given to the right, type your acronym in lowercase letters in the Change To box.

3 Click the Case Sensitive icon (Aa) to turn it on. This is important! You might search for an abbreviation such as AM, and without the Case Sensitive icon turned on, all instances of am will be changed, including in words like amnesty, cream, and so on.

4 Click once inside the empty Change Format box to open the Change Format Settings dialog box. Select Style Options from the list on the left, and in the Character Styles drop-down box, select Small Caps [**smcap**] and click OK. Then click Change All.

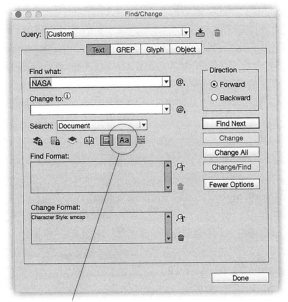

Case Sensitive icon

If you'd prefer to change *all* your acronyms at the same time in one big search, do this:

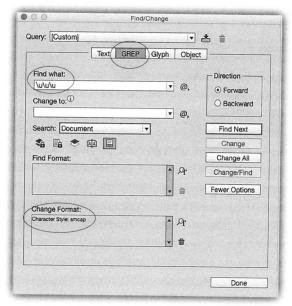

1 In Find/Change, first clear out any old searches. Then click on the GREP tab. Type \u\u\u in the Find What box. This sets up a search for any three uppercase letters in a row, which should catch all your acronyms, even if they have four or more letters.

2 Click once inside the empty Change Format box to open the Change Format Settings dialog box. Select Style Options from the list on the left, and in the Character Styles list, select Small Caps [**smcap**] and click OK.

3 Click Find Next, stop and change the first instance, then click Change/Find, and change the next. Go through the entire document this way, changing each acronym as you go.

A GREP search for \u\u\u will catch any group of three uppercase letters in a row. Since almost all acronyms are at least three characters long, this will catch them all.

Applying the References character style

It's important that your reference numbers be readable and consistent. To change all your current superscripts to the **ref** style, follow these steps:

1 In the Find/Change dialog box, clear out any old Text searches.

2 Click inside the empty Find Format box, go to Basic Character Formats in the list on the left, then in the Position field, scroll down to Superscript, select it, and click OK.

3 Click inside the empty Change Format box. Then in the Character Style list, choose **ref**, and click OK.

4 With your cursor in the text, click Find Next, then Change. Check to see if the replacement was done correctly, then click Change All.

Reference numbers are the same for footnotes and endnotes. You can adjust the appearance of your reference numbers in the **ref** character style, making them slightly larger or smaller (size), higher or lower (baseline shift), or bolder (font style).

14

Formatting your pages

Now you're ready to format your pages. You have two goals in this chapter: to rough in all the pages of your book, and to apply paragraph and character styles to every bit of text on every page.

You'll make two or three passes through your book, depending on whether your book has sidebars and images. In the first pass (in this chapter), you'll rough in your front and back matter, set up your chapters, and apply your paragraph and character styles to all the text.

In your second pass (see Part V: Adding Shapes & Color and Part VI: Adding Images), you'll add all the sidebars, images, and captions you need. (If you don't have any sidebars or images, you'll skip this pass.)

In your final pass (in Part VII: Typesetting), you'll refine your typesetting and put finishing touches on all your pages.

Why not do everything in one pass? Because after your first pass you may want to make some changes to your page design, such as modifying your chapter openings or typeface, to suit the material in *your* book. After your first pass, you'll be able to make whatever adjustments you choose by following the instructions in Part IV: Designing Your Pages.

When you're satisfied with the way your pages look, you'll do a second pass, adding shapes (such as boxes behind sidebars, see Part V: Adding Shapes & Color) and images and captions (see Part VI: Adding Images).

Changing your page design and adding shapes and images will change the flow of text in your book, and that's the reason your final typesetting refinements will be done when you're satisfied with the look of all the elements in your book, have added all your sidebars and images, and won't be making any further changes to your page design and layout. That's when you'll make the final pass through your book.

Ready to start your first pass? Applying styles to your text can be the most time-consuming stage of your book's production, so be prepared to spend some time doing it. Navigate to page 1 of your document, and start formatting your pages.

Click Type>Show Hidden Characters to display all the characters in your document that don't show up in print, such as spaces, end-of-paragraph returns, and so on. These characters will show in blue when you view your document in Normal view.

If you created an index in your manuscript in Word, you'll notice blue insertion points throughout your text wherever an index entry was added (when you are in Normal view with visible hidden characters). Be careful not to delete any of these while you're formatting your text. You'll typeset your index in chapter 54.

Roughing in your front matter

On pages 24–25 of this book you made a list of all the pages to include in your front matter. Now you'll set up those pages. Your front matter text may already be in your InDesign document if it was included in your manuscript, or you may not have it ready yet. Either way is fine. For the time being, you'll just rough in the pages.

Start with page 1. This is your title page, or your half title page if you choose to include one. If you already have your title or half title page text on page 1, then just make sure there is a page break after the appropriate text. A page break will force everything following it onto the next page. To insert a page break, use the Type Tool and click to place your cursor where you want the break to occur. Then press Enter/Return on your *numeric* keypad, or choose Type>Insert Break Character>Page Break.

Then move on to page 2. If you have a half title page on page 1, then page 2 will be blank. Just insert another page break to move everything following over to page 3. If your title page is on page 1, then page 2 will be your copyright page. Go to the bottom of your copyright page text (whatever you have there), and insert a page break. As you work through your front matter, inserting page breaks at the end of each item, you'll find your front matter starting to materialize.

If you don't have any front matter yet, you can still create your front matter pages using placeholders. For example, at the top of page 1 in front of your main text, insert the cursor with your Type Tool and simply type "Title Page," then insert a page break. On page 2, type "Copyright Page," then insert a page break. Carry on creating a new page for each item in your front matter until you've created all the necessary pages.

You may want to force a blank page. Suppose your front matter ends on a recto page. Chapter 1 or Part 1 always starts on a recto page, so you may need to add one blank page at the end of your front matter. To do so, place the cursor at the top of the page you want to be blank, and insert a page break.

When you've finished roughing in your front matter, not only will you see how many pages it will require, but you'll have added the actual pages to your book. Whether or not your front matter text is finalized isn't important at this stage. You simply want to allocate the pages for now, and you can fill them in later.

	half title
	1
blank	title
2	3
copyright ©	dedication
4	5
blank	contents
6	7
contents 2 or blank	acknowledgments
8	9
blank	introduction
10	11
introduction 2 or blank	
12	

Applying paragraph and character styles to your main text

Now that you've roughed in your front matter, your goal is to go through every page in your book and apply paragraph styles to every bit of text.

Why is it important that *all* your text has paragraph styles applied to it? There are two reasons:

1   **Every single paragraph needs a style for ebooks** There is a limited amount of formatting that ereaders recognize. They do not recognize more than one end-of-paragraph return at a time or more than one space at a time. So the amount of space after paragraphs cannot be controlled by adding several end-of-paragraph returns; rather, it must be controlled by adding space within the paragraph style settings. Same with using multiple spaces to indent paragraphs—ereaders won't recognize more than one space at a time. If your spacing is controlled exclusively by paragraph styles, then your ebook will look as expected. *Only one space and end-of-paragraph return at a time (really!).*

2   **Future design changes are easy** Suppose after your first pass you decide your type size needs to be a bit bigger. With paragraph styles applied to all your text, you can simply change the type size in your Basic Paragraph style, and just about all the type in your book will change accordingly. *And*, because you've controlled the space after paragraphs using your paragraph styles, you won't find any extra end-of-paragraph returns showing up in awkward places, such as at the top of your pages, because your text has reflowed.

Get ready to apply your styles by dragging your Paragraph Styles and Character Styles panels out of the dock so they are visible all the time. You may find it handy to assign keyboard shortcuts to the paragraph styles you are using frequently. For example, you might assign Shift+1 to your Text [**tx**] style, Shift+2 to your No Indents [**tx1**] style, and so on (see page 62).

Roll up your sleeves and get ready to go! Navigate to page 1 of your book, select your Type Tool, and get started.

Applying paragraph styles to your front matter

You'll be designing your front matter after you've finalized the design of your pages, so for the time being simply apply your Text [**tx**] style to *all* of your front matter. The box below explains several easy ways of selecting text in order to apply a paragraph style to it.

Easy ways to select text

Select one word Double-click on the word.

Select one line Triple-click anywhere in the line.

Select one paragraph Quadruple-click anywhere in the paragraph.

Select several paragraphs at a time on the same page Drag your mouse from the beginning of the first paragraph to the end of the last paragraph.

Select several pages of text Select a few words at the beginning of the first paragraph, scroll down to the page with the last paragraph, press Shift, and click at the end of the last paragraph.

Select all the text in linked text frames Put your cursor anywhere in the text and click Edit>Select All or press Ctrl/Cmd+A. This will select all text that is connected by text threads (referred to as a Story), but not any text in text frames that are separate.

Place your cursor at the very beginning of page 1, then scroll down through the pages until you reach the end of your front matter. Press Shift and click at the end of your front matter to select all the text. Then apply your Text [**tx**] paragraph style to the text by clicking the Text [**tx**] style once in your Paragraph Styles panel.

This is where you can begin using keyboard shortcuts if you wish. Refer back to page 67 to see how to set them up.

You'll notice that if there was any italicized or bolded text in your front matter, it remains unchanged despite applying the Text [**tx**] paragraph style. Any text with a character style applied will remain constant as you apply your paragraph styles to the text.

Now you'll be at the beginning of chapter 1 (or Part 1, if your book is divided into parts), starting on a recto page. If your book is divided into parts, create a page for your Part I divider by typing "Part I" and the part title, if any, at the top of your recto page, followed by two page breaks. That way, the verso page following your Part I divider will be blank, and you'll be starting your first chapter on the next recto page. You'll create paragraph styles for your part dividers later on, but for now apply your Text [**tx**] paragraph style to them.

Applying paragraph styles to your chapter openings

Start each chapter with an end-of-paragraph return at the top of the page (see facing page) by inserting your cursor just before your chapter opening and pressing Enter/Return. Then select the end-of-paragraph return and apply the Text [**tx**] style to it by clicking that style in the Paragraph Styles panel. Do this at the beginning of every chapter.

You need an end-of-paragraph return at the beginning of each new chapter so you can control how far down the page your chapter openings start. Without that, InDesign will automatically put your first element right at the top of the text frame.

You've already created all the paragraph styles you need for your chapter openings, so now you can apply them by inserting your cursor in the text and selecting the appropriate paragraph style in the Paragraph Styles panel.

Start with your chapter number. Make sure your chapter number is separate from your chapter title. You may need to insert an end-of-paragraph return after it to separate it. Then insert your cursor anywhere in the chapter number and apply your Chapter Number [**cn**] paragraph style by selecting that paragraph style in the Paragraph Styles panel. You'll see your chapter number change to the new style. If you're using the style suggested in this book, you'll want to use digits for your chapter numbers and remove the word "chapter."

Next, click on your chapter title and apply the Chapter Titles [**ct**] paragraph style to it. Do the same with your opening quote and quote attribution. You'll see the text change to the new styles.

Don't worry if the text in these styles flows onto two or more lines. You'll fine-tune these styles and choose exactly where the lines will break when you make your third pass (see chapters 50 and 51).

An end-of-paragraph
return (text [**tx**] style) at
the top of every chapter
opening allows InDesign
to recognize the "space
before" specification
in your Chapter Num-
bers paragraph style.

¶

3¶

A Caucus-Race and a Long Tale¶

A book can look good using almost any typeface;
it just depends on how the type is set.¶

—Fiona Raven, book designer¶

They were indeed a queer-looking party that assembled on the bank—
the birds with draggled feathers, the animals with their fur clinging
close to them, and all dripping wet, cross, and uncomfortable. ¶
   The first question of course was, how to get dry again: they had
a consultation about this, and after a few minutes it seemed quite
natural to Alice to find herself talking familiarly with them, as if she
had known them all her life. Indeed, she had quite a long argument
with the Lory, who at last turned sulky, and would only say, 'I am
older than you, and must know better'; and this Alice would not
allow without knowing how old it was, and, as the Lory positively
refused to tell its age, there was no more to be said.¶
   At last the Mouse, who seemed to be a person of authority among
them, called out, 'Sit down, all of you, and listen to me! I'LL soon
make you dry enough!' They all sat down at once, in a large ring,
with the Mouse in the middle. Alice kept her eyes anxiously fixed
on it, for she felt sure she would catch a bad cold if she did not get
dry very soon. 'Ahem!' said the Mouse with an important air, 'are
you all ready? This is the driest thing I know. Silence all round, if

Chapter Numbers [**cn**]
paragraph style

Chapter Titles [**ct**]
paragraph style

Opening Quotes [**quo**]
paragraph style

Quote Attributions [**quoattr**] paragraph style

No Indents [**tx1**] paragraph style is always
applied to the first paragraph following a chapter
opening or a heading.

Text [**tx**] style is applied
to all the paragraphs in
your main narrative.

Now that your first chapter opening has paragraph styles applied to it, carry on applying styles through the rest of the chapter.

Paragraph styles imported with Word

As you go through each paragraph in your first chapter, you may notice that some paragraphs already have a style applied to them. Styles imported from Word will display a download icon to the right, and they'll remain applied to your paragraphs. This can save you some time!

Simply delete the Word paragraph styles one at a time and replace them with the paragraph styles you created in chapter 10.

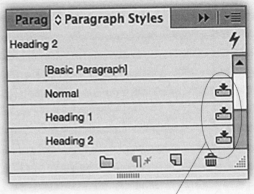

Styles imported from Word

Start with the Normal style. Delete it by dragging it onto the Trash icon at the bottom right. The Delete Paragraph Style box will open, and you'll replace the Normal paragraph style with your Text [**tx**] style by selecting it from the drop-down menu, then click OK.

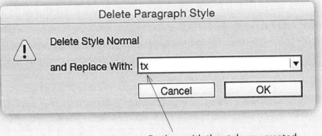

Replace with the style *you* created

Do this with every paragraph style that imported from Word. First figure out which paragraphs the style is applied to, then delete the style and replace it with a style you created in chapter 10.

Then, as you go through your chapters, you'll see that some of your styles are already applied.

Click in each paragraph (or select several similar paragraphs at a time) and look for a plus sign (+) next to the style name (see page 101). That will tell you whether the style applied properly. If it didn't, use the steps on page 101 to properly apply the style.

Applying paragraph styles to your chapters

The first paragraph following your chapter opening is not indented, so apply the No Indents [**tx1**] paragraph style to it. Then check each paragraph within your first chapter and apply the appropriate paragraph style to each one.

Main text

Apply the Text [**tx**] style to your main text even though it appears to be the same as the Basic Paragraph style. Apply the No Indents [**tx1**] style at the beginning of chapters and after any heading or paragraph separator.

You may notice a blank linespace at the bottom of a page. This is because your Text [**tx**] style is not allowing any widows, and rather than leave the last line of the paragraph stranded alone at the top of the next page, InDesign has moved a line from the bottom of the previous page over to join it. For now, this is fine. You'll fine-tune the number of lines per page during your third pass, in chapter 51.

Some lines of text may be highlighted with yellow or another color. That's because the spacing in that line is slightly tighter or looser than optimum, despite InDesign's best efforts. You'll find this information useful in chapter 51.

If paragraph styles don't apply properly

Sometimes you'll apply a paragraph style, but the text won't change properly. You'll notice the typeface didn't change, or the spacing is wrong. There'll be a plus sign (+) next to the style name in the Paragraph Styles panel. This means that something in that paragraph was changed manually, probably in your Word document, and InDesign is respecting the prior formatting.

To clear the overrides in a paragraph, place your cursor anywhere in the paragraph, then click Clear Overrides. The text will comply with the style you've applied to it. If this doesn't work, click on the paragraph 4 times, then click Clear Overrides.

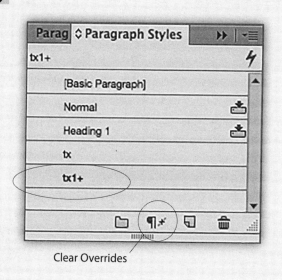

Clear Overrides

Heading 1 [**h1**] followed by No Indent [**tx1**] style

bl1 style for the first entry, and **bl2** style for the rest. We don't want a huge space between the end of the list and the head that follows, so we apply the Middle style, which has no extra space below it, to the last entry.

Heading 2 [**h2**] followed by No Indent [**tx1**] style

Extracts, Only [**exto**] style

Choosing Your Book's Trim Size

Trim size is the size of the *pages* of a book, regardless of the type of book cover. A hardcover book will appear larger than a softcover book with the same trim size because the hardcover itself is larger than the pages.

What size should your book be? You'll want to consider three things when choosing your book's trim size:

- What sizes are other books in the same genre?
- Do you want a thinner or thicker book?
- Where will your book be printed?

WHAT SIZES ARE OTHER BOOKS IN THE SAME GENRE?

Your book should fit in with other books in the same genre. Browse your bookstore or library, and see what sizes the other books are. Take a ruler with you, and measure in inches.

WHERE WILL YOUR BOOK BE PRINTED?

Standard sizes are the most cost-effective to print, and some printers and POD publishers only print certain sizes of books. To the left are some examples of standard trim sizes. Often at the design stage, you won't know where your book will be printed or published. If that's the case, select a size that will give you choices down the road.

> With all the InDesign type effects available to the self-publisher and anyone who is designing a book, it may be hard to believe that the basic guiding principle remains that a good book design goes unnoticed by the reader. Temptations abound! But reserve InDesign's showier elements for your book marketing.

Of course, you can choose any trim size for your book, but be aware that some sizes are more expensive to print and may require special binding, packaging, and shipping. Standard book sizes fit into standard shipping boxes, envelopes, and bookracks, and are

If you have a lot of text and want to keep your printing costs down, moving to a slightly larger trim size can lower your page count and save printing costs.

Inches, millimeters, points, or picas?

Historically typographers used points and picas (12 points = 1 pica, 72 points or 6 picas = 1 inch. Fonts are based on point sizes, such as 11-point Minion Italic, used in this sidebar.

Printers outside North America use millimeters because their standard paper and book sizes are metric.

If your book is set up in inches and goes to a printer that uses metric measurements, it's no problem, as long as the trim size is accurate in whatever measurement you've used.

This is sidebar text with a head. For now, keep it with the rest of the text. This example uses all four sidebar paragraph styles [**sbt**, **sb1**, **sb2**, **sb3**].

If you've just leased InDesign and need to familiarize yourself with the software, this chapter will help you get started. Your first task in InDesign is to learn the basics:

1. starting a new document
2. navigating through your document
3. learning to use the tools in the toolbox
4. using panels

Numbered Lists, First, Middle, and Last styles [**nl1**, **nl2**, **nl3**]

In chapter 3 you'll start a new document specifically for your book, but for now just make two changes to the dialog box.

Headings

Paragraph styles for headings include specifications for space before and after the heading. There is always more space before than after a heading.

Heading 3 [**h3**] followed by No Indent [**tx1**] style

This is a caption for an illustration.

Delete any extra end-of-paragraph returns before and after each heading. The paragraph following a heading should have the

Captions [**cap**] style. Keep captions in the same text frame with the book text for now as a reminder of where the illustration will go when you work on the second pass.

As you go through your chapters applying your styles, you'll probably come to some text that you haven't created an appropriate style for yet. Chances are good that you'll need to create some styles of your own to suit the material in *your* book. Remember, if you need extra white space after a paragraph, use Space After in your paragraph styles. There are easy ways of creating new styles, set out on page 108.

Paragraph separators

These are used to indicate the passage of time or a change of place within the narrative. Apply the Paragraph Separators [**sep**] style to whatever symbols you've used, and they will be centered with a linespace before and after them.

Asterisks (*) separated by em or en spaces (Ctrl/Cmd+Shift+M or N) are most commonly used for paragraph separators; however, you may prefer to use an ornament (see page 105).

Some authors use two types of paragraph separators: a single blank linespace for a short break in the narrative, and a paragraph separator with an ornament for a substantial break in time or place. If you choose to use a single blank linespace as a paragraph separator, don't just add an extra end-of-paragraph return! You'll need to create a new paragraph style for your main text that includes one blank linespace after it. Use the settings below for the new style.

Use asterisks (* * *) for separators if you plan to convert to an ebook. The spaces between the asterisks should be either em or en spaces (Type>Insert White Space>Em Space or En Space or Ctrl/Cmd+Shift+M or N), rather than multiple word spaces, because ebooks don't respect more than one word space in a row.

☐ **Text with Space After [txspaft]**
General:

                                       Parent = **tx**
Style Name = **txspaft**
Based On = **tx**

Changes from the [Basic Paragraph] style:
Indents and Spacing:

Space After = 14 pt

Whichever type of paragraph separator you choose to use, the first paragraph following the break is not indented, so apply your No Indent [**tx1**] paragraph style to paragraphs following the breaks in the narrative.

Several of the typefaces that come with InDesign include some ornaments. To open your Glyphs panel, choose Window>Type & Tables>Glyphs, or Type>Glyphs. In the Show drop-down menu, select Ornaments. Then double-click on any ornament to insert it at the cursor in your text.

If you decide to use an ornament from a different typeface from your Text [tx] style, be sure to change the Font Family in your Paragraph Separators [sep] paragraph style to that typeface.

Shift+8, any typeface, with em spaces (Ctrl/Cmd+Shift+M) between characters	* * *
Alt/Opt+8, any typeface, with em spaces (Ctrl/Cmd+Shift+M) between characters	• • •
Minion Pro ornament	⚬
Minion Pro ornament	~
Chaparral Pro ornament	↓
Adobe Garamond Pro ornament	໐

Headings

Paragraph styles for headings include specifications for space before and after the heading. There is always more space before than after a heading, so that the heading connects visually to the paragraph following it. Delete any extra end-of-paragraph returns before and after each heading. The paragraph following a heading should have the No Indent [tx1] paragraph style applied to it.

Headings should always be followed by a minimum of two or three lines of text. You may find that InDesign has left a space at the bottom of a page to keep a heading and its following lines together at the top of the next page. Don't worry if this looks awkward; you'll resolve these issues in your second pass.

Bulleted lists

The Bulleted Lists [bl] paragraph styles specify automatically adding bullets to your paragraphs. This ensures that the bullets are the same typeface and size as your bulleted lists (rather than a different typeface, such

You may need to delete any tabs that imported with your Word document bullets, as they're not needed with InDesign bullets.

as WingDings, that may have been used in your Word document). If the original bullets imported into InDesign, you'll now see two bullets at the start of each paragraph. Simply delete one. Use all three Bulleted Lists paragraph styles to get the correct spacing before and after your lists.

Numbered lists

The Numbered Lists [**nl**] paragraph styles do not specify automatic numbering. The numbering from your Word document may or may not have imported into InDesign. If not, you'll need to add numbers followed by a period and tab at the start of each item in your numbered list. Use all three Numbered Lists paragraph styles to get the correct spacing before and after your lists.

3. » This Numbered Lists paragraph begins with a number, followed by a period and a tab. The tab ensures that the first line is aligned with the rest of the paragraph. InDesign automatically places the tab for you when you set up a hanging indent.

Extracts

Use the appropriate Extracts [**ext**] paragraph styles to get the spacing right before and after your extracts.

Images and captions

If you have images to go in your book, just leave them out on your first pass. If the captions for the images are included in your main text, then apply the Captions [**cap**] paragraph style to them, but leave them in with your main text for the time being. You'll place your images and add the captions to them in chapters 43 and 44.

Sidebars: separate or linked?

The sidebars (this one, for example) in this book have been completely separated from the main text and placed on a gray (10% black) background. They are no longer linked with the main text and will stay in their current position on the page regardless of what changes are made to the main text.

During the first pass through your chapters, it's best to leave your sidebars as part of the main text, simply applying the Sidebars paragraph styles to them. Later, when your book design is finalized and during your second pass, you'll separate your sidebars and add graphic treatments to them.

Starting chapters on recto or verso pages

When you come to the end of each chapter, remember to add a page break, forcing all the remaining text onto the following page.

Traditionally chapters always began on recto pages. Nowadays it's acceptable to begin chapters on recto pages, verso pages, or a combination of both (as in this book). Sometimes the chapters themselves will dictate this for you. For example, suppose you begin all your chapters on recto pages, then discover your book has a dozen blank verso pages as a result. Today there is a higher priority on keeping both printing costs and ecological footprints to a minimum, rather than following any recto-page rules. Of course, if you have a low page count and want to expand your book as much as possible, then beginning all your chapters on recto pages is a good way to increase your page count unobtrusively.

During your first pass, let your chapters begin on recto or verso pages. In chapter 24 you'll decide whether to start them on recto pages only.

Applying character styles

You probably applied your character styles by using Find/Change in chapter 13. But as you go through your book one page at a time, you'll probably find places where you still need to apply a character style.

Run-in subheads

You'll apply the Run-In Subheads [**ris**] character style to your run-in subheads as you go through your book. Simply select the word or phrase (see page 97 for easy ways to select text), then click the character style once to apply it.

Acronyms and abbreviations

You also might find an acronym or abbreviation that needs to be changed to small caps. Follow the steps on pages 92 and 93 to search for all instances of the acronym or abbreviation, and apply the Small Caps [**smcap**] character style to them.

Easy ways to create new paragraph and character styles as needed

Sometimes, as you're formatting your text, you suddenly find that you need a new paragraph style. A simple way to create a new style is to first make the changes directly to the paragraph you're working in and then name the style you've just created. Follow the steps below.

1. Select all the text in the paragraph by quadruple-clicking, then make changes to it using the Paragraph (not Paragraph Styles) and/or Character (not Character Styles) panels, or the Control panel at the top of your screen. You may add space before and/or after, change the typeface, the size or leading, the alignment, the indents, the color, etc.

2. When you've found a look that you like, keep your cursor in that paragraph and open the Paragraph Styles panel.

3. Click on the fly-out menu at the upper right corner of the panel and select New Paragraph Style. In the General area, give the new style a name. If you only made a couple of small changes from the style you were originally using (keeping your styles family tree in mind), scroll to that style name in the Based On list. If your new style is completely different, select [No Paragraph Style] from the list.

4. Go through the other areas of the Paragraph Styles panel and look at the settings. You'll find that your new style has adopted all the settings of the selected paragraph. Think about whether you should perhaps add space above or below this new style, whether it should be hyphenated or not, and anything else that might improve it. Be sure that you've checked Apply Style to Selection in the General area of the Paragraph Styles panel. Then, any changes you make to the settings will affect the current paragraph as well as any future paragraphs that use this new style.

To create a new character style, follow the same procedure. Make changes to your selected text using either the Character (not Character Styles) panel or the Control panel. Then open the Character Styles panel, create a new style, give it a name, check the settings, and make any changes that you think will improve the style.

Even if you think you'll only use this new style once in the entire book, give it a name anyway. If you're planning an ebook, you *must* do this. Every single paragraph in an ebook needs a paragraph style! Every single character not conforming to a paragraph style in an ebook needs a character style, too!

Roughing in your back matter

Many books don't contain any back matter and, if that's the case with your book, simply skip this section. Make sure your book ends on a verso page (i.e., has an even number of pages). If it ends on a recto page, just add a blank page at the end.

If your book includes appendixes, endnotes, references, a bibliography, a glossary, resources lists, an index, or any other back matter, then you'll need to allocate some pages for them.

If you need to, return to page 25 to see the normal order for back matter elements.

Rough in your back matter the same way you did your front matter. The first back matter item always begins on a recto page, so you may need to insert an extra page break at the end of your chapters to start your back matter on a recto page.

Now go through your back matter and insert page breaks at the end of each item in the back matter to rough in the pages. If you don't have any back matter yet, you can still create your back matter pages using place-holders. For example, type "Glossary" at the top of a page, then insert one page break for each page your glossary will require. Do the same for each item in your back matter until all the pages you'll need are roughed in.

You'll create separate paragraph styles for your back matter in chapter 29. For the time being, select all the text in your back matter and apply the Text [**tx**] paragraph style to it.

You've finished the first pass through your whole book, roughing in all your pages and applying your paragraph and character styles to absolutely everything. Way to go!

15

Adding folios and running heads

Folios and running heads are your book's navigation tools. They usually go at the tops of your pages, with the chapter title on the left and the author's name or chapter title on the right.

The folios and running heads are always placed on master pages. Master pages can be described as a style for the overall look of pages, much the way paragraph styles are used to control the overall look of paragraphs. Each master page is set up with a particular format, which can then be applied to pages within your book. And each master page is based on its parent page, the A-Master.

At present you have one master page in your document: A-Master. Look at the top portion of your Pages panel, and you'll see A-Master there. Below A-Master are thumbnails of all your pages, and they all have the letter A at the top outer corners. This means that A-Master is applied to these pages.

Double-click on A-Master in your Pages panel, and the A-Master two-page spread will open. These pages are the same trim size as your whole document, and they have the margins that you specified when you set up your document.

A-Master is the master template for your whole document. This is important! This means that from now on, every time you make a change that needs to affect all the pages in your document, you'll make that change on A-Master.

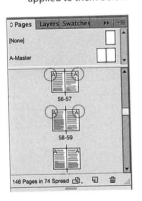

Adding folios to A-Master

Open A-Master by double-clicking it in your Pages panel. Using your Selection Tool, select Normal view in the Toolbox (or press W) so you can see the margins on A-Master. Click View>Show Rulers or press Ctrl/Cmd+R to display rulers along the top and down the left of your screen.

Most printers require a minimum of 0.5″ clearance from the top edge of the page, so your running heads and folios must be below that mark. Drag a guide to the 0.5″ mark by clicking inside the top ruler, dragging a guide down to the 0.5″ mark on the left ruler, and releasing the mouse button.

Switch to the Type Tool, and drag a new text frame anywhere in the top margin on, say, the verso page. In the Paragraph Styles panel, click the Folio [**fol**] paragraph style once to select it. Instead of typing a page number in the text frame, you'll add a Current Page Number marker by clicking Type>Insert Special Character>Markers>Current Page Number or pressing Ctrl/Cmd+Shift+Alt/Opt+N. On A-Master, the marker will appear as a capital A; however, on any page in your book with A-Master applied, the actual page number will show.

With the Selection Tool, drag the text frame into position. Align the left side with the outside margin and the top with the guide, and the bottom with the top margin; the right side can go anywhere you like.

Now you'll add a folio to the recto page. Select the folio text frame on the verso page with the Selection Tool and press Alt/Opt+Shift (to duplicate the text frame *and* keep it in the same horizontal plane as its original), while dragging the copy across to the recto page, positioning the right edge against the outside margin.

Voilà! Now go back to your Pages panel and double-click any page or two-page spread in your book. You'll see that all your pages now have page numbers.

While you are dragging a guide down, hold the Ctrl/Cmd key to make the guide extend across both pages and the pasteboard. If the guide only extends across one page, select it with your Selection Tool and press Ctrl/Cmd to extend it.

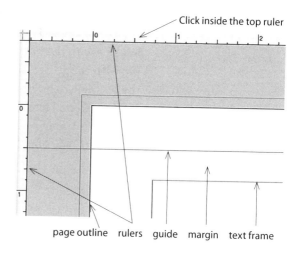

Click inside the top ruler

page outline   rulers   guide   margin   text frame

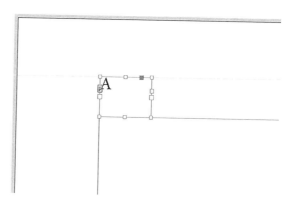

The Current Page Number Marker will appear in the top outside corner of your text frame, as the Folio [**fol**] character style applied to it specifies alignment away from the spine.

Adding running heads to A-Master

To switch from the Selection Tool to the Type Tool, press T. To switch from the Type Tool to the Selection Tool, press Esc (Windows) or V (Mac OS). Make sure no type or object is selected when you do this.

Open your A-Master page and, using the Type Tool, drag a new text frame anywhere across the top margin on the verso page. In the Paragraph Styles panel, click the Running Heads [**rh**] paragraph style once to select it, and type your book's title in the text frame.

With the Selection Tool, drag the text frame into position. Align the left side with the outside margin (yes, overlapping with the folio) and the top with the guide. Then adjust the other edges of the text frame so that the bottom is a bit below the text and the right side is aligned with the inside margin. Note that the folio's text frame is taller than the running head's text frame so that each is easy to select in the future and not stuck behind the other one.

Pressing Alt/Opt while dragging a frame with the Selection Tool will create a duplicate of the frame and its contents (whether text or an image).

Pressing the Shift key while dragging a frame will keep the frame in the same position either vertically or horizontally on the page.

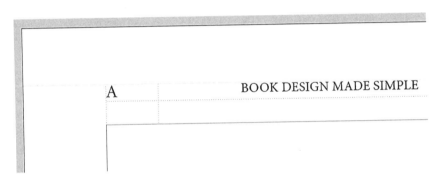

Now add a running head to the recto page. Select the running head text frame on the verso page with the Selection Tool, press Alt/Opt+Shift, and drag the copy across to the recto page, positioning the right edge against the outside margin. Switch to the Type Tool and replace the book title with the author's name or chapter title.

When you convert to an ebook, all your folios and running heads will be deleted.

Return to any two-page spread in your book by going back to your Pages panel and double-clicking any page or two-page spread. You'll see that all your pages now have folios *and* running heads. Don't worry if every recto page has the same chapter title on it. You'll put the correct chapter titles in the running heads later on, in chapter 52. It doesn't pay to use the specific chapter titles at this stage, because your chapters are probably going to shift forward and backward a bit before settling into place.

Printing pages

InDesign gives you a lot of control over how your pages print. You can print spreads (two facing pages on one sheet), scale your pages to fit standard paper sizes, and so on.

In this chapter, you'll:

1 Set up your printer to print book pages
2 Save your print settings as a preset
3 Print some pages, trim to size, and see what they look like

Open your Print dialog box by choosing File>Print or by pressing Ctrl/Cmd+P. The Print dialog box will open with the General category selected on the left.

1 Setting up your printer
General

Choose your printer from the Printer drop-down menu if it didn't automatically appear in the Printer box. Next, in the Pages: Range box, type the page numbers you want to print. To print consecutive pages, type the first and last page numbers, separated by a hyphen (e.g., 7-9). To print non-consecutive pages, type the page numbers, separated by commas (e.g., 7,9,12). Or, you can print a combination of both (e.g., 7-9,12). Note that there are no spaces between the numbers, just a hyphen or comma.

Under Options, check Print Blank Pages.

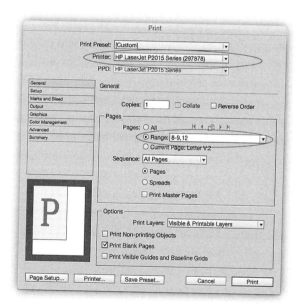

Setup

Click the Setup category on the left. Under Paper Size, the size of paper available in your printer should show there (usually US sLetter or 8.5″ × 11″ in the Americas, and A4 or 8.27″ × 11.69″ elsewhere). The Orientation is Portrait.

Under Options, keep the Scale at 100%, but change Page Position to centered. You'll see the thumbnail with the letter P in it at the left change when you change the Page Position.

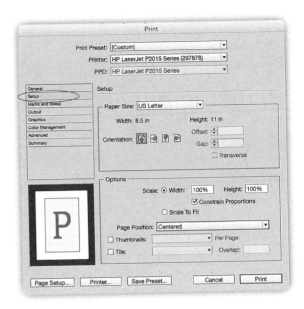

Marks and Bleed

Under Marks, check Crop Marks and Page Information. That way, when you print your pages, the crop marks will show the trim size of your pages, and the page information will print the name of the document, page number, and date and time of printing.

In the Bleed and Slug box, check Use Document Bleed Settings. That way anything that extends into the bleed area will be printed.

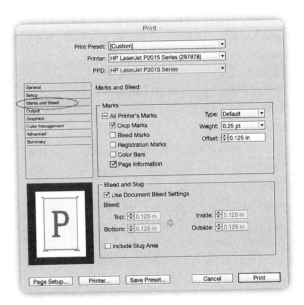

Output

This category lets you set your color parameters. For now, if you are printing on a color printer, leave the default color setting at Composite RGB. If you are printing with black ink only, change the Color to Composite Gray.

Graphics, Color Management, Advanced, Summary

No need to change any settings in the Graphics, Color Management, Advanced, or Summary categories.

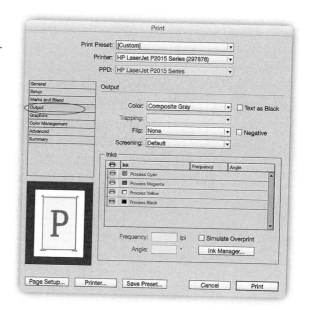

2 Saving your preset

Now that you've adjusted the settings in your Print dialog box, be sure to save them as a preset. That way, every time you print from InDesign, your settings will automatically appear.

Click the Save Preset button at the bottom left of the Print dialog box, and the Save Preset dialog box appears. Type in a name for your preset, then click OK. Now your preset will show in the Print Preset drop-down menu at the top of the Print dialog box.

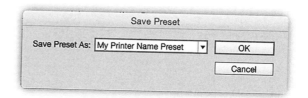

3 Printing your pages

To print pages or a whole document using these settings, simply open your Print dialog box, select your preset, choose the page numbers you want to print, and click Print.

Another way to choose the pages you want to print is by selecting them in the Pages panel. Holding the Ctrl/Cmd key, click on various thumbnails. Hover over a selected page in the Pages panel, then right-click and select Print Pages. The Range field will be filled in automatically.

The next section in this book explains how to customize the design of your book's pages at every level, starting from your book's overall trim size and going right down to the smallest details in your paragraph and character styles.

If you're satisfied with the way your book looks now, feel free to skip Part IV: Designing Your Pages and go straight to Part V: Adding Shapes & Color. If you don't need any shapes or color in your pages, then skip to Part VI: Adding Images. If you don't have any images inside your book, you'll still want to follow the instructions in chapter 23 to set up a baseline grid for your pages.

Chances are good that, even if you don't have shapes or images in your book, you'll refer back to Parts V and VI when you begin designing your book cover.

Part IV:
Designing Your Pages

17 *Changing your page design*

Now that you've applied your paragraph and character styles to all the text on your pages, look through your pages in InDesign or print them, and see if you're satisfied with the design you created following the instructions in this book. Even if you're pleased with the way your book looks (its trim size, the layout of the pages, the typeface and type size of all your text, and so on), be sure to read chapter 23 on setting up your baseline grid. Then feel free to skip the rest of Part IV: Designing Your Pages.

However, if you'd like to change some aspects of your page design to better suit your book, then Part IV is written for you! You'll be guided through changing the design of every aspect of your pages.

Part IV is set up so that the first changes you make, if you wish, are ones that affect the book and pages as a whole. These are large-scale changes that will affect the flow of text on all pages, and these changes are made globally on the A-Master page (see chapters 18–20).

Once your page size and margins are established, you'll make any changes you choose to the typeface and type size for your main text, and for other text in your book as needed. These are mid-scale changes that affect all the text in your book, and these changes are made globally to your Basic Paragraph and other paragraph styles (see chapters 21–23).

Then you'll be guided through making changes to your chapter opening pages, headings, folios and running heads, and all the other elements you set up paragraph styles for in Part II (see chapters 24–27).

And, finally, you'll design all the text and pages in your front and back matter based on the final design of your chapter pages (see chapters 28 and 29).

Now that the hard work of creating and applying your paragraph styles is done, enjoy the creative process of experimenting with changes to your book design. Have fun!

Using master pages

Master pages are used to make global changes to pages, much the way paragraph styles are used to make global changes to paragraphs. Each master page is set up with a particular format, which can then be applied to pages within your book.

At present you have one master page in your document: A-Master. This is the master page you added your folios and running heads to in chapter 15. Double-click on A-Master in your Pages panel to open it. Note that these pages are the same trim size as your whole document, and they have the same margins that you specified when you set up your document.

A-Master is the master template for your whole document. This is important. This means that from now on, every time you make a change that needs to affect *all* the pages in your document, you'll make that change on A-Master. For example, if you decide to change your margins, you'll change them on A-Master. That way, *all* your pages will be changed and get exactly the same margins at the same time.

In a typical book, A-Master controls the margins, running heads/feet, and folios. So if you decide to move your running heads/feet or folios to a different position on the page, you'll make that change on A-Master.

All of the items on A-Master will be visible on the pages to which A-Master is applied. However, you won't be able to select them using the Selection or Type tools on any pages except A-Master without specifically overriding them.

It's possible that a book with a simple layout (say, a novel) could have just one master page—A-Master. With the running heads set with the book's title on the left page and the author's name on the right page, all the pages in the book could have the same master page. You would simply delete the folios and running heads from any pages that didn't require them (such as front matter or chapter opening pages).

Pages panel with A-Master at the top and pages with A-Master applied to them below.

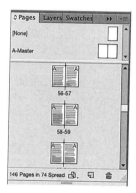

If, for some reason, you need to move, delete, or change any master page item while you're working on a book page, you can select it by holding down Ctrl/Cmd+Shift while you click on the item with any tool.

With master pages for each chapter numbered according to the chapter number, it's easy to see the chapters in the thumbnails of the Pages panel.

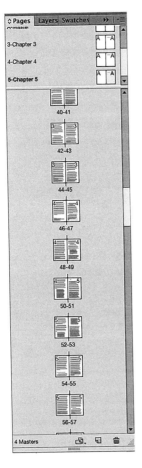

However, most books have more than one master page, usually one for each chapter (with the chapter title in the running head) and a few for the front and back matter, with all master pages being based on A-Master.

For example, this book has 75 master pages that are all based on A-Master. A-Master contains the margins, running feet, and folios, as well as columns (see page 128), guides (see page 127), and a baseline grid (see chapter 23). There is a separate master for each chapter because the chapter title in the running feet at the bottom right is different for each chapter. So it's easiest to create a new master for each chapter, *based on A-Master*, with just the chapter title changed. You'll learn how to do this in chapter 52.

For now, the important thing to remember is that any changes you make to your margins, running heads/feet, or folios will be made on A-Master.

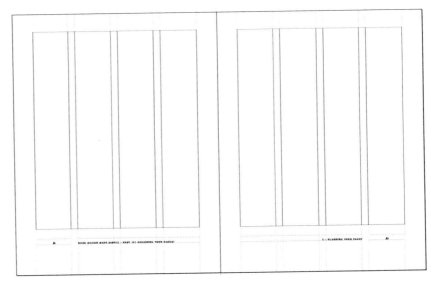

The A-Master pages for *this* book include margins, running feet, folios, columns, guides, and a baseline grid.

Changing your trim size

There are lots of reasons why you might want to change your book's trim size. For starters, it's an easy way to gain or lose several pages if you'd prefer a thicker or thinner book. Or, you may want your pages to look more or less spacious than they do now. Or, perhaps you've simply changed your mind since choosing a trim size in chapter 5.

Before changing your trim size, be sure to enable your Layout Adjustment. When Layout Adjustment is enabled, InDesign adjusts all your text frames and margins every time you make a change.

Let's say you change your trim size from 5.5″ × 8.5″ to 6″ × 9″. InDesign will move your margins so that now they are the specified distance from the new edges of your pages. InDesign will also resize all your text frames so they fit within the margins and will reflow all the text within those frames. This saves you from changing the size of every text frame manually.

You don't need to open A-Master to change your trim size; it can be done from anywhere in your document.

If you plan to print your book on a traditional offset press (as opposed to a digital press), now is the time to start thinking about your final page count. On an offset press, books are printed in groups of pages on one large sheet of paper, so the number of pages in the book must be divisible by the number of pages that fit on one sheet. Your printer will tell you this number (called a "printing number"). See more in chapter 48 about offset printing and what you need to do to plan your final page count.

Enabling Layout Adjustment

Click Layout>Margins and Columns and then check the Enable Layout Adjustment box. Click OK.

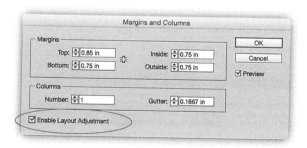

Changing your book's trim size

Click File>Document Setup to open the Document Setup dialog box. Choose your new trim size by changing the numbers in the Width and Height boxes, then click OK.

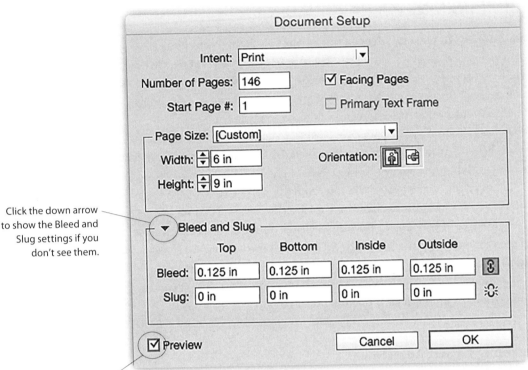

Click the down arrow to show the Bleed and Slug settings if you don't see them.

Check Preview to see your changes as you make them.

You'll see that your pages now have the new trim size, but the margins are the same distance from the edges of the pages as they were before. The size of your text frames, however, will have changed, causing your text to reflow and your page count to change.

Keeping standard printing sizes in mind

Remember, standard sizes are more cost-effective to print. Refer to pages 20 and 21 for standard printing sizes, and also check printers' websites for other available standard sizes for children's books, coffee table books, and other larger-sized books.

Changing your margins

Increasing or decreasing your margins affects both the look of your pages *and* your page count. Any changes made to your margins are always made on A-Master.

Design considerations when adjusting your margins

White space is good

It never hurts to be generous with white space. Think about your experience with reading books. If the text is too close to the spine, it's uncomfortable to read. Your hand gets sore trying to keep the book open enough to easily read all the text.

Same with the text towards the outsides and bottom of the pages. These areas are known as "thumb space." Do you have to keep moving your thumbs to read the text at the outsides or bottoms of the pages? Lack of white space in these areas makes it frustrating to read.

Margins increase as leading increases

As a general rule, type set with lots of leading looks odd with very narrow margins (left below). Conversely, type set with very little leading looks odd with generous margins (right below). If the type and leading are generous, the margins should be generous too, and vice versa.

 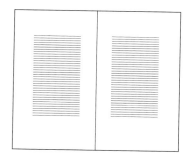

Quick notes on margin settings

Inside margin

The standard size of the inside margin is 0.75". Most books with trim sizes of 5" × 8", 5.5" × 8.5", and 6" × 9" have an inside margin of 0.75". That allows enough space for binding the book.

When a book gets to a certain thickness (usually around 400 pages), the inside margin can be a bit bigger, say 0.875" or 1". Books with sewn binding (more expensive) will lie open flatter, and the inside margin will be less of a issue. But books with perfect binding (glued) will need a bit more room on the inside margin if they are over 400 pages.

Top margin

Most books have running heads rather than running feet. If you are planning to have running heads, the top margin needs to be large enough to accommodate them.

A standard top margin in a book with running heads is 0.825" to 0.875". In books without running heads, the minimum margin is 0.5", as some printers have a minimum clearance from the edges of pages of 0.5".

Outside margin

The outside margin is often the same size as the inside margin, yet the outside margin still *appears* larger because part of the inside margin is hidden in the binding.

Bottom margin

Having an ample bottom margin is never a bad thing, and ideally it should be your largest margin. Also keep in mind that when a book is printed and bound, everything always looks lower on the page (really!). So don't be tempted to narrow your bottom margin too much (say a minimum of 0.75").

One last thing to remember: generous leading calls for generous margins, and narrower leading calls for narrower margins.

Remember that your running heads and folios appear above the top margin, so they are not counted in the margin measurements.

Remember that if you're using running feet and drop folios, they appear below the bottom margin.

Adjusting your margins

Open A-Master to get started. You'll want to see your changes as you make them. An easy way to do so is to copy and paste a 2-page spread onto A-Master. Find any 2-page spread where the text fills both pages, then select both text frames by holding Shift and clicking them with the Selection Tool. Copy the text frames by clicking Edit>Copy, then double-click A-Master to open it. Paste the text frames into A-Master in the exact place they were on your 2-page spread by clicking Edit>Paste in Place. Now you're ready to adjust your margins.

Click Layout>Margins and Columns to open the Margins and Columns dialog box. If you've set your margins following the guidelines on page 34, your Margins and Columns dialog box will look something like this:

The keyboard shortcut for Copy is Ctrl/Cmd+C.

The keyboard shortcut for Paste is Ctrl/Cmd+V.

The keyboard shortcut for Paste in Place is Ctrl/Cmd+Shift+Alt/Opt+V.

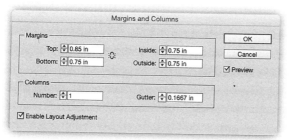

Make sure the Preview box is checked. Try changing the top margin by clicking the up and down arrows next to it. You'll see that the margin shifts each time you click it. This may take a moment or two, depending on how many pages are in your book, as InDesign will be changing all your pages at the same time.

Select both A-Master pages in the Pages panel to make changes on both pages at once.

Review the design considerations and margin settings on pages 123 and 124, and then start making your adjustments on A-Master. When you're finished, use the Selection Tool to delete the two text frames of type that you pasted into A-Master.

How wide can your margins be? That depends on your typeface and type size. Your text frame should accommodate a minimum of 27 characters per line, around 40 is optimal, and 70 is the maximum. To see how many characters fit on one line in *your* book, type a line of numbers:

The main text frame on *this* page is 64 characters wide. If the type size and leading were smaller, these lines would seem too long to be comfortably read. But at a type and size of Chaparral 10.5 pt and with generous leading of 14 pt, a line length of 64 characters is comfortable to read.

12345678901234567890123456789012345678901234567890123456789012345678901234

Using margins and columns to change your page layout

Most books are designed with one column containing the main text frame. However, some books are designed with a wider format to accommodate images, sidebars, or text in multiple columns. Examples are coffee table books, cookbooks, and how-to books, like this one.

For a larger-format book, it's often helpful to create a grid of columns rather than just, say, two. You might think the layout grid for this book is two columns (one large column toward the spine for the main narrative and a smaller column on the outside for captions), but actually it has four columns. This way, the main text occupies three columns and the captions one column, but there is also the choice of setting type or images in two equal columns side by side.

Since you have already checked the box enabling Layout Adjustment (see page 125), open A-Master and the Margins and Columns dialog box again. Under Columns, enter the number of columns you want and the gutter between them. Just make sure that Enable Layout Adjustment is checked, and click OK.

Look at any two-page spread in your book and you'll see that InDesign has reflowed your text into columns on each page, with individual text frames for each column. If you've created a two-column format, the text will have reflowed perfectly into two columns on each page with two linked text frames, and you are good to go.

But what if you don't want the text to flow into every column? Suppose you want your main text frame to be three columns wide with no text frame in the fourth column, as in this book. You simply need to trick InDesign slightly by pretending you want four columns and then switching to one column at the end. See the next page for instructions.

The page layout of *Book Design Made Simple* is based on a 4-column grid with a 0.25" gutter between them, as indicated by the light gray lines on this page.

For recipes, you might want a narrow column on the left for ingredients and a wider one on the right for instructions, but the proportions mentioned on this page will probably not work. To find the best column widths, experiment with your longest recipe until it fits well on the page, and then base all your other recipes on that layout by making a master page spread. For more cookbook tips, go to www.BookDesignMade Simple.com.

captions =
1 column wide

main text frame = 3 columns wide

By following the steps below, you will get pages that will look more like the gray outlines shown on *this* page. Make sure you're on your A-Master page and in the Normal view mode.

1   If you want to start over, undo the columns you made earlier.

Undo your most recent change by clicking Edit>Undo or by using the keyboard short-cut of Ctrl/Cmd+Z.

2   Return to Layout>Margins and Columns and uncheck the Enable Lay-out Adjustment box. Select the number of columns you want to base your grid on and the gutter between them, and click OK. On A-Master, drag vertical guides to the left and right edge of each column that you made. (Put your pointer in the ruler on the left edge of the screen and drag to the right to make the guides.) For a four-column page like this one, you should end up with eight vertical guides. Repeat this on the other page of the A-Master spread. See figure A on the next page.

vertical guides

3   Using the Measure tool (⬜), put your pointer (⬜) at the outside trim edge of one of the pages, then hold down Shift as you drag horizon-tally to the outside of the main text area that you want to create; on *this* page it would be the third guide from the outside trim (as in fig-ure A on the next page). When the Info panel pops up automatically, make a note of the width (W) of the line. Close the Info panel. The mark made by the Measure tool will disappear as soon as you click on another tool.

The Measure tool might be hiding behind the Eyedropper or the Color Theme tool.

outside edge of text frame

4   Go to Layout>Liquid Layout and in the fly-out menu click Layout Adjustment. Uncheck Allow Ruler Guides to Move, then click OK. Go to Layout>Margins and Columns and first check Enable Layout Adjustment, then change the number of columns to 1. Next, change the outside margin to the width of the line you measured in step 3. Click OK, and InDesign will reflow all your text into the new single column that you made. Your page will have an enormous outside mar-gin, with two vertical guides showing you where your outside column is, and the other vertical guides indicating the rest of your grid. Figure B on the next page shows the result.

← main text frame = 3 columns wide →

captions = 1 column wide

A

Drag vertical guides (see page 111) to the left and right edges of each column.

The light gray area represents the 4-column text frame that you created in the Margins and Columns dialog box in step 2 on page 127.

B

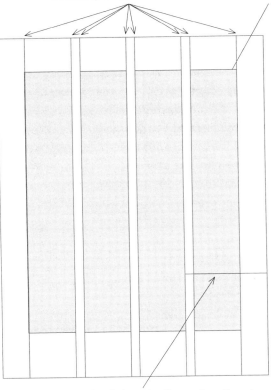

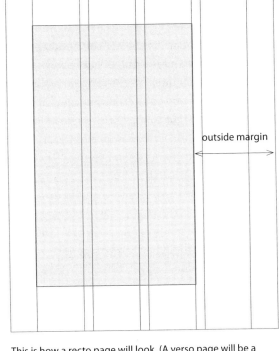

outside margin

Use the Measure tool to find out the distance from the outside trim to the outside of the area that you want for your main text frame. Look in the Info panel for the value.

This is how a recto page will look. (A verso page will be a mirror image of it.) The text frame (light gray) is only 1 column, but it's 3 columns wide. The outer column is 1 column wide. When you want to use the outer column, simply draw a text frame between the outer guides. All of the vertical guides are there when you need them to show you where to place captions or 2-column-wide text and images.

Because Layout Adjustment is turned on, InDesign automatically fills exactly the area that you want to use on each page for your main text and leaves the rest free for captions, images, and so on.

A three-column or five (or more)-column grid might work better for your book. It all depends on the page dimensions and the sizes and shapes of your images and materials.

Changing your main typeface

The single most important part of book design is ensuring that your main text is easy to read. This means you'll use a typeface suitable for long documents. Take a quick look through the books on your shelf. You'll see that most books use serif typefaces for the main text, because they are the easiest to read for long, continuous blocks of text.

Three categories of typefaces

Serif

R

Minion Pro

Serif typefaces have strokes, mostly either horizontal or oblique, added to the basic letterform. They are the easiest to read at smaller sizes, especially for long blocks of text.

Sans Serif

R

Myriad Pro

Sans serif typefaces don't have any additions to the basic letterform and are more difficult to read in continuous text. They are used for headings, running heads/feet, folios, and sidebars.

Display

R

Brush Script Std

Display typefaces are not suitable for continuous text. They are used for design elements such as chapter numbers, chapter titles, or drop caps at the beginning of chapters.

Adobe Creative Cloud has many typefaces that are suitable for books. You can search the Recommended for Paragraphs category in Typekit to find one that you like. Each typeface has different characteristics that will determine whether it is the perfect choice for *your* book.

Comparing four popular serif typefaces

Caslon Pro

This paragraph is set in Adobe Caslon Pro. This typeface is classic, and the letters look a bit old fashioned and flowery. The letters appear slightly bigger than in the typefaces below, even though the type size is the same (11/14). Caslon is ideal for historical novels, nonfiction books, and poetry.

One great thing about Caslon is its ornaments: ☒ ⚜ ⚘ ⚛ ❀ ⚘ ☙

Chaparral Pro

This paragraph is set in Chaparral Pro (as is the main text in this book). This typeface is modern, and the letters are a bit industrial-looking. See how this typeface is slightly bolder and darker on the page than the others. Chaparral is ideal for fiction, science fiction, how-to books, and friendly nonfiction.

One great thing about Chaparral is that its **bold is very BOLD.**

Garamond Pro

This paragraph is set in Adobe Garamond Pro. This typeface is classic and very easy to read at small sizes. See how much less crowded Garamond looks because of the smaller lowercase letters? Garamond is ideal for any book and is one of the most often-used typefaces for books.

One great thing about Garamond is its BEAUTIFUL SMALL CAPS.

Minion Pro

This paragraph is set in Minion Pro. This typeface is modern and clean. See how the letters are straightforward and direct. Minion is ideal for business books, nonfiction, and fiction, and it pairs well with the sans serif Myriad for titles and subheadings.

One great thing about Minion is its *gorgeous italics.*

What to look for in a font family

A font family is comprised of several related typefaces, all designed to be used together. For your book, you'll want to choose a font family that includes all the faces you'll need.

Example: Minion Pro font family

Regular (used for your main text)

lowercase: abcdefghijklmnopqrstuvwxyz !@#$%^&*()+

uppercase: ABCDEFGHIJKLMNOPQRSTUVWXYZ

oldstyle figures: 1234567890   lining figures: 1234567890

Some fonts use the term Roman for regular type—it's the traditional term for neither italic nor bold.

Italic (used for emphasis, headings, book titles, etc.)

lowercase: *abcdefghijklmnopqrstuvwxyz !@#$%^&*()+*

uppercase: *ABCDEFGHIJKLMNOPQRSTUVWXYZ*

oldstyle figures: *1234567890*   lining figures: *1234567890*

Small capitals (good for subheadings and acronyms)

regular: ABCDEFGHIJKLMNOPQRSTUVWXYZ !@#$%^&*()+

italic: *ABCDEFGHIJKLMNOPQRSTUVWXYZ*

oldstyle figures: 1234567890   lining figures: 1234567890

Semibold or Medium (good for headings)

lowercase: abcdefghijklmnopqrstuvwxyz !@#$%^&*()+

uppercase: ABCDEFGHIJKLMNOPQRSTUVWXYZ

oldstyle figures: 1234567890   lining figures: 1234567890

Semibold Italic or Medium Italic (good for headings)

lowercase: *abcdefghijklmnopqrstuvwxyz !@#$%^&*()+*

uppercase: *ABCDEFGHIJKLMNOPQRSTUVWXYZ*

oldstyle figures: *1234567890*   lining figures: *1234567890*

Bold (good for headings but not used for emphasis in main text)

lowercase: abcdefghijklmnopqrstuvwxyz !@#$%^&*()+

uppercase: ABCDEFGHIJKLMNOPQRSTUVWXYZ

oldstyle figures: 1234567890   lining figures: 1234567890

Bold Italic (good for headings but not used for emphasis in main text)

lowercase: *abcdefghijklmnopqrstuvwxyz !@#$%^&*()+*

uppercase: *ABCDEFGHIJKLMNOPQRSTUVWXYZ*

oldstyle figures: *1234567890*   lining figures: *1234567890*

Fonts: Using them legally

Most people give no thought to the legal use of fonts. But those in the publishing industry (that's you!) need to be aware of legitimate font use at all times. Luckily, Adobe Creative Cloud has simplified the issue by allowing you to use Typekit fonts without restriction—as long as you stick with Desktop use and don't stray into Web use. Web fonts have a separate license.

You may legally use the CC fonts for printing your book, making an ebook file (but see the Typekit Services Agreement for a few restrictions), and creating any kind of printed advertising or products, such as T-shirts, bookmarks, postcards, or business cards. You may also make PDFs to distribute as you like. Do not use the fonts as HTML type on your website without first signing up for Web font service.

When you uninstall the Creative Cloud package, you lose all the fonts because they were never really yours to begin with; they are just synced to your computer while you are signed up for the service.

If you would like to use some of the fonts in the future outside of CC, you will need to purchase them.

"Typeface" vs. "Font"

What's the difference? A typeface is the design that makes Caslon look different from Helvetica, for instance. A font is the delivery system for the typeface, whether it be a computer file or a set of metal type.

Fonts: How and what to buy

There are a great many websites that sell fonts. At www.BookDesignMadeSimple.com, we keep an updated list of the more commonly used sites, but you may discover others. Here are a few:

- myfonts.com
- fonts.com
- fontshop.com

Always buy OpenType fonts. When you browse for fonts online, look for the OpenType symbol (a two-color, italic "O") or the word "OpenType" in the product description. OpenType fonts are produced through a collaboration between Microsoft and Adobe, and both companies, and others, have brought their older font products into the OpenType format. That is why you might see various additional phrases that describe font software, such as "Type 1 OpenType," "TrueType flavor," "PostScript flavor," or "OpenTypeCFF." All of these are fine to use.

One great thing about OpenType fonts is that they work on both Windows and Macintosh computers. Another is all the special features that come with them, such as the various kinds of figure styles, the ability to build fractions easily, and everything else you can see in the OpenType Features dialog box in your Paragraph Styles and Character Styles panels.

Once you purchase and download the product, you'll receive a folder or file with installation instructions.

Choosing a typeface for your main text

The easiest way to choose a typeface for your main text is to experiment with some typefaces you can sync with Creative Cloud's Typekit. That way you can see what *your* words look like in different typefaces.

All the changes you make to your type at the design stage will be done within your paragraph styles. Find a 2-page spread in your document with a lot of type on it. Using your Selection Tool, click anywhere outside your document to make sure nothing is selected, then switch to Preview mode using the View Tool or by pressing W.

Double-click your Basic Paragraph style in the Paragraph Styles panel, and select Basic Character Formats on the left. Make sure the Preview box at the bottom left is checked. All the typefaces installed on your computer are contained in the drop-down menu called Font Family. At present, you'll see Minion Pro in the Font Family drop-down menu. Choose a different typeface from the menu, and you'll see all the type on your pages change to that typeface.

While your cursor is in the Font Family drop-down menu, you can use your up and down arrow keys to try every typeface on your computer. Of course, most of the typefaces won't be suitable for your main text, but it's interesting to see how different your type looks in different typefaces. Make a list of the typefaces you think have potential for your book.

These typeface changes you are viewing are only temporary while Paragraph Style Options is open. To close Paragraph Style Options without making any changes, simply click Cancel. To change your Text [**tx**] style to a different typeface, choose the typeface from the Font Family drop-down menu, and click OK.

You'll need to print several two-page spreads while you're designing your pages. Whenever you adjust your typeface, type size, leading, or margins, the overall look of your pages will change. The easiest way to check that the changes are improving your design is to print two pages, trim them to size, and tape them together in a two-page spread. Then insert the pages into a similarly sized book and see what they will look like when your book is printed and bound.

To sync a new font to use in InDesign, go into the Creative Cloud application and click on Assets>Fonts>Add Fonts from Typekit. Search by categories, click Use Fonts, choose type styles (roman, bold, italic, etc.), and click "Sync selected fonts."

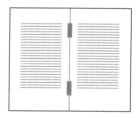

Looking more closely at type

Now that you've been looking at and thinking about typefaces for a while, you may have become curious about typographical design. How is it that the typefaces look similar but also different?

Many books have been written about the history and design of type. But to make a very long story extremely short, the design of type began in the Western world as soon as Johannes Gutenberg typeset and printed copies of the Bible in the 1450s. He based the shapes of his metal letters on the standard German handwriting of the time. As the centuries advanced and the technology spread, different typesetters developed their own styles, each time expanding the collection of typefaces. Many fonts are named after their designers, such as Garamond, Jenson, Bodoni, Caslon, and even Zapf Dingbats.

Nowadays we have access to just about every type design that has come before, and more are being introduced all the time. It's almost overwhelming (though fascinating) to browse through a font vendor's website. You can usually read a brief history of any font you choose, and often you'll discover that you can tell the difference between a very old typeface and a contemporary one at a glance. To be very untechnical about it, somehow the letters just give off a vibe from their century of origin.

To the right you'll see the names of some letter parts. Every typeface applies the shapes of these parts in a very consistent way, and the combinations of shapes and proportions are what give a typeface its look.

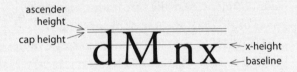

Setting type size and leading

Once you've chosen a typeface for your main text, you'll want to experiment with its size and leading (rhymes with heading). A type size of 11 pt is very common for books, and the leading is usually set two or three points above the type size. If your type size and leading are set at 11 pt and 14 pt respectively, then it's written like this: 11/14 (say 11 on 14).

You'll want to change your type size and leading if your book needs a larger type size (for example, for a younger or older readership), or if the main typeface you chose looks a bit small or crowded at 11/14.

What is the best type size and leading for your book? This will depend on marketplace standards and personal preferences. Look at several other published books in your genre and see what type sizes are used. Most type for fiction and nonfiction books is set in the 10 pt to 12 pt range. Large-print and children's books are often set in the 12 pt to 16 pt range. Find a book you like with an appropriate type size for your book, and use it as a starting point.

Try copying and pasting a paragraph from your book into a new page or document. Paste it again several times, then apply various type sizes and leading combinations in each paragraph. Print out the page and place it next to some text in another book in your genre.

Setting your type size

To set the type size for your main text, double-click the Basic Paragraph style in your Paragraph Styles panel to open the Paragraph Style Options. Make sure the Preview box at the bottom is checked so you can see changes on the fly. Select the Basic Character Formats category on the left, then change the Size drop-down menu to your new type size. You can either type in a size or select a standard size from the drop-down menu. Fractional sizes are also available, such as 11.5 pt or 10.75 pt.

When you've set your new type size, click OK to make the change throughout your main text. Print a page (see chapter 16) to see how the type looks in print. You'll see that your type size has changed but the leading is still the same, so if your type is bigger it will look more crowded, and if your type is smaller it will look more spacious.

Finding the ideal leading for your type

Leading is usually set two or three points larger than the type size. For example, if your type size is 11 pt, then your leading could be 13 or 14 pt. Leading set two points larger is the minimum you want for your book, as less will look crowded and be harder to read. Adding leading to your type is a way to create a more spacious feel for your book and make your paragraphs easier to read.

Look at the samples on page 137 to see how changing the amount of leading changes the look and feel of the type, and the color of the page as a whole. If the leading is too tight, the words look crowded. If it's too spacious, the lines begin to appear unconnected. So find a happy medium for your type—not too crowded and not too spacious. If you're in doubt, go through other books in your genre and see what looks best to you.

The main text in this book is set in Chaparral Pro at 10.5/14.

The margin captions in this book (such as this one) are set in Myriad Pro at 8/10.5.

Experiment with the amount of leading in your main text by going back into your Paragraph Style Options for the Basic Paragraph style. Select the Basic Character Formats category on the left, then change the Leading drop-down menu to a size that is two or three points larger than your type size. You can either type in the size or select a standard size from the drop-down menu. Fractional sizes are also available, such as 13.5 pt or 12.75 pt.

When you've set your new leading size, click OK to make the change throughout your main text. Print a 2-page spread to see how the type looks in print. Change the amount of leading a few times and print a two-page spread each time. Then compare the spreads to see which type and leading combination works the best for your book.

Keep in mind that increasing your leading means there could be one fewer line per page, and decreasing it could add a line to each page.

Type size and leading examples

Below are samples of type set in Adobe Garamond Pro (on the left) and Adobe Minion Pro (on the right). The lines in these columns are narrower than the lines in your book will be, but they'll give you a good idea of how type size and leading interact.

The first paragraph in each column is set in 11/14, the second in 11/13, and the third in 11/12. Notice how the different leadings affect the look of the paragraphs even though the type is all the same size. Also note that Minion requires more lines than Garamond.

This paragraph is set in Adobe Garamond Pro 11/14. The type looks spacious and is easy to read. This is a standard size of type and leading for fiction and nonfiction books. Generous leading can reduce the number of lines per page.

This paragraph is set in Adobe Minion Pro 11/14. The type looks spacious and is easy to read. This is a standard size of type and leading for fiction and nonfiction books. Generous leading can reduce the number of lines per page.

This paragraph is set in Adobe Garamond Pro 11/13. This paragraph looks slightly darker on the page than the paragraph above because of less leading, but it is still easy to read. The reduced leading may allow one extra line on every page.

This paragraph is set in Adobe Minion Pro 11/13. This paragraph looks slightly darker on the page than the paragraph above because of less leading, but it is still easy to read. The reduced leading may allow one extra line on every page.

This paragraph is set in Adobe Garamond Pro 11/12. The type is now looking a bit crowded, and it's harder for readers to find the beginning of the next line, particularly when the lines go across the whole page rather than a narrow column, such as this one.

This paragraph is set in Adobe Minion Pro 11/12. The type is now looking a bit crowded, and it's harder for readers to find the beginning of the next line, particularly when the lines go across the whole page rather than a narrow column, such as this one.

23

Setting up your baseline grid

Baseline grids are horizontal guide lines that keep lines of text consistent from page to page. Hold up a book and look at one of the pages against a lit background. The lines of type on both sides of the page should line up.

All the text and images in your book will be aligned to your margins, column(s), and baseline grid.

Baseline grids are always set to the size of the leading. If your main text has 14 pt leading, then your baseline grid is set to 14 pt. Sometimes if a book has very complex headings, subheadings, bulleted lists, etc., the baseline grid may be set to one half of the leading (say, 7 pt instead of 14 pt). This allows half-linespaces between headings and lists and can save space while still adhering to a baseline grid. But in most books, the baseline grid is simply set to the same point size as the leading.

Setting up your baseline grid

Your baseline grid will only be visible in Normal view, not in Preview. Press W to switch views while the Selection Tool is in use and nothing is selected.

Open your Grid Preferences by clicking Edit>Preferences>Grids (Windows) or InDesign> Preferences>Grids (Mac). You set some of your preferences earlier, on pages 29–33.

In the Baseline Grid box, choose a light color from the Color dropdown menu (Light Gray is a good choice). See the settings on page 139.

In the Start box, type "0 in," and in the Relative To box, select Top of Page. This Start box setting is perfect for books with running feet (such as this book); however, if your book has running heads, you'll change your Start box setting (see page 139).

Running heads and/or folios are placed two baselines above the main text. Running feet and/or folios are placed two or three baselines below the main text.

In the Increment Every box, type the size of your leading (i.e., 14 pt). Leave everything else in this dialog box with the InDesign defaults.

Click OK, and a baseline grid will appear on your A-Master. If the grid doesn't appear automatically, you may need to show it by clicking View>Grids & Guides>Show Baseline Grid and switching to Normal view. Now you'll see horizontal lines 14 pts apart across your 2-page spread from top to bottom.

The keyboard shortcut to show or hide the baseline grid is Ctrl/Cmd+Alt/Opt+'.

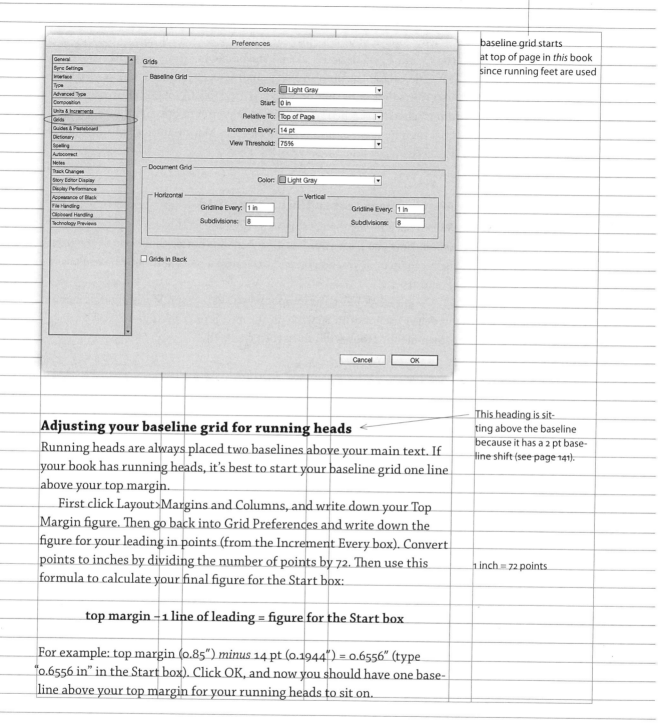

baseline grid starts
at top of page in *this* book
since running feet are used

Adjusting your baseline grid for running heads

This heading is sitting above the baseline because it has a 2 pt baseline shift (see page 141).

Running heads are always placed two baselines above your main text. If your book has running heads, it's best to start your baseline grid one line above your top margin.

First click Layout›Margins and Columns, and write down your Top Margin figure. Then go back into Grid Preferences and write down the figure for your leading in points (from the Increment Every box). Convert points to inches by dividing the number of points by 72. Then use this formula to calculate your final figure for the Start box:

1 inch = 72 points

top margin − 1 line of leading = figure for the Start box

For example: top margin (0.85″) *minus* 14 pt (0.1944″) = 0.6556″ (type "0.6556 in" in the Start box). Click OK, and now you should have one baseline above your top margin for your running heads to sit on.

Now look at your bottom margin and see where it falls in relation to the baseline grid. If you find that the bottom margin is slightly *above* a baseline, adjust the margin so it's slightly below instead. Otherwise your text won't flow onto that line. To do this, click Layout>Margins and Columns, check both the Enable Layout Adjustment box and the Preview box, then increase or decrease the Bottom Margin until it falls just below the closest baseline. Click OK.

Return to any 2-page spread by double-clicking the page icon in your Pages panel.

Aligning your text to the baseline grid

Switch back to any 2-page spread by double-clicking one in your Pages panel. Now you'll *see* your baseline grid, but notice that none of the text is lining up on it yet. You'll need to change a setting in your Basic Paragraph style.

Double-click Basic Paragraph in your Paragraph Styles panel to open it. Select Indents and Spacing on the left. From the Align to Grid drop-down menu, choose All Lines, then click OK.

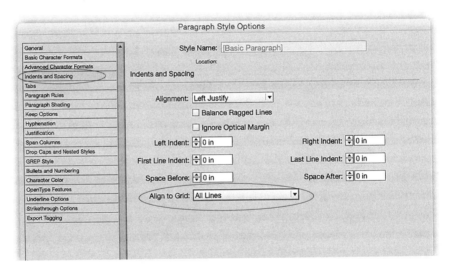

All your text *based on* the Basic Paragraph style (remember your paragraph styles family tree on page 59) will now align with the baseline grid. In other words, all the text in every paragraph style in your book should now align with your baseline grid.

Look through your pages and see how they look aligned to the baseline grid. Your main text should look fine, as will all text set with the same leading value as your baseline grid. However, not all of your text will look fine with that leading value. This includes text with smaller leading values (such as your copyright page, endnotes, index, and so on), as well as text with larger leading values (for example, titles and headings).

If you notice some text that shouldn't be aligned to the baseline grid, you can open the relevant paragraph style and, under Indents and Spacing, change Align to Grid: to None.

If you have just a bit of text that you want to take off the grid, simply remove it by selecting the Do Not Align to Grid icon in your Control or Paragraph panel (see example on page 295).

Occasions to lift off from the baseline grid

You might notice in your own book, and in this one, that the type in the Heading 2 style does not actually align with the baseline grid. There is more space than usual below the heading. That is because of the baseline shift applied to the style (see page 76). Baseline shift raises or lowers characters from their normal position but does not affect any type before or after it. To apply it, highlight all the letters that you want to move up or down, find the Baseline Shift icon (pictured at right) in the Control panel or Character panel, then type in the number of points (or even hundredths of points) that you want the type to shift. Remember to make character styles for type that uses baseline shift. You could name a style with 6 pts of baseline shift "tx+6," for instance.

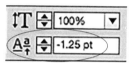

Baseline shift increments can be as small as hundredths of a point.

To typeset complex mathematics or scientific formulas, you might need to leave the principal line of the equation on the grid but allow the rest to shift up or down. Manipulating the baseline grid for fractions is a very useful tool. Here is an example:

To learn more about typesetting math, see pages 350–351.

$$\frac{(x-3)^2}{4} + \frac{(y-2)^2}{3} = 1$$

Baseline shift for type in the numerator: 6 points

No baseline shift for "+" or "= 1"

Baseline shift for type in the denominator (set on the next line): 8 points

The main line of this equation (the "+" and the "= 1") remains on the grid, but everything else is set with a baseline shift. After the math, the type goes back to aligning with the grid.

24 Designing chapter and part openings

Chapter openings are a major part of the look and style of your book. The type sizes of chapter numbers and titles are generally larger than the main text, allowing more freedom in choosing typefaces. Decorative elements can also be used. Because they set the tone of your book, chapter openings should be appropriate for your subject and genre.

What type of book do you expect to read when you see the chapter openings below?

3 The City

They were indeed a queer-looking party that assembled on the bank— the birds with draggled feathers, the animals with their fur clinging close to them, and all dripping wet, cross, and uncomfortable.

The first question of course was, how to get dry again: they had a consultation about this, and after a few minutes it seemed quite natural to Alice to find herself talking familiarly with them, as if she had known them all her life. Indeed, she had quite a long argument with the Lory, who at last turned sulky, and would only say, 'I am older than you, and must know better'; and this Alice would not allow without knowing how old it was, and, as the Lory positively refused to tell its age, there was no more to be said.

At last the Mouse, who seemed to be a person of authority among them, called out, 'Sit down, all of you, and listen to me! I'LL soon make you dry enough!' They all sat down at once, in a large ring, with the Mouse in the middle. Alice kept her eyes anxiously fixed on it, for she felt sure she would catch a bad cold if she did not get dry very soon.

'Ahem!' said the Mouse with an important air, 'are you all ready? This is the driest thing I know. Silence all round, if you please!

the City

They were indeed a queer-looking party that assembled on the bank— the birds with draggled feathers, the animals with their fur clinging close to them, and all dripping wet, cross, and uncomfortable.

The first question of course was, how to get dry again: they had a consultation about this, and after a few minutes it seemed quite natural to Alice to find herself talking familiarly with them, as if she had known them all her life. Indeed, she had quite a long argument with the Lory, who at last turned sulky, and would only say, 'I am older than you, and must know better'; and this Alice would not allow without knowing how old it was, and, as the Lory positively refused to tell its age, there was no more to be said.

At last the Mouse, who seemed to be a person of authority among them, called out, 'Sit down, all of you, and listen to me! I'LL soon make you dry enough!' They all sat down at once, in a large ring, with the Mouse in the middle. Alice kept her eyes anxiously fixed on it, for she felt sure she would catch a bad cold if she did not get dry very soon.

'Ahem!' said the Mouse with an important air, 'are you all ready? This is the driest thing I know. Silence all round, if you please!

In this chapter you'll:

1 Learn basic principles of good page design
2 Choose a look for your chapter openings
3 Try the chapter opening designs in this chapter
4 Try the part opening designs in this chapter
5 Consider some variations

1 Basic principles of good design

Three basic principles of good design are:

REPEAT ELEMENTS   RULE OF THREE   WHITE SPACE

Repeat elements

Books look professional when they have a consistent and cohesive look throughout. An easy way to accomplish this is to choose a few elements and repeat them throughout your book. Here are some options to consider:

- **alignment** Choose one method of alignment and stick to it throughout your whole book. If you like to center things, then center *everything* (except your main text, of course). Or, if you prefer aligning things to the left or to the outside margins, then make that your rule and follow it throughout your book.

- **typefaces** Choose a typeface for your main text and use that same typeface throughout your book. Try using italics or caps (large or small) as a repeating theme in your chapter openings, headings, running heads, and folios. You may want to use a second typeface for some things, such as titles and/or headings. It's fine to use two typefaces in the same book, as long as they look nice together. Try to avoid using more than two typefaces.

- **graphic elements** Repeating a graphic element throughout your book can be very effective. Something as simple as bullet points can be used

To find out which graphic elements or ornaments a typeface includes, open the Glyphs panel (or go to Type>Glyphs) and in the Show drop-down list choose Entire Font.

in your chapter opening (say, a bullet point on either side of the chapter number), as well as in running heads/feet (see the bottom of this page), and perhaps as a simple paragraph divider as well (three bullet points separated by en spaces). There are lots of graphic elements available in every typeface, such as: ~ * >> } and —. Some typefaces come with ornaments. As long as the same element is repeated (and not too loudly or too often), it can enhance your design.

Rule of three

Visual elements look best in groups of three. If a page has too many visual elements, they compete with each other and the reader doesn't know where to look first.

---

38 ALICE IN WONDERLAND

ought to speak, and no one else seemed inclined to say anything. 'Why,' said the Dodo, 'the best way to explain it is to do it.' (And, as you might like to try the thing yourself, some winter day, I will tell you how the Dodo managed it.) First it marked out a race-course, in a sort of circle, ('the exact shape doesn't matter,' it said,) and then all the party were placed along the course, here and there. There was no 'One, two, three, and away,' but they began running when they liked, and left off when they liked, so that it was not easy to know when the race was over. However, when they had been running half an hour or so, and were quite dry again, the Dodo suddenly called out 'The race is over!' and they all crowded round it, panting, and asking, 'But who has won?'

This question the Dodo could not answer without a great deal of thought, and it sat for a long time with one finger pressed upon its forehead (the position in which you usually see Shakespeare, in the pictures of him), while the rest waited in silence. At last the Dodo said, '*everybody* has won, and all must have prizes.' 'But who is to give the prizes?' quite a chorus of voices asked.

'Why, *she*, of course,' said the Dodo, pointing to Alice with one finger; and the whole party at once crowded round her, calling out in a confused way, 'Prizes! Prizes!'

Alice had no idea what to do, and in despair she put her hand in her pocket, and pulled out a box of comfits, (luckily the salt water had not got into it), and handed them round as prizes. There was exactly one a-piece all round.

'But she must have a prize herself, you know,' said the Mouse.

'Of course,' the Dodo replied very gravely. 'What else have you got in your pocket?' he went on, turning to Alice.

'Only a thimble,' said Alice sadly.

'Hand it over here,' said the Dodo.

Then they all crowded round her once more, while the Dodo solemnly presented the thimble, saying 'We beg your acceptance of this elegant thimble'; and, when it had finished this short speech, they all cheered. Alice thought the whole thing very absurd, but they all looked so grave that she did not dare to laugh; and, as she

---

{ CHAPTER THREE }

the City

They were indeed a queer-looking party that assembled on the bank—the birds with draggled feathers, the animals with their fur clinging close to them, and all dripping wet, cross, and uncomfortable.

The first question of course was, how to get dry again: they had a consultation about this, and after a few minutes it seemed quite natural to Alice to find herself talking familiarly with them, as if she had known them all her life. Indeed, she had quite a long argument with the Lory, who at last turned sulky, and would only say, 'I am older than you, and must know better'; and this Alice would not allow without knowing how old it was, and, as the Lory positively refused to tell its age, there was no more to be said.

At last the Mouse, who seemed to be a person of authority among them, called out, 'Sit down, all of you, and listen to me! I'LL soon make you dry enough!' They all sat down at once, in a large ring, with the Mouse in the middle. Alice kept her eyes anxiously fixed on it, for she felt sure she would catch a bad cold if she did not get dry very soon.

'Ahem!' said the Mouse with an important air, 'are you all ready? This is the driest thing I know. Silence all round, if you please!

39

The three visual elements on a regular page of text are the folio, the running head, and the text block. On a chapter opening page, they are the chapter opening, the text block, and the drop folio.

You'll apply the drop folio in chapter 52.

Notice that the chapter opening in the image on page 144 includes a number of visual elements: the chapter number spelled out, fancy brackets, and the chapter title. Although comprised of different elements, your chapter opening should function as one cohesive visual unit rather than a number of separate ones.

Don't be tempted to use every book design element you've ever seen. If you want to start each chapter with a drop cap, fine. If you want to start each chapter with an image or a graphic element, fine. But don't use absolutely everything at the same time. Keep it simple.

White space

You've already learned that generous margins add valuable white space to pages, giving the main text block some breathing room and allowing thumb space for your readers.

The same goes for your chapter openings. Be generous with white space. The chapter opening occupies the top portion of the page, and its length will depend on how many elements are in your chapter opening. Novels often just include a chapter number or title, whereas some nonfiction books may include a chapter number, chapter title, opening quote with attribution, and so on.

Be aware that the amount of white space in your chapter opening will affect your page count.

2 Choosing a look for your chapter and part openings

There are unlimited variations of chapter and part openings, but they can be loosely categorized as follows:

- **Classic** Use the same typeface for everything throughout your book. The type size and style will vary for different design elements. Small and all caps are used for headings. Ornaments or flourishes are used, and most elements are centered. This look works equally well for non-fiction and fiction books.

- **Modern** Use a serif typeface for main text and a sans serif for titles and headings. Sans serif type gives both novels and business books a modern edge. Modern designs are often asymmetrical, with geometric graphics such as rules and rectangles to add clean lines.

- **Characteristic** Some books need openings with character. If your story is a Western, you may want to add a touch of Mesquite or Giddyup typefaces to your chapter openings. A romance calls for a flourishy script. The key here is to add *a touch* of character, as a little goes a very long way.

Readers shouldn't be distracted by a showy design. Rather, they should be led straight into your words. Good page design is invisible.

3 Trying the chapter opening designs in this chapter

All the designs that follow are based on the paragraph styles you've created up to this point. So be sure to save a copy of your book before proceeding, just in case you want to revert back to them in the future.

The designs that follow include all the specs you need for the paragraph and character styles in your chapter openings. Find a design that suits *your* book, then change your paragraph styles accordingly.

Go to one of your chapter opening pages, then open the first paragraph style that needs changing. Make sure the Preview box is checked so you can see the changes as you're making them.

Most chapter openings only include four or five paragraph styles at most—Chapter Numbers, Chapter Titles, Opening Quotes, Quote Attributions, and possibly an ornament—so it doesn't take long to adjust the settings. If you don't like the way the changes look, simply click Cancel instead of OK, and none of the changes will be made.

The only typefaces used in the sample designs are Minion (a serif), Myriad (a sans serif), and a few display types in the Characteristic designs. Most of these typefaces are included with InDesign and demonstrate the variety of designs available to you using just those typefaces. Feel free to substitute any serif or sans serif in *your* design, and experiment with the typefaces you have available to you.

Also be sure to look at other books for inspiration. If you find a chapter opening you particularly admire, try using a similar typeface and spacing for *your* chapter openings.

Chapter title considerations

Chapter titles are all different lengths, and single-word titles must look just as good as long titles. After changing your Chapter Titles paragraph style, make sure *all* your chapter titles look equally good.

If the type size of your chapter titles is large or your titles are long, some titles may require two or more lines. If so, you can control where the lines break by adding a soft return, which forces a new line but keeps it within the same paragraph for spacing purposes. Insert the cursor where you want the line to break, then press Shift+Enter/Return. If you have chosen to show your hidden characters (Type>Show Hidden Characters), you'll notice that the soft return symbol looks like this: ¬

A chapter title should never, ever be hyphenated.

Keyboard shortcuts for ornaments commonly used in chapter openings:

asterisks (*)
Shift+8

bullets (•)
Alt/Opt+8

en dashes (–)
Alt/Opt+ -

em dashes (—)
Alt/Opt+Shift+ -

Chapter number considerations

Chapter numbers can be set in many different ways. In each case, you could set them in all caps, caps and lowercase, all small caps, or all lowercase:

Chapter One (chapter and number spelled out)
Chapter 1 (chapter spelled out, number is a digit)
One (just the number spelled out)
1 or 1 (just the digit, as an oldstyle or lining figure)
* 1 * or – 1 – or • 1 • or { 1 } (digit with an ornament on either side)
I (roman numeral)

Consider a few factors when choosing the numerals for a chapter number style.

- How many chapters are in your book? Would spelled-out numbers get longer and longer (and thus more and more difficult to read)?
- Is the typeface readable?
- Do you want the reader to pay attention to the number or just barely notice it?

DESIGN 1
Classic
chapter opening
– with –
paragraph rule

Experiment with the paragraph rule to move it up or down, make it heavier, or change its color. Keep the Preview box checked.

The chapter number and chapter title are centered, with plenty of white space above, below, and between them. This gives a classic and very comfortable and familiar look to the chapter opening page.

Notice that the drop folio is centered, too. You may choose to include drop folios on all your pages or just on your chapter opening pages. You'll apply the drop folio in chapter 52 using master pages.

CHAPTER ONE

CHAPTER OPENINGS

They were indeed a queer-looking party that assembled on the bank— the birds with draggled feathers, the animals with their fur clinging close to them, and all dripping wet, cross, and uncomfortable.

The first question of course was, how to get dry again: they had a consultation about this, and after a few minutes it seemed quite natural to Alice to find herself talking familiarly with them, as if she had known them all her life. Indeed, she had quite a long argument with the Lory, who at last turned sulky, and would only say, 'I am older than you, and must know better'; and this Alice would not allow without knowing how old it was, and, as the Lory positively refused to tell its age, there was no more to be said.

At last the Mouse, who seemed to be a person of authority among them, called out, 'Sit down, all of you, and listen to me! I'LL soon make you dry enough!' They all sat down at once, in a large ring, with the Mouse in the middle. Alice kept her eyes anxiously fixed on it, for she felt sure she would catch a bad cold if she did not get dry very soon.

'Ahem!' said the Mouse with an important air, 'are you all ready? This is the driest thing I know. Silence all round, if you please!

1

DESIGN 1: Classic with a paragraph rule, *continued*

This classic design uses the same typeface for all the elements in the design (Minion). However, other serif typefaces will work just as well. You may like to try Caslon, Chaparral, Garamond, or any other serifs you have available to you, to see which suits your book the best.

See page 176 for a part opening design that matches this chapter opener.

☐ **Chapter Numbers [cn]**

Changes from the Chapter Numbers style (see page 72):

Basic Character Formats:

Size = 11 pt

Case = OpenType All Small Caps

Tracking = 50

Indents and Spacing:

Space After = 42 pt *or* 0.5833 in

Paragraph Rules:

Rule Below = Rule On

(Fill in as shown below)

OpenType Features:

Figure Style = Proportional Oldstyle

Note that the paragraph style at the beginning of the chapter opening includes a Space Before *and* a Space After, but subsequent paragraph styles just include a Space After.

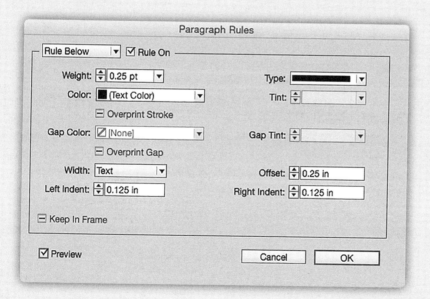

Paragraph rules affect everything in the paragraph and are not for single words on a line. For that, go to Character>Underline Options.

☐ **Chapter Titles [ct]**

Changes from the Chapter Titles style (see page 72):

Basic Character Formats:	Size = 13 pt
	Case = All Caps
	Tracking = 50
Indents and Spacing:	Space After = 84 pt *or* 1.1667 in

· · [1] · ·

CHAPTER OPENINGS

A book can look good using almost any typeface;
it just depends on how the type is set.

FIONA RAVEN, book designer

THEY WERE INDEED a queer-looking party that assembled on the bank—the birds with draggled feathers, the animals with their fur clinging close to them, and all dripping wet, cross, and uncomfortable.

The first question of course was, how to get dry again: they had a consultation about this, and after a few minutes it seemed quite natural to Alice to find herself talking familiarly with them, as if she had known them all her life. Indeed, she had quite a long argument with the Lory, who at last turned sulky, and would only say, 'I am older than you, and must know better'; and this Alice would not allow without knowing how old it was, and, as the Lory positively refused to tell its age, there was no more to be said.

At last the Mouse, who seemed to be a person of authority among them, called out, 'Sit down, all of you, and listen to me! I'LL soon make you dry enough!' They all sat down at once, in a large ring, with the Mouse in the middle. Alice kept her eyes anxiously fixed

· 1 ·

The chapter number is centered between square brackets and middle dots (these are smaller than bullets and available in the Glyphs panel), and all are separated by en spaces (Ctrl/Cmd+Shift+N).

The [**chtx1**] paragraph style is applied to the first paragraph, giving it the 2-line drop cap, and then the Small Caps [**smcap**] character style (see page 85) is applied to the first few words.

Before you decide to use a drop cap in this way, check the first paragraph of each chapter to make sure there are enough lines of type to accommodate the drop cap.

The drop folio is centered between two middle dots. En spaces separate the dots from the folio.

DESIGN 2: Classic with a two-line drop cap, *continued*

A drop cap is an attractive feature on a chapter opening page. It helps draw the reader's eye down to the beginning of the narrative. The settings are shown in the First Paragraph style.

☐ **Chapter Numbers [cn]**
Changes from the Chapter Numbers style (see page 72):

Basic Character Formats:	Tracking = 25

☐ **Chapter Titles [ct]**
Changes from the Chapter Titles style (see page 72):

Basic Character Formats:	Font Style = Bold
	Size = 13 pt
	Case = All Caps
	Tracking = 100

☐ **Opening Quotes [quo]**
Changes from the Opening Quotes style (see page 74):

Basic Character Formats:	Size = 10 pt
	Tracking = 10
Indents and Spacing:	Space After = 14 pt *or* 0.1944 in
Hyphenation:	Hyphenate = Unchecked

Use soft returns to control where the lines in your opening quotes break (Shift+Enter/Return).

☐ **Quote Attributions [quoattr]**
Changes from the Quote Attributions style (see page 74):

Advanced Character Formats:	Baseline Shift = 0
Indents and Spacing:	Space After = 70 pt *or* 0.9722 in

DESIGN 2: Classic with a two-line drop cap, *continued*

Create a new paragraph style called First Paragraph [**chtx1**] for the first paragraph in every chapter.

☐ **First Paragraph [chtx1]**
General:

Parent = **tx1**

Style Name = **chtx1**

Based On = **tx1**

Changes from the No Indents style (see page 62):
Drop Caps and Nested Styles:

Lines = 2

Characters = 1

After you create this new paragraph style, be sure to select the first paragraph in your chapter and apply it. Then you'll see the drop cap appear.

Sometimes it's necessary to adjust the space to the right of the drop cap to improve the appearance. Place the cursor before the first letter following the drop cap, then try various positive or negative values in the kerning box in the Control panel. See page 337 for more on kerning.

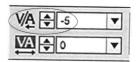

You may find that the first character in a chapter is a quotation mark. Here is an easy way to deal with this situation:

1   Delete the opening quotation mark. Now the first character in your paragraph is the drop cap.
2   Create a new text frame in the inside margin by dragging your cursor, and add an opening quotation mark (Alt/Opt+[ ). Apply the No Indent [**tx1**] paragraph style to it. In the Paragraph panel, choose Align Right.
3   Using your Selection Tool, drag the text frame so the opening quotation mark is next to the drop cap. Choose a position that looks pleasing and is close to the top of the drop cap.

It's best to deal with opening quotation marks after you've finalized your chapter opening design and page layout. Otherwise, the text frame with your opening quotation mark may get separated from the drop cap.

"The Eaglet b
  some of the
English!" said t
ing of half thos

"And the Ea
  smile: son
bly. Speak Engl
the meaning of

Move the quotation mark left to right to find the best position next to a letter.

1

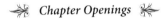 *Chapter Openings*

They were indeed a queer-looking party that assembled on the bank—
the birds with draggled feathers, the animals with their fur clinging
close to them, and all dripping wet, cross, and uncomfortable.

The first question of course was, how to get dry again: they had
a consultation about this, and after a few minutes it seemed quite
natural to Alice to find herself talking familiarly with them, as if she
had known them all her life. Indeed, she had quite a long argument
with the Lory, who at last turned sulky, and would only say, 'I am
older than you, and must know better'; and this Alice would not
allow without knowing how old it was, and, as the Lory positively
refused to tell its age, there was no more to be said.

At last the Mouse, who seemed to be a person of authority among
them, called out, 'Sit down, all of you, and listen to me! I'LL soon
make you dry enough!' They all sat down at once, in a large ring,
with the Mouse in the middle. Alice kept her eyes anxiously fixed
on it, for she felt sure she would catch a bad cold if she did not get
dry very soon.

'Ahem!' said the Mouse with an important air, 'are you all ready?
This is the driest thing I know. Silence all round, if you please!
"William the Conqueror, whose cause was favoured by the pope,
was soon submitted to by the English, who wanted leaders, and

1

DESIGN 3: Classic with ornaments, *continued*

This classic design includes ornaments on either side of the chapter title. These particular ornaments are from the typeface Arno, one of several typefaces available from Typekit that come with ornaments. Open the Glyphs panel and select Ornaments from the Show drop-down menu to see them.

For this design you'll need to create a new character style called Ornaments [**orn**] and apply it to the ornaments.

☐ **Chapter Numbers** [cn]

Changes from the Chapter Numbers style (see page 72):

Basic Character Formats: Tracking = 50

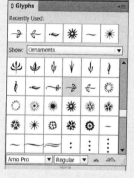

☐ **Chapter Titles** [ct]

Changes from the Chapter Titles style (see page 72):

Basic Character Formats: Font Style = Semibold italic

                                             Size = 12 pt

Indents and Spacing: Space After = 70 pt *or* 0.9722 in

☐ **Ornament** [orn] *character* style   Parent = **[None]**

General: Style Name = orn

                                             Based On = [None]

Changes from [None] character style :

Basic Character Formats: Font Family = Arno Pro

                                             Font Style = Regular

                                             Size = 18 pt

Advanced Character Formats: Baseline Shift = –1 pt

Once you've created a new character style for your ornaments, insert your cursor where an ornament is to go. Select the [orn] character style, then double-click the ornament you want in the Glyphs panel. Then add an en space between the ornament and chapter title by pressing Ctrl/Cmd+Shift+N.

DESIGN 4
Modern
chapter opening
– with –
number and title
on same line

The opening quote goes on the top line, so there is no need for an end-of-paragraph return before it (see page 99).

When the chapter number and title are on the same line, the Chapter Title paragraph style is applied, and a new Chapter Number *character* style is applied just to the number.

This style of chapter title looks best with short titles that fit on one line.

When you design your chapter opening pages, consider whether there are appendixes in your book. If so, think now about where you will place the word "Appendix." If you needed to put "Appendix" and a letter on this chapter opener page, where would they go? For suggestions, see pages 247 and 248.

Note that there is no drop folio on the opener page in this design.

A book can look good using almost any typeface;
it just depends on how the type is set.

—FIONA RAVEN
book designer

1 Chapter Openings

They were indeed a queer-looking party that assembled on the bank—the birds with draggled feathers, the animals with their fur clinging close to them, and all dripping wet, cross, and uncomfortable.

The first question of course was, how to get dry again: they had a consultation about this, and after a few minutes it seemed quite natural to Alice to find herself talking familiarly with them, as if she had known them all her life. Indeed, she had quite a long argument with the Lory, who at last turned sulky, and would only say, 'I am older than you, and must know better'; and this Alice would not allow without knowing how old it was, and, as the Lory positively refused to tell its age, there was no more to be said.

At last the Mouse, who seemed to be a person of authority among them, called out, 'Sit down, all of you, and listen to me! I'LL soon make you dry enough!' They all sat down at once, in a large ring, with the Mouse in the middle. Alice kept her eyes anxiously fixed

DESIGN 4: Modern with number and title on same line, *continued*

This modern design uses Myriad for all the elements set in a sans serif typeface (titles and headings). However, other sans serif typefaces will work just as well. Try any other sans serifs you have available to you, and see which one suits your book the best.

See page 178 for a part opening design that matches this chapter opener.

☐ **Opening Quotes [quo]**

Changes from the Opening Quotes style (see page 74):

Basic Character Formats:	Size = 10 pt
	Tracking = 10
Indents and Spacing:	Alignment = Right
	Space After = 14 pt *or* 0.1944 in
Hyphenation:	Hyphenate = Unchecked

☐ **Quote Attributions [quoattr]**

Changes from the Quote Attributions style (see page 74):

Advanced Character Formats:	Baseline Shift = 0
Indents and Spacing:	Space After = 84 pt *or* 1.1667 in

☐ **Chapter Titles [ct]**

Changes from the Chapter Titles style (see page 72):

Basic Character Formats:	Font Family = Myriad Pro
	Font Style = Light Condensed
	Size = 30 pt
	Tracking = 50
Indents and Spacing:	Alignment = Left
	Space After = 70 pt *or* 0.9722 in

To move the opening quote and attribution to the top of the page, select both (including their end-of-paragraph returns—and switch to Normal view if you don't see them). Cut the text by clicking Edit>Cut or pressing Ctrl/Cmd+X, then paste it at the top of the page by inserting your cursor at the top and clicking Edit>Paste or pressing Ctrl/Cmd+C.

DESIGN 4: Modern with number and title on same line, *continued*

Create a new *character* style called Chapter Number [**cn**] as shown below. Then insert your cursor in front of your chapter title and type your chapter number followed by an en space (Ctrl/Cmd+Shift+N). Apply the [**cn**] character style to the chapter number.

☐ **Chapter Number** [**cn**] *character* style
General:

Changes from [None] character style:
Basic Character Formats:
OpenType Features:

Parent = [None]
Style Name = **cn**
Based On = [None]

Font Style = Semibold Cond
Figure Style = Proportional Lining

Consider trying a few variations of the chapter number and title:

The first example is the one used in Design 4. You may want your title to be bolder than the number, or to change the alignment from left to right. Experiment.

1 Chapter Openings

In these examples, the chapter number is separated from the title with an en space (Ctrl/Cmd+Shift+N).

1 / **Chapter Openings**

A variation using Bold and Condensed type.

1 Chapter Openings

DESIGN 5
Modern
chapter opening
– with –
drop cap in a
different font

CHAPTER ONE

Chapter Openings

T HEY WERE INDEED a queer-looking party that assembled on the bank—the birds with draggled feathers, the animals with their fur clinging close to them, and all dripping wet, cross, and uncomfortable.

The first question of course was, how to get dry again: they had a consultation about this, and after a few minutes it seemed quite natural to Alice to find herself talking familiarly with them, as if she had known them all her life. Indeed, she had quite a long argument with the Lory, who at last turned sulky, and would only say, 'I am older than you, and must know better'; and this Alice would not allow without knowing how old it was, and, as the Lory positively refused to tell its age, there was no more to be said.

At last the Mouse, who seemed to be a person of authority among them, called out, 'Sit down, all of you, and listen to me! I'LL soon

1

This is a 3-line drop cap set in a sans serif font to match the chapter title. Start the first line of type one line below the top of the drop cap simply by adding a soft return (Shift+Enter/Return) right after the drop cap.

The drop folio is aligned away from the spine in this modern, asymmetrical design.

DESIGN 5: Modern with drop cap in a different font, *continued*

The large three-line drop cap is included in a nested style in your First Paragraph style. This means that *within* that paragraph style, a character style is assigned to the drop cap. Create a new paragraph style called First Paragraph [**chtx1**] for the first paragraph in every chapter.

☐ **Chapter Numbers [cn]**
Changes from the Chapter Numbers style (see page 72):

Basic Character Formats:	Size = 12 pt
	Case = OpenType All Small Caps
	Tracking = 50
Indents and Spacing:	Alignment = Left
	Space Before = 140 pt *or* 1.9444 in
	Space After = 14 pt *or* 0.1944 in

☐ **Chapter Titles [ct]**
Changes from the Chapter Titles style (see page 72):

Basic Character Formats:	Font Family = Myriad Pro
	Font Style = Semibold Condensed
	Size = 24 pt
Indents and Spacing:	Alignment = Left
	Space After = 70 pt *or* 0.9722 in

☐ **First Paragraph [chtx1]**

General:	Parent = **tx1**
	Style Name = **chtx1**
	Based On = **tx1**

Changes from the No Indents style (see page 62):

Drop Caps and Nested Styles:	Lines = 3
	Characters = 1
	Character Style = New
	Character Style . . .
	(see next page)

DESIGN 5: Modern with drop cap in a different font, *continued*

When you selected "New Character Style ..." from the Character Style drop-down menu (see bottom of previous page), a new dialog box appeared called New Character Style. You'll be familiar with this from setting up your original character styles (see pages 80–82). Create a character style for your drop cap as shown below, then click OK.

☐ **Drop Cap [dc]** *character* **style**
General:

Changes from [None] character style:
Basic Character Formats:

Parent = **[None]**
Style Name = **dc**
Based On = [None]

Font Family = Myriad Pro
Font Style = Condensed

After you've created the new First Paragraph [**chtx1**] style with this nested Drop Cap [**dc**] character style, be sure to select the first paragraph in your chapter and apply it. Then you'll see the drop cap appear.

Your last steps are:

• Place your cursor just to the right of the drop cap, and insert a soft return (Shift+Enter/Return). This moves the top line of text down so that the text begins in the middle of the drop cap.
• Select the first few words following the drop cap, and apply the Small Caps [**smcap**] character style to them (see page 85).

The shaded graphic behind the chapter number is created using the Paragraph Rule feature.

1

CHAPTER OPENINGS

A book can look good using almost any typeface;
it just depends on how the type is set.
FIONA RAVEN, book designer

They were indeed a queer-looking party that assembled on the bank—the birds with draggled feathers, the animals with their fur clinging close to them, and all dripping wet, cross, and uncomfortable.

The first question of course was, how to get dry again: they had a consultation about this, and after a few minutes it seemed quite natural to Alice to find herself talking familiarly with them, as if she had known them all her life. Indeed, she had quite a long argument with the Lory, who at last turned sulky, and would only say, 'I am older than you, and must know better'; and this Alice would not allow without knowing how old it was, and, as the Lory positively refused to tell its age, there was no more to be said.

At last the Mouse, who seemed to be a person of authority among them, called out, 'Sit down, all of you, and listen to me! I'LL soon make you dry enough!' They all sat down at once, in a large ring, with the Mouse in the middle. Alice kept her eyes anxiously fixed

1

The folio is aligned away from the spine and indented 0.2″ to complement this asymmetrical design.

DESIGN 6: Modern with shaded graphic, *continued*

You can add lines and shapes to your chapter opening pages manually (by creating the line or shape then copying and pasting it onto each chapter opening page); however, it's simpler if the graphic is part of a paragraph style. That way, it won't get misplaced as a result of style adjustments.

☐ **Chapter Numbers [cn]**

Changes from the Chapter Numbers style (see page 72):

Basic Character Formats:	Font Family = Myriad Pro
	Font Style = Bold
	Leading = 28 pt
	Tracking = 50
Indents and Spacing:	Alignment = Right
	Space After = 126 pt *or* 1.75 in
Paragraph Rules:	Rule Below = Rule On
	(Fill in as shown below)
Character Color:	[Paper]

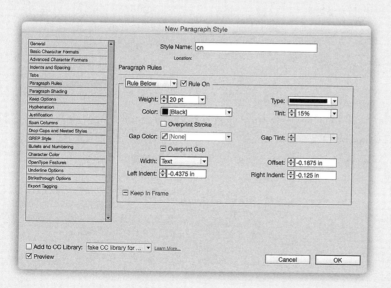

DESIGN 6: Modern with shaded graphic, *continued*

Here are the rest of the paragraph styles for Design 6.

☐ **Chapter Titles [ct]**

Changes from the Chapter Titles style (see page 72):

Basic Character Formats:	Font Family = Myriad Pro
	Font Style = Black
	Size = 12 pt
	Case = All Caps
	Tracking = 200
Indents and Spacing:	Alignment = Left

☐ **Opening Quotes [quo]**

Changes from the Opening Quotes style (see page 74):

Basic Character Formats:	Size = 10 pt
	Tracking = 10
Indents and Spacing:	Alignment = Left
	Left Indent = 0
	Right Indent = 0
Hyphenation:	Hyphenate = Unchecked

☐ **Quote Attributions [quoattr]**

Changes from the Quote Attributions style (see page 74):

Advanced Character Formats:	Baseline Shift = 0
Indents and Spacing:	Alignment = Left
	Space After = 28 pt *or* 0.3889 in

**DESIGN 7
Characteristic
chapter opening
– with –
paragraph rules
above and below
and initial cap**

CHAPTER OPENINGS

T HEY WERE INDEED a queer-looking party that assembled on the bank—the birds with draggled feathers, the animals with their fur clinging close to them, and all dripping wet, cross, and uncomfortable.

The first question of course was, how to get dry again: they had a consultation about this, and after a few minutes it seemed quite natural to Alice to find herself talking familiarly with them, as if she had known them all her life. Indeed, she had quite a long argument with the Lory, who at last turned sulky, and would only say, 'I am older than you, and must know better'; and this Alice would not allow without knowing how old it was, and, as the Lory positively refused to tell its age, there was no more to be said.

At last the Mouse, who seemed to be a person of authority among them, called out, 'Sit down, all of you, and listen to me! I'LL soon make you dry enough!' They all sat down at once, in a large ring, with the Mouse in the middle. Alice kept her eyes anxiously fixed on it, for she felt sure she would catch a bad cold if she did not get dry very soon.

'Ahem!' said the Mouse with an important air, 'are you all ready? This is the driest thing I know. Silence all round, if you please!

1

This chapter is unnumbered. Anthologies and collections of essays are often not meant to be read in any particular order, so there's no need for a numbering system.

The first paragraph has a larger indent and begins with an initial cap followed by the first few words in small caps.

This drop folio is centered and set in italics.

DESIGN 7: Characteristic with paragraph rules above and below and initial cap, *continued*

For this design you'll need rules both above and below the chapter title. Use the settings below, or experiment with your own. Be sure to check the Preview box so you can see your changes instantly.

☐ **Chapter Titles [ct]**
  Changes from the Chapter Titles style (see page 72):

Basic Character Formats:	Font Family = Myriad Pro
	Font Style = Semibold Condensed
	Case = All Caps
	Leading = 28 pt
	Tracking = 200
Indents and Spacing:	Space Before = 56 pt *or* 0.7778 in
	Space After = 112 pt *or* 1.5556 in
Paragraph Rules:	Rule Above = Rule On
	Rule Below = Rule On
	(Fill in as shown on page 167)

In the Paragraph Rules dialog boxes, here is what the terms mean:

- **Width** "Text" means *the width of the type* on the line, and "Column" means *the width of the text frame* or column you're in.
- **Indents** These are indents from the left and right edges of either the text or the column. If you want the type to extend a bit beyond the type or column, set negative indents by clicking the down arrows.
- **Offset** This is vertical distance. Instead of typing values in the box, it's easiest to click the up or down arrows.

DESIGN 7: Characteristic with paragraph rules above and below and initial cap, *continued*

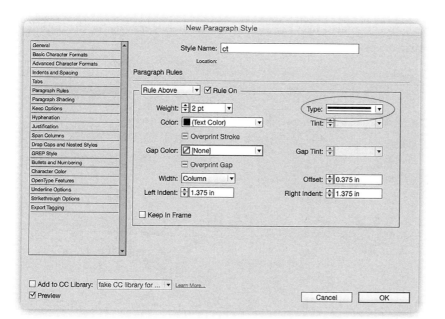

In the Type drop-down menu, choose Thick-Thin for the rule above.

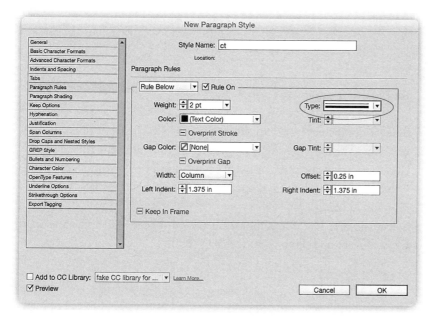

In the Type drop-down menu, choose Thin-Thick for the rule below.

DESIGN 7: Characteristic with paragraph rules above and below and initial cap, *continued*

To set up the first paragraph in this design, you'll create a paragraph style with an extra-large first line indent, and a character style for the initial cap in a sans serif typeface.

After you've created the new First Paragraph [chtx1] style, be sure to apply it to the first paragraph in your chapter.

Then when you've created the Initial Cap [ic] character style, apply it to the first character in the first paragraph.

☐ **First Paragraph [chtx1]**
General:

Parent = **tx1**
Style Name = **chtx1**
Based On = **tx1**

Changes from the No Indents style (see page 62):
Indents and Spacing:

First Line Indent: 0.375 in

☐ **Initial Cap [ic]** *character* **style**
General:

Parent = [None]
Style Name = **ic**
Based On = [None]

Changes from [None] character style:
Basic Character Formats:

Font Family = Myriad Pro
Font Style = Light
Size = 36 pt

Your last steps are:

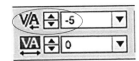

- Sometimes it's necessary to adjust the space to the right of the initial cap. Place the cursor before the first letter following the initial cap, then try various positive or negative values in the kerning box in the Control panel by clicking the up and down arrows. See page 337 for more on kerning.
- Select the first few words following the initial cap, and apply the Small Caps character style to them (see page 85).

One ᨁᨁ

They were indeed a queer-looking party that assembled on the bank—
the birds with draggled feathers, the animals with their fur clinging
close to them, and all dripping wet, cross, and uncomfortable.

The first question of course was, how to get dry again: they had
a consultation about this, and after a few minutes it seemed quite
natural to Alice to find herself talking familiarly with them, as if she
had known them all her life. Indeed, she had quite a long argument
with the Lory, who at last turned sulky, and would only say, 'I am
older than you, and must know better'; and this Alice would not
allow without knowing how old it was, and, as the Lory positively
refused to tell its age, there was no more to be said.

At last the Mouse, who seemed to be a person of authority among
them, called out, 'Sit down, all of you, and listen to me! I'LL soon
make you dry enough!' They all sat down at once, in a large ring,
with the Mouse in the middle. Alice kept her eyes anxiously fixed
on it, for she felt sure she would catch a bad cold if she did not get
dry very soon.

'Ahem!' said the Mouse with an important air, 'are you all ready?
This is the driest thing I know. Silence all round, if you please!
"William the Conqueror, whose cause was favoured by the pope,
was soon submitted to by the English, who wanted leaders, and

1

DESIGN 8
Characteristic chapter opening
– with –
rotated ornament

This chapter has a number and no title, as is often the case in novels. Spelling out the chapter number uses more space than a digit, but be aware that if you have lots of chapters, the spelled out numbers will get longer and longer (and thus more difficult to read).

The ornament is a small graphic (or image) created from a glyph and then rotated sideways. See page 170 to learn how to do this.

This drop folio is aligned away from the spine and set in semibold italics to match the chapter number. It creates a nice diagonal from the chapter number down to the folio.

DESIGN 8: Characteristic with rotated ornament, *continued*

This design requires a Chapter Number paragraph style, then the ornament is copied and pasted as an inline graphic.

☐ **Chapter Numbers [cn]**   Based On = **cn**
Changes from the Chapter Numbers style (see page 72):
Basic Character Formats: Font Style = Semibold Italic
                                                   Size = 22 pt
Indents and Spacing: Alignment = Left
                                                   Space After = 126 pt *or* 1.75 in

Never use Vertical scale or Horizontal scale on text type! But when you're creating a swash or ornament from a glyph, feel free to try any effect you like.

To make the ornament in this design, draw a new text frame and choose Minion Pro Regular 27 pt from the Control panel. Go to the Glyphs panel, choose the Greek category, and double-click the Greek small letter XI (ξ), then manipulate it in this way:

1 Highlight the character, then set the Vertical Scale (‖T) in the Control panel to 145% and the Horizontal Scale (**T**) to 80%.

2 Switch to the Selection Tool and use the Control panel to rotate the text frame counterclockwise.

3 Make the text frame smaller to fit the character closely by pressing Ctrl/Cmd+Alt/Opt+C.

4 To anchor the object in the text, select the text frame with the Selection Tool and cut it by pressing Ctrl/Cmd+X.

5 Switch to the Type Tool by pressing T, then put your cursor at the end of the chapter title and insert an en space (Ctrl/Cmd+Shift+N). Then go to Edit>Paste (Ctrl/Cmd+V), and your newly invented swash will appear next to the chapter number.

Now wasn't that fun?

Chapter Openings

They were indeed a queer-looking party that assembled on the bank—
the birds with draggled feathers, the animals with their fur clinging
close to them, and all dripping wet, cross, and uncomfortable.

The first question of course was, how to get dry again: they had
a consultation about this, and after a few minutes it seemed quite
natural to Alice to find herself talking familiarly with them, as if she
had known them all her life. Indeed, she had quite a long argument
with the Lory, who at last turned sulky, and would only say, 'I am
older than you, and must know better'; and this Alice would not
allow without knowing how old it was, and, as the Lory positively
refused to tell its age, there was no more to be said.

At last the Mouse, who seemed to be a person of authority among
them, called out, 'Sit down, all of you, and listen to me! I'LL soon
make you dry enough!' They all sat down at once, in a large ring,
with the Mouse in the middle. Alice kept her eyes anxiously fixed
on it, for she felt sure she would catch a bad cold if she did not get
dry very soon.

'Ahem!' said the Mouse with an important air, 'are you all ready?
This is the driest thing I know. Silence all round, if you please!

{ 1 }

Often in script fonts the type size looks smaller than you'd expect, and leading that is less than the type size works just fine as long as the ascenders and descenders do not crash. The example below is set in 14/12 point Brush Script.

An example on two lines

Notice above that the *p* in the first line and the *l* in the second line come close to touching each other. If they did touch ("crash"), you'd change the leading, the alignment (to left, perhaps), or the tracking.

This drop folio is enclosed in fancy brackets. You might consider putting just this folio at the top center of your recto pages, with just the chapter title at the top of the verso pages. Not every page has to have a page number.

DESIGN 9: Characteristic with display type, *continued*

Display type is very helpful in creating a mood or look for a book. There are cowboy fonts, script fonts, whimsical fonts, grunge fonts, scary or bleeding fonts, and any other kind of font you can imagine. Many display fonts are free on the Internet.

Having said that, a very little goes a long way when it comes to display fonts. Used sparingly, they can add character and charm to your book.

☐ **Chapter Titles [ct]**
Changes from the Chapter Numbers style (see page 72):

Basic Character Formats:	Font Family = Bickham Script Pro
	Font Style = Regular
	Size = 43 pt
Indents and Spacing:	Space Before = 70 pt *or* 0.9722 in
	Space After = 70 pt *or* 0.9722 in

Script typefaces often come with alternate letters, such as swash caps and swooshy tails. Open your Glyphs panel and choose Alternates for Selection from the Show drop-down menu. Then select any character in your chapter title and see what alternates are available. To select an alternate, simply double-click it.

Often the letters in a script typeface don't have perfect joins between the letters and need kerning a bit. Place your cursor between two letters that don't join properly, and click the up and down arrows in the Kern box until they line up properly. See page 337 for more on kerning. You may want to zoom in quite closely to kern the letters. To do so, hold down the Ctrl/Cmd key and hit = a few times. To zoom out, hold down the Ctrl/Cmd key and hit - a few times.

Chapter Openings

They were indeed a queer-looking party that assembled on the bank—the birds with draggled feathers, the animals with their fur clinging close to them, and all dripping wet, cross, and uncomfortable.

The first question of course was, how to get dry again: they had a consultation about this, and after a few minutes it seemed quite natural to Alice to find herself talking familiarly with them, as if she had known them all her life. Indeed, she had quite a long argument with the Lory, who at last turned sulky, and would only say, 'I am older than you, and must know better'; and this Alice would not allow without knowing how old it was, and, as the Lory positively refused to tell its age, there was no more to be said.

At last the Mouse, who seemed to be a person of authority among them, called out, 'Sit down, all of you, and listen to me! I'LL soon make you dry enough!' They all sat down at once, in a large ring, with the Mouse in the middle. Alice kept her

This is a fun chapter title set in AR HERMANN 28 pt type. It's suitable for a children's chapter book.

Note that the main text is larger for a children's chapter book (12/17 in this design).

DESIGN 9
Characteristic
chapter opening
– with –
display type,
continued

Mesquite Regular with 100
tracking at 24 pt all caps.

No matter how badly you
want to use a typeface, be
sure it's appropriate for
your book's subject matter.

To see a matching part
opener, go to page 180.

Try your chapter title in
different display type-
faces in Typekit and/or
on font websites online.

CHAPTER OPENINGS

They were indeed a queer-looking party that assembled on the bank—
the birds with draggled feathers, the animals with their fur clinging
close to them, and all dripping wet, cross, and uncomfortable.

The first question of course was, how to get dry again: they had
a consultation about this, and after a few minutes it seemed quite
natural to Alice to find herself talking familiarly with them, as if she
had known them all her life. Indeed, she had quite a long argument
with the Lory, who at last turned sulky, and would only say, 'I am
older than you, and must know better'; and this Alice would not
allow without knowing how old it was, and, as the Lory positively
refused to tell its age, there was no more to be said.

At last the Mouse, who seemed to be a person of authority among
them, called out, 'Sit down, all of you, and listen to me! I'LL soon
make you dry enough!' They all sat down at once, in a large ring,
with the Mouse in the middle. Alice kept her eyes anxiously fixed
on it, for she felt sure she would catch a bad cold if she did not get
dry very soon.

'Ahem!' said the Mouse with an important air, 'are you all ready?
This is the driest thing I know. Silence all round, if you please!

4 Trying the part opener designs in this chapter

Part openings always appear on recto pages, usually followed by a blank verso page. Sometimes, however, the verso page is used to list the chapters to come or to offer a short introduction. In *this* book, we simply used that verso page to carry on with the text, and that is fine, too, though more unusual.

By this time, you can probably predict what we are going to say about the design of your part openers: that they should be consistent with what you've done throughout your book. If you used a classic chapter opener, stick with a classic look for the part opener, and so on. In this section you'll see some selected part opening designs, each one closely related to one of the chapter openers shown in the previous pages.

The numbering system for your parts should be different from the one you used for your chapters, to avoid confusion. For instance, if you used arabic numerals for your chapters, either use roman numerals or spell out the numbers for your parts.

Part opening pages are a good place to show photos or other images at a large size, if it's appropriate for your book. Does your book use any bleeds in the design? If so, you might as well take advantage of bleeds for the part opening pages, too. Anything that bleeds off the page is visible from the outside edge of the book, which makes that page easier to find.

Check with your printer to find out whether bleeds will cause your printing costs to rise (see chapter 37 about adding a bleed).

Perhaps the idea of designing a page with very little on it is a bit intimidating. But don't panic; simply remember the basic principles of good page design:

REPEAT ELEMENTS   RULE OF THREE   WHITE SPACE

One group of elements on the page (circled above) is more pleasing to the eye than two groups would be.

First, you'll **repeat** the ideas from your chapter openings. Though you might not have as many as **three elements** on the page, simply try to consolidate everything into a single group (because odd numbers are better than even ones). As for **white space**, you'll have plenty of that.

You could begin by setting the part number using the Chapter Number [**cn**] style and part title in the Chapter Title [**ct**] style, and then make them both a bit larger. Perhaps that will be all you need. Study the designs on the next few pages to find ideas for *your* part opening pages.

Because "PART I" is such a short line, the paragraph rule settings used in the Chapter Number [**cn**] style for Design 1 (page 148) don't work here. This rule is instead set to a negative indent value, making it longer than the text.

PART I

PART OPENINGS

Notice that there is no folio on the part opener. That makes the page look more important, plus it helps keep the number of visual elements to an odd number (one), preventing unnecessary distraction.

DESIGN 1: Classic with paragraph rule, *continued*

This design is based on the chapter opening design shown on page 148. Both the part number and the part title are related to their chapter opening counterparts but are a bit larger, to make them more important and so they are not lost in all that white space.

☐ **Part Numbers [pn]**   Based On = **cn**

Changes from the Chapter Numbers style in Design 1 (see pages 72 and 149):

Basic Character Formats: Size = 14 pt

Paragraph Rules: (Fill in as shown below)

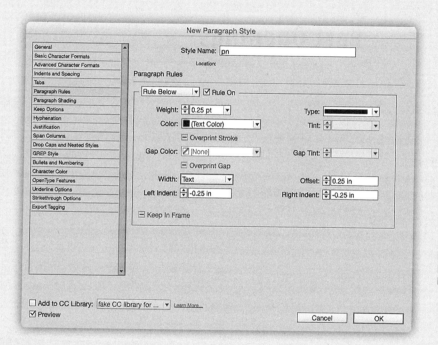

After you've created the new Part Numbers [**pn**] and Part Titles [**pt**] paragraph styles, be sure to apply them to your part numbers and part titles.

Also make sure there is an end-of-paragraph return at the top of each part opening page, before the part number, with the Text [**tx**] paragraph style applied to it (see example on page 99).

☐ **Part Titles [pt]**   Based On = **ct**

Changes from the Chapter Titles style (see pages 72 and 149):

Basic Character Formats: Size = 20 pt

Case = OpenType All Small Caps

**DESIGN 4
Modern
part opening
– with –
mini table of
contents**

Reflecting the Design 4 chapter opening (see page 156), this page has three major visual elements: an element at the upper right, another at left center, and some text below it.

The part number is centered on the chapter opening quotation in Design 4. The part title aligns with the chapter title, and the start of the mini table of contents aligns with the first text line of any chapter.

Set a tab *before* each chapter title and an em plus an en space *after* each one. Using this fixed amount of space after the title keeps the page numbers nearby and eliminates the need to look from left to right on the page. Also, it conveniently helps to keep the number of visual elements on the page to three.

Part One

Part Openings

DESIGN 4: Modern with mini table of contents, *continued*

This part opener is used to help the reader grasp the organization of the book at a glance with a mini table of contents, just as in *Book Design Made Simple*. Create the following new paragraph and character styles:

☐ **Part Numbers [pn]**   Based On = **cn**

Changes from the Chapter Numbers style (see pages 72 and 158):

Basic Character Formats: Font Family = Myriad Pro

Font Style = Light Condensed

Size = 22 pt

Tracking = 20

Indents and Spacing: Alignment = Right

Space After = 2 in

After you've created the new Part Numbers [**pn**], Part Titles [**pt**], and Part Contents [**ptoc**] paragraph styles, be sure to apply them to the text on your part opening page.

☐ **Part Titles [pt]**   Based On = **ct**

Changes from the Chapter Titles style (see pages 72 and 157):

Basic Character Formats: Font Style = Bold Condensed

Indents and Spacing: Space After = 1 in

Also make sure there is an end-of-paragraph return at the top of each part opening page, before the part number, with the Text [**tx**] paragraph style applied to it (see example on page 99).

☐ **Part Contents [ptoc]**   Based On = **tx1**

Changes from the No Indents style (see page 62):

Indents and Spacing: Alignment = Left

Left Indent = 18 pt *or* 0.25 in

First Line Indent = –18 pt *or* –0.25 in

Space After = 4 pt *or* 0.0556 in

Align to Grid = None

And, finally, select each chapter number in your part contents and apply the Part Contents Chapter Number [**ptoc-cn**] character style to them.

☐ **Part Contents Chapter Number [ptoc-cn]** *character* **style**

Based On = [None]

Changes from [None]:

Basic Character Formats: Font Style = Bold

Chances are that if your
book's chapters aren't
numbered, you won't
want to number the parts,
either. This part title is
exactly the same as the
chapter title shown on
page 174. A 10% black,
full-bleed background is
added to help the reader
find this important divider.

Before adding a bleed to
any of your design ele-
ments, check with your
printer to see whether
adding a bleed to your
design will increase your
printing costs. Then see
chapter 37 to add a bleed
to your page design.

PART OPENINGS

Display type examples

When thinking about using a display typeface, consider several factors before settling on one. 1) How appropriate is the type to your subject matter? 2) Did you (or will you) use one of these for your cover? If so, it would be smart to include it in the interior of your book instead of introducing another one. 3) Is the type readable? 4) Does it include both uppercase and lowercase characters?

Be aware that any of the typefaces below are suitable for display, but the only one suitable for book text is Myriad (for titles, headings, sidebars, and so on).

The samples below are some of the ones included when you lease InDesign, but thousands more are available online.

Sans Serif Display

Letter Gothic
1 2 3 4 5 6 7

LITHOS
1 2 3 4 5 6 7 8 9 0

Myriad
1 2 3 4 5 6 7 8 9 0

ORATOR
1 2 3 4 5 6 7 8

Poplar
1234567890

Tekton
1 2 3 4 5 6 7 8 9 0

Serif Display

Birch
1234567890

Blackoak
1 2 3 4 5 6

MESQUITE
1234567890

Nueva Condensed
1234567890

ROSEWOOD
1234567890

STENCIL
1 2 3 4 5 6 7 8 9

TRAJAN
1 2 3 4 5 6 7 8 9 0

Script

Brush Script
1 2 3 4 5 6 7 8 9 0

Giddyup
1234567890

Display number examples

Consider a few factors when choosing the numerals for a chapter number style.

- How many chapters are in your book? Would spelled-out numbers get longer and longer (and thus more and more difficult to read)?
- Is the typeface readable?

- Do you want the reader to pay attention to the number or just barely notice it?

In the examples below, both short and long numbers are shown in several display typefaces (see page 181 for more). Some interesting features but also several difficulties are immediately evident.

Myriad	FOUR	TWENTY-SEVEN	Rosewood	IV	XXVII
Brush Script	*FOUR*	*TWENTY-SEVEN*	Prestige Elite	IV	XXVII
Giddyup	FOUR	TWENTY-SEVEN	Brush Script	*IV*	*XXVII*
Lithos	FOUR	TWENTY-SEVEN	Trajan	IV	XXVII
Brush Script	*Four*	*Twenty-Seven*	Nueva	· 4 ·	· 27 ·
Giddyup	Four	Twenty-Seven	Letter Gothic	· 4 ·	· 27 ·
Tekton	Four	Twenty-Seven	Blackoak	· 4 ·	· 27 ·
Nueva	**Four**	**Twenty-Seven**	Giddyup	· 4 ·	· 27 ·
Brush Script	*4*	*27*	Brush Script	*four*	*twenty-seven*
Poplar	**4**	**27**	Prestige Elite	four	twenty-seven
Stencil	4	27	Birch	four	twenty-seven
Prestige Elite	4	27	Trajan	FOUR	TWENTY-SEVEN

5 Consider some variations

Aside from the samples and tips in this chapter, there are many more things you can do to change your chapter and part openers. You might want to try a couple of the ideas below, but, again, don't overdo it. When in doubt, leave it out.

- If you are already using a bleed somewhere else in the book, you might bring a panel of color (or gray) down from the top and put the chapter or part number in it, or from the outside and put the chapter title in it.

- How about putting the number inside a circle or other shape that's relevant to your subject matter? Keep it minimal so as not to distract the reader.

- Add a different photo for each chapter or part in a nonfiction book. Size and place it the same each time.

- If you've decided to use rules, try some different styles offered in the Paragraph Rules dialog box (Paragraph Styles>Paragraph Rules>Rule Above or Rule Below checked>Type). It's tempting, once you've discovered the possibilities, to use one of each. But don't—it's a sure sign that an inexperienced designer is at work. Stick with one style throughout the book whenever you need to use a rule.

- When choosing a display typeface or graphic, always consider whether there is some way to match your part and chapter openers to the cover.

25 *Designing headings*

There are a few factors to consider when designing a set of headings. Common sense will tell you that if there's only one level of heading, it doesn't need to be very big or bold to be noticed, but if there are multiple levels of headings, the most important ones should be bumped up a bit and given more white space so they will be more visible than the others. In this section you'll learn four ways to set up three levels of headings.

Books with one level of heading

If your book has only one kind of heading, you are lucky because you won't need to come up with a scheme to differentiate among the levels of heads. Look at the heading designs on the next several pages, and simply pick one of the Heading 1 [**h1**] or Heading 2 [**h2**] styles from the design that is closest to the one you're developing for your book.

Books with two levels of headings

Designing two heading levels is fairly uncomplicated. But even with this simple arrangement, you must still work to make the hierarchy clear. It's easy for an author to get carried away and lose track of the structure that the headings are supposed to mark for the reader. If you're confused by your own headings, try making an outline list out of them to see whether your structure is logical.

Go through the designs in this chapter and pick styles to suit the look of your book so far.

Books with three levels of headings

Now things start to get a bit complicated. But don't worry; you already set up three heading styles for your book, and at this point you just want to find a look that you like. The two options for Heading 3 styles are a stand-alone style (heading on its own line, using Heading 3 [**h3**]) or a run-in style (heading on the same line as the start of the first paragraph, using the Run-in Subheads [**ris**] character style). A stand-alone style is easier in most cases, but a run-in style will save space, and many people prefer the way it looks. Study your book to see which will work best for you.

If you decide to use a run-in style, you'll have to make two decisions: how to separate it from the text that follows and what case to use.

There are four basic choices of separators:

- A period plus an em space (**Heading here.**   Text starts here)
- No period with an em space (**Heading here**   Text starts here)
- A period plus an en space (**Heading here.** Text starts here)
- No period with an en space (**Heading here** Text starts here)

To set an em space, go to Type>Insert White Space>Em Space or type Ctrl/Cmd+Shift+M. To set an en space, go to Type>Insert White Space>En Space or type Ctrl/Cmd+Shift+N.

As for the case, you should first coordinate with your Heading 1 and Heading 2 styles; don't start a new capitalization scheme at this point. Your options are:

- Capitalize the First Letter of Major Words (Sometimes Called Title Case)
- Capitalize only the first letter of the head (called initial cap/lowercase)
- USE SMALL CAPS THROUGHOUT

Initial cap/lowercase is sometimes called sentence case.

When you study the designs on the next pages, keep these options in mind. You can easily customize one of the suggested designs to suit your needs.

Stacking heads

Sometimes one head directly follows another one, resulting in an undesirably large gap between the heads. If this happens, honor the normal space *below the first head*, and then go into the Paragraph panel or the Control panel to delete any extra space above the second head. With your cursor still in the second head, use the Paragraph Styles panel to create a new style for this heading; for instance, if a Heading 2 directly follows a Heading 1, you could call it "h2-below h1" or "h2-nospaceabove."

Alice was beginning to get very tired of sitting by her sister on the bank, and of having nothing to do: once or twice she had peeped into the book her sister was reading, but it had no pictures or conversations in it, 'and what is the use of a book,' thought Alice 'without pictures or conversation?'

HEADING LEVEL 1

Baseline shift = a quarter
of a line of space

So she was considering in her own mind (as well as she could, for the hot day made her feel very sleepy and stupid), whether the pleasure of making a daisy-chain would be worth the trouble of getting up and picking the daisies, when suddenly a White Rabbit with pink eyes ran close by her.

Heading Level 2

The semibold Heading 2 is different enough from the bold all-caps Heading 1 style so that nobody will be confused by them.

There was nothing so VERY remarkable in that; nor did Alice think it so VERY much out of the way to hear the Rabbit say to itself, 'Oh dear! Oh dear! I shall be late!' (when she thought it over afterwards, it occurred to her that she ought to have wondered at this, but at the time it all seemed quite natural); but when the Rabbit actually took a watch out of its waistcoat-pocket and looked at it, and then hurried on, Alice started to her feet, for it flashed across her mind that she had never before seen a rabbit with either a waistcoat-pocket, or a watch to take out of it, and burning with curiosity, she ran across the field after it, and fortunately was just in time to see it pop down a large rabbit-hole under the hedge.

If your book has only one level of heading, take your pick from the **h1** or the **h2** style shown here.

Heading Level 3. In another moment down went Alice after it, never once considering how in the world she was to get out again. The rabbit-hole went straight on like a tunnel for some way, and then dipped suddenly down, so suddenly that Alice had not a moment to think about stopping herself before she found herself falling down a very deep well.

For the run-in Heading 3, apply the [h3] paragraph style to the paragraph, and then apply the Run-in Subheads [ris] character style to the actual heading.

Either the well was very deep, or she fell very slowly, for she had plenty of time as she went down to look about her and to wonder

42

Classic centered headings, *continued*

These headings work well with chapter opening designs 1 or 2, shown on pages 148 and 151. Stick with the one font used throughout the book and the theme of centered elements.

☐ **Heading 1 [h1]**

Changes from the Heading 1 style (see page 76):

Basic Character Formats: Font Style = Bold

Size = 12 pt

Case = All Caps

Tracking = 50

Advanced Character Formats: Baseline Shift = 3.5 pt ←——— If you've changed the leading of *your* book text, you could also change the Baseline Shift shown here to 1/4 of a line of space.

Indents and Spacing: Space After = 0

☐ **Heading 2 [h2]**

Changes from the Heading 2 style (see page 76):

Basic Character Formats: Size = 11.5 pt

Case = Normal

Tracking = 20

Advanced Character Formats: Baseline Shift = 0

Indents and Spacing: Alignment = Center

☐ **Heading 3 [h3]** Based On = **tx1** ←——— Be sure to change the Based On setting in the General tab from **h2** to **tx1**.

Changes from the No Indents style (see page 62):

Basic Character Formats: Font Style = Regular

Tracking = 0

Indents and Spacing: Space Before = 14 pt *or* 0.1944 in

Your last steps are to apply the Run-In Subheads [**ris**] character style (see page 84) to the actual Heading 3, then choose how to separate it from the rest of the paragraph. In this design, Heading 3 has a period and an en space after it. Feel free to do it differently in *your* book (see page 185).

Alice was beginning to get very tired of sitting by her sister on the bank, and of having nothing to do: once or twice she had peeped into the book her sister was reading, but it had no pictures or conversations in it, 'and what is the use of a book,' thought Alice 'without pictures or conversation?'

Heading Level 1

Following the chapter opening style on page 156, this Heading 1 style is set in Myriad Pro Semibold with extra tracking. The paragraph rule below it helps to differentiate Heading 1 from Heading 2.

So she was considering in her own mind (as well as she could, for the hot day made her feel very sleepy and stupid), whether the pleasure of making a daisy-chain would be worth the trouble of getting up and picking the daisies, when suddenly a White Rabbit with pink eyes ran close by her.

Heading Level 2

There was nothing so VERY remarkable in that; nor did Alice think it so VERY much out of the way to hear the Rabbit say to itself, 'Oh dear! Oh dear! I shall be late!' (when she thought it over afterwards, it occurred to her that she ought to have wondered at this, but at the time it all seemed quite natural); but when the Rabbit actually took a watch out of its waistcoat-pocket and looked at it, and then hurried on, Alice started to her feet, for it flashed across her mind that she had never before seen a rabbit with either a waistcoat-pocket, or a watch to take out of it, and burning with curiosity, she ran across the field after it, and fortunately was just in time to see it pop down a large rabbit-hole under the hedge.

Heading Level 3

In another moment down went Alice after it, never once considering how in the world she was to get out again. The rabbit-hole went straight on like a tunnel for some way, and then dipped suddenly down, so suddenly that Alice had not a moment to think about stopping herself before she found herself falling down a very deep well.

Either the well was very deep, or she fell very slowly, for she had plenty of time as she went down to look about her and to wonder

Modern headings with paragraph rule, *continued*

This set of sleek, modern-looking headings coordinates with chapter opening design 4, shown on page 156. If you only need one kind of heading, simply pick one of the larger ones in this design. Remember to use the leading from *your* book if you've changed it for your main text.

☐ **Heading 1 [h1]**

Changes from the Heading 1 style (see page 76):

Basic Character Formats:

    Font = Myriad Pro

    Font Style =

        Semibold Condensed

    Size = 15 pt

    Tracking = 40

Indents and Spacing:

    Alignment = Left

Paragraph Rules:

    Rule Below = Rule On

    (Fill in as shown
      to the right)

OpenType Features:

    Proportional Lining

When you add a paragraph rule to **h1**, it will also appear in the styles based on **h1**. That's why you need to turn it off in **h2**.

☐ **Heading 2 [h2]**

Changes from the Heading 2 style (see page 76):

Basic Character Formats:

    Font Style = Semibold Condensed

    Size = 12.5 pt

    Case = Normal

    Tracking = 40

Paragraph Rules:

    Rule Below = Uncheck Rule On

If you don't see Myriad Pro in your font list, go into the Creative Cloud application and click on Assets>Fonts> Add Fonts from Typekit. Type "Myriad Pro" in the Search Typekit box. When you see the fonts displayed, click "+ Use fonts."

☐ **Heading 3 [h3]**

Changes from the Heading 3 style (see page 76):

Basic Character Formats:

    Font Style = Condensed

    Size = 11.5 pt

Alice was beginning to get very tired of sitting by her sister on the bank, and of having nothing to do: once or twice she had peeped into the book her sister was reading, but it had no pictures or conversations in it, 'and what is the use of a book,' thought Alice 'without pictures or conversation?'

Heading Level 1

So she was considering in her own mind (as well as she could, for the hot day made her feel very sleepy and stupid), whether the pleasure of making a daisy-chain would be worth the trouble of getting up and picking the daisies, when suddenly a White Rabbit with pink eyes ran close by her.

Heading Level 2

There was nothing so VERY remarkable in that; nor did Alice think it so VERY much out of the way to hear the Rabbit say to itself, 'Oh dear! Oh dear! I shall be late!' (when she thought it over afterwards, it occurred to her that she ought to have wondered at this, but at the time it all seemed quite natural); but when the Rabbit actually took a watch out of its waistcoat-pocket and looked at it, and then hurried on, Alice started to her feet, for it flashed across her mind that she had never before seen a rabbit with either a waistcoat-pocket, or a watch to take out of it, and burning with curiosity, she ran across the field after it, and fortunately was just in time to see it pop down a large rabbit-hole under the hedge.

HEADING LEVEL 3   In another moment down went Alice after it, never once considering how in the world she was to get out again. The rabbit-hole went straight on like a tunnel for some way, and then dipped suddenly down, so suddenly that Alice had not a moment to think about stopping herself before she found herself falling down a very deep well.

Either the well was very deep, or she fell very slowly, for she had plenty of time as she went down to look about her and to wonder

This heading is set in 16 pt type with 14 pts of leading. It will only work if all of the headings are one line long, because the type crashes when there are more lines.

If your book has longer headings, simply reduce the size of the Heading 1 style to 14.5 pt and the size of the Heading 2 style to 12 pt.

Modern headings with two typefaces, *continued*

In chapter opening design 5 (page 159), small caps and two different fonts are used, so you can take advantage of the variety of choices. Remember, as always, that all of the Space Before and Space After settings in the examples are based on Text [**tx**] style with 14 pts of leading. If your leading is different, change the settings to match.

☐ **Heading 1 [h1]**
Changes from the Heading 1 style (see page 76):
Basic Character Formats: Font = Myriad Pro
                                             Font Style = Semibold Condensed
                                             Size = 16 pt
Indents and Spacing: Alignment = Left
OpenType Features: Proportional Lining

☐ **Heading 2 [h2]**
Changes from the Heading 2 style (see page 76):
Basic Character Formats: Font Style = Semibold Condensed
                                             Size = 12.5 pt
                                             Tracking = 20

Be sure to change the Based On setting in the General tab from **h2** to **tx1**.

☐ **Heading 3 [h3]**   Based On = **tx1** ⟵
Changes from the No Indents style (see page 62):
Basic Character Formats: Font Style = Regular
                                             Tracking = 0
Indents and Spacing: Space Before = 14 pt *or* 0.1944 in

Your last steps are to apply the Run-In Subheads [**ris**] character style to the actual Heading 3, then choose how to separate it from the rest of the paragraph. In this design, Heading 3 has an em space after it. Feel free to do it differently in *your* book (see page 185).

☐ **Run-In Subheads [ris]** *character* **style**
Changes from the Run-In Subheads character style (see page 84):
Basic Character Formats: Font Style = Regular
                                             Case = OpenType All Small Caps
                                             Tracking = 40

**Modern headings
– with –
shaded graphic**

Alice was beginning to get very tired of sitting by her sister on the bank, and of having nothing to do: once or twice she had peeped into the book her sister was reading, but it had no pictures or conversations in it, 'and what is the use of a book,' thought Alice 'without pictures or conversation?'

HEADING LEVEL 1

So she was considering in her own mind (as well as she could, for the hot day made her feel very sleepy and stupid), whether the pleasure of making a daisy-chain would be worth the trouble of getting up and picking the daisies, when suddenly a White Rabbit with pink eyes ran close by her.

Heading Level 2

There was nothing so VERY remarkable in that; nor did Alice think it so VERY much out of the way to hear the Rabbit say to itself, 'Oh dear! Oh dear! I shall be late!' (when she thought it over afterwards, it occurred to her that she ought to have wondered at this, but at the time it all seemed quite natural); but when the Rabbit actually took a watch out of its waistcoat-pocket and looked at it, and then hurried on, Alice started to her feet, for it flashed across her mind that she had never before seen a rabbit with either a waistcoat-pocket, or a watch to take out of it, and burning with curiosity, she ran across the field after it, and fortunately was just in time to see it pop down a large rabbit-hole under the hedge.

Heading Level 3

In another moment down went Alice after it, never once considering how in the world she was to get out again. The rabbit-hole went straight on like a tunnel for some way, and then dipped suddenly down, so suddenly that Alice had not a moment to think about stopping herself before she found herself falling down a very deep well.

Either the well was very deep, or she fell very slowly, for she had plenty of time as she went down to look about her and to wonder

In a font family with many weights, it's best to skip a weight when you want the difference between two styles to be noticeable. In this case, the **h1** and **h2** are set in Black and the **h3** is set in Semibold. The Bold weight in between them was skipped.

Modern headings with shaded graphic, *continued*

Chapter opening design 6 (page 162) features a light gray box (actually a paragraph rule) behind the chapter number. Here we repeat that idea in the Heading 1 design.

☐ **Heading 1 [h1]**

Changes from the Heading 1 style (see page 76):

Basic Character Formats:
Font = Myriad Pro
Font Style = Black
Size = 12 pt
Case = All Caps
Tracking = 150

Indents and Spacing:
Alignment = Left
Space After = 0

Paragraph Rules:
Rule Below = On
(Fill in as shown to the right.)

OpenType Features:
Proportional Lining

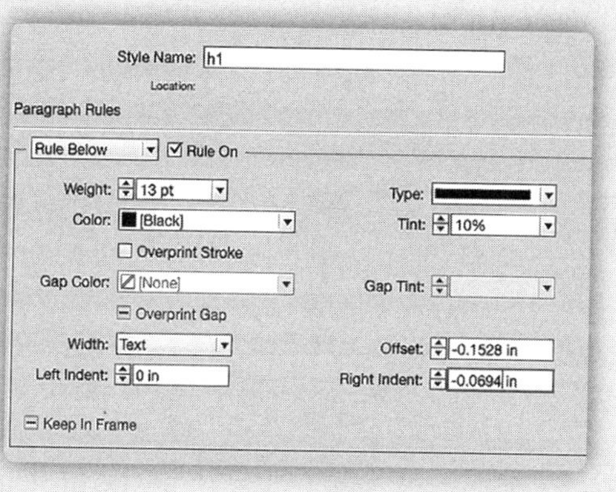

Style Name: h1
Location:
Paragraph Rules
Rule Below ▾ ☑ Rule On
Weight: 13 pt ▾   Type: ▾
Color: ■ [Black] ▾   Tint: 10% ▾
☐ Overprint Stroke
Gap Color: ☒ [None] ▾   Gap Tint: ▾
☐ Overprint Gap
Width: Text ▾   Offset: -0.1528 in
Left Indent: 0 in   Right Indent: -0.0694 in
☐ Keep In Frame

When you add a paragraph rule to **h1**, it will also appear in the styles based on **h1**. That's why you need to turn it off in **h2**.

☐ **Heading 2 [h2]**

Changes from the Heading 2 style (see page 76):

Basic Character Formats:
Font Style = Black
Size = 11 pt
Case = Normal
Tracking = 40

Paragraph Rules:
Rule Below = Uncheck Rule On

☐ **Heading 3 [h3]**

Changes from the Heading 3 style (see page 76):

Basic Character Formats:
Font Style = Semibold
Tracking = 0

26 *Designing other elements*

In this chapter you'll learn how to design some of the more complicated elements that might appear in your book. Simply skip this chapter if your book has none of the following:

- Extracts
- Display material
- Lists of all sorts
- Sidebars

Your book may have other elements, such as poetry, math, tables (charts), or footnotes. If so, you'll find solutions to typesetting that material in chapter 50.

Designing extracts

Poems (and song lyrics) that are extracts are covered in chapter 50.

You designed your extracts along with your other paragraph styles in Part II, and those extract styles should work well for most books. In this section, though, you can explore some alternatives. General rules for setting extracts are:

- Set extracts 1 point size smaller than your book text.
- Indent them the same amount as your paragraph indent, on both left and right. (An alternative is to indent them only on the left.)
- Leave one line of space above and below.
- Do not indent the first line of the extract. Extracts that are longer than one paragraph should use paragraph indents for the following paragraphs. Or, leave a full or half line of space between extract paragraphs and don't use any first line indents at all.

If you'd like to make extracts more visible on the page (and save a little space), you can use less leading than in your book text. So, if your main book text is set at 11/14, your extract could be set at 10/13 or 10/12. This extract should not sit on the baseline grid (Paragraph Style Options>Indents and Spacing>Align to Grid: None).

Quotation marks

Do not use quotation marks with extracts or chapter opening quotes. The layout and spacing of these elements signify that the text is a quotation; quotation marks would be redundant.

The Paragraph styles for the example below and the one on page 197 are laid out for you. Perhaps one of these styles (or a hybrid of your own choosing) will work for *your* extracts.

had never before seen a rabbit with either a waistcoat-pocket, or a watch to take out of it, and burning with curiosity, she ran across the field after it, and fortunately was just in time to see it pop down a large rabbit-hole under the hedge.

Extract Heading

In another moment down went Alice after it, never once considering how in the world she was to get out again. The rabbit-hole went straight on like a tunnel for some way, and then dipped suddenly down, so suddenly that Alice had not a moment to think about stopping herself before she found herself falling down a very deep well.

Either the well was very deep, or she fell very slowly, for she had plenty of time as she went down to look about her and to wonder what was going to happen next. First, she tried to look down and make out what she was coming to, but it was too dark to see anything; then she looked at the sides of the well, and noticed that they were filled with cupboards and book-shelves; here and there she saw maps and pictures hung upon pegs.

—Lewis Carroll, *Alice in Wonderland*

She took down a jar from one of the shelves as she passed; it was labelled 'ORANGE MARMALADE', but to her great disappointment it was empty: she did not like to drop the jar for fear of

ragged right text (Alignment: Left)

This extract text is one point size smaller than the main text but uses the same leading.

one linespace between paragraphs

This is one way to show the attribution. (Not all extracts have attributions, of course.)

Here are the paragraph styles for the extract shown on the previous page. You may not need all of them.

☐ **Extracts, First [ext1]**
Changes from the Extracts, First style (page 68):
Indents and Spacing: Alignment = Left
                                                           Space After = 14 pt *or* 0.1944 in

☐ **Extracts, Middle [ext2]**
Changes from the Extracts, Middle style (page 68):
Indents and Spacing: First Line Indent = 0

☐ **Extracts, Last [ext3]**
Changes from the Extracts, Last style (page 68): No Changes

☐ **Extracts, Only [ext0]**
Changes from the Extracts, Only style (page 68): No Changes

The Extracts, Only style is for an extract that is only one paragraph long.

☐ **Extracts, Head [exth]**   Based On = **ext1**
Changes from Extracts, First style:
Basic Character Formats: Style = Bold
Advanced Character Formats: Baseline Shift = 3 pt
Indents and Spacing: Space After = 0

Create the [exth] and [ext1-ffhead] paragraph styles if your extracts have headings. Then apply the styles to your extract headings and the first paragraph following them.

☐ **Extracts, First after Head [ext1-ffhead]**   Based On = **ext1**
Changes from Extracts, First style:
Indents and Spacing: Space Before = 0

If there's an attribution after the last paragraph, create the [ext3attr] paragraph style and apply it to the last paragraph instead of **ext3** so there will be no space after.

☐ **Extracts, Last with Attribution [ext3attr]**   Based On = **ext3**
Changes from Extracts, Last style:
Indents and Spacing: Space After = 0

Attributions can be set in small caps, italics, or roman (regular). Pick a character style that will work with the rest of your design.

☐ **Extracts, Attribution [extattr]**   Based On = **ext3**
Changes from Extracts, Last style:
Indents and Spacing: Alignment = Right

In the extract sample below, the type is set at 10/12, justified, with a half-linespace between paragraphs and before and after the entire block of type. Notice that even though the type is the same size as in the previous example, the first paragraph uses five lines instead of six. This is due to the justified type. So this sample saves space in three ways: leading, justification, and spacing.

the field after it, and fortunately was just in time to see it pop down a large rabbit-hole under the hedge.

Extract Heading
In another moment down went Alice after it, never once considering how in the world she was to get out again. The rabbit-hole went straight on like a tunnel for some way, and then dipped suddenly down, so suddenly that Alice had not a moment to think about stopping herself before she found herself falling down a very deep well.

Either the well was very deep, or she fell very slowly, for she had plenty of time as she went down to look about her and to wonder what was going to happen next. First, she tried to look down and make out what she was coming to, but it was too dark to see anything; then she looked at the sides of the well, and noticed that they were filled with cupboards and book-shelves; here and there she saw maps and pictures hung upon pegs.

LEWIS CARROLL, *Alice in Wonderland*

She took down a jar from one of the shelves as she passed; it was labelled 'ORANGE MARMALADE', but to her great disappointment it was empty: she did not like to drop the jar for fear of

— one half-linespace before and after the entire extract

— justified text (Alignment = Left Justify)

— one half-linespace between paragraphs

— You may find a larger space here because the paragraph following is aligned to the baseline grid.

☐ **Extracts, First [ext1]**
Changes from the Extracts, First style (page 68):

Basic Character Formats:	Leading = 12 pt
Indents and Spacing:	Space Before = 7 pt *or* 0.0972 in
	Align to Grid = None

☐ **Extracts, Middle [ext2]**
Changes from the Extracts, Middle style (page 68):

Indents and Spacing:	First Line Indent = 0
	Space Before = 7 pt *or* 0.0972 in

(continued on next page)

☐ **Extracts, Last [ext3]**
Changes from the Extracts, Last style (page 68):
Indents and Spacing: Space After = 7 pt *or* 0.0972 in

☐ **Extracts, Only [exto]**
Changes from the Extracts, Only style (page 68):
Indents and Spacing: Space After = 7 pt *or* 0.0972 in

The Extracts, Only style is for an extract that is only one paragraph long.

☐ **Extracts Head [exth]**   Based On = **ext1**
Changes from Extracts, First style:
Basic Character Formats   Style = Bold

Create the **[exth]** and **[ext1-ffhead]** paragraph styles if your extracts have headings. Then apply the styles to your extract headings and the first paragraph following them.

☐ **Extracts, First after Head [ext1-ffhead]**   Based On = **ext1**
Changes from Extracts, First style:
Indents and Spacing   Space Before = 0

Attributions can be set in small caps, italics, or roman (regular). Pick a character style that will work with the rest of your design.

☐ **Extract Attribution [extattr]**   Based On = **ext3**
Changes from Extracts, Last style:
Indents and Spacing: Alignment = Right

Dealing with display material

For math display text, see page 141.

Display text comes in many forms. It can be a mathematical or scientific expression, an important declaration (such as a rule or the moral of a story), or the reproduction of a storefront sign, for instance. Despite the diversity of material, there is one basic way to treat all of it (except complex math; see page 141): Set the type the same as your book text, but center it. Leave a full line of space above and below. Examples:

For simple display text like this, make a paragraph style called Display [**disp**] based on **tx1** except with 1) centered alignment and 2) one line of space before and after.

$$E = mc^2$$

The pen is mightier than the sword.

BRAKE FOR MOOSE

Using tabs

You can master tabs with some practice. To see the Tabs panel, go to Type> Tabs or type Ctrl/Cmd+Shift+T. Here's how each tab aligns list items:

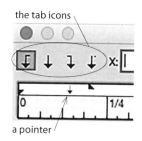

the tab icons

a pointer

left aligned	center aligned	right aligned	decimal aligned
oranges	oranges	oranges	1234.5
178	178	178	6
3	3	3	7.890

To add a tab, first make sure that all of your list copy is left aligned. Next put your cursor before the word or number where you want a tab, then hit the Tab key. (For now, the location of the tabs is not important, so even if some of your text items jump to the right or down to the next line, don't worry.) Repeat for all the items in your list, then highlight them all. In the Tabs panel, select the correct tab icon for your first tabbed column. Type a value in the "X" box, or click and drag the pointer (↓) in the white area just above the ruler. If you want to set a tab farther to the right than what shows on the ruler, hover your cursor over the ruler and a hand icon will appear. Use the hand to drag the ruler left or right. Repeat for each column in your list.

Leave the Leader box empty unless you want to fill the space before the tabbed item with something, such as a series of dots.

The "Align On" box can help you align list items on a specific character of your choice, such as an equals sign. Use the decimal tab to get access to this function, then type the character in the Align On field.

Notice that the numerals in the last column (above left) are Tabular Lining figures. Assigning Tabular figures (whether Lining or Oldstyle) assures that they line up with each other vertically.

 Tabs are very useful in printed books. However, EPUB format does not recognize them. We recommend using tabs in your printed book and then reformatting the tabbed material as a table with invisible (no color ▨) strokes for your ebook.

Designing lists

There are many kinds of lists! A well-planned book should have only a few types of lists in it, though. Aside from more details about numbered and bulleted lists, in this section you'll also find guidelines and settings for numbered paragraph, unnumbered, multicolumn, and sublists.

If your book has too many kinds of lists, reorganize or rethink.

Numbered lists

Why do we need to talk about numbered lists again if your styles are already set up? Because the list styles you have now only work for single-digit lists. If you have 10 or more entries, they will look sloppy.

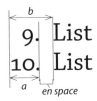

b

9. List
10. List

a   en space

The display to the left shows the ideal alignment of numbers and periods for numbered lists. The *a* value is the width of the widest number in the list plus the period. A right-aligning tab is set to the right of the period. The *b* value is where the list entries start, one en space beyond the period. The list's hanging indent is set for this location. The settings for a two-digit list in 11/14 Minion are shown below; if you're using a different font or size, continue reading.

Sometimes ragged right (Alignment = Left) works better for numbered lists. See how yours look before you decide.

☐ **2-Digit Numbered Lists, First [nl1-00]**   Based On = **tx1**

Changes from the No Indents style (see page 62):

Indents and Spacing:

	Left Indent = 0.2571 in
	First Line Indent = −0.2571 in
	Space Before = 14 pt *or* 0.1944 in
Tabs:	(Fill in as shown to the left)
OpenType Features:	Tabular Oldstyle

X: ▲▼ 0.179 in

☐ **2-Digit Numbered Lists, Middle [nl2-00]**   Based On = **nl1-00**

Changes from the 2-Digit Numbered Lists, First style:

Indents and Spacing: Space Before = 0

Remember to insert tabs before and after each paragraph number as shown on page 201.

☐ **2-Digit Numbered Lists, Last [nl3-00]**   Based On = **nl2-00**

Changes from the 2-Digit Numbered Lists, Middle style:

Indents and Spacing: Space After = 14 pt *or* 0.1944 in

For a detailed explanation of how tabs work, see page 199.

Here's how to find the values for *your* two-digit numbered lists:

Most of the time the Info panel is too distracting to have in front of you. Once you're finished using it, click the X to make it disappear.

1 Make a new text frame on the pasteboard and, using the No Indents style [**tx1**], type the widest numeral in your lists, plus a period. Then set an en space (Ctrl/Cmd+Shift+N) and type "List." Highlight the number and give it the Digits character style for your book.

2 Open the Info panel (Window>Info). This panel shows you the exact location of your cursor at any time. Place your cursor to the right of the period, and write down the X value. This corresponds to the *a* value in the demo above.

3 Place your cursor to the left of "List" and write down the X value. This is your *b* value from the demo.

4 Open the Paragraph Styles panel and start a new style called 2-Digit Numbered Lists, First [**nl1-oo**], based on your No Indents [**tx1**] style. In Indents and Spacing, add one line of space before it.

5 Also in Indents and Spacing, use *b* for the Left Indent and –*b* for the First Line Indent. This will give you the hanging indent you need.

6 In the Tabs section, select the right-aligning tab icon (↓), then type the value of *a* in the X: box. Then click OK.

7 Now set up a 2-Digit Numbered Lists, Middle [**nl2-oo**] style with zero space before, and a 2-Digit Numbered Lists, Last [**nl3-oo**] style with one line of space after, based on **nl2-oo**.

When you are formatting the lists, you must type a tab before the number and another one before the list entry, as shown at right. Also, remember to apply your Digits character style, if you're using one.

What if there's a mixture of one- and two-digit lists in your book? The best bet for most books is simply to treat them all like two-digit lists. This makes them all consistent, and you don't have to worry about mis-alignment of two different lists on the same page.

And three-digit lists? If you have any of these, make a separate style for them using the method above, and only use that style for the rare occasions when you need it. Then stick with the two-digit style for all the rest.

Numbered paragraphs

Also called paragraph lists, numbered paragraphs are easy to typeset because they are almost identical to your Text style. Simply apply your **Bold** character style to the number and period at the beginning of the paragraph, then set an en space (Ctrl/Cmd+Shift+N), and continue on with the text. Whether you want a line of space between entries is up to you. Styles for numbered paragraphs are shown on page 202.

Unnumbered (or unordered) lists

Unnumbered lists look quite simple on a page but do take some thought to set up. Look at the unnumbered lists in your book. Are they short

X value

You can set up your single-digit lists to align on the periods, too. Use the *a* value for the tab, but for the hanging indent simply use your normal paragraph indent measurement.

After reading this section, you might have noticed that in *this* book we have ignored our own instructions regarding numbered lists. This is a case of rules being made to be broken! We're striving for a minimalist look throughout, and this is just one of our design tricks. For 99% of our readers, the instructions given above will be the best method.

numbered paragraphs

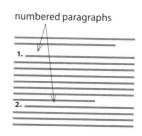

☐ **Numbered Paragraphs, First** [np1]   Based On = **tx**
Changes from the Text style (see page 62):
Indents and Spacing: Space Before = 14 pt *or* 0.1944 in

☐ **Numbered Paragraphs, Middle** [np2]   Based On = **np1**
Changes from the Numbered Paragraphs, First style:
Indents and Spacing: Space Before = 0 *or* no change

☐ **Numbered Paragraphs, Last** [np3]   Based On = **np2**
Changes from the Numbered Paragraphs, Middle style:
Indents and Spacing: Space After = 14 pt *or* 0.1944 in

or long? Are the entries short or long or a mixture? Would extra space between entries make them easier to read? Do you think they would look better in multiple columns? Do you need to save space throughout your book? Keep all of these factors in mind as you read this and the multi-column lists section that follows. Styles are shown on page 203.

Multicolumn lists

These lists can be set up in two different ways. An *anchored list* is a little easier to typeset but could cause paging headaches if it appears at the bottom of a page and needs to flow to the next. A *tabbed list* is more work to typeset but will flow to the next page with no trouble. Because of the way each is set up, the two kinds of lists are read in different ways, as shown below. This may influence which kind you choose.

Sometimes a complicated multicolumn list works better as a table. See page 342.

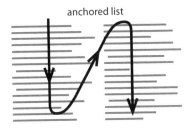

anchored list

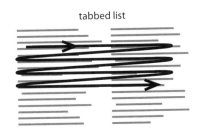

tabbed list

☐ **Unnumbered Lists, First** [unl1]   Based On = **tx1**

Changes from the No Indents style (see page 62):

Indents and Spacing: Alignment = Left

                                               Left Indent = 0.4 in

                                               First Line Indent = −0.2 in

                                               Space Before = 14 pt *or* 0.1944 in

☐ **Unnumbered Lists, Middle** [unl2]   Based On = **unl1**

Changes from the Unnumbered Lists, First style:

Indents and Spacing: Space Before = 0 ←

If your lists are a bit hard to read, consider adding 1/4 to 1/2 of a linespace between entries. If you add extra space, change your Align to Grid setting to None under Indents and Spacing.

☐ **Unnumbered Lists, Last** [unl3]   Based On = **unl2**

Changes from the Unnumbered Lists, Middle style:

Indents and Spacing: Space After = 14 pt *or* 0.1944 in

Anchored list   To typeset an unnumbered anchored list, set up the styles shown on page 204. The good news about an anchored list is that you need only the Middle style [**mcl2**] and perhaps the Column Head style [**mcl-colh**]. (The others are for tabbed lists.) Now complete these steps:

If your anchored multi-column list is bulleted or numbered, simply use the Middle styles you already have set up for those kinds of lists.

1   Make a new text frame the same width as your basic text frame, then go to Object>Text Frame Options and specify the number of columns and width of the gutters (the space between the columns). A gutter measurement that usually works well is 0.25″.

2   Highlight the list text that is on your page(s), copy it, place your cursor at the top left of the text frame you just made, and paste it. The text should flow into the columns.

3   Make the columns equal length, more or less, by dragging the center bottom handle of the text frame up or down. In any multicolumn list, it's desirable to make the left column(s) longer than the right one(s) if they cannot all be the same length. To force copy into the next column, type a soft return (Shift+Enter/Return).

4   Anchor the list to the book text this way: With the Selection Tool, select then cut the text frame containing your list (Ctrl/Cmd+X). With

the Type Tool, place your cursor at the end of the text line above where you want the list to go, press Enter/Return to make several extra lines of space, apply your **tx1** style to those lines, and then paste the list in the last blank line (Ctrl/Cmd+V). The text frame should appear just where you expected it, but if not, you may need to press Enter/Return once or twice more, or perhaps delete some of the blank lines. If you need to, you can resize the anchored text frame at any time.

The main problem with an anchored list is that if it doesn't all fit on the page and needs to flow to the next page, the entire thing moves as

You'll need to point this list out to your ebook conversion service so they can anchor it in place without using the extra linespaces.

☐ **Multicolumn Lists, First** [**mcl1**]   Based On = **tx1**
Changes from the No Indents style (see page 62):
Indents and Spacing: Alignment = Left
Left Indent = 0.2 in
First Line Indent = −0.2 in

For a tabbed list, add tabs. A sample tab setup for 3 columns is shown on the next page.

Space Before = 14 pt *or* 0.1944 in
Tabs: Add tabs for tabbed list only

For an anchored list without column heads, you only need the Middle style.

☐ **Multicolumn Lists, Middle** [**mcl2**]   Based On = **mcl1**
Changes from the Multicolumn Lists, First style:
Indents and Spacing: Space Before = 0

☐ **Multicolumn Lists, Last** [**mcl3**]   Based On = **mcl2**
Changes from the Multicolumn Lists, Middle style:
Indents and Spacing: Space After = 14 pt *or* 0.1944 in

The Column Head style can double as a head for the entire list.

☐ **Multicolumn Lists, Column Head** [**mcl-colh**]   Based On = **mcl1**
Changes from the Multicolumn Lists, First style:
Basic Character Formats: Style = Bold *or* Italics

☐ **Multicolumn Lists, First after Head** [**mcl1-ffh**]   Based On = **mcl1**
Changes from the Multicolumn Lists, First style:
Indents and Spacing: Space Before = 0

a unit. One way out of this awkward layout situation is to give the list a title (use the **mcl-colh** style provided on the previous page) and then place the entire list at the top or bottom of the same page or a nearby one, on the same spread if possible. Then in the text, refer to the list by its title, rather than by saying "the list below."

Another way out of the situation is to make a tabbed list instead.

Tabbed list This method is definitely more laborious, but it's also more flexible, as it will flow from one page to the next without any problem. First, set up the multicolumn list paragraph styles shown on the previous page. To typeset the list, use left-aligning tabs (↓) to set up a number of columns of equal width. Be sure to include all the tabs in the **mcl1** paragraph style. A sample tab panel for a two-column list is shown below. Yours will probably be different.

To typeset the list, go *across* the page rather than down, like this:

This is entry one, and it is »more than one line long.

» This is entry two, and it turns over¶
» » onto a second line.¶

This is entry three, and it is »longer than one line.

» This is entry four, and it's short.¶

Tab for turned lines in left column

Tab for start of right column   Tab for turned lines in right column

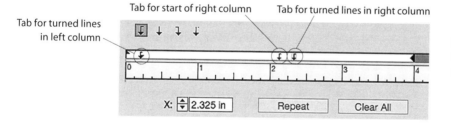

For a detailed explanation of how tabs work, see page 199.

Bulleted lists

You set up bulleted list styles in chapter 10, and most likely you can keep them just as they are. But if for some reason you don't like the bullet that comes with your book text font, simply change it. Here's how:

1   Open your **bl1** paragraph style in the Paragraph Styles panel and select Bullets and Numbering from the list on the left. In the List Type menu, make sure it says "Bullets."

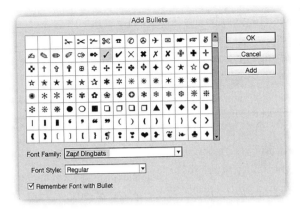

2 In the Bullet Character area, click on Add. The Add Bullets dialog box pops up, and you can browse through various typefaces. Start with your Text typeface. If that doesn't satisfy, try looking in Zapf Dingbats (shown to the left) or Wingdings, and choose a character you like.

3 If your new bullet is part of a different font family from your book text, check the "Remember Font With Bullet" box. Click Add, then OK.

4 Return to the Bullet Character chart in the Paragraph Style Options dialog box for **bl1**, and click on the new bullet to highlight it. This character will now appear in all your bulleted lists.

5 To change the color or size of your new bullet, make a character style for it while you're still in the Bullets and Numbering dialog box. Select New Character Style from the Character Style drop-down list. Name the style simply "bullet." This style should include *only the differences* from your **bl1** style, such as the font for the bullet, the new size, the baseline shift, the new color or tint of black, etc. There's no need to fill in every blank in the dialog box. Click OK to close the dialog box, then OK to finish.

Choose New Character Style from the list and name it "bullet."

Sure, it's fun to experiment with bullet characters, but don't get carried away. Unless bulleted lists are a major feature in your book, they shouldn't stick out like a sore thumb.

Sublists

Sometimes a list entry has subentries below it—bullets below numbers, letters below bullets. The number of variations is huge. You've learned how to set up lists, so a few suggestions should be all you need at this stage to create good-looking sublists. The marker (bullet, number, or letter) for any sublist entry should align with the main entry (not the marker) above it, and then the subentry should indent more: add the same amount of indent that you used in the main list. The example to the right shows the alignments. Here are a couple of general rules:

- Lowercase or uppercase letters align *at left* with each other.
- Roman numerals align *on the periods*, as for numbered lists.

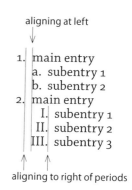

aligning at left

1. main entry
   a. subentry 1
   b. subentry 2
2. main entry
    I. subentry 1
   II. subentry 2
  III. subentry 3

aligning to right of periods

Designing sidebars

Along with chapter numbers and titles, sidebars are often the most noticeable design feature in a book. Indeed, if readers find your sidebars to be especially entertaining or instructive, they will often seek them out before reading the rest of the text.

You set up your original **sb** styles on page 70.

In the next several pages you'll find some basic sidebar designs and the style settings for each. A few of these designs require making shapes and using layers and colors (even if your book is going to be printed in black ink only). Part V: Adding Shapes & Color will show you how.

And in every one of these designs, your first step will be to cut the sidebar copy from your main text and paste it into a new text frame.

In addition to the designs shown on the next several pages, you'll find a few more suggestions in the list below. Mix and match some of the ideas to find the best look for *your* book.

- Bleed a background box across a two-page spread.
- Use a drop cap to start the sidebar text.
- Design a heading area for the sidebar title.
- If your book text is justified, set sidebars ragged right (Alignment = Left).
- Run the title vertically if the same title repeats with each sidebar.
- Set the first few lines the full width and the rest in two or three columns.
- Place a vertical rule to the left of the sidebar text.

Whatever design you use should work for *all* of your sidebars. Go through each one and think about its features—the amount of copy, lengths of headings, and kinds of lists—before making a final decision.

Classic
two-column
sidebar
– in –
one-column text

Leave 2–3 lines of white
space between the
text and the sidebar.

If your sidebar has a title,
make a separate text frame
for it. Place it so the base
of the title is 2 baselines
above the base of the
first line of sidebar text.

Sidebar text is 1 pt size
smaller than the text,
with 2 pts less leading.

This style of sidebar should
always appear at the top
or bottom of the text
page—never in the middle.

Alice was beginning to get very tired of sitting by her sister on the bank, and of having nothing to do: once or twice she had peeped into the book her sister was reading, but it had no pictures or conversations in it, 'and what is the use of a book,' thought Alice 'without pictures or conversation?

So she was considering in her own mind (as well as she could, for the hot day made her feel very sleepy and stupid), whether the pleasure of making a daisy-chain would be worth the trouble of getting up and picking the daisies, when suddenly a White Rabbit with pink eyes ran close by her.

There was nothing so VERY remarkable in that; nor did Alice think it so VERY much out of the way to hear the Rabbit say to itself, 'Oh dear! Oh dear! I shall be late!' (when she thought it over afterwards, it occurred to her that she ought to have wondered at this, but at the time it all seemed quite natural); but when the Rabbit actually took a watch out of its waistcoat-pocket and looked

SIDEBAR TITLE

For a minute or two she stood looking at the house, and wondering what to do next, when suddenly a footman in livery came running out of the wood—(she considered him to be a footman because he was in livery: otherwise, judging by his face only, she would have called him a fish)—and rapped loudly at the door with his knuckles.

It was opened by another footman in livery, with a round face, and large eyes like a frog; and both footmen, Alice noticed, had powdered hair that curled all over their heads. She felt very curious to know what it was all about, and crept a little way out of the wood to listen. The Fish-Footman began by producing from under his arm a great letter, nearly as large as himself, and this he handed over to the other, saying, in a solemn tone, 'For the Duchess. An invitation from the Queen to play croquet.' The Frog-Footman repeated, in the same solemn tone, only changing the order of the words a little, 'From the Queen. An invitation for the Duchess to play croquet.' Then they both bowed low, and their curls got entangled together.

42

Classic two-column sidebar in one-column text, *continued*

...ng the top or bottom of the
...e sidebar text (Ctrl/Cmd+X)
...rl/Cmd+V) into a new text
...and specify two columns with a
...the column lengths by moving
...r down. You can force type into
...Shift+Enter/Return) where you
...ar are shown below.

In multicolumn text it is always more desirable for the left column to be longer than the right one if they cannot be equal in length.

...ge 70):

Font Style = Regular

Font Size = 10 pt

Leading = 12 pt

Left Indent = 0

Right Indent = 0

Space Before = 0

Align to Grid = None

Drop Caps Lines = 2

Drop Caps Characters = 1

See page 153 for how to deal with a drop cap that has a quotation mark before it.

...age 70):

First Line Indent = 12 pts *or* 0.1667 in

Drop Caps Lines = 0

Drop Caps and Nested Styles:

☐ **Sidebars, Last** [sb3]

Changes from the Sidebars, Last style (see page 70): No changes

☐ **Sidebars, title** [sbt]

Changes from Sidebars, Title style style (see page 70):

Basic Character Formats:	Case = OpenType All Small Caps
Indents and Spacing:	Alignment = Center
Drop Caps and Nested Styles:	Drop Caps Lines = 0

Check Out Receipt

Central Library

Thursday, December 10, 2020
12:14:54 PM

Kendrick, Daniel Nathan

Title: Book design made simple
Material: Soft Bound
Due: 12/31/2020

You just saved $59.95 by using your library. You have saved $504.78 this past year and $504.78 since you began using the library!

Thank You!

Modern sidebar
– with –
text wrap and a
bleed background

The type in this sidebar is on the baseline grid, looking nice and neat next to the main text. Also note that the sidebar text aligns at left with the folio.

1. Format the sidebar type in its own text frame.
2. Give the new text frame a text wrap.
3. Position the top and bottom of the text frame on the closest available baselines. Then position the outside edge to align with the folio below. Move the inside edge to the center of the page (you'll see a guide appear when you reach the center line).

If ithe sidebar text were any wider the letter spacing and word spacing in the main text would probably look very poor—either too tight or too loose.

Alice was beginning to get very tired of sitting by her sister on the bank, and of having nothing to do: once or twice she had peeped into the book her sister was reading, but it had no pictures or conversations in it, 'and what is the use of a book,' thought Alice 'without pictures or conversation?

So she was considering in her own mind (as well as she could, for the hot day made her feel very sleepy and stupid), whether the pleasure of making a daisy-chain would be worth the trouble of getting up and picking the daisies, when suddenly a White Rabbit with pink eyes ran close by her.

There was nothing so VERY remarkable in that; nor did Alice think it so VERY much out of the way to hear the Rabbit say to itself, 'Oh dear! Oh dear! I shall be late!' (when she thought it over afterwards, it occurred to her that she ought to have wondered at this, but at the time it all seemed quite natural); but when the Rabbit actually took a watch out of its waistcoat-pocket and looked at it, and then hurried on, Alice started to her feet, for it flashed across her mind that she had never before seen a rabbit with either a waistcoat-pocket, or a watch to take out of it, and burning with curiosity, she ran across the field after it, and fortunately was just in time to see it pop down a large rabbit-hole under the hedge. In another moment down went Alice after it, never once considering how in the world she was to get out again. The rabbit-hole went straight on like a tunnel for some way, and then dipped suddenly down, so suddenly that Alice had not a moment to think about stopping herself before she found herself falling down a very deep well. Either the well was very deep, or she fell very slowly, for she had plenty of time as she went down

SIDEBAR TITLE

For a minute or two she stood looking at the house, and wondering what to do next, when suddenly a footman in livery came running out of the wood— (she considered him to be a footman because he was in livery: otherwise, judging by his face only, she would have called him a fish)—and rapped loudly at the door with his knuckles.

It was opened by another footman in livery, with a round face, and large eyes like a frog; and both footmen, Alice noticed, had powdered hair that curled all over their heads. She felt very curious to know what it was all about, and crept a little way out of the wood to listen.

Modern with text wrap and a bleed background, *continued*

To make this sidebar, first cut the sidebar text (Ctrl/Cmd+X) from the main text frame, paste it (Ctrl/Cmd+V) into a new text frame, then place it next to the main text. Give the sidebar text frame a text wrap (in your panels at the right of your screen or Window>Text Wrap) with the settings shown to the right. Finally, position your sidebar as described on page 210.

Text wrap settings for sidebar text frame

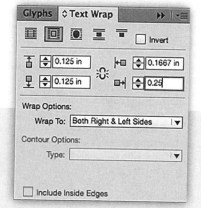

☐ **Sidebars, First [sb1]**

Changes from the Sidebars, First style (see page 70):

Basic Character Formats:	Font Family = Myriad Pro
	Font Style = Condensed
	Font Size = 10 pt
Indents and Spacing:	Left Indent = 0
	Right Indent = 0
	Space Before = 0
Paragraph Shading:	Shading = On
	(Fill in as shown to the right.)

☐ **Sidebars, Middle [sb2]**

Changes from the Sidebars, Middle style (see page 70):

Indents and Spacing:	First Line Indent = 12 pt *or* 0.1667 in

☐ **Sidebars, Last [sb3]**

Changes from the Sidebars, Last style (see page 70): No changes

☐ **Sidebars, Title [sbt]**

Changes from Sidebars, Title style (see page 70):

Basic Character Formats:	Font Style = Bold Condensed
	Case = All Caps
Indents and Spacing:	Alignment = Left

Adjust the Left value to extend to the outside edge of the bleed in *your* book (outside margin + 0.125").

For sidebars on recto pages, create a second set of identical paragraph styles except reverse the Left and Right values.

Modern sidebar
– with –
graphic and title

The title aligns with the fourth line of text.

In this design the graphic icon and the title always appear in the outer margin area, aligning toward the spine. So on a recto page the icon and title are on the right, aligning left.

The sidebar's text frame is the same width as the main text frame, minus 0.125" so that the type doesn't touch the inside edge of the background box.

It would be smart to construct an empty sidebar—complete with graphic (if any), title text frame, and background box—for a verso page and another for a recto page and then put them both into a library. Then whenever you need a sidebar you can drag one or the other out of the library, all ready to use. See chapter 39 for more about libraries.

SIDEBAR TITLE

For a minute or two she stood looking at the house, and wondering what to do next, when suddenly a footman in livery came running out of the wood—(she considered him to be a footman because he was in livery: otherwise, judging by his face only, she would have called him a fish)—and rapped loudly at the door with his knuckles.

It was opened by another footman in livery, with a round face, and large eyes like a frog; and both footmen, Alice noticed, had powdered hair that curled all over their heads. She felt very curious to know what it was all about, and crept a little way out of the wood to listen.

The Fish-Footman began by producing from under his arm a great letter, nearly as large as himself, and this he handed over to the other, saying, in a solemn tone, 'For the Duchess. An invitation from the Queen to play croquet.' The Frog-Footman repeated, in the same solemn tone, only changing the order of the words a little, 'From the Queen. An invitation for the Duchess to play croquet.' Then they both bowed low, and their curls got entangled together.

Alice was beginning to get very tired of sitting by her sister on the bank, and of having nothing to do: once or twice she had peeped into the book her sister was reading, but it had no pictures or conversations in it, 'and what is the use of a book,' thought Alice 'without pictures or conversation?'

So she was considering in her own mind (as well as she could, for the hot day made her feel very sleepy and stupid), whether the pleasure of making a daisy-chain would be worth the trouble of getting up and picking the daisies, when suddenly a White Rabbit with pink eyes ran close by her.

There was nothing so VERY remarkable in that; nor did Alice think it so VERY much out of the way to hear the Rabbit say to itself, 'Oh dear! Oh dear! I shall be late!' (when she thought it over afterwards, it occurred to her that she ought to have wondered at this, but at the time it all seemed quite natural); but when the Rabbit actually took a watch out of its waistcoat-pocket and looked at it, and then hurried on, Alice started to her feet, for it flashed across her mind that she had never before seen a rabbit with either a waistcoat-pocket, or a watch to take out of it, and burning with curiosity, she ran across the field after it, and fortunately was just in time to see it pop down a large rabbit-hole under the hedge. In another moment down went Alice after it, never once considering

This design works in any trim size that is wide enough to allow for an outer column. You could try any number of variations on what you see above. The background box could bleed left and/or right. The sidebar text could be set in one column. The title could appear above the text instead of next to it. The icon could be removed and the title moved up. You could set the first few words in small caps. Look again at the list on page 207 for other variations that would suit *your* book design.

Modern with graphic and title, *continued*

To make this sidebar, first format the sidebar text in its own two-column text frame that is 0.125" narrower than the main text frame. Place the title in a different text frame. Make a 10% black background box that is the full width of the type area and 0.2917" taller than the sidebar text. Place the top of the background box 0.125" (9 pts) above the top of the text and either behind it (Object>Arrange>Send to Back) or on its own layer.

For a detailed explanation of how to set up a two-column text frame for a sidebar, see the top of page 209. See chapters 31 and 33 for how to make shapes and apply colors.

☐ **Sidebars, First** [sb1]
Changes from the Sidebars, First style (see page 70):

Basic Character Formats:
    Font Family = Myriad Pro
    Font Style = Regular
    Font Size = 10 pt
    Leading = 12 pt

Indents and Spacing:
    Alignment = Left
    Left Indent = 0
    Right Indent = 0
    Space Before = 0
    Align to Grid = None

☐ **Sidebars, Middle** [sb2]
Changes from the Sidebars, Middle style (see page 70):

Indents and Spacing:
    First Line Indent = 12 pts *or* 0.1667 in

☐ **Sidebars, Last** [sb3]
Changes from the Sidebars, Last style (see page 70): No changes

☐ **Sidebars, Title** [sbt]
Changes from Sidebars, Title style (see page 70):

Basic Character Formats:
    Font Style = Bold Condensed
    Font Size = 12 pt
    Case = All Caps
    Tracking = 25

Indents and Spacing:
    Alignment = Towards Spine

Modern sidebar
– with –
rounded corners

This design could also work with a narrower trim size, as in the design on page 208.

The background box for the title is 60% black, which contrasts well with the white type.

See the opposite page for instructions on how to make these boxes with some square corners and some rounded corners.

Alice was beginning to get very tired of sitting by her sister on the bank, and of having nothing to do: once or twice she had peeped into the book her sister was reading, but it had no pictures or conversations in it, 'and what is the use of a book,' thought Alice 'without pictures or conversation?'

So she was considering in her own mind (as well as she could, for the hot day made her feel very sleepy and stupid), whether the pleasure of making a daisy-chain would be worth the trouble of getting up and picking the daisies, when suddenly a White Rabbit with pink eyes ran close by her.

There was nothing so VERY remarkable in that; nor did Alice think it so VERY much out of the way to hear the Rabbit say to itself, 'Oh dear! Oh dear! I shall be late!' (when she thought it over afterwards, it occurred to her that she ought to have wondered at this, but at the time it all seemed quite natural); but when the Rabbit actually took a watch out of its waistcoat-pocket and looked at it, and then hurried on, Alice started to her feet, for it flashed across her mind that she had never before seen a rabbit with either a waistcoat-pocket, or a watch to take out of it, and burning with curiosity, she ran across the field after it, and fortunately was just in time to see it pop down a large rabbit-hole under the hedge.In another moment down went Alice after it, never once considering how in the world she was to get out again. The rabbit-hole went

SIDEBAR TITLE

For a minute or two she stood looking at the house, and wondering what to do next, when suddenly a footman in livery came running out of the wood—(she considered him to be a footman because he was in livery: otherwise, judging by his face only, she would have called him a fish)—and rapped loudly at the door with his knuckles.

It was opened by another footman in livery, with a round face, and large eyes like a frog; and both footmen, Alice noticed, had powdered hair that curled all over their heads. She felt very

curious to know what it was all about, and crept a little way out of the wood to listen.

The Fish-Footman began by producing from under his arm a great letter, nearly as large as himself, and this he handed over to the other, saying, in a solemn tone, 'For the Duchess. An invitation from the Queen to play croquet.' The Frog-Footman repeated, in the same solemn tone, only changing the order of the words a little, 'From the Queen. An invitation for the Duchess to play croquet.' Then they both bowed low, and their curls got entangled together.

42 RUNNING HEAD

In this design the text frames *are* the background boxes. This is a useful technique to learn (and could be used for the sidebar design on page 210, too). Once you've made the text frames, you can either use object styles for them (chapter 38) or put them into a library (chapter 39). Either method will remember and store your work for future use.

Modern with rounded corners, *continued*

To make the text frame for the sidebar text as its own background box:

1 Make a text frame the full width of the type area in your design.
2 Select the box with the Selection Tool, go to Object>Text Frame Options, fill in the dialog box as shown to the right, and click OK.
3 With the text frame still selected, open the Corner Options dialog box (Object>Corner Options) and fill it in as shown below.
4 With the text frame still selected, open the Swatches panel, and specify 10% black for the fill and None for the stroke. (See chapter 31 to learn how to apply colors.)

Unlinked chain symbol allows each setting to be different.

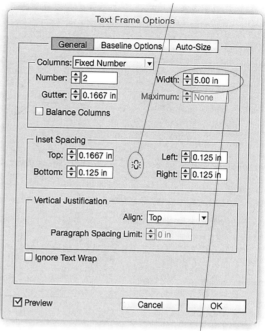

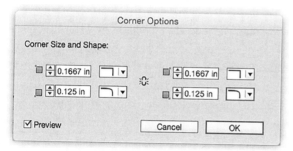

These widths will be the width of your text frame.

To make the text frame for the sidebar title as its own background box:

1 Make a text frame the full width of the type area in your design and one baseline high.
2 Using the Selection Tool, click on the box. Then go to Text Frame Options (Object>Text Frame Options), fill in the dialog box as shown to the right, and click OK.
3 With the text frame still selected, open the Corner Options dialog box and fill it in as shown on the next page, and click OK.

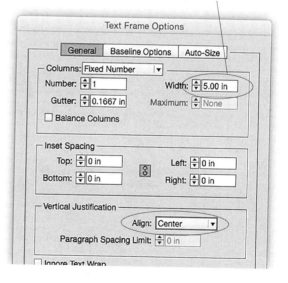

Modern with rounded corners, *continued*

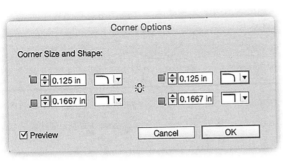

Corner options for the sidebar title text frame

4 With the text frame still selected, open your Swatches panel, and specify 60% black for the fill and None for the stroke.

5 Apply the paragraph styles shown below and on the next page to your sidebar text and title, then cut the sidebar text (Ctrl/Cmd+X) from the main text frame and paste it (Ctrl/Cmd+V) into your new text frame. Do the same with your sidebar title.

After all of your sidebar text is flowed into its text box and formatted, use the Selection Tool to drag the center bottom handle up (or down) just enough so that the last lines of type do not disappear.

Your final job is to place the title box above the text box and group them together. Select the text box with the Selection Tool and enlarge your view (Ctrl/Cmd+=) so you can work with precision. Drag the title box so its base just touches the top of the text box and the square corners line up. Now select both boxes at once, and group them (Object>Group or Ctrl/Cmd+G). This will ensure that the whole sidebar will stay together even if you move it. If you ever need to do more work on the box, simply ungroup it first (Ctrl/Cmd+Shift+G).

☐ **Sidebars, First [sb1]**
Changes from the Sidebars, First style (see page 70):

Basic Character Formats:	Font Family = Myriad Pro
	Font Style = Regular
	Font Size = 10 pt
	Leading = 12 pt
Indents and Spacing:	Left Indent = 0
	Right Indent = 0
	Space Before = 0
	Align to Grid = None

Modern with rounded corners, *continued*

☐ **Sidebars, Middle** [sb2]

Changes from the Sidebars, Middle style (see page 70):

Indents and Spacing: First Line Indent = 12 pt *or* 0.1667 in

☐ **Sidebars, Last** [sb3]

Changes from the Sidebars, Last style (see page 70): No changes

☐ **Sidebars, Title** [sbt]

Changes from Sidebars, Title style (see page 70):

Basic Character Formats: Font Style = Black

                                   Font Size = 11 pt

                                   Case = All Caps

                                   Tracking = 50

Indents and Spacing: Alignment = Center

Character Color: [Paper]

By this time you've become a real designer, and you're probably coming up with better ideas as you progress. This is a good time to stop and look closely at your book as a whole to see whether all of your design elements still hang together. If not, which elements please you the most? Is there a way to take something from them and replace something that you did earlier that no longer fits with the rest? On the other hand, you might find a way to use your favorite parts of the design in your running heads and folios, which you will read about in the next chapter. Remember that consistency, with two or three distinctive visual elements throughout, is the key to a successful book design.

27

Designing folios and running heads

Folios and running heads (or feet) are your book's navigation tools, so they need to be very clear and simple. There are many ways you can position them, and this will depend on your book's design and your personal preferences. Running heads are more common than running feet and are recommended for fiction and nonfiction because the layout is more forgiving. For example, if some of your pages are one line shorter or longer for typesetting reasons, it's not so obvious. In this chapter, you'll learn:

Your folios and running heads are on A-Master. Refer back to chapters 15 and 18 if you need to.

1 Where to place your folios and running heads
2 What text to include: book title and . . . ?
3 Alignment: centered or away from spine?
4 How to choose typefaces and sizes
5 Fine-tuning folios and running heads

1 Where to place your folios and running heads

Folios and running heads are placed at the top of pages, two baselines above the main text. In other words, there is one blank linespace between the running heads/folios and the main text.

When you convert to an ebook, you'll delete all your folios and running heads or feet.

Running feet are placed at the bottom of pages, two or three baselines below the main text so there are one or two blank linespaces between the main text and the running feet and folios.

On the first page of each chapter, the running heads are removed, and usually the folio is moved from the top of the page to the bottom (called a *drop folio*) or eliminated altogether.

Running foot aligned away from spine 3 lines below main text block

Folio centered in outside column

And, of course, rules are made to be broken. This book has running feet on the first page of each chapter. Some books have folios on recto pages only, and perhaps the book title only on verso pages. There are many variations. Choose a configuration that looks good and gives readers everything they need to navigate your book.

2 What text to include: book title and . . . ?

In a novel, the book title usually goes on the left and the author's name on the right. In nonfiction books, the book title usually goes on the left and the chapter title on the right. These are just guidelines, and you can put whatever you like in the running heads. Look at several books and you'll see a variety of options.

When choosing text to include in your running heads, always consider your readers first. How will they make their way through your book? In novels, often there are no chapter titles or table of contents, so the book title and author's name is sufficient. In nonfiction, readers navigate from the table of contents or index, so it's helpful to see chapter titles in the running heads. In *this* book, the book title and part title are on the left and the chapter number and title are on the right. Choose running heads that will be most helpful for readers navigating your book.

3 Alignment: centered or away from spine?

Folios are most often aligned to the outside margins, and running heads are either centered or left/right aligned a short distance away from the folios. But again, there are many possible variations.

A good rule of thumb is to keep everything consistent. If your chapter title and headings are centered, center your running heads too. If your chapter title and headings are left or right aligned, then align your running heads away from the spine. See the examples to the right and on the next page.

folio   Everything else is centered

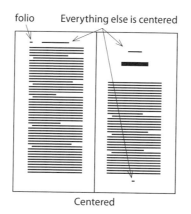

Centered

folio   All left or right aligned

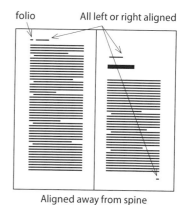

Aligned away from spine

author's name in small caps, centered

book title in small caps, centered

Consider saving space by putting folios and running heads in the outer column—if they won't interfere with your book's content.

chapter number and title on verso, current heading 1 on recto

Gray-to-white gradient bleeds top.

part number and title (separated by a dingbat) on verso

chapter number and title (separated by a dingbat) on recto

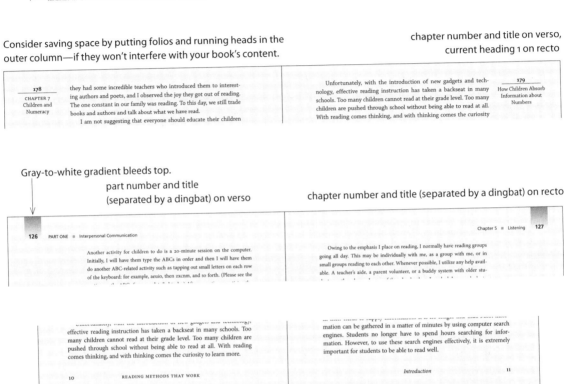

book title in small caps, centered

chapter title in upper and lowercase italics, centered

unnumbered part title on verso

unnumbered chapter title on recto

Vertical rules bleed bottom and separate folios from running feet.
Folios appear outside the normal text area.

4 How to choose typefaces and sizes

Folios

If your design uses any sans serif type for sidebars, tables, captions, or display, use that type for your folios. Sans serif numerals are just a bit easier to read at a glance. If you're using oldstyle numbers throughout, stick with them for folios. On the other hand, if you have a lot of numbers in the text, you're probably using lining figures, so use them for folios, too. Folios can be the same size as the text or a bit smaller—or, if your book makes major use of an index (such as in a reference book or cookbook), bigger.

Now set up a **Folio** paragraph style (see page 78), and remember that in Indents and Spacing you can set the alignment to Towards Spine, Away From Spine, or Centered to make this style simple to use.

Running heads

Design your running heads to match either your text style (probably a serif typeface) or your folio style (possibly a sans serif). Since you've already determined that the two typefaces match each other nicely, it is fine to mix them here.

Running heads can be the same size as the folios or a bit smaller. Study the examples on the previous page to see whether any of these general ideas would work in your book. The main thing is to be sure that your entire navigation system is readable at a glance.

Set up a **Running Head** paragraph style (see page 78). Under Indents and Spacing, choose Towards Spine, Away From Spine, or Centered. In the Align to Grid drop-down menu, choose All Lines.

5 Fine-tuning folios and running heads

Look at several of your 2-page spreads and see whether your folios and running heads look okay. You may want to apply Small Caps or Italics character styles to your running heads/feet, or change your folios to lining figures.Sometimes it helps to look at other books to see how they've handled folios and running feet.

There are no hard and fast rules here, so go with what you think looks best. Print a few 2-page spreads to be sure.

28

Designing your front matter

You've done a lot of work and are perhaps getting a bit weary at this point, hoping that now you can simply stick the front matter at the front of the book and be done with it. But this chapter and and the next (Designing your back matter) are actually very important, so take care with them.

On page 24 you learned all the elements that might go into your front matter, with only the title page and copyright page being absolutely required. You've also roughed in the pages (chapter 14). In this section we'll discuss all the common front matter items in more detail, and you'll create and apply paragraph styles throughout your front matter. You'll also set up a page numbering system, as the front matter is numbered separately from the rest of the pages, in lowercase roman numerals.

Title page

The title page is supremely important. Your goal is to give the reader a positive and accurate first impression by integrating design elements from the interior and the cover of the book. If your design is a classical one with centered headings and conservative chapter openings, don't switch to left or right alignments or jazzy typefaces on this page. Stick with your own look.

The title page will appear either on page i or—if you are going to use a half title page—on page iii. You should place the elements on the title page more or less as shown on the next page, with the title first and the publisher at the bottom. As you move them around, reduce the page size on the screen and squint at them to see which elements form groups. The title, subtitle, and edition (if any) should be in a group. The author's name should be somewhat close to the title but not quite in the same group. The publisher (and possibly the city) should always be by itself, flush bottom on the page. Move the title group up and down a bit and see what looks balanced, then carefully place the author. And remember the

Pages in the front matter coming before the Contents do not have visible page numbers.

At the end of this chapter, on page 245, you'll assign lowercase roman numerals to your front matter pages. For now, arabic numerals are fine.

basic principles of good design: repeat elements, the rule of three, and white space.

Try aligning elements much the way you have in the rest of the book. If headings are generally flush left, try placing type flush left on this page, too. If you use a particular type ornament or other graphic throughout the book, see whether it works here, too. If you're in love with the image on your front cover, you may repeat all or part of it on this page, as long as the typeset information remains very readable. Study other books to find out how they have used the space on their title pages, and be creative within the design you've already established.

The title page contains much of the official information about the book—in other words, whatever is on the title page will be entered into a library's database, plus that of the Library of Congress or Library and Archives Canada. Do not include quotations or any other copy (although artwork is fine).

You don't need to use the baseline grid on the title page.

See chapter 59 for ways to isolate a section of your cover image, or to fade it back.

A title page includes:
Title [**ttl**]
Subtitle [**subttl**]
Edition (2nd edition +) [**ed**]
Author(s) [**au**]
Author Affiliation(s) [**auaffil**]
Publisher [**pub**]
Publisher's Location [**city**]

Design your title page (*left*) first, then base the half title page on the title page.

Sun Showers
on a Sunday

a memoir by
Felicity Menendez

Felicity's Press
Whitehorse

Sun Showers
on a Sunday

Half title page

If you're going to use a half title page (sometimes called a bastard title), base it on the title page. Here you will set only the book title—no author, no subtitle, no ornaments. You might use the same typeface you used for the title on the title page or, if you used a display face on the title page, use a more conservative one here. If the title page title is on two or more lines, you could set it that way on the half title page, too. The type size should be smaller than on the title page, and in most books, the half title is centered. Consider placing it at the same height on the page as the title on the title page so that the reader's eye doesn't have to jump up or down when turning the page.

Sometimes a half title page is used again on the recto page just before the start of the main text. If you want to do this, use the Selection Tool to select the type on your first half title page, copy it, and paste it in place (Edit>Copy, then Edit>Paste in Place) on the second half title page so that this page is an exact copy of the first one.

Family names

Over the centuries of bookmaking, some interesting jargon has developed.

A **widow** is the last line of a paragraph, stranded by itself at the top of a new page. Widows are simply not allowed.

An **orphan** is defined in a couple of different ways: a very short final line of a paragraph, or the opening line of a paragraph, placed as the last line on a page. Orphans of both kinds are to be avoided whenever possible.

A **bastard** is another name for a half title page.

In InDesign, you've used **parent and child** styles when setting up your style sheets. These family terms are newer ones.

How did these references to family members (and nonmembers) come about? Good question! But if you remember the typesetter's socially outdated rule that a widow has no future and an orphan has no past, it will help you remember at least those two terms.

Copyright page

Another mandatory front matter element, the copyright page always appears on the verso after the title page.

A complete, annotated copyright page is shown on page 226.

Many new authors find the copyright page confusing and intimidating. Below is an explanation of each item and how to get the information you need. Be sure not to leave any of it for the last minute.

- **Publisher's address** A URL or email address is passable, but these do change, perhaps more often than a physical address. You need to include an address of some kind so that someone can contact you if they want to quote from your book later on.

- **Copyright notice** Include a minimum of the © symbol, year, and the name of the copyright owner. Canadian authors have automatic copyright protection, so they may simply write a copyright notice of their choosing. Authors in the U.S. have three options:

When should you complete your copyright page? A complete schedule of the self-publishing process is laid out on pages 478–479.

  1. Obtain an official copyright from the Library of Congress. This may be done before publication or up to three months after publication. At this writing, the cost is $35.
  2. Invent a copyright notice of your own, or copy one from another book, without the backing of the Library of Congress.
  3. Protect yourself by doing the following: Make two hard copies of the manuscript and put them both into mailing envelopes addressed to yourself. Write a statement saying "I __[your name]__ am putting this manuscript in an envelope on __[add date]__." Make two copies of the statement and have them notarized separately. Mail each manuscript and its notarized statement to yourself separately, using certified mail with a return receipt for each, and keep the tracking numbers, then track the package online and print out the tracking information. When you receive the packages, *do not open them*. This process will show that you were in possession of the written material on a certain date; therefore, if someone steals your words later on, you will have proof of this to show to your attorney. You'll have a witness (the notary public), evidence (the package), and a date and time (the tracking information). The second package will remain unopened as untampered evidence to use in court.

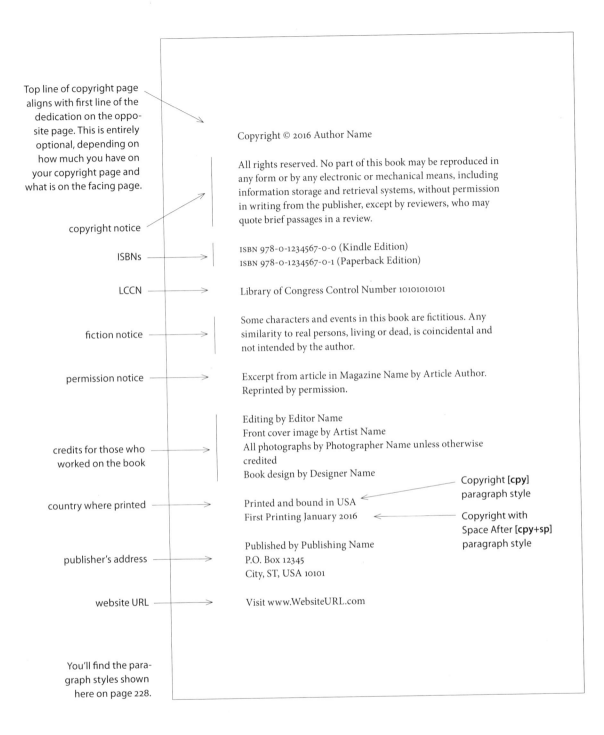

Top line of copyright page aligns with first line of the dedication on the opposite page. This is entirely optional, depending on how much you have on your copyright page and what is on the facing page.

copyright notice

ISBNs

LCCN

fiction notice

permission notice

credits for those who worked on the book

country where printed

publisher's address

website URL

You'll find the paragraph styles shown here on page 228.

Copyright © 2016 Author Name

All rights reserved. No part of this book may be reproduced in any form or by any electronic or mechanical means, including information storage and retrieval systems, without permission in writing from the publisher, except by reviewers, who may quote brief passages in a review.

ISBN 978-0-1234567-0-0 (Kindle Edition)
ISBN 978-0-1234567-0-1 (Paperback Edition)

Library of Congress Control Number 10101010101

Some characters and events in this book are fictitious. Any similarity to real persons, living or dead, is coincidental and not intended by the author.

Excerpt from article in Magazine Name by Article Author. Reprinted by permission.

Editing by Editor Name
Front cover image by Artist Name
All photographs by Photographer Name unless otherwise credited
Book design by Designer Name

Printed and bound in USA
First Printing January 2016

Published by Publishing Name
P.O. Box 12345
City, ST, USA 10101

Visit www.WebsiteURL.com

Copyright [cpy] paragraph style

Copyright with Space After [cpy+sp] paragraph style

- **Copyright date** This can be a bit tricky. If you get your copyright from the U.S. Library of Congress on a certain date, use that year for your copyright date. Otherwise, use the year of publication. If you print the book near the end of the calendar year, though, use the following year for your copyright date. The more recent the date, the happier potential readers will be, especially for non-fiction and how-to books.

- **Edition number** Include this only if the book is in its second or higher edition. A second printing is *not* a new edition. If you make slight changes for a second or subsequent printing—perhaps adding some new book reviews or a new foreword—that's not a new edition, either. A new edition must be substantially changed from the previous one, with new information, rearranged and rewritten chapters, etc.

Front matter resources

U.S. copyright
United States Copyright Office
   copyright.gov

ISBN (International Standard Book Number)
Canada: Library and Archives Canada
   www.bac-lac.gc.ca/eng/services/isbn-canada/Pages/isbn-canada.aspx
U.S.: R. R. Bowker LLC
   myidentifiers.com

CIP (Cataloging-in-Publication) data
Canada: Library and Archives Canada
   www.bac-lac.gc.ca/eng/services/cip/Pages/cip.aspx

LCCN (Library of Congress Control Number)
U.S.: United States Library of Congress
   loc.gov/publish/pcn/

- **ISBN (International Standard Book Number)** All books need a number if they are to be sold. You may purchase the number from the resources listed in the sidebar above. See chapter 68 for more details on where to purchase ISBNs, how many to buy, and how to assign them to the different editions of your book.

- **Cataloging-in-Publication (CIP) data or (U.S.) Library of Congress Control Number (LCCN)** In the U.S. and Canada, the national libraries will give publishers library cataloging data to put on their copyright pages. But in the U.S., this is offered only to large publishers, and that is probably not you (yet). So in the U.S., ask the Library of Congress for a control number (LCCN). Librarians everywhere are happier to accept a book with a number. The numbers are given at no charge.

CIP data can be obtained from private sources. See www.BookDesignMadeSimple.com/Resources for a current provider.

See chapter 41 for much more on permissions.

- **Credits for artwork and permissions** For copyrighted quotes, song lyrics, and artwork, you need written permission (an email message is acceptable). Write for permission as soon as you decide to use the material, because it can take months to track down the copyright owner and come to an agreement. You may have to pay to use the material. Have a backup plan in case you don't receive permission in time or it's denied altogether. Often the permission will come with specific wording that the owner wants to see in your book. Be prepared to send a free copy of your book to the copyright owner.

- **Credits to those who helped you** Some authors like to list some or all of their paid assistants: editors, proofreaders, printer, etc. This is not the place for acknowledgments, though—simply a list.

- **Country of printing** This is mandatory for customs reasons. Simply state "Printed in the United States of America," "Printed in Canada," or the appropriate country.

Study copyright pages in other books and the example on page 226 to see how others have dealt with all of this information. Set up the two paragraph styles below for your copyright page. Feel free to change the suggested type size and leading so that all the material will fit properly on *your* copyright page.

☐ **Copyright [cpy]**   Based On = **tx1**
Changes from the No Indents style (see page 62):
Basic Character Formats: Font Size = 9 pt
                                                            Leading = 11 pt
Indents and Spacing: Alignment = Left
                                                            Align to Grid = None

☐ **Copyright with Space After [cpy+sp]**   Based On = **cpy**
Changes from the Copyright style:
Indents and Spacing: Space After = 11 pt *or* 0.1528 in

Dedication page

The dedication almost always appears on the recto that faces the copyright page. Keep it simple. There is no need for a heading or to say "Dedicated to" here, as everyone knows what this page is for. Place the dedication about one-third of the way down the page, on the baseline grid. It's customary, although not mandatory, to set it in italics and center each line. Use the same typeface and size as your Text style.

If you are going to print offset rather than digital and don't have room for a dedication page, you can place it at the top of the copyright page.

Drag the top of the text frame down to position your dedication vertically on the page.

For my sisters and brothers
with love

Be careful how you break the lines in the dedication.

For my sisters
and brothers with love

means something different from

For my sisters and brothers
with love

Set up your Dedication using the paragraph style shown below. Feel free to change the indents to suit your copy. Be thoughtful about the line breaks, and use hard returns between the lines.

☐ **Dedication [ded]** Based On = **tx1**
Changes from the No Indents style (see page 62):

Basic Character Formats: Font Style = Italic
 Tracking = 10

Indents and Spacing: Alignment = Center
 Left Indent = 0.75 in
 Right Indent = 0.75 in

Hyphenation: Hyphenate = Unchecked

Epigraph

Place this on the next recto after the dedication page, with a blank verso page in between. Using the same typeface and size as your Text style, start the quotation on the same baseline as the dedication, and indent it left and right equally, so that it's a compact block of type. Set the attribution on the next line.

Drag the top of the text frame down to position your epigraph vertically on the page.

If your epigraph is poetry, see pages 352–355 for how to align the lines properly.

> History would be an excellent thing
> if only it were true.
>
> —Leo Tolstoy

From *Crimson Snow* by David Shone

An epigraph can be set in italics or roman. Each line can be centered, or left aligned with the text block centered. The attribution, as you saw on pages 151 and 156, can be centered or right aligned. The paragraph styles offered below are for the epigraph on this page. If your indents result in a lopsided page, simply increase or decrease the indents until everything is centered and the attribution aligns at right with the longest epigraph line.

☐ **Epigraph [epi]**   Based On = **tx1**
Changes from the No Indents style (see page 62):
Basic Character Formats: Tracking = 10
Indents and Spacing: Alignment = Left
                                                  Left Indent = 0.87 in
                                                  Right Indent = 0.87 in
                                                  Align to Grid = None

☐ **Epigraph Attribution [epiattr]**   Based On = **epi**
Changes from the Epigraph style:
Indents and Spacing: Alignment = Right
                                                  Space Before = 7 pt *or* 0.0972 in

Front and back matter titles

You'll design a paragraph style for the titles of your front and back matter sections—"Contents," "Preface," "Glossary," "References," and so on. Sample paragraph styles are offered in the next few pages. Base your front and back matter titles on your Chapter Title [**ct**] paragraph style, but use less space before and after them. For example, if your chapter titles are a quarter of the way down the page, put your front and back matter titles at the top. This distinguishes them from chapter titles and saves space.

First create a paragraph style for your front and back matter titles (see the Front and Back Matter Title [**fbt**] paragraph style samples on pages 233 and 236), then apply the style to your front and back matter titles.

Contents

Begin the table of contents (TOC) on the next recto after the epigraph and a blank verso. Or, if your Contents are going to fill only two pages, you might want to place this section on a spread instead—pages iv–v, for instance. Don't leave a blank recto page before a Contents spread, though.

Before you start designing the Contents, you'll need to make two basic decisions:

Novels almost never include a table of contents.

1   How many levels of headings do you want to show? If you have plenty of space to fill, you might include headings 1–3; on the other hand, if you are squeezed for space, you might only include chapter numbers and titles. Consider your reader in this decision, too. If your chapters are quite long, will the reader be able to find everything he or she needs if you list only chapter titles? Also think about the potential buyer, who might very well use the Contents to decide whether to buy, either in a store or online.

2   Where do you want to put the page numbers? If you place them flush right in the text block, will they be so far from the titles that they are hard for the reader to figure out? Should you perhaps place them a set distance from the titles or headings themselves, not lining up flush right at all (as in *this* book)? Study examples in other books and the ones on the following pages to get ideas for your Contents.

If you have a very simple TOC with just a few entries, you might consider just applying the paragraph and character styles you create to your typed TOC. However, there are two benefits to using an automatic TOC: 1) it'll update page numbers automatically, and 2) it'll generate a navigation system when converted to an ebook.

Once you have set up the paragraph styles for your Contents, you'll learn how to generate an automatic TOC (see pages 240–244), which "types" the entire list, including page numbers, for you.

 An automatic table of contents is especially useful in an ebook, where it becomes a navigation chart.

DESIGN A
Classic contents
– with –
part and
chapter titles

These sections are part of the front matter but appear *after* the Contents in the book. Their paragraph style in the TOC is **toc-fbt**.

TOC Part Title [**toc-pt**] with TOC Part Number character style [**toc-pn**] applied to the part number

TOC Chapter Title [**toc-ct**] with TOC Chapter Number character style [**toc-cn**] applied to the chapter number

Tabular Oldstyle figures are used in all the TOC styles so that the numbers line up neatly below each other.

Folio but no running head or foot

CONTENTS

· v ·

From *Sassy Gal's How to Lose the Last Damn 10 Pounds* by Sharon Helbert

Classic contents with part and chapter titles, *continued*

This Contents design is related to the classic chapter opening with two-line drop cap (Design 2) on pages 151–153. Page numbers are flush right in the text frame because the chapter titles in this example are long enough so that it's easy to locate the correct page number for each. If your chapter titles are short, consider putting the page numbers one em space after each title (see page 238) or adding a dot leader to the tab (see below). Use the following style settings to set up the table of contents on page 232.

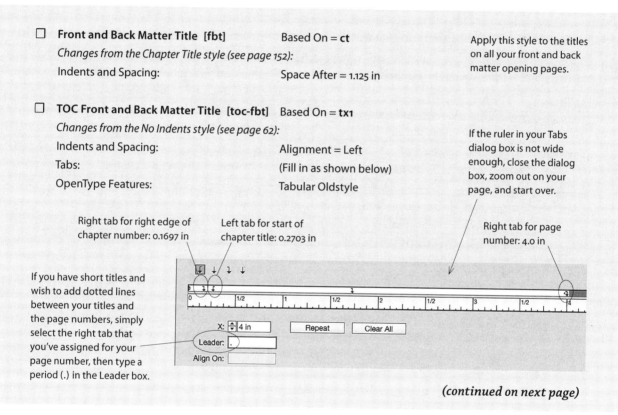

☐ **Front and Back Matter Title [fbt]**   Based On = **ct**

Changes from the Chapter Title style (see page 152):

Indents and Spacing:

Space After = 1.125 in

Apply this style to the titles on all your front and back matter opening pages.

☐ **TOC Front and Back Matter Title [toc-fbt]**   Based On = **tx1**

Changes from the No Indents style (see page 62):

Indents and Spacing:

Alignment = Left

Tabs:

(Fill in as shown below)

OpenType Features:

Tabular Oldstyle

If the ruler in your Tabs dialog box is not wide enough, close the dialog box, zoom out on your page, and start over.

Right tab for right edge of chapter number: 0.1697 in

Left tab for start of chapter title: 0.2703 in

Right tab for page number: 4.0 in

If you have short titles and wish to add dotted lines between your titles and the page numbers, simply select the right tab that you've assigned for your page number, then type a period (.) in the Leader box.

X: 4 in   Repeat   Clear All

Leader: .

Align On:

(continued on next page)

The tabs above should work for your book if you have changed neither the trim size of 5.5" × 8.5" nor the margins from the original settings in chapter 2. If you have changed trim size or margins, you'll need to move the rightmost tab to the right edge of your text frame.

Classic contents with part and chapter titles, *continued*

Set up the rest of your paragraph and character styles as shown below.

☐ **TOC Part Title [toc-pt]**   Based On = **toc-fbt**
Changes from the TOC Front and Back Matter Title style (see page 233):
Basic Character Formats: Font Style = Semibold
Indents and Spacing: Space Before = 14 pt *or* 0.1944 in
                                                                      Align to Grid = None

☐ **TOC Chapter Title [toc-ct]**   Based On = **toc-fbt**
Changes from the TOC Front and Back Matter Title style (see page 233):
Indents and Spacing: Left Indent = 0.2703 in
                                                                      First Line Indent = −0.2703 in
The Back Matter Title, First   Space Before = 4 pt *or* 0.0556 in
is self-explanatory. Extra   Align to Grid = None
space is needed before this
title to distance it from the
last chapter. Use the **toc-fbt**   ☐ **TOC Back Matter Title, First [toc-bmt1]**   Based On = **toc-fbt**
style for any subsequent   *Changes from the TOC Front and Back Matter Title style (see page 233):*
back matter heads. See   Indents and Spacing: Space Before = 28 pt *or* 0.3889 in
an example on page 238.

Insert an em space   ☐ **TOC Part Number [toc-pn]** *character* **style**   Based On = **[None]**
between the part num-   Basic Character Formats: Case = All Caps
ber and the part title.   Tracking = 50

Type a tab before and   ☐ **TOC Chapter Number [toc-cn]** *character* **style** Based On = **[None]**
after the chapter number.   Basic Character Formats: Font Style = Semibold
                                                                      Size = 14 pt

Now generate an automatic TOC for Design A by following the example on pages 240–242). Then add your part numbers, followed by an em space, and apply the **toc-pn** character style to them. Add your chapter numbers, with a tab before and after, and apply the **toc-cn** character style to them. Apply the **toc-bmt1** style to the first back matter entry, and make any other adjustments needed.

Notice that the heading
for the table of contents is
always simply "Contents."

Contents

From *Storytelling in Words and Pictures* by Janet Stone

toc-fbt TOC Front and
Back Matter Title style

toc-ct TOC Chapter Title
style

toc-h1 Heading 1 on its
own line with a page
number

toc-h2 Level 2 headings
grouped together with no
page numbers. Because the
sections are short, often
more than one Heading 2
appears on the same page
in the book, so it would
be easy for the reader to
find them without being
given a page number. Also,
this method saves space.

Modern contents with headings run together, *continued*

This table of contents design is compact and easy to read, with the second-level headings grouped together without page numbers. It corresponds with Design 4, Modern chapter opening with number and title on same line, pages 156–158. The paragraph and character styles for this design are:

(see page 157)

Apply this style to the titles on all your front and back matter opening pages.

☐ **Front and Back Matter Title [fbt]**   Based On = **ct**
Changes from the Chapter Title style (see page 157):
Indents and Spacing:
Space Before = 9 pt *or* 0.125 in
Space After = 45 pt *or* 0.625 in

☐ **TOC Front and Back Matter Title [toc-fbt]** Based On = **tx1**
Changes from the No Indents style (see page 62):

Basic Character Formats:
Font Family = Myriad Pro
Font Style = Light Condensed
Tracking = 40

Sometimes you can't see the entire ruler in the Tabs dialog box. If that is the case, click and hold down the mouse on the main part of the ruler and you'll see a hand. Drag the hand to the left to expose the right end of the ruler.

Indents and Spacing: Alignment = Left
Tabs: Set a right tab at 4 in
    (see example on page 233)
OpenType Features: Figure Style = Tabular Lining

☐ **TOC Chapter Title [toc-ct]**   Based On = **toc-fbt**
Changes from the TOC Front and Back Matter Title style:
Basic Character Formats: Size = 13 pt
Indents and Spacing: Left Indent = 0.2 in
    First Line Indent = −0.2 in
    Space Before = 22.5 pt *or* 0.3125 in
    Align to Grid = None

☐ **TOC Back Matter Title, First [toc-bmt1]**   Based On = **toc-fbt**
Changes from the TOC Front and Back Matter Title style:
Indents and Spacing: Space Before = 28 pt *or* 0.3889 in

☐ **TOC Heading 1 [toc-h1]**   Based On = **tx1**

Changes from the No Indents style (see page 62):

Indents and Spacing: Alignment = Left

                                              Left Indent = 0.3 in

                                              First Line Indent = –0.1 in

Tabs: Set a right tab at 4 in

                                                 (see example on page 233)

Hyphenation: Hyphenate = Unchecked

OpenType Features: Figure Style = Tabular Lining

☐ **TOC Heading 2 [toc-h2]**   Based On = **toc-h1**

Changes from the TOC Heading 1 style:

Indents and Spacing: Left Indent = 0.4 in

                                              Right Indent = 0.5 in

                                              First Line Indent = 0

                                                                                To delete the tab set at
Tabs: No tabs ←   4", simply drag it down-
                                                                                ward and it'll disappear.

☐ **TOC Chapter Number [toc-cn]** *character* style Based On = [None]

Basic Character Formats: Font Style = Semibold Condensed

                                              Size = 13 pt

OpenType Features: Figure Style = Tabular Lining

Now generate an automatic TOC for Design B by following the examples on pages 240 and 243. Then you'll need to check that the page numbers are lining up on your right margin. If not, open the **toc-fbt** paragraph style, and drag the right tab into position (you'll see the page numbers shift as you do this). Do the same tab adjustment in the **toc-h1** paragraph style. Next, run the level 2 headings together by deleting the hard return after each one (except the last in each group). Set an en space, a solidus (/), and another en space between entries (or choose another character, such as a bullet). Use soft returns between lines (if needed), and never begin a line with a solidus. Add your chapter numbers, followed by a tab, and apply the **toc-cn** character style to them. Finally, apply the **toc-bmt1** style to the first back matter entry (see page 238).

It helps in this operation if you can see the hidden characters. If you're not seeing them, go to Type>Show Hidden Characters.

On the next page you'll see the TOC from the same book laid out in a different way.

DESIGN C
Modern contents
– with –
headings stacked

one em space

In this example the amount of space between each heading and its page numbers is one em space (Ctrl/Cmd+Shift+M).

The first back matter head **[toc-bmt1]** has its own style with space above.

Use the Front and Back Matter Title **[toc-fbt]** style for the rest of the back matter headings.

vii

From *Storytelling in Words and Pictures* by Janet Stone

This is the same table of contents as in Design B, but the level 2 heads are typed in a list instead of being run together. Most of the headings are very short and the page numbers are placed a uniform distance after each, making them easy to find.

Most of the paragraph styles are identical to those shown for Design B on pages 236–237 except for the one shown below. What makes this design different is that the page numbers are separated from the titles and headings by an em space rather than a tab. In this design the figures look better as Proportional Oldstyle, and this is the only difference between the following paragraph style and the one on page 237.

☐ **TOC Heading 1 [toc-h1]**   Based On = **tx1**
Changes from the No Indents style (see page 62):

Indents and Spacing:	Alignment = Left
	Left Indent = 0.3 in
	First Line Indent = –0.1 in
Tabs:	Set a right tab at 4 in
	(see example on page 233)
Hyphenation:	Hyphenate = Unchecked

In this style the figures (page numbers) remain Proportional Oldstyle, as in the **tx1** style. So they are not mentioned here; compare with the almost identical style on page 237.

If you like, naturally you can type your own TOC. Simply use one of the suggested designs or make up your own, then apply the paragraph and character styles to everything. The following pages of instructions, though, are for those who want to take advantage of InDesign's full power, ensure accuracy, and automate the system for easy updating.

Now that you've set up your styles, you'll learn how to generate an automatic table of contents. It may seem complicated at first, but it's worth the effort to learn, because any changes that you make in the book can be updated in the TOC with just a couple of clicks. Also, in an ebook, all of the items in the TOC will be hyperlinked to the content.

Generating an automatic table of contents

Begin by going to Layout>Table of Contents. Your dialog box will look something like the one below. Click the More Options button at the right if you don't see all the choices shown.

The "Contents" title

The paragraph styles in your book, some of which will appear in the table of contents

The TOC paragraph styles that will be used in the actual table of contents (**toc-ct**, **toc-h1**, etc.)

Style and placement of page numbers

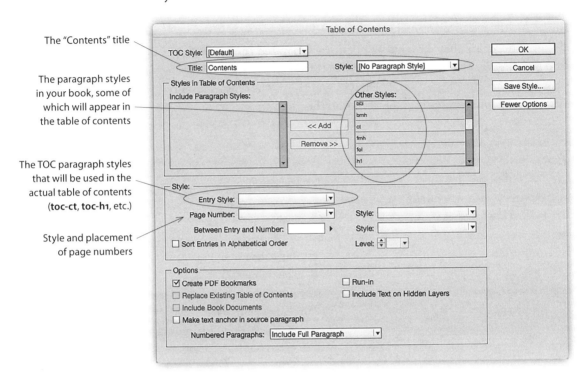

How it works

The Table of Contents dialog box allows you to control every aspect of your TOC. First you'll assign a paragraph style to the title that reads "Contents." Then you'll choose which paragraph styles you want to include in your TOC (part titles and chapter titles, for example) from the box on the right and add them to the box on the left. For each one, you'll assign an entry style, which is the TOC paragraph style you just set up on the preceding pages. After that, you'll instruct InDesign where to place the page number and what character style to use for it. And finally, you'll save your settings as a TOC style. Let's go through the process step by step for designs A, B, and C next.

Automatic table of contents for Design A

To generate an automatic TOC for Design A (page 232), fill out the Table of Contents dialog box as shown below.

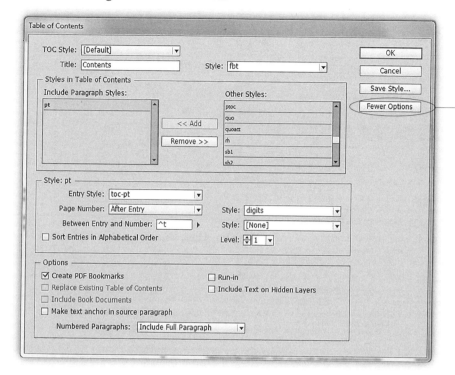

If you don't see all the options in the Style and Options sections, click the More Options button to display them.

1. To the right of "Title: Contents," choose the **fbt** style from the drop-down list. This will give the title "Contents" the style you want.
2. Select the **pt** style in the Other Styles column, click the Add button, and the **pt** style will move to the Include Paragraph Styles column.
3. In the Entry Style drop-down list, choose **toc-pt**, the style you set up for your TOC part titles. Don't worry about the part number character style for now; you'll apply that later.
4. Between Entry and Number (meaning page number) you want a tab, so leave "^t" as it is. In the upper Style box, enter the **digits** character style. Ignore the lower Style box. Assign Level 1 to every entry.

Now repeat these steps for your chapter titles (entry style = **toc-ct**) and your front and back matter titles (entry style = **toc-fbt**).

It doesn't matter what order the paragraph styles are listed in. InDesign will create your TOC in the order of the page numbers each style appears on.

Select each style in the Include Paragraph Styles column after adding it, and then make changes.

Next, save your work by clicking on Save Style and naming your TOC style. When you're finished, your dialog box should look more or less like this:

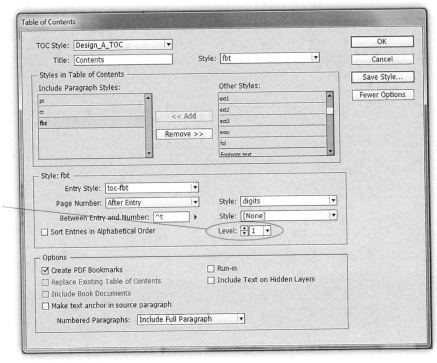

If you had not made different paragraph styles for each of your title levels, you could use the Level numbers to indent the titles for you, but the results would be rather crude.

Be sure to flow your automatic TOC into a text frame that isn't linked to the text in your book. It needs to be separate in order to update properly.

Now click OK. This closes the dialog box and loads your cursor with the TOC text, so go to the page you set up for your Contents, then click to flow it into a new text frame. The result may not come out exactly as you planned, but it'll be close enough that you only need to adjust a few things on your page, such as applying the character styles to your part and chapter numbers. Follow the instructions on page 234 to finalize your TOC. You can also change your TOC paragraph styles now, if you want, and see the changes take place on your TOC page just as you would on any other page.

Automatic table of contents for Design B

Design B on page 235 has the level 2 headings run together without page numbers, and the rest of the headings with page numbers flush right. You'll use the Table of Contents dialog box as explained for Design A (pages 241–242), with one exception: For the **h2** paragraph style, you'll indicate No Page Number, as shown below:

Design B doesn't include part titles, so you'll add your **fbt**, **ct**, **h1**, and **h2** styles to the automatic TOC.

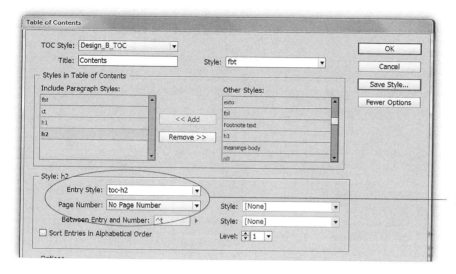

No Page Number is selected for the **toc-h2** style.

Now click Save Style and give the style a name, then click OK. Go to the page you set up for your Contents (see page 239), then click to flow it into a new text frame. You'll notice the level 2 headings are not run together the way you planned, and you'll also need to apply your character style [**toc-cn**] to each chapter number. Follow the instructions on page 237 to finalize your TOC.

If you subsequently make any changes to your book, such as adding pages or moving text, simply go to Layout>Update Table of Contents. You'll be notified that your Contents has been updated. Then look at the TOC and you'll see that the page numbers have changed accordingly.

Whenever you go into the Table of Contents style dialog box to make a change to your TOC structure—adding a new level of heading, for instance—you must click on Save Style. Then click OK to generate the newly designed TOC.

Automatic table of contents for Design C

In Design C (page 238), each heading has its page number a set space after the entry. You'll use the Table of Contents dialog box as explained for Design B (page 243), with one exception: You'll select Em Space from the Between Entry and Number drop-down list, as below. Repeat this for each TOC paragraph style.

First select and delete anything in this box, then use the drop-down list to find Em Space, and InDesign fills in the field for you.

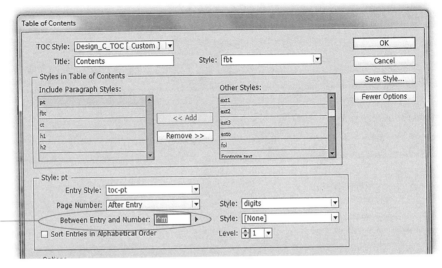

Now click Save Style, give the style a name, then click OK. Go to the page you set up for your Contents, then click to flow it into a new text frame. The only adjustment you need to make now is to apply your character style [**toc-cn**] to each chapter number.

Chances are that *your* table of contents will not quite resemble any of the samples we've shown on these pages, as your titles, headings, and page numbers will differ. But the principles remain the same no matter how many levels of titles and headings you have. Pick and choose from what you see in the samples, or find a more appealing style in another book. Once you understand how the TOC paragraph styles and the Table of Contents dialog box work, you'll be able to design and generate just the right TOC for your book.

Preface, Foreword, and Introduction

If your book has these sections, you probably already have all the paragraph styles you'll need for them. For the titles, apply the Front and Back Matter Title paragraph style [**fbt**] that you set up for your Contents. For the text, apply your regular text styles.

Note the correct spelling of Foreword (not Forward!).

Controlling your page numbering system

Your front matter will have a separate page numbering system from the rest of your book, using lowercase roman numerals. To make your page numbering system work this way, follow the instructions below.

In the Numbering & Section Options dialog box, the lower section (not shown) deals with chapters. You won't need to use automatic chapter numbering in your book.

Go to the Pages panel, click on the thumbnail image of the first page of the book to highlight it, then find Numbering & Section Options in the Pages fly-out menu. Select Start Page Numbering at 1, and the lowercase roman numeral style, as shown to the right. Click OK, and all the pages will now be numbered with lowercase roman numerals.

Next, in the Pages panel, click on the thumbnail of the first page of chapter 1 (a recto page). On the other hand, if your first chapter begins with a 2-page spread, make the page before that spread be page 1 by inserting a half title page. If your book is divided into parts, then the recto page for Part I will be page 1.

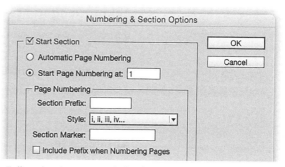

Follow the above example for the very first page of your book.

Then find Numbering & Section Options in the Pages fly-out menu. Check the Start Section box, then select Start Page Numbering at 1, and the arabic numeral style. Click OK, and this page will be numbered 1 with all the pages after it continuing in order, with arabic numerals.

Notice that on the Pages panel, the first page of each page numbering section is marked with a small triangle above it.

If you delete or add pages at any time in the future, the new pages will tuck neatly into the numbering scheme you have just set up.

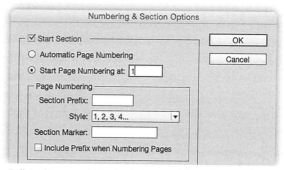

Follow this example for the first page of the main part of your book.

Designing your back matter

In chapter 14 you roughed in your back matter pages. All of these sections should match the style of the rest of your book, but each has its own conventions. The most common back matter sections are reviewed below.

Back matter titles follow the same style as front matter titles (see page 233). Simply apply your **fbt** paragraph style to the title of each back matter section, and the page numbers will continue on from the chapters. The first page of the back matter always starts on a recto page.

Acknowledgments

If you did not put your Acknowledgments in the front matter, put them just after the end of the text. Set this section just as you did the Preface, Foreword, and/or Introduction (see page 245), using your **fbt** style for the title, and your regular styles for the text.

Appendix(es)

If you have more than one appendix, you may treat the opening pages the same as your chapter openers, but set "APPENDIX A" (or "B," "C," etc.) in place of the chapter number (see example on page 247). If there's only one appendix, you could simply run the word "APPENDIX" and a colon in with the rest of the main title.

Appendix text and headings may be treated the same as in the rest of the book, or you may use smaller type and less leading, requiring new paragraph styles. If you decide to use a different column arrangement, make new master pages for appendixes (see index example on page 369).

Because appendix copy may come in the form of tables, narrative, lists, legal language, scientific or mathematical formulas, and so on, we are not offering paragraph styles. However, you'll see appendix opener samples on the next two pages.

APPENDIX TITLE

Alice was beginning to get very tired of sitting by her sister on the bank, and of having nothing to do: once or twice she had peeped into the book her sister was reading, but it had no pictures or conversations in it, 'and what is the use of a book,' thought Alice 'without pictures or conversation?'

So she was considering in her own mind (as well as she could, for the hot day made her feel very sleepy and stupid), whether the

A drop cap at the beginning of a chapter or section is usually used with narrative. Even if an appendix consists of narrative, it does not normally begin with a drop cap.

The appendix opener above is based on chapter opening Design 1 (page 148), with the "number" and title the same size as in the chapter opener, but notice that they are closer together and placed at the top of the page.

Use the paragraph settings below for this design.

☐ **Appendix Letters [appl]**   Based On = **cn**
Changes from the Chapter Numbers style (see page 149):
Indents and Spacing: Space Before = 0
                                            Space After = 0.0625 in
Paragraph Rules: Rule Below = Rule On
                                            Offset = 0.125 in

☐ **Appendix Titles [appt]**   Based On = **ct**
Changes from the Chapter Titles style (see page 150):
Indents and Spacing: Space After = 0.56 in
                                            Aligned to Grid = None

There is a line of space (**tx** style) above the appendix number, just as for most of the chapter opener examples in this book.

Appendix A

Appendix Title

If you were to place the related chapter opening page and this appendix opening page next to each other, you'd see that the beginning of the appendix text lines up with the chapter title.

Alice was beginning to get very tired of sitting by her sister on the bank, and of having nothing to do: once or twice she had peeped

Here you see an opening page that is based on both the chapter opening Design 4 on page 156 and the part opening Design 4 on page 178. Paragraph styles for this design are shown below.

☐ **Appendix Letter [appl]**   Based On = **pn**
Changes from the Part Numbers style (see page 179):
Basic Character Formats: Size = 18 pt
Indents and Spacing: Space Before = 9 pt *or* 0.125 in
                                                                  Space After = 9 pt *or* 0.125 in

☐ **Appendix Titles [appt]**   Based On = **pt**
Changes from the Part Titles style (see page 179):
Indents and Spacing: Space After = 1.125 in

Endnotes

Endnotes take the form of a numbered list. Usually they appear at the end of each chapter, with the numbers beginning again at 1 in each chapter, but sometimes they continue on in one overall numbering scheme and appear in the back matter. You might find that using a two-column format will save you space.

In the sample below you'll see two different styles: left justified type with indented paragraphs in the left column, and ragged right (Alignment = Left) type with hanging indents in the right column. Paragraph styles for both can be found on the next page. Try both one- and two-column formats; you might be surprised by which will save more space. Another option is to add space (a few points to half a line) between entries.

So the paragraph styles shown on the next page are simply suggestions to get you started on designing your endnotes pages. If you decide to use more than one column, make a new master page (use one you previously set up for your appendix, or see index example on page 369).

Endnotes placed in your back matter are entitled "Notes" rather than "Endnotes."

To format endnote reference numbers (the superscript numbers within your main narrative), see pages 85 and 93.

---

and then put them both into a library. Then whenever you need a sidebar you can drag one or the other out of the library, all ready to use. See p. 123 for more about libraries.

14. The inside edge of the sidebar is at the center of the page. If the sidebar text were any wider, the letter spacing and word spacing in the main text would look very poor—either too tight or too loose.

15. This shows corner options for the sidebar title text frame.

CHAPTER 14

1. When you convert to an ebook, you'll delete all your folios and running heads or feet.

2. Pages in the front matter coming before the Contents do not have visible page numbers.

3. Shone, David. *Champagne Haze.* Kettering, OH: Hour Glass Books, 2009.

4. Some of the online publishing services offer a free ISBN. You may use theirs if you like, but we believe it's best to own and control your own ISBNs. Also, the numbers you receive in a bunch will be more or less sequential and thus better organized.

5. Wray, David. *The Secret Roots of Christianity: Decoding Religious History with Symbols on Ancient Coins.* Needham, MA: Numismatics and History, 2012.

whenever you need a sidebar you can drag one or the other out of the library, all ready to use. See p. 123 for more about libraries.

14. The inside edge of the sidebar is at the center of the page. If the sidebar text were any wider, the letter spacing and word spacing in the main text would probably look very poor—either too tight or too loose.

15. This shows corner options for the sidebar title text frame.

CHAPTER 14

1. When you convert to an ebook, you'll delete all your folios and running heads or feet.

2. Pages in the front matter coming before the Contents do not have visible page numbers.

3. Shone, David. *Champagne Haze.* Kettering, OH: Hour Glass Books, 2009.

4. Some of the online publishing services offer a free ISBN. You may use theirs if you like, but we believe it's best to own and control your own ISBNs. Also, the numbers you receive in a bunch will be more or less sequential and thus better organized.

5. Wray, David. *The Secret Roots of Christianity: Decoding Religious History with Symbols on Ancient Coins.* Needham, MA: Numismatics and History, 2012.

Left justified with indented paragraphs

Left aligned with hanging indents

Styles for the justified example in the left column, page 249:

Notice that the list numbers in this design are set in **bold** character style. Set an en space after each number and period.

☐ **Endnotes Text [end]**
Basic Character Formats:

Indents and Spacing:

Based On = **tx1**
Size = 9 pt
Leading = 11 pt
Tracking = −5
First Line Indent = 11 pt *or* 0.1528 in
Align to Grid = None

The type and leading sizes shown here are just suggestions; quite possibly you'll find that different sizes work better for you.

☐ **Endnotes Chapter Numbers [end-cn]**
Changes from the Endnotes Text style above:
Basic Character Formats:

Indents and Spacing:

Based On = **end**

Font Style = Semibold
Case = OpenType All Small Caps
Tracking = 0
Alignment = Center
Space Before = 11 pt *or* 0.1528 in

Styles for the ragged right example in the right column, page 249:

☐ **Endnotes Text [end]**
Basic Character Formats:

Indents and Spacing:

Based On = **tx1**
Size = 9 pt
Leading = 11 pt
Alignment = Left
Left Indent = 14 pt *or* 0.1944 in
First Line Indent = −14 pt *or* −0.1944 in
Align to Grid = None

Type a tab before each number and another tab before each entry.

Tabs:

Set a right tab at 0.125 in

☐ **Endnotes Chapter Numbers [end-cn]**
Changes from the Endnotes Text style above:
Basic Character Formats:

Indents and Spacing:
OpenType Features:

Based On = **end**

Font Family = Myriad Pro
Font Style = Semibold Condensed
Case = All Caps
Tracking = 20
Space Before = 11 pt *or* 0.1528 in
Figure Style = Proportional Lining

Glossary

Readers may refer to the glossary often, so use larger type than you did for the endnotes. If you have enough space, simply use the same size and leading as your text style.

A hanging indent usually works well. Or don't use any indents but add space between entries. Set the glossary term in semibold or bold, then set an en or em space before the definition. If you like, you can add the book page where the term first appears, as shown below. Put this number in parentheses and set the number (but not the parentheses) in italic.

The Find function (Edit> Find/Change) is very helpful for locating the first use of your glossary terms.

signatures (*3*) Groups of book pages that are printed on the same sheet and folded. The number of pages in a signature varies according to the size of the paper and the size of the book pages. Common numbers of pages in a signature are 16 and 32, but 24 and 48 are also used.

small caps (*69*) Capital letters that are the same size as the lower-case letters in a font. Commonly used for acronyms and terms such as A.M., P.M., B.C., and A.D.

soft return (*128*) A line return that forces a new line but keeps it within the same paragraph. Place the cursor where you want the break, then press Shift + Enter. See also hard return.

softcover (*240*) Commonly called a paperback, but soft covers can also be made of a

blind stamping, the design is pressed into the cover with no ink or foil.

swatch (*260*) A small sample of a color. The Swatches panel lists all the named colors in the document.

tabular lining or oldstyle figures (*18*) Numerals, either lining or oldstyle, that are spaced evenly so that they can be aligned in columns.

text block (*34*) The area on a page in which the main body of text is placed. The text block does not include the running head (or foot) or the folio, or any material in a side column.

text frame (*16*) A box in which type is placed

text wrap (*208*) The method for allowing type to run around the edges of a graphic shape or image rather than flowing across it

In addition to the paragraph style below, you might want to create a character style for the glossary terms. You could add tracking, set the terms in your sans serif font, use semibold rather than bold, and so on.

You'll find another glossary example on the next page.

☐ **Glossary Text [gloss]**   Based On = **tx1**

Changes from the No Indents style (see page 62):

Indents and Spacing:

Left Indent = 14 pt *or* 0.1944 in

First Line Indent = −14 pt *or* −0.1944 in

In your book, a one-column glossary might work better. The design below uses a half-linespace between entries, and so the type is taken off the baseline grid.

> **signatures**   Groups of book pages that are printed on the same sheet and folded. The number of pages in a signature varies according to the size of the paper and the size of the book pages. Common numbers of pages in a signature are 16 and 32, but 24 and 48 are also used.
>
> **small caps**   Capital letters that are the same size as the lower-case letters in a font. Commonly used for acronyms and terms such as A.M., P.M., B.C., and A.D.
>
> **soft return**   A line return that forces a new line but keeps it within the same paragraph. Place the cursor where you want the break, then press Shift + Enter. See also hard return.
>
> **softcover**   Commonly called a paperback, but soft covers can also be made of a plastic material.
>
> **spiral**   A type of binding that uses one continuous metal wire (plastic coated or not), curled into a spiral, to hold the pages together.

In this example, an em space is set after each term (Ctrl/Cmd+Shift+M).

☐ **Glossary Text [gloss]**   Based On = **tx1**
Changes from the No Indents style (see page 62):
Indents and Spacing: Space After = 7 pt *or* 0.0972 in
                                                  Align to Grid = None

☐ **Glossary Term [glossterm]** *Character* **Style** Based On = [None]
Basic Character Formats: Font Family = Myriad Pro
                                                  Font Style = Semibold

As with the endnotes designs (pages 249–250), these glossary samples are meant to show you options so that you can design the best glossary for *your* book. Change or combine the given features as much as you need to for the best results.

Bibliography or References

Treat this section much the same as the endnotes (pages 249–250), with smaller type and less leading than your Text style. Add space between entries, or use a hanging indent. Use one or two columns. If you divide the list into sections with headings, design the headings the same as those in your endnotes, to match your overall design.

Garabedian-Weber, Dawn. *Become Aware: A New Life Has Begun.* Worcester, MA, 2008.

Hager, Margaret Henderson. *Farewell, Samsara: Selected Poems.* Philadelphia, 2014.

Helbert, Sharon. *Sassy Gal's How to Lose the Last Damn 10 Pounds or 15, 20, 25 . . .* Boston: Alegcris Press, 2014.

CHAPTER 2

Kriger, Shlomit, ed. *Marking Humanity: Stories, Poems, & Essays by Holocaust Survivors.* Toronto, ON: Soul Inscriptions Press, 2010.

Muñoz-Jordan, Ana S. *How Turtle Became a Dolphin: A Story about Adapting to Life's Changes.* Jupiter, FL: Tortuphina Press, 2009.

Poole, Scott. *The Sliding Glass Door.* Spokane: Colonus

Garabedian-Weber, Dawn. *Become Aware: A New Life Has Begun.* Worcester, MA, 2008.

Hager, Margaret Henderson. *Farewell, Samsara: Selected Poems.* Philadelphia, 2014.

Helbert, Sharon. *Sassy Gal's How to Lose the Last Damn 10 Pounds or 15, 20, 25 . . .* Boston: Alegcris Press, 2014.

CHAPTER 2

Kriger, Shlomit, ed. *Marking Humanity: Stories, Poems, & Essays by Holocaust Survivors.* Toronto, ON: Soul Inscriptions Press, 2010.

Muñoz-Jordan, Ana S. *How Turtle Became a Dolphin: A Story about Adapting to Life's Changes.* Jupiter, FL: Tortuphina Press, 2009.

Poole, Scott. *The Sliding Glass Door.* Spokane: Colonus Publishing, 2011.

Sarich, Angie. *Leaving Parma.* Spokane: Colonus House,

Left justified with space between   Left aligned with hanging indents

Styles for the justified example in the left column above:

☐ **References Text [ref]**

Basic Character Formats:

Indents and Spacing:

Based On = **tx1**

Size = 9 pt

Leading = 11 pt

Space After = 4 pt *or* 0.0556 in

Align to Grid = None

☐ **References Chapter Numbers [ref-cn]**

Changes from the References Text style above:

Basic Character Formats:

Indents and Spacing:

Based On = **ref**

Font Style = Semibold

Case = OpenType All Small Caps

Alignment = Center

Space Before = 7 pt *or* 0.0972 in

References styles continue on the next page.

Styles for the ragged right example in the right column, page 253:

☐ **References Text [ref]**   Based On = **tx1**
Basic Character Formats: Size = 9 pt
                                                  Leading = 11 pt
Indents and Spacing: Alignment = Left
                                                  Left Indent = 14 pt *or* 0.1944 in
                                                  First Line Indent = −14 pt *or* 0.1944 in
                                                  Align to Grid = None

☐ **References Chapter Numbers [ref-cn]**   Based On = **ref**
Changes from the References Text style above:
Basic Character Formats: Font Family = Myriad Pro
                                                  Font Style = Semibold Condensed
                                                  Case = All Caps
                                                  Tracking = 20
Indents and Spacing: Space Before = 11 pt *or* 0.1528 in
OpenType Features: Figure Style = Proportional Lining

Index

The index is complex and deserves a section of its own (see chapter 54).

Congratulations! You've successfully designed every element in your book's pages, and applied appropriate paragraph and character styles to every bit of text in your book. Well done!

Next, in Parts V and VI, you'll add shapes, images, and captions to your book, if needed. This will constitute the second pass through your book. If you don't have any shapes, images, or captions inside your book, skip to Part VII: Typesetting, and that's where you'll do your final pass through your pages.

Part V:
Adding Shapes & Color

30

Working with shapes

In Parts V and VI, you'll add shapes, colors, images, and captions to your book, which will constitute the second pass through your pages. If your book pages don't require shapes or color, then feel free to skip to Part VI: Adding Images for the time being (you'll refer back to Part V when you design your book cover).

Shapes are used for lots of reasons: to make sidebars stand out, to draw your reader's attention to something, to create an illustration or diagram, or to simply add color. And they're fun to create!

Before getting started with shapes and color, make sure you've already set up a baseline grid (see chapter 23), as you'll use the grid to easily align shapes on your pages.

Adding shapes and images during your second pass may increase the number of pages. If you'll be printing on an offset press, refer to chapter 48 for ways to control your page count.

The text in *this* box has been cut from the main narrative and pasted into this rectangle shape.

Using shapes in conjunction with text

There are two ways to combine text with shapes:

1   Leave the text where it is in the main narrative and create a shape behind it, as in *this* box.

2   Cut the text out of the main narrative and paste it into a separate text frame (as in the example to the left).

Every shape that you make has an assigned purpose: graphic or text (or unassigned, meaning neither one). If you mistakenly use the Type Tool to draw a shape to place behind your sidebar text, your shape will be a text frame. You can easily change that by selecting it with the Selection Tool, going to Object>Content, and choosing Graphic.

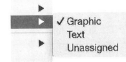

If you think about this, you'll realize that you could use a circle or polygon as a text frame. Go ahead—try it! Draw a circle or polygon, change its content to Text, and type something in there.

InDesign: CMYK, RGB, and
[Y]K colors for your pages and
three types:

rs used on a printing press—
it or not, all the beautiful full-
ally printed with just four ink
ing for your book cover and
or if they'll be printed in color,
, you'll use the default [Black]
ercentages of the K) for gray.

played on all monitors and
take a photo with your digital
our scanner, the image will have
ment into InDesign, if there
be RGB, too. RGB color usually
ng.

RGB images are now
accepted by some POD
and digital printers,
such as CreateSpace.

SPOT colors are ink colors that are premixed by companies such as Pantone. Premixing inks allows a greater color range than is possible by just using the four CMYK ink colors. Spot colors are often more brilliant and include neon and metallic colors. Company logos often use spot colors. If you use a spot color in your book, it will be more expensive to print, requiring an extra ink color on the press. Also, the spot color will need to be separated from the other colors in your digital files when you package them for the printer. This is beyond the scope of this book.

Spot colors are only available in offset printing.

Organizing the colors in your Swatches panel

Start by opening and getting familiar with the Swatches panel (to open it, click Windows>Color>Swatches). Your Swatches panel will look something like this:

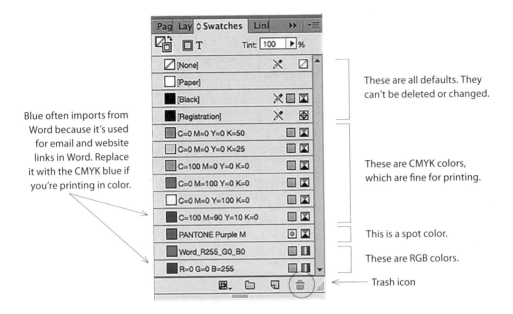

Blue often imports from Word because it's used for email and website links in Word. Replace it with the CMYK blue if you're printing in color.

These are all defaults. They can't be deleted or changed.

These are CMYK colors, which are fine for printing.

This is a spot color.

These are RGB colors.

Trash icon

It's a good idea to keep the colors in your Swatches panel organized by deleting any RGB and spot colors. To delete a color, drag it onto the trash icon at the bottom right to open the Delete Swatch dialog box. If you're printing with black ink only (like most book pages), simply replace the swatch with the default [Black] as shown below. If you're printing with color, replace the swatch with a similar CMYK color.

See page 260 for how to create a new defined swatch.

Applying colors to your shapes and type

You'll apply up to two colors to every shape you create: one for the fill (the inside of the shape) and one for the stroke (the outline of the shape). The two boxes at the top left of your Swatches panel control the color of the fill and stroke.

Click the Fill box (upper left) or Stroke box (lower right) to bring it to the front.

Click the curved arrow to swap the colors. In this example, the fill becomes black and the stroke gray.

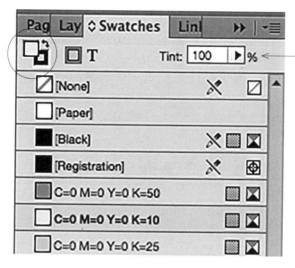

Use of Tint (less than 100% of a color) not recommended (see note at bottom of page 261).

The upper left box controls the fill (the inside) of your shape. To fill a shape with a color, bring the Fill box to the front by clicking it. Then click one of the colors in the Swatches panel to apply it to the fill of your shape.

The lower right box controls the stroke (the outline) of your shape. To add a stroke, bring the Stroke box to the front by clicking it. Then click one of the colors in the Swatches panel to apply it to the stroke of your shape. (See page 272 to set the attributes of the stroke.)

The same principles apply if you want to add color to type. Select the type with the Type Tool, then pick a color fill from the Swatches panel. You could also add a stroke to the type, but that would only be appropriate in a large heading or on your cover. The stroke will be 1 pt in weight by default, but you can change the weight (thickness) in the Weight field of the Stroke panel. Any weight less than 0.25 pt will not print reliably, however. See chapter 35 for more details.

Stroke = 100% black
Fill = 10% black

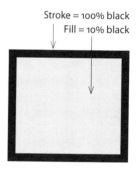

To add a color to a paragraph or character style, specify it in the Character Color section of the appropriate paragraph or character style.

Changing or adding color swatches

There's a good chance the colors in your Swatches panel are not the exact colors you'll need for your book. It's easy to either change an existing color or add a new one.

To change an existing color, double-click the color in the Swatches panel to open the Swatch Options box. Simply move the sliders to change the color, then click OK.

To add a new color, click the Swatches Panel fly-out menu and select New Color Swatch. In the New Color Swatch dialog box, move the sliders to get the color you want, click Add, then click Done.

If you like, you can name your swatch—call it "sidebar," for instance. In this example the swatch is named with its color values.

You can change an existing RGB color to a CMYK color simply by changing the Color Mode.

To change an existing color or create a new color, move the sliders, or type color values in the percentage boxes.

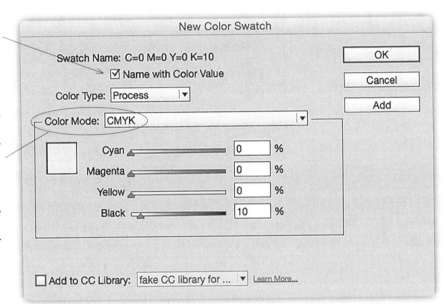

How do you know you've chosen a "good" color?

You don't! But there are a couple of ways you can check. You can refer to Pantone Process color samples or other printed samples that show the CMYK values of the printed colors. Or, you can simply get some pages or your cover printed at your local copy store on their color printer and see how they look.

Creating a color for shapes behind sidebars and text

Most shapes placed behind text are a light gray color. Light gray is a good color choice because 1) the text remains easy to read, 2) gray is a neutral color (plays nicely with other colors), and 3) gray is available for pages that are printed with black ink only.

The most common light gray color used is 10% black (used for the sidebar boxes in *this* book).

To create a 10% black color, add a new color as explained and shown on page 260, and move the Black slider to 10%. Done! Now you'll be able to create shapes and apply your 10% black color (or any other color you choose) to a shape's fill. Usually the color applied to the stroke is None; in other words, the shape doesn't have a stroke.

Many printers will insist that no percentage below 5% be used in a solid block of color because it will not print reliably.

A quick word about the Tint feature

You can enter a percentage into the Tint box to fade the color of a fill or stroke. For example, you could select the default [Black] color and then choose a Tint of 10% to fade the color from black to gray.

That works fine for the shape currently selected. However, if you are using a tint in more than one place (for example, in all the sidebar boxes in your book), it's better to create a swatch specifically for that tint. That way, if you want to change the tint globally from, say, 10% to 15%, you can simply move the slider(s) on that color.

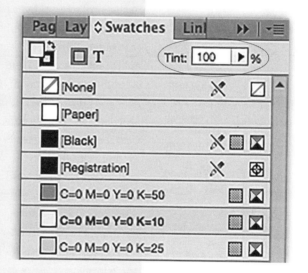

The sidebar boxes in *this* book have a color value of C=0 M=0 Y=0 K=10 (see the swatches to the right). They are not the default [Black] with a 10% tint applied.

linear
gradient

radial
gradient

short drag

long drag

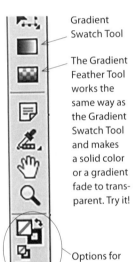

Gradient
Swatch Tool

The Gradient
Feather Tool
works the
same way as
the Gradient
Swatch Tool
and makes
a solid color
or a gradient
fade to trans-
parent. Try it!

Options for
applying the
gradient

Making and using gradients

A gradient is a smooth-looking transition between or among colors or tints. The two types available in InDesign are shown to the left. The strategic use of gradients can boost a design nicely, but don't overuse them.

Applying a gradient

Before creating your own gradient, you need to understand how gradients work and how to apply them. First, locate the Gradient panel either at the right of your screen or by going to Window>Color>Gradient. Draw a shape (see chapter 33), select it with the Selection Tool, make sure that Fill is in front in the Swatches or Toolbox, then open the Gradient panel and choose either Linear or Radial from the Type drop-down list. Your shape will be filled with the default gradient that's shown in the panel. Try clicking on the little arrows to reverse the direction of the gradient, and entering positive or negative values in the Angle field to see the effects.

Now, with your shape selected, click on the Gradient Swatch Tool (▮) in the Toolbox, and your cursor will become a small crosshair. Click anywhere inside or even outside your shape and drag in any direction. Repeat this several times, clicking and dragging from various points in different directions each time. If you drag a short distance, the change of color is rapid and condensed; if you drag beyond the edges of the shape, the change is more gradual (see examples above left). If you hold down the Shift key while dragging, the direction will be strictly horizontal or vertical, or at a 45° angle. Try these techniques with both linear and radial gradients to find out how they work. With a radial gradient, start in the middle of the shape and drag outward. Once you've tried that, start in other spots and drag in other directions to see the various effects. And don't forget that you can reverse the colors anytime by clicking on the Reverse arrows in the Gradient panel.

You can apply gradients to type as well as shapes. To do this, first type some large text in its own text frame. Next click on your type frame with the Selection Tool, then the Gradient Swatch Tool, and lastly on the "T" near the bottom of the Toolbox. Now choose Linear or Radial in the Gradient panel. Your type will take on the selected gradient. You can then use the Gradient Swatch Tool crosshairs to change the angle and length of the gradient just as with a shape.

Gradients look smooth, but they are actually made up of a series of shades between the colors. You can avoid obvious visible banding (see example to the right) if you follow these guidelines:

- Lighter colors work better than darker ones.
- Stick with similar colors; a drastic change between colors (e.g., green to orange) can result in banding.

- If you're using two shades of the same color, a higher percentage of color change (10% to 70%, for instance) will work better because there will be a greater number of smaller steps between the ends of the gradient.
- Use gradients in relatively small areas rather than across an entire page.

banding

Creating a gradient

Now that you're familiar with how gradients work, you can make your own by following these steps:

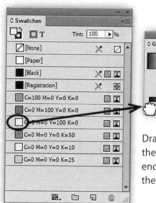

1 In the Swatches panel, make a swatch (see page 260) for each end of the gradient.
2 Drag the Swatches panel out from the dock, and open the Gradient panel. This way you can work with both at once.
3 Choose Linear or Radial in the Type list. Drag one of your new swatches to the left end of the gradient display in the Gradient panel. When a hand with a plus sign appears, you have hit the target and can let go of the swatch with the mouse or trackpad. Repeat this at the other end of the gradient with the second color. Your gradient should now show the two colors you intend to use. If you like, you can add a third color to the gradient by making another swatch and dragging it somewhere between the ends of the current gradient in the Gradient panel. You can also slide any of the colors left or right.
4 You may now drag the thumbnail of the new gradient from the Gradient panel over to the Swatches panel if you like, so you'll have the gradient handy if you want to reuse it. Double-click on "New Gradient Swatch," then type in a new name for the swatch.

Drag your swatch from the Swatches panel to one end—or anywhere along the length of the gradient.

Return the Swatches panel back to the dock when you're finished.

Adobe offers a good tutorial on using and creating gradients if you want more details and tricks.

32

Using layers for shapes

Using the Layers panel will help you keep all the elements on your pages or cover organized. You can easily arrange elements so that some are in front of others (such as text being in front of a shape). You can also lock layers to keep some things in place while you move others around. And you can turn layers on and off to control what you see and/or print.

The layer itself is transparent; the objects on the layer are not. You can shuffle the stack of layers anytime, and you can move objects from one layer to another.

It's useful to have two layers for your pages if you're adding shapes: one for text and one for shapes. The Shapes layer includes all your elements that are *behind* everything else. And the Text layer is *in front* of all other layers, and includes all your text frames.

To set up your layers, open your Layers panel at the right of your screen or by clicking Window>Layers. You'll see there is one layer, called Layer 1. Select any text frame with your Selection Tool and its outline will be the same color as shown for Layer 1. To change the name of Layer 1 to "Text," double-click Layer 1 to open your Layer Options dialog box, change the name to Text, then click OK.

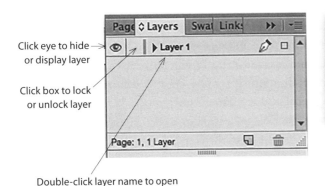

Shape on lower layer, type on upper layer   Shape on upper layer, type on lower layer

Click eye to hide or display layer

Click box to lock or unlock layer

Double-click layer name to open Layer Options dialog box

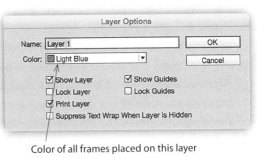

Color of all frames placed on this layer

Add a new layer by clicking the Create New Layer icon on the Layers panel (see example below). A new layer called Layer 2 will appear above your Text layer. The color for this layer is probably red. Double-click Layer 2, change its name to Shapes, and click OK. Then, because everything on the Text layer should be in front of or *above* everything on the Shapes layer, drag the Shapes layer down so it appears *below* the Text layer.

The layer at the top of the list is in front. The layer at the bottom of the list is behind. You can change their order anytime by dragging layers up or down the list.

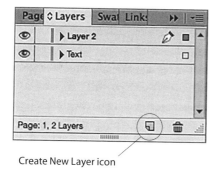

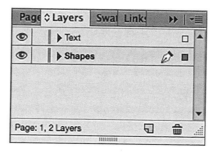

Create New Layer icon

Another way to create a new layer or access the Layer Options dialog box is by clicking the fly-out menu on the Layers panel and choosing those options there.

Now, whenever you add a shape to your pages, first select the Shapes layer in your Layers panel so that your shape will be added to that layer and appear on the page *behind* your text. While adding shapes, you may find it easier to lock your Text layer (click once in the Lock box to turn the lock on or off) so you don't select a text frame by mistake. You can also turn a layer on or off by clicking once in the Visibility box (the eye icon).

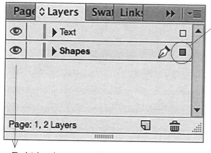

To hide a layer, simply click once in the Visibility box.

Select a frame and you'll see which layer it's on by the color of the box in the Layers panel and the color of the frame. Drag this box to another layer to move the frame. The box and frame will change color to match the new layer.

To lock a layer, simply click once in the Lock box.

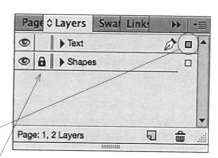

Using the shape tools

Three shape tools are in your Toolbox—Rectangle, Ellipse, and Polygon (click and hold the visible one to see the others). Take a moment to check this out. Select any shape tool, then drag to create that shape. Hold the Shift key while you drag to keep the width and height equal (the Rectangle Tool creates a square, the Ellipse Tool creates a circle, and the Polygon Tool creates a regular polygon). The shape will acquire the fill and stroke colors selected in the Swatches panel (you learned about the Swatches panel in chapter 31). You can delete your experimental shapes by simply selecting the shape with the Selection Tool and pressing the Delete key.

Creating rectangles to go behind text in the main narrative

The most common shapes used in book pages are rectangles placed behind text to make it stand out from the main narrative. Here are the steps you'll take when creating these shapes:

Line up your rectangle with your baseline grid and margins or column(s).

If you have trouble moving the handles precisely, your guides might be the problem. Go to View>Grids & Guides and check or uncheck Snap to Guides. Keep this in mind anytime you move an object.

1 Open your Layers panel and select the Shapes layer (see Chapter 32). Lock your Text layer to make it easier to work with the shapes you'll draw on the Shapes layer (otherwise the text frame above the shape will get selected by default because the Text layer is above the Shapes layer).
2 Select the Rectangle Tool and draw a shape by clicking and dragging.
3 Switch to your Selection Tool and drag the edges of the frame to make it the right size and shape. Switch to Normal view by pressing W and line up the edges of the rectangle with your baseline grid, margins, and column(s), as shown with *this* box.

4 Select appropriate fill and stroke colors for your shape (see chapter 31 about working with color and the Swatches panel).

5 Add a corner option to your rectangle, if you wish (see page 273 about adding corner options).

6 Create an object style for your sidebar boxes. Thought you were finished with styles? Not just yet. Object styles make it easy to create lots of shapes with the same characteristics (for example, same color, corner options, fill, and stroke). See chapter 38 about object styles.

This rectangle has rounded corners, one of the Corner Options available (see page 273).

NOTE: Remember that during your second pass you'll add your shapes and images *at the same time* as you progress through your pages. Adding shapes and images will change the flow of your text, so you'll finalize the layout of each page as you go.

In addition to creating rectangles with the Rectangle Tool, you can also use the Ellipse Tool to create ovals and circles, and the Polygon Tool to create starbursts. Any of these tools can be used to add a shape to your pages or cover.

Using the Polygon Tool

The Polygon Tool is a bit different from the Rectangle and Ellipse Tools, in that you can choose the number of sides and the optional star inset.

Double-click the Polygon Tool in the Toolbox to open Polygon Settings and choose the number of sides and inset of the points. Then click OK.

Also in your Toolbox, you'll notice Rectangle, Ellipse, and Polygon *Frame* Tools. These look the same as the Rectangle, Ellipse, and Polygon Tools except they have an X across them. They are used for placeholders. For example, you might add a rectangle frame where you intend to add type or an image later. The X in the frame will make it easier to see in Normal view, while it's still empty (see below).

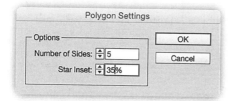

5 sides, 35% star inset
1 pt solid stroke, color fill

25 sides, 50% star inset
No stroke, color fill

7 sides, 0% star inset
1 pt solid stroke, color fill

34

Using the drawing tools

There are three drawing tools in your Toolbox—the Line, Pen, and Pencil tools. These can be used to create any kind of line or shape. Use the Line Tool for single straight lines; the Pen Tool for straight lines, curves, and shapes; and the Pencil Tool for drawing freehand lines and shapes.

Any time you use a drawing tool, the line or shape you draw will include the stroke and fill colors selected in your Swatches panel (see chapter 31).

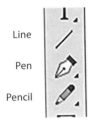

Line

Pen

Pencil

Using the Line Tool

With the Line Tool selected, it's easy to create a straight line. Simply click and drag a line anywhere on your page. If you want the line to be horizontal, vertical, or at a 45° angle, press the Shift key while you drag. Once you've created a line, use the Selection Tool to move it or change its length, or the Free Transform Tool (⬚, see page 289) to rotate it.

Once your line is positioned where you want it, choose a stroke color in the Swatches panel (see page 259), and use the Stroke panel to choose the weight (thickness) and type of stroke (see page 272).

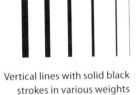

Vertical lines with solid black
strokes in various weights

Using the Pen Tool

The Pen Tool is very versatile and allows you to create both straight and curved lines that can be adjusted at will. Anchor points are created wherever you click the Pen Tool, connected by straight or curved lines, and together they form adjustable paths.

Drawing shapes with straight lines

The simplest use of the Pen Tool is to create a shape using straight lines. Click (don't drag) the Pen Tool anywhere to get started, and you'll see a small solid square appear (your first anchor point). Click again (don't

First anchor point

drag) in another spot, and a second anchor point will appear with a connecting line. Note that this anchor point is solid, and now the first anchor point is hollow. Keep clicking, and you'll create more anchor points connected with lines.

To complete your path, you can:

1 Close it by returning to your first anchor point (you'll see a small circle next to the Pen Tool:) and clicking on the first anchor point; or
2 Leave it open by pressing Ctrl/Cmd and clicking anywhere outside an object, or by pressing Enter/Return and switching to a different tool.

Once your path is complete, you can select stroke and fill colors in the Swatches panel (see page 259) and use the Stroke panel to choose the weight and type of stroke (see page 272).

To move any of the anchor points after the path is complete, drag the anchor point using the Direct Selection Tool (the white pointer in your Toolbox).

Drawing shapes with curved lines

Curved lines are drawn a bit differently from straight lines. When you set a new anchor point for a curved line, you'll drag instead of clicking. Dragging creates an anchor point with handles that allow you to control the amount and direction of the curve. Here's an example:

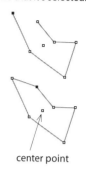

A solid anchor point shows that it's selected.

center point

Direct Selection Tool

If you click or drag in the wrong place by mistake, undo the anchor point by pressing Ctrl/Cmd+Z or clicking Edit>Undo.

Set the first anchor point by clicking and dragging in the direction you want the curve to go in. Drag about 1/3 of the distance to the next anchor point.

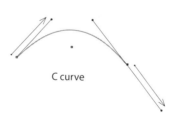

C curve

Set your second anchor point by clicking and dragging in any direction. As you drag, you'll see the curve developing. Stop dragging when the curve is where you want it.

It is worth the effort to practice this method until you get a smooth movement going, because the resulting curves are very graceful.

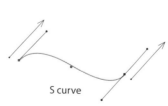

S curve

Drag your second anchor point in a different direction to create a C curve (top) or in the same direction to create an S curve (bottom).

You can create curved lines that consist of a combination of C and S curves by changing the direction in which you drag after clicking anchor points.

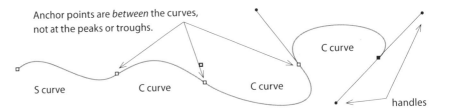

Anchor points are *between* the curves, not at the peaks or troughs.

S curve   C curve   C curve   C curve   handles

To complete your path, you can:

1. Close it by returning to your first anchor point (you'll see a small circle next to the Pen Tool: ✎₀), clicking on the first anchor point, and dragging; or
2. Leave it open by pressing Ctrl/Cmd and clicking anywhere outside an object, or by pressing Enter/Return and switching to a different tool.

Once your path is complete, you can easily adjust it using the Direct Selection Tool. Move any of the anchor points by selecting and dragging them, or change the curve between anchor points by selecting the curve, then dragging the handles.

Add color to your path by choosing stroke and fill colors in the Swatches panel (see page 259), and use the Stroke panel to select the weight and type of stroke (see page 272).

This curved line is shown in the example above right but has been rotated 90° and has a 2 pt black dotted stroke applied with a barbed arrow at the end.

Using the Pencil Tool

The Pencil Tool is for freehand drawing. Simply grab the tool (✎), position the pointer where you want to start, and begin to draw with your mouse or on your keypad. You'll find that the resulting shape will have many more anchor points than something you'd draw with the Pen Tool, and you might want to smooth out some of your lines. As an example, we'll improve the flower sketch to the left. Your drawing will be different, of course, so you may not need all of the options listed on the next page.

The original flower with dozens of anchor points. The starting and ending points are not connected.

- To fill in the little gap near the center of the shape, zoom in, get the Direct Selection Tool, and drag a small rectangle around the first and last anchor points to select them both. Then go to Object>Paths>Close Path *or* Join. An alternative is to use the Direct Selection Tool to drag the last anchor point so it overlaps the first anchor point. If you're drawing a curved line like the one at the top of the previous page, you don't need a closed path.

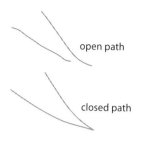

open path

closed path

- To smooth out the path, get the Smooth Tool (, in the same group as the Pencil Tool), and draw on or near the sections of the path that need smoothing. This will delete some of the anchor points and smooth out the lines somewhat. If you double-click the Smooth Tool in the Toolbox, you'll see a dialog box similar to the one below. Move the slider to achieve a smoother line, click OK, and try smoothing again.

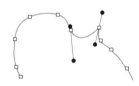

After using the Smooth Tool

- You can also move, delete, and add anchor points. To move one, select it with the Direct Selection Tool and drag it to a new position. To delete a point, use the Delete Anchor Point Tool (, in the Pen Tool group) to click on the point. To add a point, get the Add Anchor Point Tool ( ) and click on the existing line where you want the new point.

- You can manipulate the handles that emanate from the anchor points. This action changes the direction and size of the curves between the anchor points. To access the handles, click between two anchor points, or directly on one anchor point, with the Direct Selection Tool.

After dragging the handles at two anchor points

To achieve smooth curves right from the start, you can set the Pencil Tool preferences before you begin to draw. Double-click on the Pencil Tool, and a dialog box like the one below will appear. Use the Smoothness slider and experiment. The flower to the right was drawn using the settings shown here.

A new flower with Smoothness set at 83%. The Smoothness setting for the original flower was zero.

There are many more tricks for using all of the drawing tools. Refer to www.Book DesignMadeSimple.com for links to tutorials.

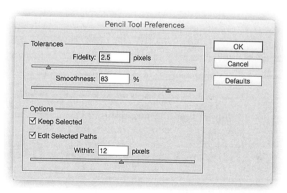

Pencil Tool Preferences

Tolerances
Fidelity: 2.5   pixels
Smoothness: 83   %

OK
Cancel
Defaults

Options
☑ Keep Selected
☑ Edit Selected Paths
Within: 12   pixels

35

Using the Stroke panel

As you saw on page 259, the *color* of a stroke is selected in the Swatches panel. However, the Stroke panel is where you'll choose the weight and type of stroke. Open your Stroke panel at the right of your screen or by clicking Window>Stroke, and it'll look something like this:

The thinnest line acceptable to offset printers is 0.25 pt. So don't use the "hairline" option unless you're sure you won't be printing offset.

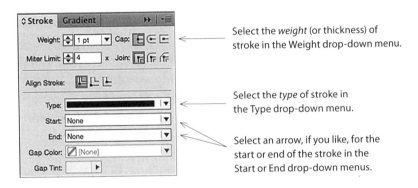

Select the *weight* (or thickness) of stroke in the Weight drop-down menu.

Select the *type* of stroke in the Type drop-down menu.

Select an arrow, if you like, for the start or end of the stroke in the Start or End drop-down menus.

To add a stroke to text, select the text with your Type Tool, then use the Stroke panel to apply a stroke.

Strokes can be applied to shapes created with shape tools (see chapter 33), to lines created with the Line Tool, Pen Tool, or Pencil Tool (see chapter 34), and even to text and image frames.

Select your shape, line, or frame using your Selection Tool, then select the type and weight of the stroke in the Stroke panel. Here are some examples:

Solid, 0.75 pt

Thick - Thick, 4 pt

Thick - Thin, 5 pt

Dashed, 2 pt

Straight Hash, 5 pt

Dotted, 3 pt

Wavy, 4 pt

Solid, end arrow, 0.25 pt

Adding corner options to rectangles and polygons

There are five different corner options you can add to rectangles and polygons, shown to the right.

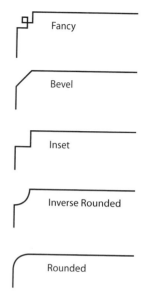

Fancy

Bevel

Inset

Inverse Rounded

Rounded

To add corner options to a shape, first either create a rectangle using the Rectangle Tool or a polygon using the Polygon Tool, or select an existing shape using your Selection Tool. Click Object>Corner Options to open the Corner Options dialog box (shown below).

The default corner options are for four square corners. You can change all four corners at the same time by leaving the link icon in the middle locked. Click one of the drop-down menus to see the five corner options and try a few to see how they look (with Preview checked, you can see the options as you try them). Make the corner option larger or smaller by clicking the up and down arrows next to the size. You can change any corner independently by clicking the link icon to unlock it.

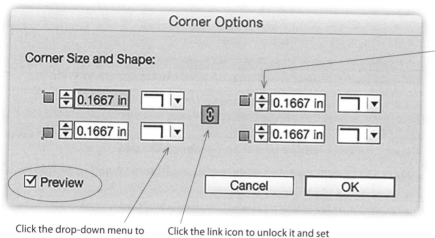

Click the up and down arrows to make the corner option bigger or smaller, or type in a value.

Check Preview to see the corner options as you try them.

Click the drop-down menu to try different corner options.

Click the link icon to unlock it and set each corner option independently.

Rectangle with 1 pt black stroke
No corner options added at top
0.125" rounded corners at bottom

9-sided polygon
with 40% star inset
10% black fill
0.1" bevel corners

Rectangle with 25% black fill

0.125" inverse rounded corners

36

Putting objects into groups

There are many instances where you may want to group two or more objects together so they don't get separated. For example, in *this* book, there are lots of diagrams with images, circles, arrows, and text, all meant to stay together (for example, the two diagrams opposite). You can select multiple objects by clicking on them individually while holding the Shift key. To deselect any object from the ones you've already selected, hold the Shift key while clicking on it.

How do you make sure various objects stay together? Using the Selection Tool, drag to select all the objects you want to stay together, then click Object>Group (or press Ctrl/Cmd+G). You'll see a dotted line around the group (see sample at left). To ungroup your objects, click Object>Ungroup (or press Ctrl/Cmd+Shift+G).

You can also group objects in stages. Say you group a few objects, then add a caption. Group the caption with your existing group by selecting the group and caption and pressing Ctrl/Cmd+G.

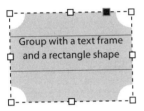

Group with a text frame and a rectangle shape

You can change text in an existing group by selecting it with the Type Tool. To change a shape or image, select it with the Direct Selection Tool (below).

Using the Pathfinder panel to combine shapes

Shapes can be combined to create new and different shapes by grouping them using the Pathfinder panel. Go to Window>Object & Layout>Pathfinder to see all the interesting ways you can combine and manipulate shapes and lines. Below are two examples of how you can combine a square and ellipse by either adding them together or subtracting one from the other. Have fun experimenting!

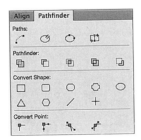

Pathfinder panel

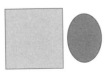

two separate shapes

ellipse in front of square, Object>Pathfinder>Add

ellipse in front of square, Object>Pathfinder>Subtract

Adding a document bleed

Bleed is a printing term referring to anything printed beyond the edge of the page. When a shape, color, or image goes to the edge of a page or cover, it actually must print *past* the edge because trimming the paper after printing is imprecise. If a shape, color, or image ends right where the paper will be trimmed, there's a chance that a strip of unprinted paper will be left showing. To avoid this problem, all shapes, colors, and images that you want to go to the edge of your page or cover will actually have to extend ⅛″ or 0.125″ *past* the edge of the paper.

You probably included a bleed when you originally set up your document (see page 34), but if not, adding a bleed area to your document in InDesign is easy and can be done anytime from anywhere in your document (see below). Click File>Document Setup, then the triangle next to Bleed and Slug, to open the full Document Setup dialog box. In the Bleed area at the bottom, make sure the link icon at the far right is unbroken, then type 0.125 in the box at the left and press Tab. The same setting will fill in all the boxes. Click OK.

Switch to Normal view and you'll see that InDesign has added a red line 0.125″ *outside* the edges of all your pages or cover. Now whenever you add a shape, color, or image to your pages or cover that goes right to the edge, make sure it extends to the edge of the bleed rather than the edge of the page.

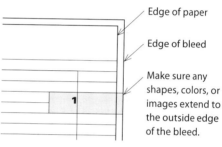

Edge of paper

Edge of bleed

Make sure any shapes, colors, or images extend to the outside edge of the bleed.

First make sure the link is unbroken.

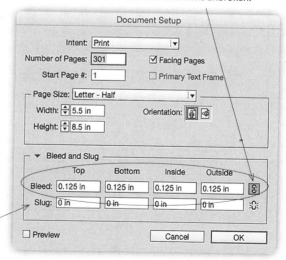

Ignore the Slug settings.

38

Using object styles

An object style contains a group of settings that makes an object (a shape, line, or frame) appear a certain way. Object styles control objects in a way similar to how paragraph styles control paragraphs.

Object styles are super-handy for making sure any text frames, shapes, and images you use frequently throughout your book are consistent. If you'll be constantly drawing arrows or circling things to point out features or applying text wraps to your images, it's quick and easy to set up an object style and apply it as you go. Consider creating an object style for image frames with text wraps, arrows, shapes, sidebar boxes, and even text frames for captions (see chapter 44).

Below are two examples of object styles used throughout *this* book:

This is the Screenshot object style, with rounded corners and a drop shadow.

The arrow shown above is used throughout this book. The Arrow object style is set for a 0.25 pt solid stroke with a simple arrow at the end.

Object styles control settings for fill and stroke, corner options, paragraph styles, text wrap, drop shadows, and much more. Besides keeping objects looking consistent, object styles make it easy to change objects globally. For example, you can change *all* your sidebar boxes to a different color just by changing that setting in your Sidebar object style. Or you can change its corner options. Any changes you make to an object style will change *all* the objects in your book with that style applied.

There are two steps involved in using object styles: 1) *creating* the object styles, and 2) *applying* the object styles.

Creating object styles

To create an object style, first select a shape, line, text frame, or image frame that is already set up the way you want it, then create a new object style for it. Here are the steps:

1 Open your Object Styles panel by clicking Window>Styles>Object Styles.
2 Using your Selection Tool, select a shape, line, or frame.
3 Click the fly-out menu in the Object Styles panel, then select New Object Style. Fill in the dialog box as shown below, then click OK.

Add a name here.

Later you can change any of the Style Settings by opening the appropriate setting and adjusting it as needed.

Make sure the Apply Style to Selection and Preview boxes are checked.

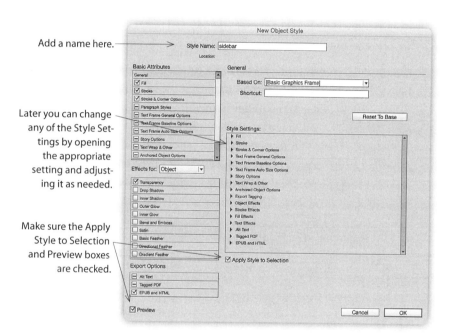

Object Styles panel fly-out menu

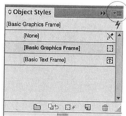

Drag your Object Styles panel into the dock at the right of your screen for easy access next time.

Applying object styles

Now that you've created an object style, it's easy to apply it to your objects. Using your Selection Tool, select the object you want to apply the object style to, then click that style in the Object Styles panel. Voilà!

As you add shapes, lines, text frames, or image frames to your pages, apply the appropriate object style to each one.

You might need to click the Clear Overrides icon (⬚⚡) at the base of the Object Styles panel to force the object to accept the style.

39

Using a library

The library function in InDesign is a very handy tool and easy to use. You simply set up a library (formally called an Object Library) for anything out of the ordinary that you use repeatedly in the book, such as graphics, inline art, fractions, foreign phrases, and so on. Whenever you want to use one of the items, you can simply open the library, which appears as a panel similar to any of your other panels, and drag the item onto the page. Here's how:

Some InDesign users have a strong preference for libraries and other users for object styles. Find your own best use for either one, or use both—it's up to you.

1   Choose File>New>Library, and the CC libraries box might appear (see below). If it does, click No, then name your new library and save it to the same folder with your InDesign file. Note that it will have an .indl extension and that you will see it as an independent file in your folder.

2   In order to make the library always ready to use, dock it with the other panels on the right side of your screen. If you choose not to dock it, you can let it float

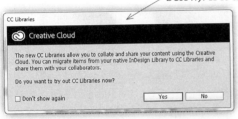

A Creative Cloud Library is an asset-sharing tool used among Adobe applications, devices, and users. You might find it useful, but it's not what we are discussing here.

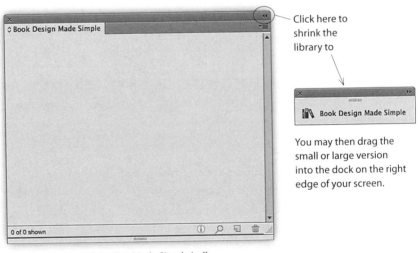

Click here to shrink the library to

You may then drag the small or large version into the dock on the right edge of your screen.

Book Design Made Simple.indl

in front of the document, or you can close it for now and then open it again anytime (File>Open).

3   With the library open, find an object that you want to add to it and use the Selection Tool to drag the object onto the Library panel. If it's type that you want to add, copy the type into its own text frame first, then drag the whole frame.

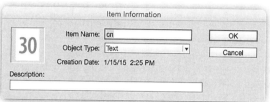

4   Double-click the object in the library, and name it in the space below the box in the library that it's now sitting in. The objects will arrange themselves alphabetically.

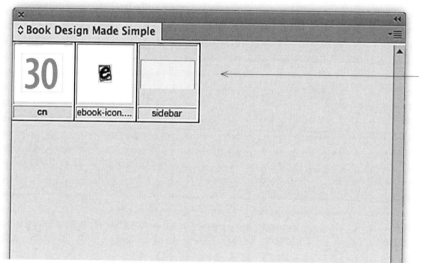

Left to right: a text frame with type in it, an image, and a graphic shape

5   When you want to use a library object, simply open the library and use the Selection Tool to grab the object and drag it onto your page or pasteboard. It will appear at full size, ready to use, while leaving the library object in place.

To change or replace a library object, drag it to the trash icon and answer Yes to the dialog box that appears (right). Then drag your new object into the libary and name it.

Now that you've learned how to add shapes to your book and apply color and object styles to them, your next step is to learn how to add images and optimize them for printing (see Part VI: Adding Images).

Adding shapes and images to your pages usually affects the flow of text, and that's why it's important to add both to your pages at the same time. This constitutes the second pass through your pages, and you're almost there!

Part VI:
Adding Images

40

Preparing to add images

If you're including images in your book, Part VI: Adding Images is for you! You'll have already set up your baseline grid in chapter 23 (which will help you to align your images nicely within margins and/or columns), and you'll also have learned about creating and applying object styles in Part V: Adding Shapes & Color (which will be useful for applying consistent text wraps to your images and captions).

If you don't have any images inside your book, feel free to skip to Part VII: Typesetting, where you'll do your final pass through all your pages. If you skip Part VI: Adding Images now, you'll come back to it when you design your book cover, to learn about getting permission to use images, as well as placing, sizing, and optimizing them for print.

In Part VI: Adding Images, you'll be using what you learned in previous chapters of this book about baseline grids, using a bleed, and using object styles. You'll also learn to use Adobe Mini Bridge—a useful and labor-saving tool for organizing your images.

Adding images and captions will increase your page count. If you'll be printing on an offset press, you'll want your page count to fit into signatures. See chapter 48 for ways to adjust it to fit.

You may want to read through chapters 41 to 44 in this section while working on the first image in your book. That way, you'll be able to add a text wrap, caption, credit, and/or bleed to it right away and decide on its final size. All these things will affect the flow of text for the remainder of your chapter, so it's good to resolve each image, in order, as you progress through your pages.

So read on, or if there are no images in your pages, skip Part VI for now and come back to it later when you need it.

Getting permission to use images

Chances are you'll use at least one image in your book—the author photo! And commonly, you'll have front and back cover images and some photos, drawings, and/or illustrations on some of your pages.

Requesting permission is not only the law but also a common courtesy. Imagine how you'd feel if you found that someone used the material in *your* book without asking. So, when do you need to get permission? Simply put, if any of the images you're using were photographed, drawn, or created by someone else, you need to get permission.

Make a list of all the images used in your book, exactly where you got them, and who created them. Here are some of the possibilities.

- **online image bank**   If you searched for your image in one of the many online stock photo providers, first read the fine print about licensing. When you begin your search, you can restrict the listing to royalty-free images, which are the best choice in most cases. A *royalty-free* image can generally be used for any purpose as often as you like—once you purchase it, of course. On the other hand, a *rights-managed* image or a *licensed* image will have restrictions, and you will pay only for the one intended purpose. You might find yourself using one of these if you want famous images or images of famous people. Start with a royalty-free search, then move on to rights-managed or licensed images if you can't find what you want.

- **elsewhere on the Internet**   If you found an image somewhere else on the Internet, make sure you have permission to use it. You might assume that photos on sites such as Wikimedia Commons or Google Images are copyright-free, but that is not always the case. Read the fine print, and copy and paste the exact wording of the credit line into your list of permissions. If you need permission, get it.

- **a museum**   Most museums charge a fee for use of their images, and they all have strict rules about how they can be used, so follow them

Visit www.BookDesign MadeSimple.com/ Resources or look on page 379 of this book for a listing of some of the many image banks.

Even if you found your image on the Adobe Stock website, you must purchase a license to use it in your book.

Always use the exact credit or permissions wording you are given by any image provider.

If all your images are created by the same person,
with the exception of a
few, add a credit to the
copyright page like this:

All photos by Glenna Collett
unless otherwise credited.

and then add a credit to
specific photos by adding
to the end of the caption:

Photo credit: Fiona Raven

If your images don't have
captions, add the credit
underneath or up the
side of the photo (see
pages 295–297). The credit
can be in very small type.

to the letter. Before the institution grants permission, they will want to know how large the image will be on the page, whether it will be printed in color or black and white, and the topic under discussion. You'll need additional written permission if you want to crop. Allow plenty of time (months, in many cases) for the permissions process.

- **historical photos**   These may be copyright-free, but they are often owned by an organization, such as a historical society. Ownership will be noted somewhere on the site you're visiting. Ask for permission.
- **public domain**   This term simply means works that have run out of their copyright and are now owned by the public—for instance, music by Beethoven. With images, this is a bit tricky, because although the object itself may be in the public domain, an image of it may not. An example would be a photo of a painting of an early American president. Think twice before assuming anything is in the public domain.
- **a photographer you've hired**   If you've hired someone to take any photo in your book—and this goes for illustrators too, of course—find out what wording they want for their credit line and follow it exactly.

How to write for permission

Search using the term
"permission to use image" +
the name of the institution.

You can sometimes find a permissions request form for a specific institution on the Internet. If there's no form, write a letter (email is fine) respectfully asking to use the image and telling the title of your book, the chapter title, and the topic of discussion. Tell the size at which you want to use the image and whether it will be black and white or color. Ask about fees and their preferred credit verbiage. Keep a record of all correspondence.

Where to list credits and permissions in your book

If you have only a very few, put them on the copyright page. If you have a great many, list them in your back matter under the heading "Photo [or Image or Illustration] Credits." You might list them in groups by creator or in numerical order by page number.

Another option is to place a credit line in small type next to each image (see page 297) or include it at the end of the image caption. There are many ways to deal with credits, so look in other books to see how they have handled them.

Organizing your images

Keeping your images well organized is one of those tasks you'll be glad you took the time to do. Here is a simple method: Give each image a number that shows what chapter it's in and its position. For instance, "03-06" would be the sixth image in chapter 3. (If you've already assigned numbers to your images and captions, simply follow your own numbering system.) Feel free to use descriptive information in the file name, but put the numbering scheme first so the files will always be in the correct order when listed (e.g., "03-06_orange_cat" would be followed by "03-07_brown_cow"). If it helps you, make a different folder for each chapter or part in your book.

Using Mini Bridge

If you have a large number of images in your book, consider using Mini Bridge as an efficient way to keep track of them. In Mini Bridge, images are displayed as thumbnails, and you can place an image by simply dragging its thumbnail onto your page. If you are visually oriented, you might find this method more logical than using the Place command, which requires you to remember a file name—see page 288.

To use Mini Bridge, you first need to install Bridge. Click the Bridge icon on your Control panel to automatically open Creative Cloud and download Bridge. Once the download is complete, open Mini Bridge by clicking Window>Mini Bridge or by pressing Shift and clicking on the Bridge icon. When your Mini Bridge panel opens, click Launch Bridge and it will look something like the panel shown to the right.

Use the navigation area at the left of the panel to locate the folder with your image files in it. Double-click that folder and your

It is a good idea to use short file names for ebook conversions.

Adobe Bridge and Mini Bridge come with the full Creative Cloud package. If you leased InDesign only, you won't have them.

 Bridge icon

The Mini Bridge panel

images will appear in thumbnails to the right. You can determine the size of the thumbnails with the slider at the bottom of the panel.

You can dock your Mini Bridge panel with the panels on the right of your screen. Dock it near the top so that when it's open you can drag the bottom of the panel down far enough to see several images at once. And as with other panels, you can resize it to better fit the way you work.

The full version of Bridge is also available to you. It's a very robust application that allows you to organize your images in any way you like. While looking at them all at the same time, you can rename them, compare and rate them, get information (metadata) about them, and even make contact sheets of them to share with others—basically it's a full-screen, full-function version of Mini Bridge. View an Adobe or lynda .com tutorial to find out all the ways that Bridge can help you to work more efficiently.

Navigate to the folder containing your images by double-clicking in the list on the left, and your progression of folders is displayed at the top.

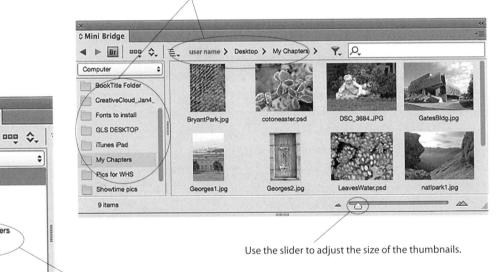

Next time you use Mini Bridge, go directly to Recent Folders or Recent Files.

Use the slider to adjust the size of the thumbnails.

Placing and positioning images

A picture is worth a thousand words, right? So your book's pictures need to be as high quality as you can possibly make them, and they must be well and intelligently placed. Before you learn the details of preparing your images for printing, you'll lay them out in your pages and make decisions about sizing and cropping.

First and most important: *Every image in your book must be a free-standing file.* In other words, each image will be saved on your computer with its own file name, as a specific file type (such as PSD, TIF, JPG, PNG, GIF, BMP, AI, EPS, and so on).

If some or all of your images are in your Word document, you'll need to extract them before proceeding.

Extracting images from a Word document

In Word you may have inserted some images, but once they were embedded they became unusable by InDesign or Photoshop. This is why you deleted them before placing your manuscript in InDesign (see page 44). In doing that, though, you should have kept a copy of the original image files and can use them in your book. If not, here is how to extract images from a Word document:

1 Open the Word document with your images in it.
2 Save the document in Web Page (.htm) format. The result will be a folder containing an HTM file and a list of image files called "image001," image002," and so on.
3 Select (single-click) each image in this folder (many of them will be listed two or more times). Find the highest-quality file for each image—almost always the largest file—and put it in a separate folder, ready to be used in your book. Don't worry about file format at this stage.

Placing images on the page

Links panel before any images are placed

Images are always *placed* in InDesign, never copied and pasted. Why? Because if you copy and paste an image onto a page, it becomes embedded in your InDesign document, bloating your document's file size and making it impossible to optimize the image in Photoshop.

Conversely, when you *place* an image in InDesign, a link is created between the original image file and your InDesign document. The image exists as a separate file that can be sized, cropped, and optimized, and it still remains linked to your page in InDesign. You'll have control over your linked images through the Links panel. To open your Links panel, first look in your docked panels; if it's not there, click Window>Links.

Placing images using the Place command

Using your Selection Tool, first click outside of any frames to make sure nothing is selected. Then click File>Place (or press Ctrl/Cmd+D) to open

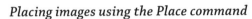

the Place dialog box. Browse for the file you want to place, then click Open. You'll see a miniature version of the image attached to your mouse pointer. Click once anywhere on your page or pasteboard, and the image will be placed in your document.

You can place multiple images at a time by selecting multiple images from a folder (hold Ctrl/Cmd while selecting images), then clicking Open. Your mouse pointer will be loaded with all the images you selected, and you'll place one each time you click on the page or pasteboard.

Placing images using Bridge or Mini Bridge

If your placed image is much larger than your page or even the pasteboard, simply zoom out (Ctrl/Cmd+-) until you can see the entire image frame. Using the Free Transform tool ( ), click on one corner of the frame, hold down the Shift key, and drag inward to resize it.

If you have a large number of images, you may want to organize them in Bridge or Mini Bridge, applications that are included in the Adobe CC package (see page 285). You can place an image from Bridge or Mini Bridge by first clicking on the image icon in Bridge or Mini Bridge to select it, dragging it onto your page, and then clicking anywhere on the page or pasteboard to place the image. Review chapter 42 for details on using Bridge.

Sizing and cropping images

After you've placed an image on a page, there are two easy ways to size and crop it: using the Free Transform Tool and using the Selection Tool. You'll probably find using a combination of both is easiest, perhaps starting with the Free Transform Tool and fine-tuning with the Selection Tool.

1 Using the Free Transform Tool (⚡) The Free Transform Tool is best for making large adjustments to an image, such as reducing its size and rotating it. To change the size of your image, press and hold the Shift key, then click and drag on any corner of the image's frame. (Pressing the Shift key prevents the image from becoming distorted.) Feel free to reduce the size of the image as much as you like, but only enlarge it a bit, as images become blurry and pixelated if they are enlarged too much from their original size.

Position your image on your page by dragging it. You'll want to align the image with your baseline grid, margins, columns, and text.

Rotate your image by hovering anywhere outside the image frame and you'll see a curved arrow. Drag vertically or horizontally and you'll see your image rotating. You can also see your changes (amount of rotation) in the Control panel.

2 Using the Selection Tool (▶) The Selection Tool is best for fine-tuning the size of your image frame and cropping the image. Click on an image with your Selection Tool, and you'll see the frame around it (also called the bounding box). Drag your image into its final position on the page, then drag each side of the frame or bounding box as needed to fit the image exactly within a specific space.

If you want to keep the frame or bounding box at a certain size but crop the image within it, first hover over the image with the Selection Tool until a doughnut appears in the center (called the content grabber). Hover directly over the doughnut and a grabber hand appears. Click once on the doughnut, and you'll see a frame with a different color appear around the image. You can now resize, rotate, and move the *contents* of the frame (i.e., the image) independently of the bounding box until you're satisfied. This is one way you can crop your image in InDesign.

Switch from the Selection Tool to the Free Transform Tool by pressing E. Switch from the Free Transform Tool to the Selection Tool by pressing V.

Use the Free Transform Tool for sizing and rotating images.

In positioning images, try to be as precise as possible. If you are having trouble with this, your guides might be the cause. Go to View>Grids & Guides and check or uncheck Snap to Guides. Keep this in mind anytime you move an object.

You can move an object a tiny amount with the Selection Tool and an arrow key. Every time you hit the key, the object moves one point.

link OK symbol   frame

handles

content grabber

The image frame or bounding box defines the edges of the *visible* image. Select it with the Selection Tool.

Use the content grabber to select the *contents* of a frame (i.e., the entire image).

Alternatively, you can use the Direct Selection Tool ( ) to select the contents.

Commonly in InDesign, a file that you place will look very rough on the page. But before you panic, print out that page, and likely you'll discover that the image is fine. This is simply something you'll have to get used to; you can trust the way the file looks in Photoshop.

Cropping is a powerful tool. If you chose to cut a sibling out of a family portrait, for instance, it would send a strong message to your family. In less extreme cases you can still affect how your readers interpret what you're showing. So be as thoughtful when working with photos as you were when writing your manuscript, for this is visual editing.

Experiment with your images to see how they look best. Move the image around in its frame using the content grabber to find the best position and size for the main focus of the image. Crop anything distracting in the background, and feature the most important part of your image prominently.

In this image, the water is uninteresting, the muddy shoreline is unattractive, and the second bird and the log are distracting.

The focus is now on the important part of the image.

If you look at all of your images together (try using Adobe Bridge or Mini Bridge; see page 285), you might be able to come up with a conscious cropping style. Perhaps you'd like all the portraits to show only the face. Or you might want all the photos of buildings to show the surrounding area as well—trees, neighboring buildings, and the like.

Try to crop and size your images so they fit within your baseline grid and also your vertical guides, the invisible grid you may have set up when constructing your A-Master page (see page 120). This will keep your pages neat and allow the first line of your captions (when you add them) to start on the baseline grid.

another possible photo width

older than you, and must know better'; and this Alice would not allow without knowing how old it was, and, as the Lory positively refused to tell its age, there was no more to be said.

At last the Mouse, who seemed to be a person of authority among them, called out, 'Sit down, all of you, and listen to me! I'LL soon make you dry enough!' They all sat down at once, in a large ring, with the Mouse in the middle. Alice kept her eyes anxiously fixed on it, for she felt sure she would catch a bad cold if she did not get

First line of caption is sitting on the baseline grid.

← Top of photo aligns with the top of a line of type. Bottom of photo is on the baseline grid.

You might also consider framing an image inside a non-rectangular shape. To do so, first create the desired shape with the Ellipse or Polygon Frame Tool (see chapter 33). Make sure the shape's fill color is None. Then select the shape with the Direct Selection Tool and place (File>Place) your image file in it. The image will appear at full size inside the shape, and you can size and crop it using the Direct Selection Tool or content grabber.

Whenever you size and crop an object—in this case, an image—your Control panel displays what you're doing. After you've finished making your photo look good, check to make sure the image is still proportional in size to the original. Both width and height scale percentages should match, as shown below. If they don't, type the correct value in one of the scale percentages boxes, make sure that the chain symbol is unbroken, and press Enter/Return. This will result in a proportional image.

When enlarging or shrinking your image, hold the Shift key to keep its width and height proportional.

Width and height of image or bounding box. If you want to change the size by typing in a new value (but also keeping it proportional to its original size), make sure the chain symbol is unbroken.

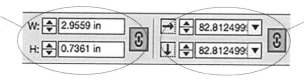

Scale percentages of the image itself. These values will be the same if your image was sized proportionately.

Positioning images on your pages

Generally it's best to position images at the top or bottom of the page, although naturally there are exceptions. For instance, if you have an outer column, you can place images anywhere north-south in the column, wherever they are the most useful (such as in *this* book). Just be sure not to leave only a few lines of type stranded at the top or bottom of a page above or below an image, as readers will not notice them.

Unless you're required to use entire, uncropped photos (which is usually the case when you're reproducing museum pieces), you have the opportunity to interpret the meaning and importance of each image in your book. It probably seems obvious that a full-page image is more important than a postage-stamp sized one. This is the time to decide which images need to be emphasized over others. Make a list of all images for each chapter and give each one a rating of A, B, or C to signify its importance. This will help you solidify your thoughts about them and set up your layout scheme for the chapter.

If you notice that all the most significant images are bunched together in one part of the chapter, consider rearranging your copy a bit. Showing all the largest illustrations close to each other not only will unbalance the chapter but also will create some difficult layout problems.

Generally it's best to size your images no larger than the type area on the page, unless you want to use a bleed (see below). You'll find that if you use the type column width for photos as often as possible, they will look neater than if you use random widths. (On the other hand, if you have a side column like the one in this book, use that width as often as you can.) When you're sizing photos, leave room for captions, whether they'll appear below or to the side.

If your image will bleed off the page, make sure to align the edge(s) with the red bleed lines that are 0.125″ outside the edge of your page.

If you decide to use a bleed for your image, be sure to extend it the full amount of the bleed, which is usually ⅛″ (0.125″). Your bleed area should appear in red around the edges of your pages in Normal view—see page 275 to set this up if you haven't already. Of course, you must make sure that the most important part of your image is not going to bleed off the page or fall into the gutter between pages, and beware of cutting images of people awkwardly. Also, remember that your printer is not going to trim your book's pages precisely the same for each book; the trimming can vary as much as ⅛″.

It's also possible to place an image across the gutter or spine of a 2-page spread. Whenever an image, shape, or line is placed across two adjoining pages, it's called a crossover. Images can look very attractive placed across a 2-page spread. Just make sure that the portion of the image that disappears into the spine or binding of the book isn't an important part of your image (such as a face).

The rectangle at the top of this 2-page spread has a 0.125" bleed off the top of both pages, and it also forms a crossover, being placed across the gutter (or spine) of two adjoining pages.

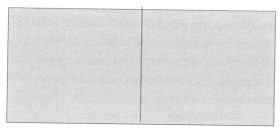

This image is a crossover and bleeds on all four sides. Its caption could be placed on the previous or following page.

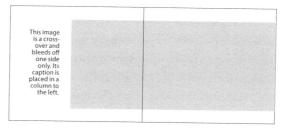

This image is a crossover and bleeds off one side only. Its caption is placed in a column to the left.

If you're pairing images of dissimilar shapes on a page, try to make them both the same height (next to each other), both the same width (one above the other), or overlapping (see right). This way, they look like a matched pair and not just two images that happen to be sitting near each other. When you're satisfied with your pairing, you'll find the images easier to move if you group them first by selecting both images, then pressing Ctrl/Cmd+G. (Later, if you want to ungroup the images, select the group and press Ctrl/Cmd+Shift+G.)

As you work with your images, check each one in the Links panel (toggle the arrow in the lower left corner to reveal the Link Info section) to make sure its effective resolution is at least 300 ppi. If the value is below 300 ppi at your image's current size, try using the image at a smaller size on the page. You can see the effective ppi changing in the Links panel as you change the size of your image. (If you really want to use the image at a size where its effective resolution is less than 300 dpi, you'll need to resample the image in Photoshop as described on page 304).

Ideally, your image's Effective PPI should be a minimum of 300.

44

Adding captions and text wraps

Once you've placed an image on your page and positioned it approximately in its final position, you'll want to add its caption and a text wrap to both of them (so the text runs around the image and caption, not on top of them). That way you'll be able to see how the image and caption affect the flow of text on your pages, then adjust their size and placement for the most pleasing layout.

Adding captions

If all of your captions are going to be the same width, consider putting an empty caption text frame into a library (chapter 39) to save time. With your cursor inside the caption text frame, select the **cap** paragraph style (but don't add any type), then put the text frame into the library. Now all of your captions will automatically take on the **cap** style when you insert them into the frame.

Chances are your captions are still within your main narrative and have the Caption [**cap**] paragraph style applied to them. To extract a caption from the main narrative, select the whole caption by quadruple-clicking it with the Type Tool, then cut it from the main narrative by clicking Edit>Cut or pressing Ctrl/Cmd+X.

Next, create a new text frame for the caption by dragging the Type Tool. Paste the caption in the new text frame by clicking Edit>Paste or pressing Ctrl/Cmd+V. Now that your caption is in its own frame, use your Selection Tool to position the frame below or beside the image.

If your captions are not already within your main narrative, simply create a new text frame by dragging your Type Tool, then type the caption in it and apply the Caption [**cap**] paragraph style to it (see page 78).

Placement considerations for captions

The most common types of captions are summarized below, but note that these ideas are very general. Work out a good style and method for your book and stick with it as much as possible.

1 **Put captions below the images** in books that have a single column of type. Set them in the italics of your book text or in a contrasting

typeface, about 1 pt smaller, to differentiate them from the narrative. Align them at left with the image.

Your Caption paragraph style (see page 78) includes aligning the first line of your caption to the baseline grid. This creates a consistent amount of space between the bottom of your image and the top of the caption (see top right).

If an illustration appears at the bottom of a page, place the last line of the caption flush with the last line of type. To do this, you must stop the first line of your caption from aligning to the grid. Place your cursor anywhere in the caption, then select the Do Not Align to Baseline Grid icon in your Control or Paragraph panel (see right).

Caption goes here.

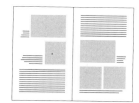

Do Not Align to
Baseline Grid icon

2. **Put captions beside the images** if you have a column for that purpose (as in *this* book). Use a different typeface, possibly a sans serif if your book text uses a serif font, or use the italic font of your book text. Make the captions smaller than the book text but still readable. The type can be set to align toward the image, and usually side captions are placed to the outside of the image (i.e., away from the spine).

3. **Captions in art books** get a different treatment. Often each image is numbered, so give the label and number (e.g., "Plate 12.4") its own style and color (create a character style with small caps and a different color, for example). For a full-page illustration, the caption can appear on the facing (or even the previous) page, perhaps with a directional note ("left," "opposite page," "overleaf") in italics at the beginning of the caption text. Consider using arrows or triangles as pointers if you think they will help (e.g., ▶ ▷). You can find them in the Glyphs panel (Type>Glyphs). If the typeface for your captions doesn't include an appropriate symbol, try a dingbat or symbol typeface. Examples: Zapf Dingbats, Webdings, Wingdings, and Symbol. Create a new character style for the pointer, specifying its typeface, color, and size.

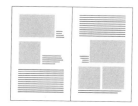

Images toward the spine (above) are preferable to images away from the spine—notice the big empty hole in the middle of the spread below.

4. **Place captions *above* charts and tables.** Your readers will go through the material in a linear fashion, left to right and top to bottom, so it's best to give them the general explanation of the table in the caption before they start.

Adding a text wrap

Since the advent of desktop publishing, we often see photos sticking into the text with the text running around them. That's because this is now a very simple procedure called Text Wrap. Start by opening your Text Wrap panel (click Window>Text Wrap), and dock it with your other panels.

The following explains a simple way to add a text wrap to an image and the caption placed below it. If your captions are positioned below your images, then this method is for you! If not, page 298 explains all the ways that text wrap can be used for your images and captions.

Adding text wrap to an image

Make sure your image is in *front* of the type you want to wrap around it (text wrap only affects text *behind* it). To put one frame in front of another, select the frame, then click Object>Arrange and choose Bring to Front, or press Ctrl/Cmd+Shift+].

Select an image frame using your Selection Tool, then choose the Text Wrap options shown below left. Note there is no space *below* the image. That's because your caption will be placed below the image. Then create a new object style called **images**, following the instructions on page 277, and apply the **images** object style to every subsequent image you place.

Adding text wrap to a caption

If you prefer, you can use a library instead of object styles to achieve the same goal.

Select a caption frame using your Selection Tool, then choose the Text Wrap options shown below right. Note there is no space *above* the caption. That's because your image will be placed above the caption. Then create a new object style called **captions** and apply the **captions** object style to every subsequent caption you place.

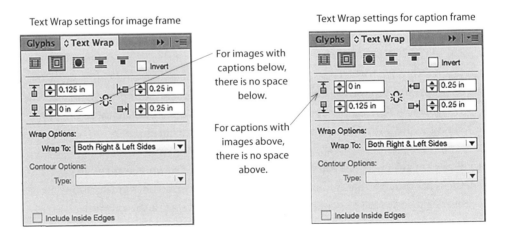

Text Wrap settings for image frame

For images with captions below, there is no space below.

For captions with images above, there is no space above.

Text Wrap settings for caption frame

Adding a credit to the side of an image

If you're planning to place credits up the side of your images, you'll need to create a new object style for credits, specifying the amount of space between the top of the credit text frame and the credit text. That way, all your credits will be an equal distance away from the edge of your images.

Create a new text frame by dragging your Type Tool, and type in the image credit text. Add an inset space to the top of your credit text frame by clicking Object>Text Frame Options and making the selections shown to the right and click OK. Then switch to the Selection Tool and create a new object style called **credits**, following the instructions on page 277, and apply the **credits** object style to this and all subsequent credit text frames.

Finally, rotate the credit text frame by clicking the Rotate 90° Counter-clockwise icon in the Control Panel (⟳). Place the credit frame alongside your image, and align the top of its frame flush with the right side of your image.

Because the text wrap applied to your image only affects text *beneath* it, the text in your credit text frame shouldn't be affected by the text wrap around the image. If the text wrap *is* affecting it, then bring the credit text frame to the front by selecting it with your Selection Tool, then clicking Object>Arrange and choosing Bring to Front, or pressing Ctrl/Cmd+Shift+].

With your credit text frame selected, click the lock icon to unlock it, then set your Top Inset Spacing to suit.

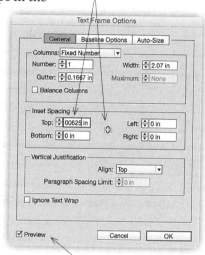

Check the Preview box so you can see the changes as you make them.

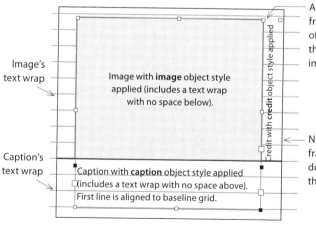

Image's text wrap

Image with **image** object style applied (includes a text wrap with no space below).

Caption's text wrap

Caption with **caption** object style applied (includes a text wrap with no space above). First line is aligned to baseline grid.

Align the credit text frame with the right side of the image frame. Note the space between the image and the credit.

Note that the image frame's text wrap does not affect the credit text.

Create a new paragraph style for your credits based on **tx1**, but with small type (6 or 7 pt, depending on the typeface you're using).

Different options for using a text wrap

There are lots of ways you can use the text wrap features in InDesign. Click on any image or text frame, then hover over the top row of options in the Text Wrap panel. From left to right, they are:

- **No text wrap** means that the text runs right over the image. If you want this effect, don't use the text wrap feature at all, and simply place the image behind the type (Object>Arrange>Send to Back).
- **Wrap around bounding box** is most likely the option you'll use. The bounding box is the frame around your image or caption.
- **Wrap around object shape** is best for when the object has an interesting shape (see left, or the two rubber duckies on page 299). Use sparingly, for special effect.
- Use **Jump object** if you've put an image in the middle of the page and want the text to jump right over the image and continue.
- **Jump to next column** makes the text stop just above the image and then start up again at the top of the next column or page.

Once you've chosen an appropriate text wrap option, you'll need to set up your inset (white space) measurements. As you've done before, click on the chain link in the middle of the panel to make all the values either the same (link closed) or independent of each other (link open). Experiment with measurements until you are happy with the amount of space between the frame and the type.

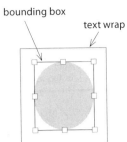

bounding box

text wrap

Wrap around bounding box

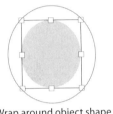

Wrap around object shape

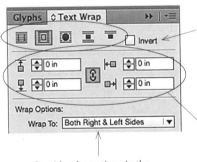

General text wrap options, left to right: No text wrap, Wrap around bounding box, Wrap around object shape, Jump object, and Jump to next column

Amount of white space above, below, to left, and to right of image

Consider the options in the Wrap To drop-down list, too.

Combined with the Wrap around object shape option, the Invert feature places type *inside* the shape instead of wrapping type around it, as shown to the right.

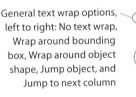

Combined with the Wrap around object shape option, the Invert feature places type *inside* the shape instead of wrapping type around it.

The text wrap options shown on the previous page are easy to implement—just select your image and choose one of the icons at the top of the Text Wrap panel. But suppose you want to create a custom shape for your text wrap?

bounding box

text wrap

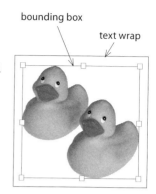

The image to the right shows two rubber ducks on a white background inside a rectangular frame or bounding box. Applying a regular text wrap will form a rectangle around the bounding box, but a text wrap that follows the shape of the ducks (like the one to the left) is more interesting. When you have shapes like this isolated on a white or transparent background, InDesign can detect the shape in the image. Choose the options shown in the Text Wrap panel to the right.

Alternatively, you may want the text wrap to create a completely different shape. In chapter 34 you learned how to create and edit shapes using the Pen Tool and the Direct Selection Tool. These same tools can be used to change the shape of the text wrap.

First select the image and apply any text wrap other than No Text Wrap. Switch to the Pen Tool (or press P).

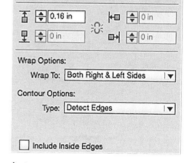

Create a new anchor point by clicking anywhere between anchor points, and delete an anchor point by clicking directly on it (you'll see a small plus or minus sign next to the Pen Tool). Switch to the Direct Selection Tool temporarily by pressing Ctrl/Cmd to move anchor points or drag handles (as described in chapter 34). Have fun creating custom shapes for your text wrap!

There are other, more complicated, ways to use text wrap, but chances are you won't need them for your book. If you're interested, refer to an InDesign tutorial for instructions.

When you've placed all your shapes and images, added captions to them, and added text wraps where needed, you're ready to package all your linked images into a folder. This is explained in chapter 45.

Packaging your book

Once you've placed all your images, you're ready to package your book. Packaging saves a *copy* of your latest InDesign document, together with all the images used in your book, into a new folder. The images will be linked to your InDesign document. If you choose to optimize any of your images (see chapter 46), you'll make changes to the images in your new folder, while your original images remain intact in their current locations.

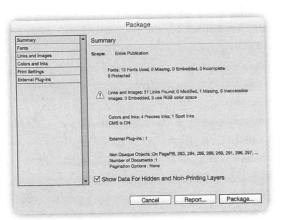

Click File>Package to open the Package dialog box. You'll see it's divided into sections on the left for Fonts, Links and Images, and so on. You may see some warnings, but just ignore these for the time being, as you'll make any necessary repairs in chapter 46. Then click Package.

The next dialog box you'll see is for Printing Instructions, so just click Continue for now. Next you'll see a Create Package Folder dialog box like the one at the lower left. Check the boxes at the bottom as shown, navigate to the place where you'll save your new folder, and type a name into the Save As box. Then click Package.

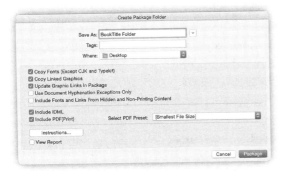

Now your InDesign document, image files, and document fonts are all together in one folder. You'll be using this set of linked images from here on, but you still have your originals in case you need them at any point down the road.

NOTE: Close the InDesign document you are working on *right now* before proceeding any further. Open the new document in the new folder you just created, and proceed with that one.

Optimizing your images

Now that you've placed all your images, applied text wrap to them, added captions and/or credits, and packaged them into a new folder, it's time to decide whether or not you need to optimize your images.

What, exactly, *is* optimizing? It's improving an image by adjusting its colors or contrast, making it look sharper, increasing its resolution, and making any other changes so the image looks better *in print*.

To optimize or not to optimize?

If your book will be printed with a POD printer such as CreateSpace or IngramSpark, you probably don't need to optimize your images. When you create a PDF to upload to the printer (see chapter 71), Acrobat will automatically do a number of things to optimize your images: reduce any higher-resolution images to 300 dpi, convert the colors in your images if needed, and crop them to their frames. Simple, right?

Of course you'll want to first check any PDF you'll be uploading to your printer, to make sure all the images look fine. If any happen to need extra attention, you can spend some time improving them, using this chapter as your guide.

If you have some images with effective resolutions *below* 300 dpi, or if any colors are looking dull or lacking contrast in the PDF, you may want to optimize those images individually. This chapter will guide you through a number of steps to help your images look their best.

At what stage should images be optimized?

The best time to optimize your images is when the design and layout of your cover and pages are finished. That way, you'll be sure there are no further changes to the size, placement, and cropping of your images, and you'll optimize them just before creating your final PDF for the printer.

If you choose to optimize any images individually, you'll be taking the following steps:

1   Checking the image in the Links panel
2   Making sure its effective resolution is at least 300 ppi, and cropping the image if needed
3   Converting the colors to a color profile
4   Improving colors and/or contrast
5   Saving the updated image in an appropriate format for printing
6   Relinking the updated image to your InDesign file

You'll use Photoshop to optimize your photographs and Illustrator to optimize any vector images you may have. In this chapter you'll learn the simplest methods to accomplish the essentials of what you may need. If you prefer, you can ask your printer's prepress department to do this for you (for a fee, of course). To execute more complex changes to your images, you may need to take an online tutorial from Adobe, sign up for lynda.com lessons, go through the steps in a how-to book, or take a class. See the Resources section at www.BookDesignMadeSimple.com for links.

1 Checking your images in the Links panel

The Links panel displays a wealth of information about each image (look in your docked panels or click Window>Links to open it). In the upper section of the panel you'll see a list of your images with their page numbers to the right. You'll also see any alerts for missing or outdated links. (See the example opposite.)

Click on any image with your Selection Tool. You'll see the image's file name highlighted in the upper section, and in the lower section all the information for it is shown. If you don't see the lower section called "Link Info" at the bottom of the list of images, click the arrow at the bottom left of the panel, and it will appear.

The only items on this long list of specifications that are important to you right now are: **Actual PPI**, **Effective PPI**, **Color Space**, and **Format**. Later in this chapter you'll optimize these aspects of your images, but for now here is a simple summary of these items:

In the upper left corner of any image on your page you'll see a link OK symbol (⬡), a modified file symbol (⚠), or a missing file symbol (❓). The latter two symbols have the same meanings as in the Links panel.

- **Actual ppi** is the number of pixels per inch in your original image file. **Effective ppi** is the number of pixels per inch in the image *at the size it is used* in your book. (If there is no actual or effective ppi showing in your Links panel, that means it's a vector image and you don't need to worry about resolution.) If effective ppi is less than 300, that means either the actual ppi is too low, or you have enlarged the image too much on your page and thereby reduced its ppi. Either way, the image will look fuzzy when printed. If this is the case, you have four choices:

  1 obtain a higher-resolution image from your image source,
  2 use the image at a smaller size so that it will be printed at 300 ppi,
  3 resample the image in Photoshop (see page 306), or
  4 pay the printer's prepress department to fix this problem for you.

- **Color space** must be either CMYK, Grayscale, or Bitmap. RGB, the color mode used by digital cameras, scanners, computer monitors, and ebooks, is not used in printed books unless your printer specifically states that it is okay. (At the time of writing, CreateSpace accepts images in RGB format.) You'll convert your images to CMYK or grayscale in either Photoshop (see pages 308–310) or Illustrator (see pages 311–312), or alternatively pay your printer's prepress department to do it for you. Remember that if your book is going to be printed with black ink only, *all* of the images used on your pages must be in either grayscale or bitmap format.

- **Format** This should say PSD (Photoshop), TIFF (or TIF), JPG, PNG, BMP, AI, or EPS. If you come across a different file extension, check under **Creator** and see whether the file was created in Photoshop or Illustrator, as you may still be able to work with it. After you've optimized your images, you'll save them as PSD or JPG files in Photoshop, or as AI files in Illustrator (see pages 314–316).

Get started by checking your first image in the Links panel. Look at the settings for Actual PPI, Effective PPI, Color Space, and Format, to see whether any need optimizing for print. If so, make the necessary adjustments by following the instructions in this chapter.

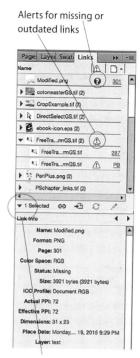

Alerts for missing or outdated links

Click the arrow in the Links menu to see the information about each file.

You'll optimize PSD, TIFF (or TIF), JPG, and PNG files in Photoshop, and AI and EPS files in Illustrator.

2 Sizing, cropping, and resolving ppi issues in Photoshop

You don't need to worry about sizing or resolution in images created in Illustrator. They are vector images, made up of lines and curves that are defined with mathematics, and the math stays the same no matter the size.

If you're new to Photoshop, you'll find it similar to InDesign in a number of ways. For starters, both have a Control panel across the top, a Toolbox down the left, and panels docked on the right. Open Photoshop and InDesign at the same time and, if possible, size their screens so you can see both at once, side by side. If not, just jump back and forth between programs as you proceed.

You've already selected an image in InDesign and checked its actual and effective ppi in the Links panel. If its effective ppi is *close to or greater than 300 ppi,* you only need to size and crop the image in Photoshop. However, if the effective ppi of your image is *much smaller than 300 ppi* (say, 280 ppi or less), you'll need to resample the image in Photoshop.

Sizing and cropping an image

Optimize the images in the new packaged folder you created in chapter 45 (all the linked images will be in the Links folder).

Open your image in Photoshop by clicking File>Open, browse for your image, then click Open. You'll adjust the size and resolution of your image and crop it to size all at the same time using the Crop Tool in Photoshop.

First find the exact size of your image's frame or bounding box in InDesign. Switch to InDesign, select your image with the Selection Tool, then look for the width and height displayed in the Control Panel at the top. Write down the dimensions and also note how the image is cropped.

Switch back to Photoshop and click on the Crop Tool (�) in your Toolbox on the left. The crop menu will appear at the top of your screen. Make the selections as shown below, and type in your image dimensions (followed by "in" for inches). You'll see a crop frame in front of your image, changing size and shape as you do this.

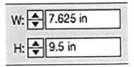

Width and height shown in the Control panel.

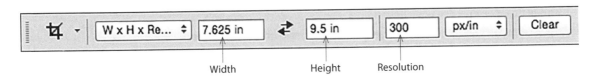

Width Height Resolution

Cropping in Photoshop gets rid of unneeded data and keeps your book's file size down.

Drag any handle on the crop frame and the frame will get proportionately larger or smaller. Use this frame to crop your image to the way it looks in InDesign. When you're satisfied, press Enter/Return. Now your image is 300 ppi at the exact size it's placed in InDesign. Voilà!

An easy workflow for optimizing your images

There are so many instructions and options in this chapter! To help you make sense of it all, this sidebar offers a summary of the steps to optimize an image and then put your improved image on your book page in place of the old one. These are the most important procedures, gathered into one place. Here's what you do:

To optimize PSD, TIF, JPG, or PNG files

1 Open Photoshop and InDesign at the same time. In InDesign, select an image with the Selection Tool. Find the width and height of the image in the Control panel. Write down the dimensions, noting how the image is cropped.

2 In Photoshop, if the effective resolution is 300 ppi or higher, size and crop the image. Using the Crop Tool ( ), fill in the width and height and 300 px/in in the top menu, adjust the frame around the image until it matches the visible parts on your book page, then press Enter/Return (see page 304); *or*, if the effective ppi is too low, resample the image (see page 306).

3 Convert the image to the correct color mode: CMYK, Grayscale, or Bitmap. To convert to CMYK or Grayscale, click Edit>Convert to Profile, then choose the appropriate color profile from the Profile drop-down menu under Destination Space (see pages 307–309). To convert to Bitmap, see page 310.

4 If you need to improve the colors and/or contrast in your image, complete the steps on page 313.

5 Flatten the layers (if you choose to do so) by clicking Layer>Flatten Image (see page 314).

6 Save the image as a PSD file by clicking File>Save As and choosing PSD (see page 315).

7 Return to InDesign and relink the image. Select the image frame with your Selection Tool, then open your Links panel, click on Relink ( ), and find your new optimized file (see page 317).

To optimize AI or EPS files

1 Open Illustrator and InDesign at the same time.

2 In Illustrator, convert the image to the correct color mode, CMYK or Grayscale. To convert to CMYK, click Edit>Assign Profile, then choose the appropriate color profile from the Profile drop-down menu (see page 311). To convert to grayscale, select the entire image by dragging over it from outside the top left corner to beyond the bottom right corner. Click Edit>Edit Colors>Convert to Grayscale (see page 312).

3 Convert any type in the image to outlines. Select the type with your Selection Tool, then click Type>Create Outlines (see page 312).

4 Save the image as an AI file by clicking File>Save As and choosing AI (see page 316).

5 Return to InDesign and relink the image. Select the image frame with your Selection Tool, then open your Links panel, click on Relink ( ), and find your new optimized file (see page 317).

Remember that you packaged your links in chapter 45. So your original images are still in their old locations, and you're now going to optimize the images in the Links folder of your new package. You can name your optimized files with the same file names as the originals (although they may have new file extensions) without worrying about mixing them up or losing your original image files in case you need them later.

Resolving too-low ppi issues by resampling

Let's say you're using an image in your book that you've found on the Internet (with permission, of course). When you check the actual ppi of the image in your Links panel in InDesign, it's 72 ppi (the standard resolution of images intended for viewing onscreen).

Make a good effort to find a higher resolution version of your image before using this method.

In addition to this, you may have enlarged and/or cropped the image when you placed it in InDesign, so its effective ppi is now even lower. Yikes! You could simply change the resolution of your image to 300 ppi in Photoshop, but you'll likely end up with a very blurry image, one that isn't good enough quality to print in your book.

If you want to use an image at a much larger size than its current resolution allows, you'll need to resample the image by enlarging it to an enormous size, sharpening it, then reducing it back to the size you want. Use this type of drastic resampling as a last resort, only if you really can't find a better or higher-resolution version of the image. The results are almost never as sharp as you'd like.

Here are the steps:

- First you'll enlarge your image. In Photoshop, open your Image Size dialog box by clicking Image>Image Size. Fill in the dialog box as shown below. Experiment with other setting in the Resample box while looking at the preview. Then click OK, and Photoshop will do its best to make the resulting huge image look good.

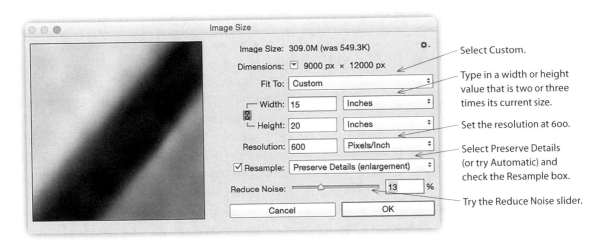

Select Custom.

Type in a width or height value that is two or three times its current size.

Set the resolution at 600.

Select Preserve Details (or try Automatic) and check the Resample box.

Try the Reduce Noise slider.

- Now your image will be huge—in fact, it probably won't fit on your screen. Reduce its display size so you can see the whole image on your screen by pressing Ctrl/Cmd+- (hyphen) as many times as you need to.

- Next, you'll sharpen your image. Open the Unsharp Mask dialog box by clicking Filter>Sharpen>Unsharp Mask. With the Preview box checked, you'll be looking at a small sample of your image. Hover over the sample with your mouse and you'll see a hand tool you can use to move around within your image. Or you can click anywhere in the image itself to see a sample of that area to view the most important parts of the image as you work. Move the three sliders left and right until you get the best possible effect. At this size, no image is going to look great, so use the little zoom tools to see smaller and larger views. You can always undo your work with Ctrl/Cmd+Z, or Edit>Undo, or Edit>Step Backward. If you need more fine-tuning, try the Filter>Noise>Reduce Noise sliders.

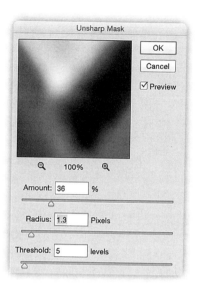

- Finally, you'll size and crop your image to the exact size it's placed at in InDesign. To do this, follow the instructions under Sizing and Cropping an Image on page 304.

3 Converting your images to a color profile

Your images will most likely be printed with black ink only (for book pages) or with CMYK ink colors (for color pages and your book cover). Before you optimize any of the colors in an image or change the level of contrast, you'll want to see how that image will look when it's printed. Converting an image to a suitable color profile will show you that.

Images coming from cameras and scanners are in RGB color. There is a much larger range (or gamut) of colors available in RGB than in CMYK. An image may look fabulous onscreen, with lots of light, bright greens and glowing oranges, but you may find those lustrous colors can't be printed using the four CMYK ink colors. That's why color profiles are helpful.

If you already know where your book will be printed, find out from your printer what color profile you should use. POD printers, such as IngramSpark and CreateSpace, don't provide color profiles, but Photoshop comes with lots of generic color profiles to choose from.

See page 257 for an explanation of RGB and CMYK colors.

If your printer provides you with a color profile, it'll be a file with the extension .icc. Unzip it if necessary, and save the file to your desktop. To install it in Windows, right-click the file and select Install Profile. To install it on a Mac, copy the file to Computer\Macintosh HD\Library\ColorSync\ Profiles. Once it's installed, you can select the profile in Photoshop and Illustrator.

Converting RGB images to CMYK in Photoshop

You've checked the color space of your images in the Links panel in InDesign, and chances are you have at least a few RGB images to convert to CMYK. So open your image in Photoshop, then open the Convert to Profile dialog box by clicking Edit>Convert to Profile.

Below you'll see the Convert to Profile dialog box. The Source Space shows which profile your image is in right now. It probably says Adobe RGB (1998) or another RGB profile.

You'll choose a CMYK color profile for your Destination Space. Read the options below, then choose a profile for your Destination Space:

- **CreateSpace, IngramSpark, and other POD printers** POD printers don't specify color profiles; however, their PDF instructions include exporting to the default "Working CMYK - U.S. Web Coated (SWOP) v2" color profile, so you'll be fine choosing that one.
- **Offset printer** Find out which color profile your printer uses from their website and download it, or ask them to provide it to you.
- **Not sure?** If you're in doubt, choose U.S. Sheetfed Coated v2 for color images on your cover and color pages.

Check the Preview box.

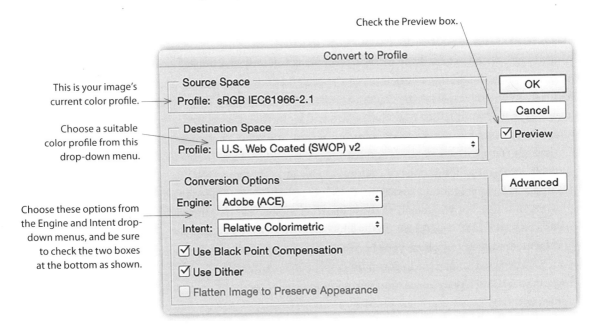

This is your image's current color profile.

Choose a suitable color profile from this drop-down menu.

Choose these options from the Engine and Intent drop-down menus, and be sure to check the two boxes at the bottom as shown.

Converting color images to grayscale in Photoshop

If your pages will be printed with black ink only, then you'll need to convert any color *photographs* to grayscale. If you have any images that are black and white only (with *no* shades of gray), those images are considered "line art" and will be treated differently (see below).

Grayscale means that, in addition to black and white, your image contains many shades of gray (such as in a photograph).

To convert a color image to grayscale, open your image in Photoshop, then open the Convert to Profile dialog box by clicking Edit>Convert to Profile. In the Destination Space drop-down menu, choose the Gray Gamma 2.2 profile. You'll see your image change to grayscale right away. Select the options shown below, and click OK.

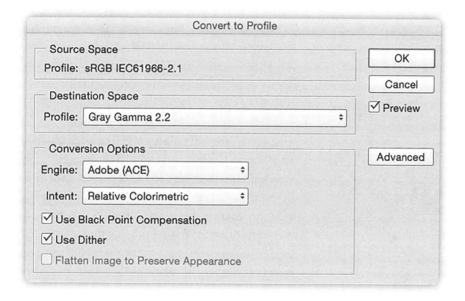

Converting black and white images to bitmap in Photoshop

If you have an image that's black and white (with *no* shades of gray), you'll convert it to a bitmap (unless it's an EPS or AI file, in which case you'll convert the color in Illustrator; see page 312).

Line art differs from photographs because it needs to be saved at a much higher resolution (1200 ppi) so it doesn't look blurry. The bitmap format (BMP) saves high-resolution images at a very small file size because it only saves black pixels (white areas become transparent in InDesign).

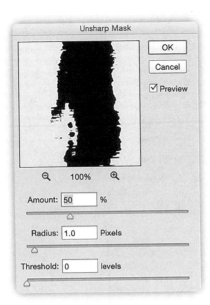

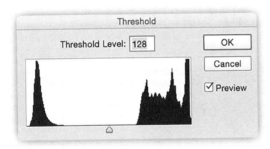

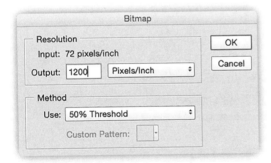

50% Threshold means that any shade of black higher than 50% will become black, and anything less will become white.

Here are the four steps to creating bitmaps:

- First add some contrast to your image using Image>Adjustments>Brightness/Contrast.

- Then you'll use Unsharp Mask to sharpen the edges of your image. This creates a sharp difference between the black and white, to help differentiate them as much as possible. So click Filter>Sharpen>Unsharp Mask to open the Unsharp Mask dialog box. Adjust the settings as shown at left, then click OK. Now you'll repeat this step once more, but can now do so quickly by clicking Filter then Unsharp Mask (which now shows at the top of the Filter drop-down menu), or by simply pressing Ctrl/Cmd+F.

- Next, click Image>Adjustments>Threshold to open your Threshold dialog box (see left). Move the slider to the left and right to see how the threshold level affects your image. Find a place on the slider where the blacks in your image are solid, yet there aren't any black spots or specks in the white areas. You'll probably find you need to move the slider a bit to the right from its default setting of 128 to get solid blacks and clear whites. Then click OK.

- Finally, convert your image to a bitmap by clicking Image>Mode>Grayscale. You'll get a message asking whether it's okay to discard color information, so click Discard. Then click Image>Mode>Bitmap to open your Bitmap dialog box. Set Output to 1200 ppi and choose 50% Threshold, as shown at left. Then save as a PSD file (see page 315).

Converting RGB images to CMYK in Illustrator

Start by opening your image in Illustrator. If the image was created in a previous version of Illustrator, you might get a warning screen that says "This file contains text that was created in a previous version of Illustrator. This legacy text must be updated before you can edit it." Click Update.

To find out the current color space of the image, look at the tab at the top of your screen, where the file name is shown. If it says RGB, then open the Assign Profile dialog box by clicking Edit>Assign Profile.

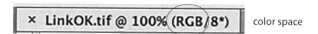 color space

Aside from the color space, the tab also shows the current zoom level (100% in this example).

Below you'll see the Assign Profile dialog box. Read the menu options, then choose a CMYK profile for your image:

- **Createspace, Ingram Spark, and other POD printers** POD printers don't specify color profiles, however their PDF instructions include exporting to the default "Working CMYK - U.S. Web Coated (SWOP) v2" color profile, so you should be fine choosing that one.

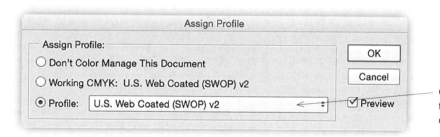

Choose a color profile from the Profile drop-down menu.

- **Offset printer** On your printer's website, find out which color profile your printer uses and download it, or ask them to provide it to you. If you receive one, it will be a file with the extension .icc. Unzip it if necessary, and save the file to your desktop. To install it in Windows, right-click the file and select Install Profile. To install it on a Mac, copy the file to Computer\Macintosh HD\Library\ColorSync\Profiles.
- **Not sure?** If you're in doubt, choose U.S. Sheetfed Coated v2 for color images on your cover and color pages.

These are the same instructions given on page 307. If you already have the profile, there's no need to install it again.

Converting color images to grayscale in Illustrator

Open your image in Illustrator. If the image was created in a previous version of Illustrator, you might get the same warning screen as described on page 311. If so, click Update.

Using your Selection Tool (it looks just like the Selection Tool in InDesign), select the entire image by dragging over it from outside the top left corner to beyond the bottom right corner. Click Edit>Edit Colors>Convert to Grayscale. All the artwork in your image will turn to black and shades of gray.

Converting type to outlines in Illustrator

If your image has any type in it, and especially if the illustration was drawn by someone else, you should convert all of the type to outlines. (If someone else drew the illustrations, instruct them to do this before they send the art to you.) This action converts the letters to shapes so they'll always print properly, regardless of whether or not you have the exact typeface installed on your computer. After the type is converted to outlines, the words can no longer be edited. So before you work with this file, be sure to save it as a copy (File>Save a Copy) or give it a new file name so you can go back to the original later if necessary.

Select the type by clicking on it with your Selection Tool (it looks just like the Selection Tool in InDesign), then click Type>Create Outlines. Notice that each letter suddenly has many anchor points and you could alter its shape if you wanted to (but don't). Repeat this operation until all of the type in your image has been converted to outlines.

Anchor points in Illustrator are like the ones you see when you draw a shape in InDesign. Each point is movable (see page 268) with the Direct Selection Tool.

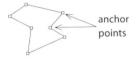

anchor points

Select some type and you'll see a line under it. →

← After the type is converted to outlines, it'll have anchor points just like shapes in InDesign.

You might find it interesting to note that you can create type outlines in an InDesign file, too, using this same method. In that way, you can insert an image inside a letter, using the letter shape as the image frame.

4   Improving the colors and/or contrast in your images

In this section you'll try to make your images look better in just a few quick and easy steps in Photoshop. Save different versions of the image so you can easily get back to earlier ones if you like them more.

Use these suggestions for color or grayscale photographs (but not for bitmaps, EPS, or AI files).

- **Basic levels** Open your photo. Click Image>Adjustments>Levels and, with the Preview box checked, click Auto (right). If you think the photo is improved, click OK. If not, click Cancel.

- **Brightening** You can enhance what you did in the previous step with the Brightness/Contrast feature. Click Image>Adjustments>Brightness/Contrast. Use the sliders to change whatever you like (see below). Have fun playing with the effects, but it's best to be conservative. A good rule of thumb is to make changes of less than 20% to keep your photos looking realistic.

- **Sharpening** If you'd like to sharpen or soften your photo a bit, click Filter>Sharpen>Unsharp Mask. With the Preview box checked, you will be looking at a small sample of the photo, and if you hover over the sample with your mouse you'll see a hand tool that you can use to move around to view the most important part of the photo as you work. Now move the three sliders left and right until you get the effect that you want (see top of page 310).

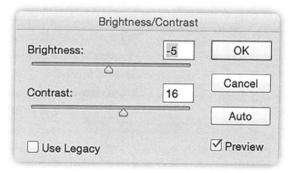

- **Beyond the basics** Since the entire reason for Photoshop's existence is to improve the way photos look, there are dozens of other things you can do to your images. Feel free to explore and experiment, but don't forget to save, save, save!

5 Saving your image files

Now that you've optimized your images, in either Photoshop or Illustrator, be sure to save your files. When you packaged your InDesign file (in chapter 45), copies of all your original image files were saved in a new folder together with your InDesign file. That is the folder you're working in now, so all your original image files are still intact in their original locations. That's good, as you may want to go back to one of those uncropped RGB images down the road.

You'll want to use your RGB images in your ebook.

Image file size is an especially important issue in an ebook.

All of your updated images will be saved in your new packaged folder under the same names, although some will have different file extensions. So there's no need to worry about overwriting your original images or losing any original image files.

Flattening layers in Photoshop—yes or no?

Photoshop and Illustrator files include layers, just as InDesign files do. You may have purposely created layers in your image file, or your camera or scanner might have automatically saved your image onto a layer. Open your Layers panel by clicking Window>Layers to see whether you have any layers aside from the default Background layer.

Saving an image with layers in Illustrator does not affect its file size, so there's no need to flatten any images in Illustrator.

Saving an image with layers in Photoshop adds to its file size, so if file size is an issue, it makes sense to flatten the layers (i.e., reduce the layers down to a single Background layer) before saving the image for use in your InDesign file. One larger file size isn't a big deal, but if you have several images that aren't flattened, you'll notice a difference. Look at the status bar at the bottom left of your screen and you'll see your flattened/

Flattened file size on the left and unflattened file size on the right.

unflattened file sizes (see example at left). Base your decision on whether or not to flatten the file on the difference in file size. Also be aware that flattening an image adds a white background to any transparent areas within the image, so if your image has transparent areas, don't flatten it.

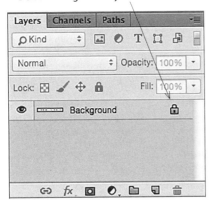

Default Background layer

If you decide to use your layered file in InDesign, save it as a PSD file (see page 315) and place it in your InDesign document. To get back to it quickly for editing while you're working in InDesign, open the Links panel, select the image, go to the flyout menu, choose Edit With, and then choose your version of Photoshop from the list.

If you choose to flatten an image, first save the PSD file *with* its layers intact, in case you want to re-edit the image in the future. Once saved, flatten the layers by clicking Layer>Flatten Image. Click File>Save As to save a flattened copy, and add FLAT to the file name so you'll know it's the flattened file. Then relink it to your InDesign document (see page 317).

Create a separate folder for archiving your layered PSD files. That way they'll be available down the road.

Saving files in Photoshop

Save your optimized images in Photoshop in PSD, TIFF, JPG, or PNG format (in order of preference). PSD is favored for a number of reasons: 1) it saves *all* the image data, unlike the JPG format, which discards much of it to keep the file size small, 2) PSD files can contain more than one layer (although saving with layers will increase the file size), 3) PSDs can be saved with areas that remain transparent when placed in InDesign (see page 403), and 4) PSDs can be edited from within InDesign (see page 314).

Save your file by clicking File>Save As and choosing a format from the Save as type (PC) or Format (Mac) drop-down menu (below left). Photoshop should default to saving this new file in the same location as the previous one (in the Links folder, where you packaged your InDesign file). If not, browse for the correct folder.

Every time a JPG file is saved, more data is stripped away to reduce the file size. If you want to use this format, work on the image in Photoshop (PSD) format, then save to JPG when you are completely finished with it.

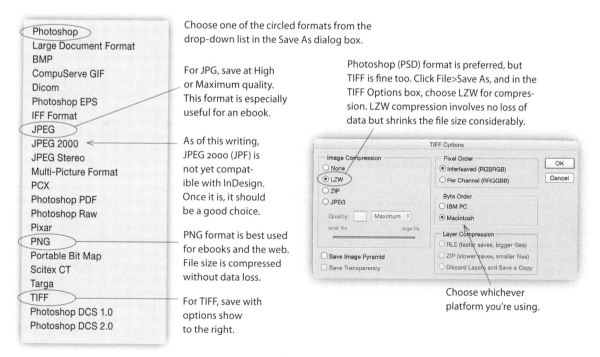

Choose one of the circled formats from the drop-down list in the Save As dialog box.

For JPG, save at High or Maximum quality. This format is especially useful for an ebook.

As of this writing, JPEG 2000 (JPF) is not yet compatible with InDesign. Once it is, it should be a good choice.

PNG format is best used for ebooks and the web. File size is compressed without data loss.

For TIFF, save with options show to the right.

Photoshop (PSD) format is preferred, but TIFF is fine too. Click File>Save As, and in the TIFF Options box, choose LZW for compression. LZW compression involves no loss of data but shrinks the file size considerably.

Choose whichever platform you're using.

Saving files in Illustrator

Save your optimized image in Illustrator by clicking File>Save As and choosing AI from the Save as type (PC) or Format (Mac) drop-down menu (see top and left below). It should default to saving this new file in the same location as the previous one (in the Links folder, where you packaged your InDesign file). Then click Save and you'll see the Illustrator Options dialog box appear with the default settings as shown at the bottom right. Click OK to save your image.

Choose AI as your file type.

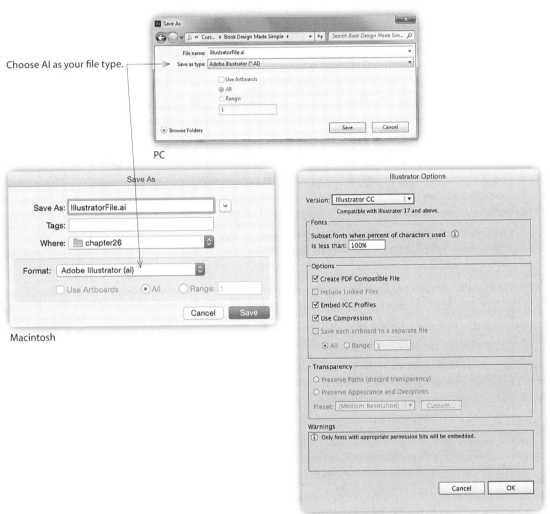

PC

Macintosh

6   Relinking your images to the InDesign file

When you've finished optimizing and saving an image, you'll need to relink it in your InDesign file. Go back to your InDesign file and select the image using your Selection Tool. You'll see that the image file name is highlighted in the Links panel (the old, pre-optimized file name, possibly with a file extension that you have since changed).

To link your selected image with its newly optimized file, click the Relink icon (⊖), browse for your optimized file, then click Open. If you resized the image in Photoshop, it won't be positioned in the frame exactly the way you had it before, so press Ctrl/Cmd+Alt/Opt+E to refit the image to the frame.

If you optimized an image and itsmation point symbol next to the image file name in the Links panel. Click on the Update Link icon, and the linked file will be updated. Again, if the image isn't positioned in the frame exactly the way you had it before, press Ctrl/Cmd+Alt/Opt+E to refit the image to the frame.

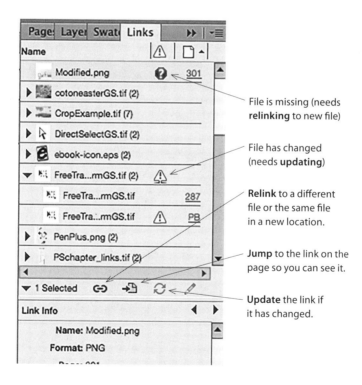

File is missing (needs **relinking** to new file)

File has changed (needs **updating**)

Relink to a different file or the same file in a new location.

Jump to the link on the page so you can see it.

Update the link if it has changed.

In Part VI: Adding Images, you set up your baseline grid and added all your images and captions to your pages. This changed the flow of text on your pages and probably created more pages than you had before.

And now that you've designed all the elements on your pages and applied paragraph, character, and object styles to them, your text and images are pretty much in their final places.

That's a huge accomplishment!

You're ready to do your third and final pass through your book. In Part VII: Typesetting, you'll fine-tune your text, paragraphs, and pages so that every 2-page spread looks perfectly professional.

You're nearly there!

Part VII: Typesetting

Planning your final pass

Your book pages are now substantially complete. You've added styles to all your text and placed your images and captions. You're ready for your final pass through all the pages.

Why do another pass? You've probably noticed that even though you've added styles to all your text, some of the text still requires some polishing. When you placed your images, your type probably moved around a good deal. And, if you intend to print more than 1,000 copies of your book, you'll probably use an offset press, so you'll want to review chapter 48 and adjust the page count in your book for the most cost effective printing.

Once you've finalized all your pages, you'll create a separate master page for each chapter in your book (unless it's a novel) and apply the appropriate one to all your chapters. At this stage, your book will be ready for proofreading and, after you've made the proofreading corrections to your pages, it'll be ready for indexing (if you intend to include an index). Adding and typesetting the index is the last thing you'll need to do.

So get started on your final pass. If you'll be using a print-on-demand printer or digital printing, skip chapter 48 about page count, and carry on with chapter 49.

Page count for offset printing

If your book will be printed digitally, there's no need to worry about page count, because your book can have any even number of pages.

However, if your book will be printed on a press, you'll need to consider your page count. Because large sheets of paper are used on presses, several pages of your book will be printed on one sheet of paper, then folded and trimmed. Depending on the printer's sheet size and the trim size of your book, each sheet usually holds 8, 16, 32, or 48 pages. The folded sheets are called signatures, and the signatures are bound together to form a book.

Reminder: In a book, every single page is counted, whether a page number is showing or not.

Example of an 8-page signature

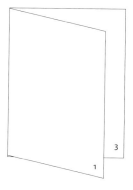

Take a sheet of paper and fold it in half. You'll have 4 pages.

Fold it in half again, and you'll have 8 pages.

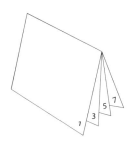

Number the pages as if they are pages in a book, then unfold your sheet of paper. The two sides of your paper will look like this:

L	8
4	5

⌐	ᄅ
6	3

The way the pages are positioned on each side of the sheet is called imposition, and your printer will do this for you. One sheet of paper with 8 pages printed on it is an 8-page signature.

Why page count is important for offset printing
Signatures

Ask your printer for the number of pages per signature for *your* book.

Books printed on a press need to have their pages fit into signatures. It is most cost-effective to print in 32-page signatures for a sheet-fed press or 48-page signatures for a web press (explained on page 22).

Perceived value

If you have a slim volume, consider increasing your page count to give potential readers a greater perceived value and to command a higher price for your book. For example, you may want your novel to be over 200 pages so it will be a similar size to other novels selling for the same price.

Minimizing production costs

If you have a tight budget, you can reduce your page count to keep your production costs lower. With a lower page count, your proofreading, indexing, printing, and shipping costs will all be lower.

How close is your current page count to signatures?

Check the chart below. What is the closest page count you can work toward? If your book currently has, say, 232 pages, you can work toward 224 or 256 pages (32s) or 240 pages (48s).

	32-page signatures (for an offset sheet-fed press; best if you have top-quality images for coffee-table or children's books)	**48-page signatures** (for an offset web press; cheaper if you have b&w images only and don't need top-quality images)
1	32	48
2	64	96
3	96	144
4	128	192
5	160	240
6	192	288
7	224	336
8	256	384
9	288	432
10	320	480
11	352	528
12	384	576
	etc.	etc.

If your page count lands between two signatures, then consider including a half-signature. This usually costs very slightly more but is often well worth it.

Some printers allow quarter-signatures. Again, the cost is slightly more, but may be worth it to you.

Easy ways to increase your page count

See which ideas will work the best for *your* book. It's easiest to implement these changes before adding shapes and images as the text will reflow.

1 **Add blank pages at the back** Easy, right? Simply add blank pages at the back of your book if you're a few pages short of your optimum page count. No one will notice. Two blank pages actually become only one blank sheet of paper, so even if you have six or eight blank pages at the back, there will only be three or four blank sheets.

2 **Add testimonials at the front** Add two new pages at the very front of your book and put testimonials or reviews there. If you have a lot of these, you may need to add several pages, but always add an even number so your title page or half title page starts on a recto page.

3 **Spread out your front matter** Add a half title page followed by a blank page, so that your title page is now on page iii. That will add two pages to your front matter. Sometimes the Contents can be spread over two pages rather than one full page. Consider adding an epigraph on a recto page, followed by a blank page, thereby adding two more pages. If your front matter is fairly lengthy (more than, say, six pages), consider adding two pages at the end of it, just before chapter 1, with a second half title page on the recto side and a blank page following it. Having spacious front matter is a good way to create extra pages without having to change any of your chapters.

4 **Start each chapter on a recto page** Add a blank verso page to the end of every chapter that ends on a recto page. It's an easy way to add a few extra blank pages without being obvious. However, if this creates way too many blank pages, then reconsider. You don't want your book to look padded.

5 **Start each chapter farther down the page** Add more space before your Chapter Number (**cn**) and Chapter Title (**ct**) paragraph styles. They don't have to be at the top of the page. This can give some chapters an extra page, thereby adding to your overall page count.

6   **Create new parts** Divide your book into parts. Add two new pages at the beginning of each part. On the recto page, put the part number and title (see chapter 24), and leave the verso page following it blank.

7   **Increase your margins** Generous margins look attractive. The margins in your current document (as set up in chapter 7) are very conservative to keep your page count and production costs as low as possible. However, if you want to create more pages, then increasing your margins is a good way to do so (see chapter 20).

8   **Increase your type size and/or leading** Even a slight increase—from, say, 11/14 to 11.5/14.5—can create extra pages (see chapter 22). Remember to change your baseline grid to match the new leading.

9   **Change your trim size** It sounds drastic but can be a simple fix. If your trim size is 6″ × 9″, changing it to 5.5″ × 8.5″ or 5″ × 8″ can make a difference of several pages (see chapter 19).

10 **Use drop folios** Books often have running heads and folios in the top margin. Moving the folios to the bottom of the page requires a larger bottom margin, thereby reducing the number of text lines per page.

Decorative rules allow this page to be 4 lines shorter.

11 **Add a decorative rule to the top and bottom of each page, between the text block and the running head and folio** This is a great way to reduce the number of text lines on each page by two or four without being obvious. The top and bottom margins will be even bigger, to allow a horizontal line to separate the running heads at the top and folios at the bottom from the text block.

12 **Spread out your back matter** Redesign your back matter headings so they occupy more space at the top of the page. Increase the type size and leading (but never make these larger than your main text type). Decrease the number of columns in your endnotes and index. Add a recto page inviting readers to visit your website, followed by a blank page. Add a page about the author, with a photo and bio.

Easy ways to decrease your page count

1 Remove all unnecessary blank pages Your title page, chapter 1, and the first section of your back matter must all begin on recto pages, but everything else can just follow on.

2 Condense your front matter Don't include a half title page. Use a smaller type size on the copyright page and include the acknowledgments and/or dedication on the copyright page.

3 Condense your chapter openings Start each chapter at or close to the top of the page. Consider placing your chapter number and title on the same line to save space (see page 158).

4 Running chapter titles To save even more space, start each chapter immediately below the previous chapter (see example at right). Create a two- to four-line Space Before in the Chapter Title (**ct**) paragraph style to make the chapter openings obvious so your readers can easily identify them.

5 Create new parts by adding a part number and/or title just before the chapter title that follows it Instead of using two whole pages for a part divider, add a heading at the top of a new page (Part II—Title, for example), followed immediately by the next chapter title.

6 Decrease your margins Reducing your margins can make a difference to your page count, as long as your pages don't look cramped (see chapter 20). Most printers require a minimum of 0.5″ on all margins, except 0.75″ for the inside margin.

a running chapter title

ALICE IN WONDERLAND

two people! Why, there's hardly enough of me left to make ONE respectable person!'

Soon her eye fell on a little glass box that was lying under the table: she opened it, and found in it a very small cake, on which the words 'EAT ME' were beautifully marked in currants. 'Well, I'll eat it,' said Alice, 'and if it makes me grow larger, I can reach the key; and if it makes me grow smaller, I can creep under the door; so either way I'll get into the garden, and I don't care which happens!'

She ate a little bit, and said anxiously to herself, 'Which way? Which way?', holding her hand on the top of her head to feel which way it was growing, and she was quite surprised to find that she remained the same size: to be sure, this generally happens when one eats cake, but Alice had got so much into the way of expecting nothing but out-of-the-way things to happen, that it seemed quite dull and stupid for life to go on in the common way.

So she set to work, and very soon finished off the cake.

THE POOL OF TEARS

'Curiouser and curiouser!' cried Alice (she was so much surprised, that for the moment she quite forgot how to speak good English); 'now I'm opening out like the largest telescope that ever was! Good-bye, feet!' (for when she looked down at her feet, they seemed to be almost out of sight, they were getting so far off). 'Oh, my poor little feet, I wonder who will put on your shoes and stockings for you now, dears? I'm sure _I_ shan't be able! I shall be a great deal too far off to trouble myself about you: you must manage the best way you can;—but I must be kind to them,' thought Alice, 'or perhaps they won't walk the way I want to go! Let me see: I'll give them a new pair of boots every Christmas.' And she went on planning to herself how she would manage it. 'They must go by the carrier,' she

28

7 **Decrease your type size and/or leading** Even a slight decrease—from, say, 11/14 to 10.5/13.5—can reduce the number of pages (see chapter 22).

8 **Change your trim size** If your trim size is 5″ × 8″, changing it to 5.5″ × 8.5″ or 6″ × 9″ can make a difference of several pages (see chapter 19).

9 **Decrease the type size and/or leading in your back matter** Back matter is often set one or two points smaller than the main text, particularly for bibliographies, references, glossaries, and indexes. Increase the number of columns in your endnotes and index. (Sometimes, though, adding a column produces the opposite effect and actually adds pages!)

As you can see, there are many ways to increase or decrease your page count. Some are easy, and some are a bit more complicated, requiring changes to paragraph styles.

During your final pass, keep in mind your goal of increasing or decreasing your page count. You may find ways of adding a page to or removing a page from every chapter.

Adding, deleting, and moving text, pages, and styles

As you go through your final pass, you may find places where you want to add or remove pages, or perhaps move some pages to a different place in your book (say, move your Acknowledgments from the front matter to the back matter). You can even move pages to a different book! You might want to do this if you're planning two different editions or a series.

This chapter explains how to:

- Link and unlink text frames
- Add new pages
- Remove pages
- Move pages within the same document or to a new document
- Transfer styles from one InDesign document to another

InDesign has some ways of handling text flow that aren't immediately apparent. For example, if you delete a page using the Pages panel, you'll find that the text is still there within your linked text frames, and InDesign has simply added a new page to the end of your book so that no text is hidden (remember Smart Text Reflow was enabled in your Preferences, on page 30).

Linking and unlinking text frames

Before you decide to move pages in your book, think about whether linking or unlinking text frames might accomplish your objective. It's important to understand how text threads work so you can change them if necessary. Make sure you can see your text threads before you begin (View>Extras>Show Text Threads), then follow the steps on the next pages for the variations on linking and unlinking text frames.

Linking a new empty text frame

In InDesign you can easily insert a new, empty text frame into a chain of already linked frames. Here's how:

If you draw a frame with the Selection Tool or a shape tool, you can convert it to a text frame in one click by going to Object>Content and choosing Text, or by clicking inside it with the Text Tool.

1 Draw a new text frame with the Type Tool.
2 Using the Selection Tool, click on the out port of the frame you want to appear *before* the new frame.
3 Click the loaded text icon inside the new text frame and the text from the previous frame will flow into the new one. Text that follows will also be threaded from the new frame.

Linking a full text frame

Anytime you're in the middle of an operation, with a loaded text icon to place, and you change your mind, simply go to the Toolbox and click on any tool. Your original operation will be cancelled and you can start over.

If you have a text frame that already has text in it, you can link it to the beginning of a series of full, threaded frames, or to the end, but not to the middle of the series. To add a full frame to the *beginning* of a series, follow these two steps:

1 Click on the out port of the new full frame.
2 Click the loaded text icon at the upper left of the frame you want to link to. Your text will flow together.

To add an already full frame to the *end* of a series:

1 Click on the out port of the last full frame in the series.
2 Click the loaded text icon at the upper left of the frame you want to add. The text will flow together.

To link text in the *middle* of a series of threaded frames, you'll copy and paste instead:

1 Use the Type Tool to copy (Ctrl/Cmd+C) or cut (Ctrl/Cmd+X) the text you want to add.
2 Put your cursor in the text where you want the copy to appear and paste (Ctrl/Cmd+V) the copy.
3 Using the Selection Tool, delete the text frame that it came from.

Unlinking text frames

This operation is simple. In order to unlink text frames, do the following:

1 Using the Selection Tool, double-click on the out port of the frame you want to keep. The type disappears from the second frame.
2 The first frame will have the red overset text symbol (⊞) at the out port. Either extend the text frame to fit the overset text, or make a new text frame, click on the out port, and then click again inside the new text frame. The overset text will flow into the new frame.

Perhaps you simply want to delete one text frame from a series. All you have to do is to delete it using the Selection Tool, and the copy that was in it will flow to the next frame.

Overset text is text that does not fit in the text frame.

Keep in mind that Smart Text Reflow was enabled in your Preferences on page 30, and InDesign will auto-matically create more pages to reflow overset text. If you want to manually control the flow of your text frames, just uncheck this feature in Preferences>Type.

Adding, deleting, and moving pages

Before you add, delete, or move any pages, look at your Pages panel. Go to the fly-out menu, and make sure that Allow Document Pages to Shuffle and Allow Selected Spread to Shuffle are checked. "Shuffling" in InDesign means that if you add one page, the one after it will move down to the next spread, and all pages after it will move forward too. Without check-ing these two shuffle options, you could end up with more than two pages in your spread, as in the example to the right.

You also have the option of disabling Smart Text Reflow by going to Preferences (InDesign>Preferences on a Mac)>Type and unchecking the Smart Text Reflow box. This will prevent InDesign from adding new pages at the end of your book every time you make a change. If you've fin-ished adding images to your book, you'll find this especially helpful.

Oops! If this happens to you, undo your work (Ctrl/Cmd+Z), check the Allow Document Pages to Shuffle option in the Pages menu, and start over.

Adding new pages

Maybe you have overset text at the end of your book, or you simply need to add a page in the middle. There are two basic ways to do this. Review both methods that follow before you decide which will work better for your circumstance.

Insert a page break

Insert a page break by pressing Enter/Return on your *numeric* keypad, or choosing Type>Insert Break Character>Page Break.

The first method is to simply insert a page break somewhere in your text. A blank page will appear where your cursor is. If Smart Text Reflow is on, all your text will move forward, and a new page will be added at the end of the book.

This might not be the effect you wanted, though, especially if you've already added images to your book, because the images will stay where they were but the text will move forward. If this is the case, try the next method instead.

Use the Pages panel

Open the Pages panel, highlight the page before the one(s) to be inserted, then go to the fly-out menu and select Insert Pages. The dialog box will look something like this:

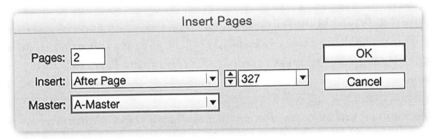

If your layout has elements that need to remain on either verso or recto pages (recto-only chapter openers, for instance), it's best to add an even number of pages.

Type in the number of pages you want to add, which existing page they should follow (Insert: After Page) or precede (Insert: Before Page), and which master page should be applied to the new page(s). Most of the time, A-Master is the correct choice here. If you want a completely blank page, choose [None].

The new pages will be blank, except for folios and running heads. To flow your text onto the new pages, use the Selection Tool to click the out port on the page you want text to flow from, place the loaded cursor at the top of the new page, and click. The text will flow onto the page. Repeat this for all the new pages where you want text to appear. If you look at your text threads now (View>Extras>Show Text Threads), you'll see that the new text frames are joined with the rest. Your new pages will be numbered in sequence (pages 328 and 329 in the example above), and the original pages in this example will be renumbered, starting with 330.

Removing pages

If you delete a page in InDesign, your threaded text does not disappear along with the page; it simply flows forward. To remove pages, go to the Pages panel, select the page(s) you want to delete, and click on the trash can at the bottom of the panel. The following warning will pop up:

If you've disabled Smart Text Reflow, or if your page contains unthreaded material, such as images, you'll only see the upper part of this warning.

You can see from the warning that you'll be adding another page at the end of your book unless you go back and uncheck Smart Text Reflow. If the material on the page is not part of your text flow (some images or a table, for instance), you'll get the same warning but without mention of Smart Text Reflow. If you click OK, any unlinked objects will disappear.

Maybe you want to get rid of a page of copy and also the page itself. To do that, cut (and perhaps paste it somewhere else) or delete the text itself using the Type Tool. You'll see other text flowing onto the page, but that is okay. Next, go to the Pages panel, select the page you want to delete, click on the trash can, and when you see the warning shown above, click OK.

Moving pages in the same document

At any time you can change your mind about where things should go in your book. You might want to move a full-page sidebar somewhere else, or transfer your Acknowledgments from the front matter to the back matter. Because all the text frames in your main narrative are linked, moving pages requires some thought so that your text will still flow properly in your text frames. Choose the best approach for moving *your* pages.

Using the Move Pages feature to move pages with no linked text

In the Pages panel, highlight the page(s) you want to move. Then in the Pages fly-out menu, select Move Pages, and a dialog box will pop up, similar to the one shown below.

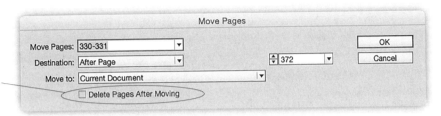

The correct pages should appear in the Move Pages area, so just type in where they should move to, and click OK. The only problem with this method is that any existing text threads move with the pages. This can result in a terrible tangle, with links jumping from page 329 to page 373, 374, and then back to page 330, in this example. Even a small jump in the text threads can be very confusing, so if you have linked text consider using one of the methods listed below, depending on your situation.

Sometimes it's even easier to move pages by dragging thumbnails in the pages panel to new positions.

Moving pages with linked text

1 Using the Type Tool, select all the text on the pages you want to move, then cut it by pressing Ctrl/Cmd+X (the linked text frames will reflow).
2 Go to the new location and insert your cursor at the top of the page. Paste the text there by pressing Ctrl/Cmd+V, and the text will flow in.

Moving pages with linked text, images and captions

If you are moving pages with different types of frames (some linked and some not), then use this method. In InDesign, you can't simultaneously select frames that are on different spreads, so if you're moving pages on different spreads, you'll have to repeat steps 1–4 as many times as necessary.

Uncheck Smart Text Reflow in Preferences>Type to avoid confusion.

1 Add one or two new blank pages in the new location (see page 330).
2 Using the Selection Tool, drag across a whole page or 2-page spread to select all the frames, then press Ctrl/Cmd+X to cut them.

3   In the Pages panel, double-click the page(s) you just added to go there.

4   Still using the Selection Tool, go to Edit>Paste in Place, and the frame(s) will appear on the new page(s). If they were previously threaded together on a spread, they will still be threaded *to each other* on the new pages, but the threads to other pages will now be broken.

5   Go back to the original location, and look at the page immediately following. You'll see that InDesign didn't delete the text in the frames you cut, but just moved it into the next text frame. Select the text you moved using the Type Tool, and delete it by pressing the Delete key.

6   Go to the new location and rethread the text frame(s) to your main narrative (see page 328) if need be.

7   In the Pages panel, select the page(s) you want to delete, and click on the trash can at the bottom of the panel.

Moving pages from one document to another

When you move pages from one document to another, several things move along with them: the paragraph, character, and object styles that are in use on the pages; and the master pages in use.

To move pages from Document A to Document B, go to the Pages panel in Document A and highlight the thumbnails of the pages you want to move. Then in the Pages fly-out menu, select Move Pages. You'll see the dialog box pictured on page 332. Select Document B from the Move to drop-down list and decide whether you want to delete them from Document A or not.

Now check Document B's Pages menu and locate your new pages to make sure they are in the right place. Check your Paragraph Styles and Character Styles panels to make sure that the styles imported along with the copy.

Any document that is open will appear in the Move to drop-down list, so make sure that Document B is open.

Transferring styles from one InDesign document to another

Being able to transfer styles between documents can save you a lot of work if you start a new project. Use the method described on the next page to transfer paragraph, character, and object styles. Paragraph styles are used as an example, but the steps are the same for all.

The same process can be used to transfer color swatches, too. See chapter 31 for more about color.

1   Open the document you want to transfer paragraph styles *into*. Go to the Paragraph Styles fly-out menu and choose Load Paragraph Styles (or Load All Text Styles if you want to deal with your character styles at the same time). In the dialog box, find the document you want to get the styles from, and click Open.

2   You'll see a dialog box like the one below.

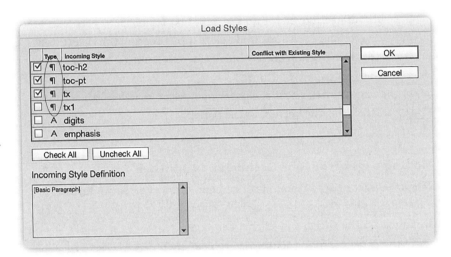

If you choose Load All Text Styles, you will see both paragraph styles (¶) and character styles (A) in the same list.

3   If you want to import all the styles, click on the Check All button. If you only want to select a few styles, click the Uncheck All button, then choose the individual styles you want. If you need a reminder of the settings for any particular style, look at the Incoming Style Definition area, where the settings are described. Then click OK.

4   The styles you want will now appear among your new document's paragraph styles.

You will discover a conflict in style names if you've named your styles the same in both documents. You could rename your styles in one of the documents, or you could use one of the methods described below to deal with this situation:

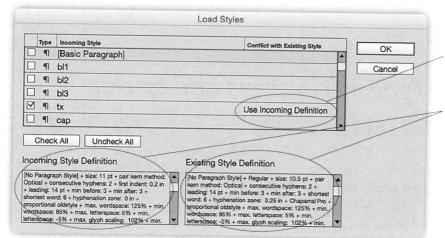

When you highlight a style that has a name conflict, you're given a choice of Use Incoming Style Definition or Auto-Rename. Both the new and the existing styles are defined in the lower part of the dialog box to help you make the decision.

- **To replace the existing style with the new one** If there's a conflict, your Load Styles dialog box will look something like the one above. When you highlight the style that has a conflict, you'll be presented with a menu of choices in the Conflict with Existing Style column. Both style definitions are shown so that you can figure out whether or not to overwrite the existing style with the new style. If you decide to do so, choose Use Incoming Style Definition. Your existing style will disappear.

- **To keep both styles** Highlight the style with the conflict, and choose Auto-Rename in the Conflict with Existing Style column. This will simply import the new style and add "copy" to the end of the style name. You can decide later which style you want to keep, or you can rename or repurpose one of the styles.

You can now see that there are many ways to rearrange your text and pages both within your current document and between documents. We hope these procedures have made it easier for you to avoid confusion while putting everything in your book into the proper order. Once you've accomplished this, save your file with a new file name.

50

Typesetting tips and tricks

Different types of text require different treatments, and you'll learn tips and tricks to make your text look its best, including:

- Kerning for better-looking headings
- Finding and using special characters
- Typesetting punctuation
- Typesetting charts and tables
- Typesetting footnotes
- Adjusting in-line art
- Typesetting math and fractions
- Typesetting poetry

Before you begin, tidy up your Paragraph Styles and Character Styles panels to remove any unused styles. Click on the fly-out menu in each panel, choose Select All Unused, then click the trash can at the bottom. The Delete Paragraph Style dialog box will pop up, and you can replace the styles in question with Basic Paragraph. Check the Apply to All box at the bottom, and click OK.

Now sort your styles into alphabetical order. Click on the fly-out menu in each panel, choose Sort by Name, and your styles will be reordered alphabetically.

Kerning for better-looking headings

To kern is to change the amount of space between two characters. You set up your Basic Paragraph style to use optical kerning, and usually it works quite well, but sometimes adjustments are needed. To kern manually, insert your cursor between two characters. Then either type a number in the kerning box in the Control panel, or use the arrows to fix the space as needed. As with tracking, kerning is measured in thousandths of an em.

In chapter titles and other headings where the type is large, use kerning between letter pairs that look poorly spaced. In general, two letters with straight strokes look better when they are separated a bit, and two letters with curves look better closer together. But every typeface is a bit different, and every pair of letters is a new situation. It's easier to see how the type looks if you're in Preview mode, as InDesign will highlight the kerned letters. (You specified that in Preferences>Composition on page 32. If you find the highlighting distracting or annoying, go to Preferences>Composition and uncheck Custom Tracking/Kerning.)

Check each of your chapter titles and chapter numbers (whether spelled out or arabic numerals), and kern them so that all the characters look evenly spaced. Note that if you kern between some characters and then use tracking in that same paragraph, the kerning values are not affected by the tracking.

What, exactly, is the difference between kerning and tracking? Kerning adjusts the space between two characters, making them farther apart or closer together. Tracking stretches or shrinks the spacing between all the characters and spaces selected (usually several lines or a paragraph) for the purpose of improving the look of the whole paragraph or page.

Finding and using special characters

You may sometimes find yourself trying (and failing) to find a special character on your keyboard. Are you searching for a multiplication sign? A foreign language accent? You'll probably find whatever you need in the Glyphs panel (Type>Glyphs). Make sure you are looking at the correct font, then select the kind of character you need from the Show drop-down list, or look at the entire font. When you move your pointer over the glyphs, their Unicode values and names pop up.

kerning

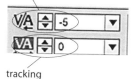

tracking

optical kerning

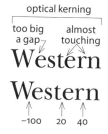

too big a gap   almost touching

−100   20   40

With manual kerning, the spacing within the word looks more even.

The footnote references in your main text may be hard to read, especially if they directly follow quotation marks. Use Find/Change to locate each reference number (**ref** style), then manually add space between the quotation mark and the number, as shown below.

optical kerning

quote."123

quote."123

kern value = 40

If you need to create your own special character, see page 350 for how to add it into your line of type.

Ligatures are pairs or groups of letters that are stuck together as a single character. You set up your Basic Paragraph style to use ligatures automatically. Some examples:

æ ff ffi fl

Ligatures were invented to save space and time when metal type was set by hand. Some fonts have no ligatures at all.

Put the cursor where you want the glyph to appear in your text, then scroll down in the Glyphs panel until you find the character, and double-click it. It will then appear in your text. If you need the same glyph more than once, chances are you'll see it in the Recently Used area at the top of the panel, and you won't have to search for it again. (If you don't see a Recently Used area at the top, click on the up-and-down arrows icon just to the left of the word "Glyphs" in the panel.)

You can learn a lot from studying the Glyphs panel for your typeface. Try comparing oldstyle and lining figures, or discover which ligatures, if any, your font comes with. You might learn some new currency symbols, such as the various signs for the euro and the yen, or the sign for the old Spanish currency, the peseta (₽), that you see highlighted below. And the next time you need an oddball character, you'll know exactly where to start your search.

Recently used glyphs ——→

Choice of glyph set—in this case, the entire font.

Some of the more specialized glyph sets include Basic Latin (Roman alphabet), Extended Latin (with foreign language accents), symbols, math symbols, currency symbols, and Greek.

Your typeface and style ——

Typesetting punctuation
Ellipses

Ellipses (also called ellipsis points) are the series of three or four dots or periods that indicate the omission of words in a quotation, or sometimes a pause. For most written material, they work this way:

- **Use three dots in the middle of a quoted sentence** The dots should have space between them. Don't use the ellipsis character that comes with Word and with InDesign, as *it isn't correct for typesetting.* Instead, set the three dots like this: nonbreaking space, period, nonbreaking space, period, nonbreaking space, period, space. This will force all the dots to appear on the same line. To set a nonbreaking space, go to Type>Insert White Space>Nonbreaking Space, or press Ctrl/Cmd+Alt/Opt+X. It's fine to end a line with the three-dot ellipsis.

- **Add a period if needed** If the ellipsis appears after the end of a sentence, add a normal period for the sentence, then set the space-dot-space-dot-space-dot-space ellipsis, using nonbreaking spaces as before. The period can be on the first line, with the ellipsis following on the next line if necessary.

- **Add other punctuation** If the omission in the quotation occurs just *before* other punctuation, such as a question mark or semicolon, set the ellipsis first, then a space, and the other punctuation. If the omission occurs just *after* other punctuation, set the punctuation, then a space, then the ellipsis.

Very often, the situation is more complicated than in these examples. Ask your editor if you're confused, or consult *The Chicago Manual of Style,* which has the definitive answers for all things relating to ellipsis points.

The Chicago Manual of Style explains the whys and wherefores of ellipses, hyphens, dashes, and punctuation in great detail. This book is every typesetter's friend.

This sentence is interrupted . . . and then continues.

The first quoted sentence ends. . . . Something is omitted, and the quotation continues.

This demonstrates how to use an ellipsis with other punctuation marks . . . ; the semicolon appears *after* some words that were omitted.

This demonstrates how to use an ellipsis with other punctuation marks; . . . the semicolon appears as part of the first phrase, *before* the omitted words.

Hyphens and dashes

Here's what you need to know about hyphens and dashes:

If InDesign hyphenates a word in an awkward place, insert your cursor where you'd prefer to hyphenate the word and press Ctrl/Cmd+Shift+hyphen. This will insert a "soft hyphen" which lets InDesign know where to split the word, if needed.

There is an actual minus sign glyph, and it is slightly different, so you should use that if you have serious math in your book. See pages 350–351.

- **Use a hyphen** (-) in hyphenated words and in phone numbers. Most of the time, hyphens will be set automatically by InDesign at the ends of lines, but if you need a hyphen to stay in place even if it's not at the end of a line, just hit the hyphen key.

- **Use an en dash** (–) between numbers, but not in phone numbers. Type Alt/Opt+hyphen. There is no space before or after an en dash. Never begin a line with an en dash. Note that an en dash can also be used as a minus sign, in which case, *do* set a word space both before and after it in an equation.

  In some countries (such as the UK and Australia), en dashes are used in place of em dashes, with a space before and after them. The best way to set en dashes in books with this style specified is to use a nonbreaking space (Ctrl/Cmd+Alt/Opt+X), then the en dash, followed by a regular word space. That way, the en dash never lands at the beginning of a line of type.

- **Use an em dash** (—) to indicate a sudden break or change of topic within a sentence. Type Alt/Opt+Shift+hyphen. In North America, do not set a space before or after the dash. In some European languages, a thin space (Type>Insert White Space>Thin Space) is used before and after it. Never start a line with an em dash that is used in this way. You may have noticed that many people use a space, en dash, and another space instead of the method just described; this is normal usage in the UK and Australia, but not in North America (see en dashes, above). Never use more than two em dashes in the same sentence—one before the extra phrase and one after it, as in this sentence—otherwise the reader will not understand where you are going with it.

  Another use for an em dash is at the beginning of an epigraph or extract attribution (discussed in chapter 26). Do not set a space between the dash and the writer's name.

Punctuation: roman or italic?

Should punctuation be set in the same style (roman or italic) as the text it follows? Word often makes this decision correctly for you, but you should know the basic rules:

- **Commas** May be set in the same style as the phrase the comma follows (this is more traditional). Or you may set commas always in roman (this is more current). Discuss this issue with your editor, then pick a style and stick with it.

- **Colons, semicolons, question marks,** and **exclamation points** Should almost always be set in the style of the main text surrounding them. But if they are in the middle of a book title or a heading, like the one at the top of this page, set them in the same style as that element.

- **Parentheses ( ) and square brackets [ ]** Are almost always set the same as the surrounding text rather than the text that's enclosed (e.g., [*apparently*]). If an entire italicized parenthetical phrase is sitting on a line by itself, though, set the whole thing in italics. Example:

  (continued on the next page)

  You might notice that the final letter of the italicized type sometimes crashes with the parentheses or brackets (e.g., the final letter in *all*). You should kern (page 337) or set a thin space (Type>Insert White Space>Thin Space) to eliminate this.

- **Periods** Never worry about periods being set in italics, because they look the same both ways.

Punctuation: roman or bold?

For the most part, italics rather than bold type should be used for emphasis. However, if you've used bold type you need to know how to handle the punctuation that accompanies the words. In each instance you should decide whether the punctuation belongs with the bold type or not. See the examples to the right.

Either way is fine.

You may have three, *and only three,* wishes granted. italic

You may have three, *and only three,* wishes granted. roman

What? Only *three*? roman

Maybe you should read *Is This Genie for Real?* italic
Not only is he *real*; he is a genuine genie genius. roman

bold
Hey! What are you doing there?

Didn't you read the sign saying **Keep Out**? roman

Typesetting charts and tables

The table-making function in InDesign is impressively robust, offering more options than you'll find in a word processor. You can import tables from Word and spreadsheets, or create them from scratch in InDesign.

Before you jump into this, though, you might want to explore the available options for your table and learn to use the table selection functions by setting up an experimental table. Make a new text frame on the pasteboard, go to Table>Insert Table, and set up some rows and columns. Hover over the upper left corner of the table with the Type Tool cursor, and an arrow (↘) will appear. Click to select the entire table, then open the Table panel (Window>Type & Tables>Table) to see the range of choices. Once you are familiar with this and how to select rows, columns, and the entire table, you may proceed. But you'll find it helpful to keep your experimental table on the pasteboard so you can try various effects.

Adobe provides video tutorials explaining the many effects you can create, and how to insert graphics and even other tables within the table.

Importing tables

When you imported your Word document, chances are that your tables came in with the rest of the text. And chances are also that they don't fit on your page or something has happened to them in the transition. It's probably best to cut and paste each table into its own new text frame, possibly reimporting them from Word, as described below.

Here are some tricks to try if your imported tables are a real mess:

1 Take the table out of your original Word document and put it in a new Word file.
2 Make a new text frame that's the correct width for your book page. Put your cursor in it, then go to File>Place. Select Show Import Options at the bottom of the panel. Find your Word table file, select it, and click Open.
3 When the Import Options panel appears, in the Formatting area, choose Remove Styles and Formatting from Text and Tables, and "Convert Tables To: Unformatted Tables," unless you *really* need to keep specific layout details of your original table intact.

Though it may be counterintuitive, remember to use the Type Tool to select both type and cells in a table. The Selection Tool won't help at all.

Once your table is imported, continue with these steps:

1   Hold the text cursor over the edge of the table or its columns, and it becomes an arrow (↓, →, ←→, etc.). You'll find that you can stretch or shrink the table and individual columns to fit your space. Note, though, that any table cell with a red dot in the lower right corner has overset text, so resize with caution. You don't need to fix the problem right away, as it might be solved by changing your Table Body paragraph style or your cell inset settings (page 346).

2   Click the type cursor to the left or right of the table, and it becomes the same height as the table (you may need to insert the cursor above or below the table and use the arrow keys to get there). You can then align the table left, right, or center in the text frame by clicking on the appropriate alignment symbol in the Control panel (≣ = left, ≣ = centered, and ≣ = right).

3   To fine-tune the table, select the whole table by clicking your Type Tool at the top left corner, then use the Table>Table Options tools to control the number of rows and columns, add color and rules (called "strokes"), and more. Go to Table>Cell Options to control the appearance of the text in the cells, add strokes and fills, and more.

4   If you have more than one table in your book, save your table style in the Table Styles panel (Window>Styles>Table Styles). Changing the style later will affect all your tables accordingly.

5   Create paragraph styles for your table text using the styles on page 344. If you need more styles—such as numbered or bulleted lists—within your tables, adapt them from others in your book, naming them **tbnl** or **tbbl**, for instance. Styling details for various kinds of table entries are shown on page 345.

6   For a multipage table, you might want to use a footer saying "*(continued on next page)*" in italics at the bottom right of each page (or only on the recto page). The footer looks best if it appears below the table and not as part of the table.

Tables are not easy! But if you've learned how to work with a table that you typed in Word, you can also work with it in InDesign.

Create the styles for text in the tables as paragraph styles. Create styles for other features of the table, such as rule weights, insets, and background colors as table styles, using the Table Styles panel. See page 344.

Even if you don't want or need to save a table style, saving cell styles might cut down on your work within the same table (Window>Styles>Cell Styles).

☐ **Table Body** [tb]   Based On = **tx1**

Changes from the No Indents style (see page 62):

Use Tabular Lining figure style if your tables have numbers that need to line up; otherwise use Proportional Oldstyle.

Basic Character Formats: Size = 10 pt

                                Leading = 11 pt

Indents and Spacing: Align to Grid = None

OpenType Features: Figure Style = Tabular Lining

☐ **Table Column Heads** [tch]   Based On = **tb**

Changes from the Table Body style:

Basic Character Formats: Style = Bold

                                Case = Small Caps

Indents and Spacing: Alignment = Center

☐ **Table Footnotes** [tbftn]   Based On = **tb**

Changes from the Table Body style:

Basic Character Formats: Size = 8.5 pt

                                Leading = 10 pt

The Table menu in the Control panel offers more options than this Table panel, but the panel is sometimes quicker to use, and it's the place to store your table and cell styles. When you're not using it, dock it under the Paragraph Styles panel.

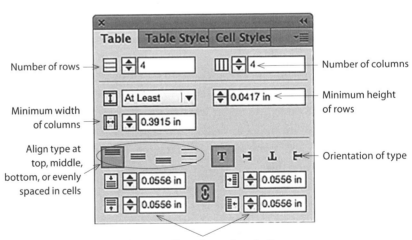

Number of rows

Minimum width of columns

Align type at top, middle, bottom, or evenly spaced in cells

Number of columns

Minimum height of rows

Orientation of type

Amount of inset from edge of cells

Numerals are set up in the Table Body [tb] paragraph style as Tabular Lining so they will line up neatly in columns.

Use a decimal tab (↓) to align whole numbers at right with each other.

Align column heads at the bottom of the cell.

STUB HEAD[2]	TABLE TEXT	TABLE CURRENCY	TABLE DECIMALS	TABLE WHOLE NUMBERS	TABLE DATES
		SPANNER HEAD FOR FOUR COLUMNS[1]			
First category	Description of first category	$1234.59[3]	89.572	764	Jan. 17, 1950
	Another description of first category	467.92	3.4	12	Dec. 17, 1960
Second category	Description of second category	13	9425.467	1,456	July 7, 2012
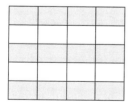	Description of this category	3693.21	15.246	468	Mar. 7, 2004
	With a horizontally split cell	32.01			
Fourth category	Second and fourth categories have a 10% black background.	145.67	468.34		

1 A spanner head relates to more than one column head and is centered over those columns. Always merge columns (select the relevant cells, then go to Table>Merge Cells) for a spanner head.

2 The first column head is sometimes referred to as the *stub head*. It can be centered over the column, or flush left over the column even if the other column heads are centered.

3 When setting up tabs for numbers in a table, simply select the whole column, then use the tabs panel (Type>Tabs) to place a decimal tab. The numbers in the column will automatically align on the tab; don't press the Tab key.

To fill a cell with an image, put your cursor in the cell and go to Table>Cell Options>Graphic. Set all cell insets to 0, check Clip Contents to Cell, and click OK. Then File>Place the image. Move and resize the image inside the cell with the Direct Selection Tool if necessary.

Use a decimal tab (↓) to align decimals and numerals in a column. Slide the tab left or right until the longest number in the column is centered. Whole numbers also align as if they had a decimal.

Table text can be centered vertically in the cell or aligned at the top or bottom (Cell Options>Text).

Use Cell Options to make diagonal lines.

To make the strokes disappear between footnotes, go to Cell Options and make the stroke weight 0.

Alternating rows of a background color can make a table much easier to understand if you want readers to read left to right. If you want them to read down instead, you can make alternating columns.

To the right are the settings for the alternating rows in the simple table on the left (Table>Table Options>Alternating Fills).

| Table Setup | Row Strokes | Column Strokes | Fills | Headers and Footers |

Alternating Pattern: Every Other Row

Alternating

First: 1 Rows   Next: 1 Rows
Color: ■ [Black]   Color: ☑ [None]
Tint: 10% ☐ Overprint   Tint: 100% ☐ Overprint

Skip First: 0 Rows   Skip Last: 0 Rows

☐ Preserve Local Formatting

Building tables in InDesign

InDesign offers so many options that it's sometimes difficult to decide what to choose. Look for tables in other books and figure out what options were used there. Choose a style you like, and if it fits in with the rest of your book design, imitate it.

You can rearrange columns and rows after your table is made. See the Adobe tutorial on that topic.

Naturally, you can also typeset your tables right in InDesign. The principle is the same as for importing tables, but you need to do a bit of prep work before you can start typing your data. Study the example on the previous page. Also, if you haven't done so already, open your Tables panel (Window>Type & Tables>Table). Its functions are shown on page 344.

1   Draw a text frame for the table, or put your cursor at the insertion point in your text (on a new line). Go to Table>Insert Table. Type in the number of columns and rows, and how many of the rows are for headers (column heads, which can be repeated on each page if you so specify) and footers. Include a row for each table footnote that you anticipate having. Then click OK.

2   Type your column heads and data in the cells. Merge or split cells as needed using the options in the fly-out menu on your Table panel.

3   Add paragraph styles (page 344) to all the heads and data.

4   Resize columns and rows using the pointer arrows (↓, →, ↔, etc.), which you access by hovering with the Type Tool. Using these arrows, you can also add and delete columns and rows by first selecting a column or row, then choosing Table>Insert [or Delete]>Row [or Column]. Another option is to make columns equal widths by selecting some adjacent columns and going to Table>Distribute Columns Evenly. Similarly, you can make all adjacent rows equal in height by selecting them and going to Table>Distribute Rows Evenly.

To control strokes and fills, highlight the relevant cells, then go to Table>Cell Options>Strokes and Fills. You'll see a box like the one below with blue outlines representing the sides of the cells. The stroke settings you choose will affect all the blue outlines of the cells. If you don't want a stroke applied to a side, click on that blue side to *deselect* it, then specify the stroke for just the selected sides.

5   Highlight a column of text or numbers, then set up a decimal tab to make them align properly (see examples on page 345). You do *not* need to hit the Tab key to get the text or numbers to line up. Alternatively, you can specify the inset from the left or right side of a column (or an individual cell). Highlight the text in the relevant cells, then go to Table>Cell Options>Text and adjust the Left and Right insets by clicking on the up or down arrows until the material looks centered.

6   Apply stroke and fill styles as needed, including alternating background colors for rows or columns. You can make a table without any visible strokes by specifying "0 pt" as the weight for all strokes in Table Setup, Table Options, and Cell Options. If you want a bit of blank space between columns or rows, insert an empty column or row.

BOOK DESIGN MADE SIMPLE · PART VII: TYPESETTING

Fitting tables on the page

You might find that your table simply doesn't fit on the book page as well as it did in your Word document. Here are some basic ways to deal with a table that's too wide:

- Squeeze the column widths by dragging the sides
- Reduce the type size by adjusting the paragraph styles
- Use a turned table; in other words, turn it 90° counterclockwise on the page. To do this, select the text frame of the table with the Selection Tool, then click once on the counterclockwise arrow (↺) in the Control panel. Squeeze or stretch the table to fit the page dimensions. Once you've sized it properly, you can rotate the table back to its normal orientation to edit it and apply styles as needed, and then rotate it again to place it on the page. If the turned table is smaller than the width of the page, place it so the top or bottom of the table is touching the outside margin.
- Set the table across a two-page spread. You can accomplish this within one table by creating a very wide column in the center, equal to the total width of your two inside margins, or 1″ wide at the very least. If necessary, make a white box (see page 256 and 259) to cover visible elements in that middle column so that it appears to be blank space.

To rotate a table 90 degrees, it'll need to be in its own text frame. To separate a table from the main narrative, select the whole table by hovering the Type Tool over the top left corner to get a diagonal arrow, then clicking once. Cut the table (Ctrl/Cmd+X), drag a new text frame on your pasteboard, and paste the table in it (Ctrl/Cmd+V). Swtich to your Selection Tool, and rotate the table as described to the left.

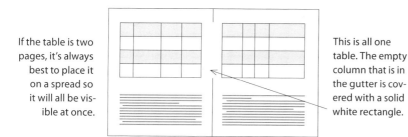

If the table is two pages, it's always best to place it on a spread so it will all be visible at once.

This is all one table. The empty column that is in the gutter is covered with a solid white rectangle.

If your table is too tall, continue it onto another page. Your column heads will automatically repeat at the top of each new page (see step 1 in the instructions on page 346). If the table doesn't completely fill the two pages, it might look better if both pages are of equal length. This is easier said than done, however, so don't waste too much time over it if it's just not working out.

Almost any question you might still have about tables will be answered by a Creative Cloud tutorial. Go to the CC icon on your screen (or open Creative Cloud) and under the Apps tab, click on View Tutorials under InDesign.

Typesetting footnotes

Footnotes in InDesign work much the same way as in Word. If you inserted footnotes in your manuscript, they'll appear at the bottom of the appropriate pages in your book.

If, on the other hand, you want to type or import the footnotes as you go along, put your cursor in the position on the page where the note reference (the asterisk or superscript number) will appear, go to Type>Insert Footnote, then start typing (or copy and paste from another document) the footnote text. It will automatically appear at the bottom of the page, with the proper number in both the reference location and at the start of the note.

Create a paragraph style for your footnotes using the specifications below. Notice that both the type size and the leading are two points smaller than in your Text [**tx**] style.

To fine-tune the footnote layout, open the Footnote Options dialog box by clicking Type>Document Footnote Options. Under the Numbering and Formatting tab, fill in the boxes as shown on page 349. These settings are fine for most books. If you have only a few footnotes, choose the asterisk numbering style, but if you have more than four per chapter, choose arabic numerals.

The Formatting area of the Document Footnote Options refers to the footnote references in the text, so choose "Apply Superscript" next to "Position" if you are using numbers (but not if you are using asterisks). Your Character Style should be None. Under Footnote Formatting, scroll down and select the Footnotes paragraph style [**ftn**] that you just created. The Separator is the space between the footnote number and the footnote

To create the **ref** character style for your footnote reference numbers, see page 85.

Footnote references that are not numbered use a specific set of symbols, in this order:

*, †, ‡, §, **, ††, ‡‡, etc.

In each chapter, start over with *.

If the footnote references in your main text are crashing with quotation marks, kern as shown on page 337.

☐ **Footnotes [ftn]**
Changes from the Text style (see page 62):
Basic Character Formats:

Indents and Spacing:

Based On = **tx**

Size = 9 pt
Leading = 12 pt
First Line Indent = 12 pt *or* 0.1667 in
Align to Grid = None

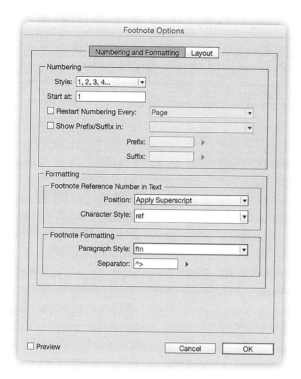
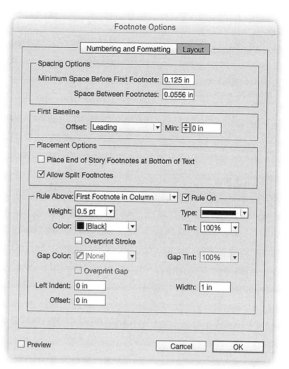

text. Use the drop-down list to go to En Space, which appears as "^>" in the dialog box. If other symbols show up in the box, simply delete them.

Moving on to the Layout tab (above right), set the minimum space before the first footnote at 0.125 in. This will provide at least one line of white space between the text and the first footnote. If you want more space, type in a higher value. Set the Space Between Footnotes at 0.0556 in (4 pts).

Under Placement Options, selecting Place End of Story Footnotes at Bottom of Text means that you want to use endnotes instead of footnotes; this was discussed on pages 249–250. Allow Split Footnotes means that when a note is too long it will continue onto the next column or page. This is a perfectly standard practice, so check this box.

If you want a short rule to appear above the first footnote in the column or page, choose this option from the drop-down list, and check Rule On. Change the weight to 0.5 pt, and leave the rest of the options as they appear in the illustration.

Choose all the footnote settings carefully, keeping in mind the requirements of *your* book.

Adjusting inline art (anchored objects)

Sometimes words alone just don't do the trick, and you need to show a small piece of art in your text. Here's how you make that happen:

1 Make your symbol in InDesign or another program (e.g., ⬡). You can even use a photo file.
2 Place the symbol on the pasteboard (File>Place) next to your page in InDesign and make it the right size for your line of type (◯).
3 Select the symbol using the Selection Tool, and copy it (Edit>Copy).
4 Switch to the Type Tool, put your cursor where you want the symbol to go in the text, then paste the symbol (Edit>Paste).
5 Chances are that the symbol will be too high on the line. Highlight it with the Type Tool, then use the baseline shift arrows (or input box) in the Control panel to lower it into its proper place.

Baseline shift increments can be as small as hundredths of a point.

Typesetting math and fractions

There are three basic kinds of fractions: level, or on-line, fractions (1/2); case fractions (usually ½, or ⅓); and built-up fractions ($\frac{1}{2}$). Each is discussed below.

Use **level fractions** if you're not discussing math but need to insert an occasional fraction or mathematical expression, such as $(a + b)/c$ or $(12 + 9)/3$, in line with the rest of your text. Oldstyle numerals are distracting in math, so use lining figures. (Highlight your numerals, then go into the Character panel fly-out menu and select OpenType>Tabular Lining, or create a new character style as shown below.) For the slash in the fraction, simply use the one on the keyboard, which is also called a solidus. Also note that in $(a + b)/c$, only the letters are in italic—not the parentheses or the solidus. In $(12 + 9)/3$, nothing is set in italic.

If you are typesetting a cookbook, experiment with the various kinds of fractions to find the most readable format, and increase the leading if necessary. Ingredient lists need to be very clear and easy to read.

☐ **Lining Figures [lfig]** *character* style   Based On = **[None]**
OpenType Features: Figure Style = Tabular Lining

A few commonly used **case fractions** are probably provided with your font; look in the Glyphs panel. If you need to set fractions not included with your font, you can construct your own. There are three options:

- Type the numbers with the slash, highlight them, go the fly-out menu in the Character panel, and choose OpenType>Fractions. Bingo! InDesign even converts the solidus to a fraction slash for you. Examples: ½, ⁵⁄₁₆, and ³⁵⁄₄₂ were all set using this method; note that they are identical to the fractions in the next option.

- You'll find both numerators and denominators for each numeral in the Glyphs panel (read the labels that appear as you hover over the glyphs), as well as a "fraction slash." Simply set the numbers and fraction slash (put your cursor in place on the page, then double-click each glyph), and you'll probably discover that no kerning is needed. Examples: ½, ⁵⁄₁₆, and ³⁵⁄₄₂ were all set using glyphs from the panel.

- If you're using a font that doesn't come with numerators and denominators, you can use superscripts and subscripts for the numerals, but you will have to use kerning and baseline shift to make them look good. If a fraction slash is not provided, try typing a regular slash and setting it in italic.

If you do discuss a good deal of math in your book, you should use **built-up fractions** with full-size numerals. Be sure to use Tabular Lining figures, and remember to take numerators and denominators off the baseline grid (Control panel or Paragraph panel> ≡≡). See page 141 for an example of how to use baseline shift to place the numbers properly. You might also want to use underline options to make the horizontal bar. To do this, highlight the characters that need the underscore, then go to Underline Options in the Character panel fly-out menu. Here you can select a line weight and move the bar up or down for best appearance. While you're at it, create a character style for future use.

In most cases you should treat these full-size built-up fractions as display material. Set the math on its own line(s), not running in with other text. You may either center each set of math expressions or indent them all equally from the left—usually a paragraph indent.

If you're not using an OpenType font, the Open-Type features aren't available to you, but read on to learn how to build fractions by hand.

keyboard slash (solidus)
fraction slash

Math plug-ins are available for use with InDesign. Go to the Resources page at www.BookDesign MadeSimple.com to find the latest. Another alternative is to hire a math typesetting service.

In the Glyphs panel you will find a minus sign:

en dash
minus sign

It's common to align several lines of math on the equals signs. (This may or may not be appropriate for your book.) Review the section on using tabs, on page 199, for instructions.

Typesetting poetry
Occasional poems

Treat poems that show up occasionally in your book as Extracts and create the paragraph styles shown below. Use the Extracts, Poetry, First style at the beginning of each stanza, as this will add a linespace between stanzas. If the poem has an attribution, treat it the same way as a quotation attribution (see pages 194–198). For the extra indents seen in many poems, set one or a series of em spaces (Type>Insert White Space>Em Space, *or* Ctrl/Cmd+Shift+M). See the next page for an example of a simple poetry extract.

You must use em spaces rather than word spaces for extra indents if you want to make an ebook. Neither ebooks nor websites can recognize more than one word space in a row.

Use this style for the first line of the poem and the first line of a new stanza, too.

☐ **Extracts, Poetry, First** [extpo1]   Based On = **ext1**
Changes from the Extracts, First style (see page 68):
Indents and Spacing: Left Indent = 0.4 in
                              First Line Indent = −0.2 in

☐ **Extracts, Poetry, Middle** [extpo2]   Based On = **extpo1**
Changes from the Extracts, Poetry, First style:
Indents and Spacing: Space Before = 0

Use this style for the very last line of the poem, but only if it has no attribution.

☐ **Extracts, Poetry, Last** [extpo3]   Based On = **extpo2**
Changes from the Extracts, Poetry, Middle style:
Indents and Spacing: Space After = 14 pt *or* 0.1944 in

If your attribution sticks out to the right a lot more than the longest line of the poem, change the settings to give the attribution a larger right indent.

☐ **Extract Attribution** [extpoattr]   Based On = **extpo3**
Changes from Extracts, Last style:
Indents and Spacing: Alignment = Right

☐ **Extracts, Poetry, Title** [extpot]   Based On = **expo1**
Changes from the Extracts, Poetry, First style:
Basic Character Formats: Bold

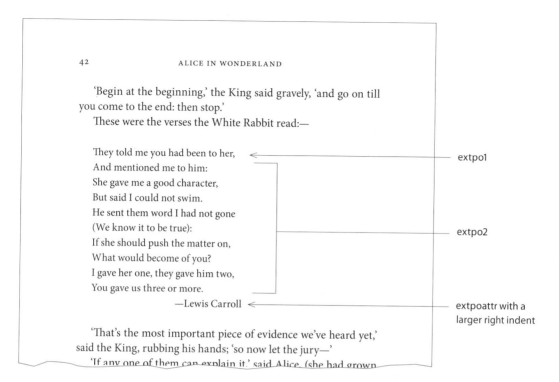

'Begin at the beginning,' the King said gravely, 'and go on till you come to the end: then stop.'

These were the verses the White Rabbit read:—

> They told me you had been to her,   ← extpo1
> And mentioned me to him:
> She gave me a good character,
> But said I could not swim.
> He sent them word I had not gone
> (We know it to be true):   ← extpo2
> If she should push the matter on,
> What would become of you?
> I gave her one, they gave him two,
> You gave us three or more.
>   —Lewis Carroll   ← extpoattr with a larger right indent

'That's the most important piece of evidence we've heard yet,' said the King, rubbing his hands; 'so now let the jury—'

'If any one of them can explain it,' said Alice, (she had grown

A book of poetry

For an entire book of poetry, you'll need a different approach. The idea is to set all the lines with left alignment and then center each poem left-to-right (called *east-west*) on its own page.

Begin by setting up the Poems paragraph styles on page 355.

Next, go to your A-Master page and draw a rectangle on one of the pages, making it the full width of the type area. With the rectangle selected, drag a vertical guideline to the middle of the rectangle. Repeat this process on the other page of the spread. Now delete both of the rectangles that you drew. Return to your text pages and notice the vertical guide in the center of every page in the book. You will use these to center your poems later.

Now format each poem using the styles given on page 355. Begin each poem at the top of a new page. Add space between stanzas or verses by using the Poem with Space After [**pospaft**] style. If a poem is a few lines too long for the page, just end it on the next page, but try to have *at least*

Each poem should begin at the top of a text page. Even if it is very short, don't be tempted to move it down to center it north-south on the page. If *all* of your poems are short, use an extra-large top margin.

Note that the running head is a bit smaller than usual, with extra space below it (a large top margin, see page 125 to increase the top margin) so as not to interfere with the poem titles.

The poem title is at the top of the text area, centered.

The poem is also centered east-west in the text frame, using the method described on page 355.

The Evidence

They told me you had been to her,
And mentioned me to him:
She gave me a good character,
But said I could not swim.
He sent them word I had not gone
(We know it to be true):
If she should push the matter on,
What would become of you?
I gave her one, they gave him two,
You gave us three or more;
They all returned from him to you,
Though they were mine before.
If I or she should chance to be
Involved in this affair,
He trusts to you to set them free,
Exactly as we were.
My notion was that you had been
(Before she had this fit)
An obstacle that came between
Him, and ourselves, and it.
Don't let him know she liked them best,
For this must ever be
A secret, kept from all the rest,
Between yourself and me.

Centered drop folios (see page 362 for style) emphasize the centeredness of the page.

43

☐ **Poems [po]**   Based On = **tx1**
Changes from the No Indents style (see page 62):
Indents and Spacing: Left Indent = 11 pt *or* 0.1528 in
   First Line Indent = −11 pt *or* −0.1528 in

☐ **Poems with Space After [pospaft]**   Based On = **po**
Changes from the Poems style:
Indents and Spacing: Space After = 14 pt *or* 0.1944 in

Use the Poems with Space After style for the last line of each stanza or verse.

☐ **Poem Titles [pot]**   Based On = **po**
Changes from the Poems style:
Basic Character Formats: Bold
Indents and Spacing: Alignment = Center
   First Line Indent = 0 (change this setting before changing Left Indent)
   Left Indent = 0
   Space Before = 14 pt *or* 0.1944 in
   Space After = 14 pt *or* 0.1944 in

four lines on the continuing page. Breaking between stanzas is always preferred. Running the first page a couple of lines short is better than having the continuing page with fewer than four lines on it. And never leave a single line of a stanza by itself at the top or bottom of a page.

The next steps will give your poems the finishing touch. On each page, do the following:

There are many variations on poetry book layouts. Look at other books for something that will work in *your* book.

1   Select the text frame with the Selection Tool, then grab the center right handle of the frame and move it to the left until it almost touches the longest line of the poem, being careful not to cause any type to bump over to the next line.
2   With the text frame still selected, move the whole frame to the right until it is centered on the vertical center guide on the page. Both the poem and its title should now be centered east-west on the page.

Remember that you can drag an object straight in one direction by holding the Shift key as you drag.

Repeat these steps on each page. Yes, it's laborious, but entirely worth the effort to achieve a professional look.

51

Improving your page layout

You've fine-tuned all the parts of your text that needed special typeset-ting, so now you're ready to look critically at the pages in your book, fix-ing any problems as you go.

You'll go through each chapter as a separate unit, making sure all your facing pages align at the top and bottom, and there are no instances of awkward hyphenation, widows or orphans, and other page layout no-nos.

Some of these typesetting rules have been mentioned already in this book, but seeing them in one place should help you put them all together now. All of the book layout rules below are interconnected, so it might be helpful to first read through the chapter before you get started.

Pages and spreads should align at top and bottom

Always, always begin your pages at the top margin. Even your chapter and part opening pages start at the top margin, with an end-of-para-graph return set in your Text [tx] paragraph style. The only exception is on pages that have an illustration that extends above the top margin.

Ideally, the only pages that won't line up with your closest baseline above the bottom margin are the last pages in each chapter and a few of the pages in your front matter (your title page, copyright page, Contents, and epigraph, if you have one).

As you go through your book, look at each two-page spread to make sure the two pages align with each other at the bottom margin. There may be several instances where they don't. This is because the Basic Para-graph style (Keep Options) is set up so that the last line of a paragraph cannot be alone at the top of a page (a widow). InDesign will pull the pen-ultimate line of that paragraph to the top of the page as well, to remove the widow. As a result, the previous page will be left one line short.

What can you do when this occurs? Try the following adjustments, which are shown in order of preference:

- Reword some text to make it longer or shorter.
- Resize an illustration.
- Use tracking to gain or lose lines (see below).
- Shorten the two page frames so they are both one line short. Spreads that run one line long are discouraged—especially if your book uses running feet—but can be tolerated if you have run out of other options. Be sure your *next* spread is normal length.
- Add or delete extra space above (but never below) headings. Adjust the space the same amount above all equal headings on the 2-page spread. In order for this to work, you may have to take the text off the baseline grid on this page.

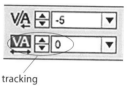

tracking

Using tracking to balance the number of lines on facing pages

So you start going through your pages and notice that several pages are one line short. Ack! What to do?

Start with the first instance of a short page in your chapter. Make sure you're in Normal view so you can see your baseline grid and end-of-paragraph returns. On that short page, do you see any paragraphs that end very close to either the beginning or end of a line? If you can't reword, you might be able to make those paragraphs one line shorter or longer using tracking.

Select the paragraph in question by quadruple-clicking it with your Type Tool. Using Tracking in the Control panel (see above), first try –10 or +10 to see whether you can shrink or expand the paragraph to lose or gain a line. If so, great! Focus on that paragraph, and try to get the Tracking value as small as possible, otherwise the paragraph could look squished or stretched.

If you can't find a paragraph on that page to shrink or stretch, look at the previous page. Any possibilities?

If you absolutely can't find any way of making the two pages the same length, then drag the bottoms of the text frames up so that *both* pages are one line shorter.

Don't apply tracking to whole pages, or both pages of a 2-page spread. Instead try to minimize the amount of tracking within a paragraph, so the reader won't notice that it's been squeezed or stretched.

There are exceptions to the page balancing rule. Some books, such as cookbooks, workbooks, and teachers' manuals, present a different topic or issue on each page. In these books, pages should still align at the top, but a "ragged bottom" look is fine. The same goes for poetry books. In fiction and most nonfiction books, however, page balancing is a must.

One other interesting exception is children's picture books and art books, which are laid out to make each 2-page spread look balanced and attractive.

Widows and orphans

Orphans are discouraged in headings, too, by the way.

We have discussed widows and orphans dozens of times already, but we bring them up here again to emphasize just how interlocked all the typesetting and layout conventions are. When you fix one problem, another one can arise. Just do your best! And read on.

Letter spacing and word spacing

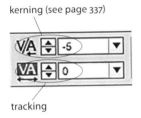

kerning (see page 337)

tracking

Your text becomes highlighted after it's tracked or kerned so you can easily see (in Normal view) which paragraphs have been affected. If it annoys you, go to Preferences (InDesign>Preferences on a Mac)>Composition and uncheck Custom Tracking/Kerning.

Look at a single paragraph in your book. Do you see lots of white space between letters or words on some lines? On the other hand, do any of the lines look crammed in? This can be caused by several factors, such as columns—or lines wrapped around an illustration—that are too narrow, your hyphenation settings, or possibly your justification settings.

Tracking is usually the best way to adjust spacing in any block of type—see the sidebar on page 357. Tracking values are measured in thousandths of an em, so if you type 10, it's a 1% increase in spacing. As a general rule, it's best not to use values lower than –10 or higher than 10 in regular book text.

Check the justification settings for your Text [tx] style and compare them to those on page 40. If your settings are okay but you're still having a problem with a specific paragraph, you can change the justification for that one paragraph by clicking the fly-out menu on the Paragraph panel, choosing Justification, and changing some settings there.

The next three sections in this chapter address similar issues that affect spacing. Read them before you decide which action to take in each situation.

Fine-tuning hyphenation and word breaks

You may find some instances where InDesign has hyphenated a word in a very awkward or unusual place. You specified the hyphenation settings for your Basic Paragraph style on page 39, but occasionally you may need to change the settings for a single paragraph.

First, try adding a soft hyphen to break the word in your preferred place. Insert your cursor where you'd prefer the word to break, then press Ctrl/Cmd+Shift+hyphen. A soft hyphen is inserted, which means that InDesign will break the word there if a hyphen is needed, but if not, no hyphen will show. For example, if you end up adding tracking or new copy to that paragraph down the road, and the word no longer needs to be hyphenated, you won't be stuck with an unwanted hyphen in the middle of your word.

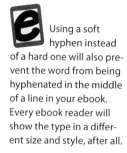 Using a soft hyphen instead of a hard one will also prevent the word from being hyphenated in the middle of a line in your ebook. Every ebook reader will show the type in a different size and style, after all.

If that doesn't work, insert your cursor in the problem paragraph, then open the Hyphenation dialog box by clicking the fly-out menu in the Paragraph panel and choosing Hyphenation. Check the Preview box, then try changing different settings to see what helps improve your paragraph. Move the Spacing slider left and right, perhaps try reducing the number of letters from 3 to 2, and check and uncheck the boxes at the bottom. Remember, you're just changing the settings for this one paragraph. After you've changed the settings, look at the paragraph style name for that paragraph in the Paragraph Styles panel. You'll see a plus sign next to the style name, reminding you that some settings have been changed.

Awkward page or line breaks confuse the reader

Check the last line of each recto page. Has the text broken in the middle of a phrase that should be kept together? Here are some word groups to avoid breaking between pages, and even between lines:

- dates (e.g., 25 / B.C., or May / 13)
- names (e.g., John / Allen Lerner, John Allen / Lerner, J.A. / Lerner)
- hyphenated words with an extra hyphen (e.g., self-sus- / taining)
- phone numbers, or two numbers separated by an en dash
- addresses (e.g., 38250 / Willow Street)
- prefixes (e.g., Mr., Ms., or Dr., separated from the surname)
- page or chapter numbers (e.g., page / 24, or chapter / 2)

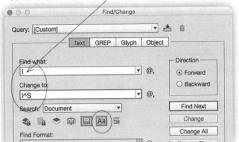

ladder

This little paragraph demonstrates three things discussed in this section. **Ladders** are three or more
hyphens in a row. A **stack**
appears when your text is
appropriately full of words
approved by your editor
that unfortunately don't
work well on the page. A
river shows up when the
spacing is difficult; perhaps the column is too narrow (like this one).

stack   river

InDesign can help you prevent such breaks. Select the text you want to keep together, then either 1) open the Character panel and select No Break from the fly-out menu or 2) select No Break from the drop-down list at the far right of the Control panel.

A great way of keeping two words together is to use a nonbreaking space between them (Ctrl/Cmd+Alt/Opt+X). Use the Find/Change feature (Ctrl/Cmd+F) to search for the words, and change the space to a nonbreaking space.

Here are some examples showing the nonbreaking space character inserted to keep words together:

Ms.ˆCollett   Chapterˆ4

1234ˆMy Street   Augustˆ7

Avoiding ladders, stacks, and rivers

A **ladder** is a series of three or more hyphens in a row at the ends of lines. In your paragraph styles, you set up your hyphenation options to avoid ladders (see page 39), but it's still a good idea to look through your book just in case some snuck in where you typed hard returns.

A **stack** is the appearance of the same series of characters at the start or end of three or more consecutive lines. These become very obvious once you start looking for them, and they can attract the reader's eye unnecessarily. The words don't even have to be the same each time; if you stacked "ate," "create," and "obliterate" above each other, it would look like a stack of *ate*'s just the same. Use tracking or soft hyphens to fix the problem.

A **river** is an unfortunate arrangement of white spaces that happen to line up in such a way as to look like white worms or a meandering stream of water on the page. They can appear everywhere once you start looking, but don't worry about minor ones. If there are really obvious rivers, reword slightly, or use tracking or soft hyphens, to make these disappear. A soft, or discretionary, hyphen is invisible unless needed to break a word. Put your cursor in the word and go to Type>Insert Special Character>Hyphens and Dashes>Discretionary Hyphen, or press Ctrl/Cmd+Shift+hyphen.

No blank recto pages

The heading says it all. Never, ever leave a recto page blank unless it's at the very end of your book. A blank right-hand page signals THE END to the reader.

No really short pages

Very short pages usually show up only at the end of a chapter. Not only do they look silly, but they also might make some readers think that the typesetter is either inexperienced or is deliberately trying to pad the book. A good rule of thumb is to have a minimum of six typeset lines on a page.

As you apply these layout and typesetting rules to your pages, you'll find that you can use one layout rule to help you resolve a problem with another rule. This takes practice, so take it slowly at first. Go through one chapter at a time and scan for trouble spots; sometimes it helps to highlight the problem by temporarily changing the color of the type in the trouble spot using the Swatches panel. Then start over in the chapter and remedy each problem in turn. Very often you'll discover that when you've fixed one, you've also solved one on the next page in the process. Or you may have even caused trouble for yourself on the next page. This can be frustrating, but remember that at this point you're doing the real work of page layout, and you will get better at it as you go along. We hope you'll come to enjoy the problem solving and start to think of your book as one big, challenging, and enjoyable puzzle.

Remember to return all your type to black after fixing each chapter.

Congratulations once again! Your chapters are now in fine shape, and you have only a few remaining steps before you can send your book to the printer. You'll finalize your running heads or feet, deal with proofreading corrections, and add your index.

52

Creating and applying chapter master pages

Now that your pages are finalized, you'll create and apply master pages.

Creating B-Master for chapter opening pages

Chapter opening pages usually differ from regular chapter pages in that they don't have running heads/feet and usually have a drop folio (a page number at the bottom). It's easy to create a separate master for chapter opening pages and, once applied, this makes it easy to see where new chapters start in your Pages panel.

In your Pages panel, open A-Master by double-clicking it, then click the fly-out menu and select New Master. Fill in the New Master dialog box as shown below, and click OK.

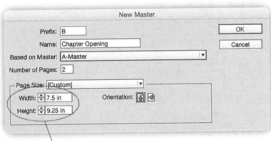

Fill in *your* book's trim size here.

You'll see that you can't select any of the text frames on the B-Master, as they're based on the A-Master page, and so are locked in place. To unlock a frame, press Ctrl/Cmd+Shift and click on it with any tool. Unlock and delete the running head/feet frames, and move the folio frames down to two or three baselines below the bottom margin. Decide whether you want the drop folios to be centered on the page or on the outside.

If your Folio paragraph style is aligned Away From Spine, but you want your drop folios centered, you need to create a new paragraph style:

Apply this paragraph style to the two drop folios on your B-Master page.	☐ **Drop Folios [dfol]** *Changes from the Folio style:* Indents and Spacing:	Based On = **fol** Alignment = Center

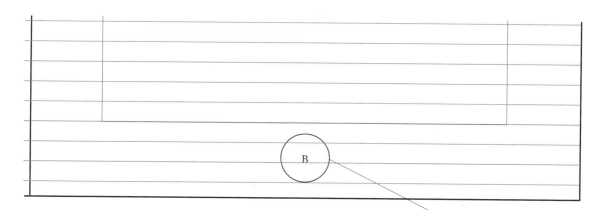

Note that the Current Page Number marker says "B" on B-Master.

Creating a separate master page for each chapter

One possible way to make your life easier is to create a separate master page for each chapter or part of your book. But this only helps if both of the following are true:

- The running heads change with each chapter or part
- Most of your chapters are more than a couple of pages long

To create a new master page for each chapter or part, open the Pages panel and select New Master from the fly-out menu. In the Prefix box type the chapter number—even if you're not using numbers—so that the chapters will be listed in the correct order (you can use 0 for your front matter). In the Name box type in the chapter title or an abbreviated version of it. In the Based On Master area, select A-Master. Then select 2 for the number of pages, and click OK. You'll now see the master page you've just created.

The only thing you'll want to change on this new master page is the number and chapter title in the running head. To make the running head text frame on your new master page editable, hold down Ctrl/Cmd+Shift, then click on the text frame. Select the copy you need to change, then type the correct words there. You don't need to touch the folios.

Repeat this process for every chapter or part in your book, including each section of your back matter. When you're finished, you'll have a separate master page for each one. (See page 369 for creating columns on the master page for your index.)

Using the method described here, *Book Design Made Simple* has 77 master pages!

Wondering what to type as a running head for the front matter? Try the name of the longest front matter section that you have in your book—"Preface," for instance. You'll need to remove many of the running heads later (see page 365) and change some others. On the other hand, if you have no pages in the front matter that are going to use running heads, create your front matter master page with no running heads at all.

Applying your master pages

Print your Contents or make a list so you have all the page numbers handy for each chapter, then apply the correct master pages to all the pages in your book. Start with your front matter:

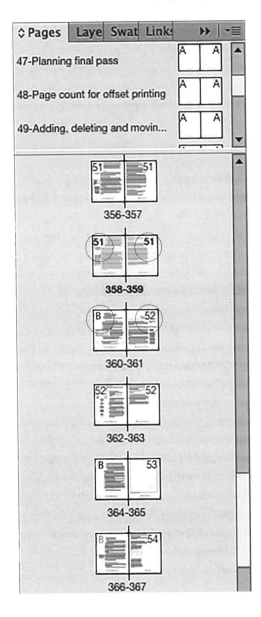

- Open your Pages panel fly-out menu
- Choose Apply Master to Pages
- Select 0–Front Matter from the Apply Master drop-down menu
- Add the page range separated by a hyphen (e.g., i-xvi)
- Click OK

Now scroll down your Pages panel and make sure all your front matter pages have the 0–Front Matter master page applied.

Next apply B-Master to the chapter opening page for chapter 1. You can use the method above, but it's simpler to just drag the B-Master icon onto the appropriate page thumbnail. You'll see a B displayed in the corner of that page thumbnail when it's applied.

Repeat the steps above for every chapter, first applying B-Master to the chapter opening page, then applying the chapter master to the rest of the chapter pages using Apply Master.

When you're finished, every page in your book will have a master page applied to it, and every page thumbnail in your Pages panel will display a letter or number in its outside corner (see example to the left).

If you change the titles of any chapters later on, simply change the running head on its master page, and all the running heads in the chapter will automatically change too.

Removing running heads and folios from certain pages

Now that you've applied master pages to every page in your book, they'll all display running heads and folios except the chapter opening pages, which will only display drop folios.

There are certain pages that never display running heads or folios:

• All the front matter before the Contents
• All blank pages

So you'll need to take one more quick trip through all your pages, and remove the running heads and folios from the pages listed above.

Navigate to page i, hold Ctrl/Cmd+Shift (to override the master page), and click the running head text frame to select it. Press Delete. Do the same for the folio text frame. Or, you can drag to select both frames at the same time (if they're near each other), then press Delete. Be sure not to delete any other content from your pages!

Go through all your chapters, deleting the running heads and folios from any blank pages.

If a page you deleted the text frames from ends up having text or images on it later on, simply go into the Pages panel and drag the master page icon back onto the page thumbnail to reapply the master page elements.

53 *Final proofreading corrections*

A proofreader is someone who reads proofs. This means that he or she never sees your pages until *after* they have been laid out. The proofreader should be a different person from the editor because a fresh set of eyes will see many things that you and even your editor never noticed. Also, the proofreader will check your running heads, hyphenation, and other issues that may have arisen during the layout process. It is always worthwhile to hire a good proofreader.

The proofreader's corrections might come to you in PDF format. Or they might come handwritten on a hard copy. If you receive a PDF, the corrections will probably have been made using the Comments feature. In Acrobat, click View>Tools>Comment>Open—or simply click on "Comment" in the toolbar to the right of the workspace—to see a list of comments docked at the right of your screen. You'll be able to click each comment in the list to see it displayed on the appropriate page.

If you receive handwritten corrections, however, the proofreader may have used many markings that are new to you. A chart of proofreading symbols appears on the opposite page.

You'll no doubt have lots of corrections to make, so be sure to save your InDesign file with a new name or date, and get started.

Once you've entered and double-checked all the corrections, go back and review one last time for spacing, hyphenation, tracking, page alignment, and all the other issues you took care of earlier (chapters 48–51).

Once your final proofreading corrections are finished, you'll forward your pages to your indexer for indexing. Or, if your book won't include an index, feel free to skip to Part IX: Preparing to Publish, where you'll create a high-resolution PDF of your pages for printing.

Congratulations on a job well done.

$\wp$	Delete	*ital*	Set in <u>italic</u>
$\subset$	Close up; delete space	*rom*	Set in roman
stet	Let it stand as it was originally	*bf*	Set in <u>boldface</u>
#	This is the symbol for space. You might see −# or +#	*lc*	Set in lowercase
eq#	Make space between words (or between lines) equal	*caps*	Set in <u>caps</u> (CAPITAL letters)
$\P$	Begin new paragraph	*sc*	Set in <u>small caps</u>, like this: SMALL CAPS
$\square$	Add one em space (the amount equal to the type size measured in points)	*wf*	Wrong font; set in correct type
$\boxtimes$	Add one en space (half the size of an em space)	X	Check type for a blemish
$\rbrack$	Move right	$\wedge$	Insert something here
$\lbrack$	Move left		Insert comma
$\rbrack\lbrack$	Center		Insert apostrophe or single quotation marks
$\sqcap$	Move up		Insert quotation marks
$\sqcup$	Move down		Insert period
fl	Flush left		Insert semicolon
fr	Flush right		Insert colon
‖	Align vertically	=	Insert hyphen
tr	Transpose		Insert em dash (a dash that is equal in length to the type size)
bb	Bad break, as in a word hyphenated wrong at the end of a line		Insert en dash (a dash that is half as long as an em dash); these are used almost exclusively between two numbers
sp	Spell out		Insert parentheses

Common proofreader's marks on hard copy

54 *Adding your index*

You create your index (or finalize it, if you built it in Word) after your book has been proofread and all the corrections entered. That way, you'll be sure that none of your text will reflow on your pages, and the page numbers in your index won't change.

Most authors choose to have a professional indexer create their index. A professional indexer will sort out the important from the unimportant and organize the index to make it easier for readers to find the information they're looking for. A good index not only helps the reader but also is a sign of a well-made book.

If you don't see your index markers in Normal view, click Type>Show Hidden Characters.

Did you already add index entries to your manuscript in Word? If so, your index imported into InDesign with your Word document. You'll see blue insertion points ($_\wedge$) dotted throughout your text when you're in Normal view.

Before working with an indexer, it's a good idea to study indexes in other books on your topic. Read the main entries and see what subentries are listed under them. Try looking up an obscure term to see whether it's listed; if so, is it in a logical place in the index? Can this index serve as a model for your own? Use it as a starting point and discuss its pros and cons with your indexer. Also discuss your audience and the number of pages you want the index to fill. That way, your indexer will be able to produce a helpful and appropriate guide for your readers. When your index is ready, your indexer will supply your index in Word.

If you are printing your book on an offset press, make sure your index will fit into an optimum page count for signatures (see chapter 48).

Setting up the first page of your index

If you haven't already done so, add a new page (see page 329) at the back of your book for the index, and apply to it the master page you created for your index on page 363.

If you created your index in Word, your index entries may have flowed in at the back of your manuscript and already appear in your text. If so, select the index heading and all the entries and delete them (really!). That index was static, so you'll generate a new one using InDesign's Index feature that will update automatically.

So now you have a blank page at the back of your book with the index master page applied to it.

Adding columns to your index master page

Open your index master page by double-clicking its icon in the top section of your Pages panel. The 2-page spread should look the same as all your other master pages, except the running head says Index.

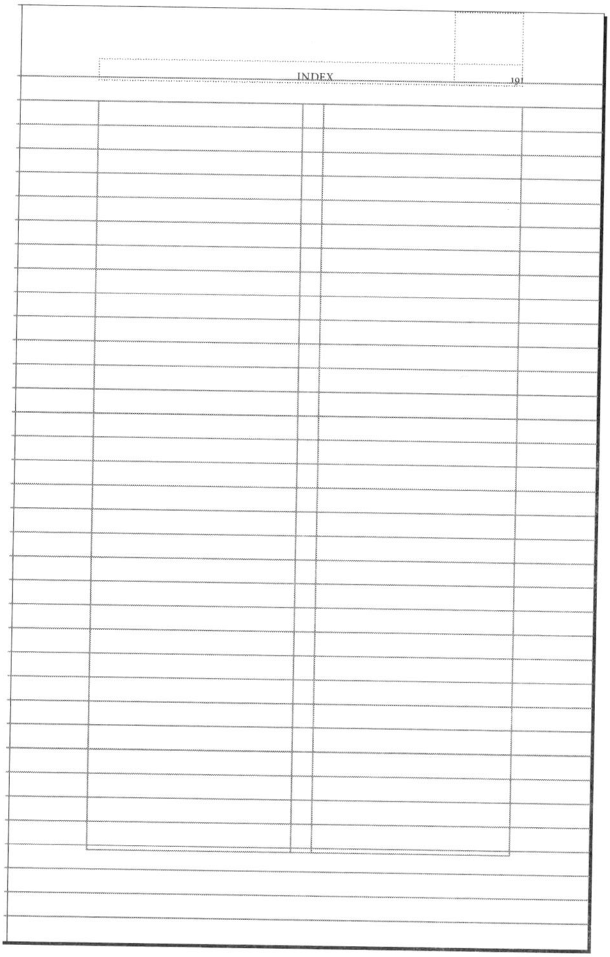

To add columns, click Layout>Margins and Columns. In the Margins and Columns dialog box, fill out the Columns section as shown below to create two columns. (The Margins area will show the measurements for *your* book.)

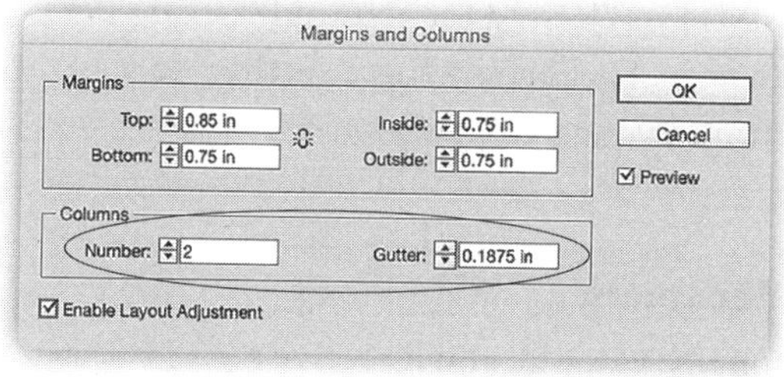

```
                    Margins and Columns
┌─ Margins ─────────────────────────────────┐        ┌──────────┐
│  Top:  [÷]0.85 in      Inside:  [÷]0.75 in │        │    OK    │
│                    ⊹                       │        └──────────┘
│  Bottom: [÷]0.75 in    Outside: [÷]0.75 in │        ┌──────────┐
└────────────────────────────────────────────┘        │  Cancel  │
┌─ Columns ─────────────────────────────────┐         └──────────┘
│  Number: [÷]2          Gutter: [÷]0.1875 in│         ☑ Preview
└────────────────────────────────────────────┘
☑ Enable Layout Adjustment
```

If your book has wider pages, or your index entries are very short, you may prefer a three-column index. You'll be able to change the number of columns easily using the Margins and Columns dialog box. Make sure the Preview and Enable Layout Adjustment boxes are both checked, and that way you can change the number of columns even after your index text is placed.

Creating paragraph styles for your index

Take a look through your index, and see what type of indentation scheme your indexer (or you) have used. It's very important to preserve the hierarchy that has been set up. Notice how many levels of entries there are.

Indexes with two or three levels of entries are the most common. Here is an example of an index with three levels:

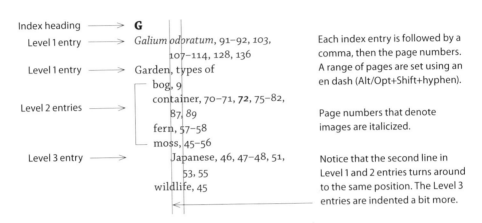

Index heading ⟶ **G**

Level 1 entry ⟶ *Galium odoratum*, 91–92, 103, 107–114, 128, 136

Level 1 entry ⟶ Garden, types of

Level 2 entries ⟶ bog, 9
container, 70–71, **72**, 75–82, 87, 89
fern, 57–58
moss, 45–56

Level 3 entry ⟶ Japanese, 46, 47–48, 51, 53, 55
wildlife, 45

Each index entry is followed by a comma, then the page numbers. A range of pages are set using an en dash (Alt/Opt+Shift+hyphen).

Page numbers that denote images are italicized.

Notice that the second line in Level 1 and 2 entries turns around to the same position. The Level 3 entries are indented a bit more.

Now create the paragraph styles you'll need for your index using the settings shown on the opposite page. You'll apply these settings to your index text after you've flowed it into your index pages.

Placing your index Word document

If your book has been professionally indexed, you'll receive a Word document containing your index. (If you created your own index with your original manuscript, then skip this section and follow the instructions in the next one instead.)

First navigate to your first index page. You'll see a blank page with two columns like the example on page 369. Place your Word document in the left column. If necessary, add one more index page, then click in the out port and hold down the Shift key to autoflow the text to the second index page. InDesign will create as many new pages as needed to flow all the text in your index into columns.

Now skip to "Applying your index paragraph styles" on page 372.

☐ **Index Level 1 [ind1]**   Based On = **tx1**
Changes from the No Indents style (see page 62):
Basic Character Formats: Size = 9 pt
                                                 Leading = 11 pt
Indents and Spacing: Alignment = Left
                                                 Left Indent = 27 pt *or* 0.375 in
                                                 First Line Indent = –27 pt *or* –0.375 in
                                                 Align to Grid = None

☐ **Index Level 2 [ind2]**   Based On = **ind1**
Changes from the Index Level 1 style:
Indents and Spacing: First Line Indent = –13.5 pt *or* –0.1875 in

☐ **Index Level 3 [ind3]**   Based On = **ind2**
Changes from the Index Level 2 style:
Indents and Spacing: Left Indent = 36 pt *or* 0.5 in
                                                 First Line Indent = –9 pt *or* –0.125 in

☐ **Index Heading [indh]**   Based On = **ind1**
Changes from the Index Level 1 style:
Basic Character Formats: Font Style = Bold
                                                 Size = 10 pt
Indents and Spacing: Space Before = 11 pt *or* 0.1528 in

Generating your manuscript index in InDesign

If you created your own index in your manuscript, your next step is to generate your index using InDesign's automated index feature.

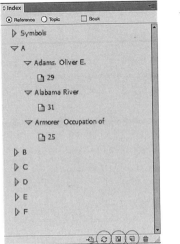

Open the Index panel by clicking Window>Type & Tables>Index. You'll see your index entries sorted alphabetically. You can examine individual entries by clicking the arrows next to the letters to reveal the entries. If you click the arrow next to the entry, you'll see the page number(s) displayed (see example to the left).

To generate your index, first navigate to your index page. You'll see a blank page with two columns like the example on page 369. Click the Generate Index icon at the bottom of your Index panel, and then fill in the Generate Index dialog box as shown below.

Click OK, and your cursor will·be loaded with the index text. Place your cursor in the left column and hold down the Shift key to autoflow the text. Your index text will flow into the two columns on your index page, and InDesign will create as many new pages as needed to flow all the text in your index into columns.

Using the Index panel, you'll be able to add new index entries using the Create New Index Entry icon.

Update Preview   Generate Index   Create New Index Entry

If you make any changes to your index, either by adding or removing material from your pages or by adding or changing entries, first open this dialog box, check Replace Existing Index, and click OK. You'll see a box with confirmation that your index has been updated.

Then in future simply click the Update Preview icon at the bottom of your Index panel.

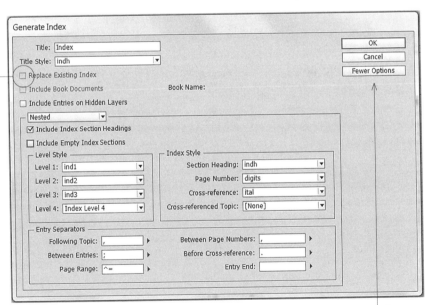

If you don't see the lower options, click the More Options button.

Applying your index paragraph styles

Now that your index text is placed in columns, you'll apply your new paragraph styles to the text.

First check to see whether the entries already have paragraph styles applied to them. They probably do, as indexers and the automatic InDesign Index feature both supply text with styles attached.

Follow the instructions on page 100 to delete the imported styles and substitute them with the styles you just created. That will save a lot of time. If no styles were imported, simply apply them manually.

Typesetting your index

Don't apply your B-Master Chapter Opening page to the first page of your index, as B-Master has a single-column format. Instead you'll mimic the chapter opening page on the first page of your index. Drag down the tops of the text frames to make some space, and create a new single-column text frame at the top that extends right across the columns. Add your usual chapter opening for your back matter [**fbt**], using the title Index.

Then delete the running head and folio from the top of this page by pressing Ctrl/Cmd+Shift and selecting them, then pressing the Delete key. Add a drop folio to the bottom of the page by opening B-Master, copying the drop folio (select the text frame with the Selection Tool and press Ctrl/Cmd+C), then going back to the first page of your index and pasting it in place (Ctrl/Cmd+Shift+Alt/Opt+V).

Now drag the tops of the two index text frames to the same baseline where all the other material in your back matter begins.

Look through your index pages and see how the entries have flowed. Ideally, each column begins with an entry (rather than a line of just page numbers) and ends just above your bottom margin. Keep in mind that these entries aren't aligned to your baseline grid.

Starting on the first page, make sure the second column doesn't start with a line of page numbers, and that the columns have the same number of lines. You may need to apply tracking or soft returns to some entries to balance the number of lines in the columns (see page 357). It's acceptable to make all the columns on a 2-page spread one line shorter, if that helps to balance the columns.

The only hard and fast rule for index layout is: Never begin a column with a page number.

In your index, always set "See" and "See also" (referring readers to other index entries) in italics. Use Find/Change to help you.

If your index is too long (needs to fit within fewer pages), consider: 1) deleting the alphabetical headings and simply adding one blank line between sections and/or 2) increasing the number of columns on your index master page (see page 369).

If your index is too short, consider: 1) changing the settings in your Index Heading [**indh**] paragraph style to increase the amount of space before (from 11 pt to, say, 22 pt) and/or 2) increasing the type size and leading in your Index Level 1 [**ind1**] paragraph style to, say, 10/12 (this will increase the size in all your other index paragraph styles, too).

Finally, make the columns on the last page of your index the same length. If this is not possible, make the left one longer than the other(s). And you're done!

Now that you've finished working through Part VII: Typesetting, your book pages should be completely finished. What a huge accomplishment!

In Part VIII: Designing Your Book Cover, you'll learn how to set up your book cover template in InDesign and then get started with your cover design.

Or, you can skip straight to Part IX: Preparing to Publish and generate a high-resolution PDF of your book pages to upload to your printer.

Part VIII:
Designing Your Cover

55

Researching your target market

The first step in designing a compelling book cover is learning about your target market. Who is likely to buy your book? What group of people did you have in mind when you wrote your book?

Before you wrote your book, you were perhaps not very concerned with other books that would compete with yours in the marketplace. Or, it's possible that you wrote your book specifically to improve on or challenge others that were already out there. Either way, you'll want to research your target market, and here's why.

Your book needs to have a look and feel that is similar (but not *too* similar) to the others in the same category so that potential readers are not thrown off by it at first glance. When they browse in a bookstore or library, they have certain expectations—whether they are aware of them or not—about the kind of book they are looking for. These people are your target market, and you'll be catering specifically to them. Planning early to make your book the right size and to grab your reader's attention will help you hit the bullseye.

In this chapter you'll be:

- Defining your target market
- Comparing your book with others
- Planning your front cover to appeal to your market

Defining your target market

Chances are that your book is not going to appeal to every single person on this earth, so just what kind of person did you have in mind as you were writing your book? Think about those people now. Where do they live? Are they a certain age? What kind of clothing do they wear? What is their income level? Where do they shop? More specifically, where are they most likely to shop for books?

What kinds of images came to mind while you were picturing your audience? Did you visualize any colors? Bright and loud ones? Muted tones? Do you have a mental picture of stripes in primary colors? Tweed jackets? Fragrant flowers? Make a nice long list of any impressions you have about these readers of yours.

Now define the category your book fits into. Perhaps it fits into more than one (e.g., nonfiction + history + Civil War + collectibles), and if so, list them all, and then look at the list. See whether you can trim it down to two or at most three categories that are the most closely related to the main point of your story, and thus the most realistic for selling your book.

If your book is nonfiction, try going to some online bookstores. What keywords work best for finding books like yours? These words should help you define *your* category, too. If you plan to sell your book online, start listing your own keywords for that purpose now.

On Amazon.com, there are specific categories already set up for you. To find them, simply start a search for your general topic, and a list of categories will appear on your screen (on the left on a desktop computer). Click on a category and subcategories will appear. Continue doing this until you find the best match for your book.

Comparing your book with others

Next, make a trip to your local bookstore or library. Take a notebook and ruler with you (for measuring in inches), and do some market research.

Once you've found the section of the store or library where your book will be displayed, study the other books. Use your ruler to measure their pages (horizontal × vertical inches) and note which size is the most prevalent. Notice whether the books have hard or soft covers. You want your book to fit in nicely with the others on the shelf. If you were to decide to make yours oversized, for whatever reason, it would probably have to be stored on a different shelf—not very good for sales!

While you're at it, write down the prices of these books and see whether they have fewer or more pages, illustrations, or information than yours. Are the pages printed in color or black ink? Try to determine objectively whether each book's perceived value matches its price, and begin to figure out where your book should fit within the range of prices.

Now start over, and examine their front covers. Do certain colors predominate? Does almost every cover feature a photograph, do they show illustrations, or do they simply use type? Which ones are the most eye-catching, which of them appeals to you the most, and why? Make notes about your impressions.

If you've already designed your book's pages, you made your trim size decisions earlier, and this is just a refresher.

Once again, start over, and read their back covers. You'll probably notice that they all have pretty much the same kinds of information on them. You are going to put very similar information on the back cover of your book, too.

Planning your front cover to appeal to your market

Here's where your thinking about the target market comes in. Get out that list you made of your impressions of your future readers. Which of the listed items still really resonate with you? Now that you've studied some competing books, which of the listed items did you see reflected in those books? Do your ideas seem to jibe with what other people think about the same audience?

Start a new list now. Write down descriptive words for the kind of feeling you want readers to get the instant they pick up your book. Remember that the front cover grabs, and the back cover sells. So on the front, you want potential customers to get the intended feeling right away. Some possible items on your list might be: active, exciting, calm, feminine, masculine, fun, serious, techie, conservative, mysterious, etc.

Now that you've pinpointed your target market's demographic and researched other competing books in the marketplace, you're ready to start designing your front cover.

Starting your front cover design

56

Most front covers have the same basic format as the cover on *this* book: a title, subtitle (optional), author's name, and graphic elements (images or simply color). Your goal is to find a combination of type and image(s) that will appeal to your target market and look professional.

In this chapter you'll be:

- Finding images to experiment with
- Creating a cover design file in InDesign
- Placing your images on the pages
- Experimenting with title layouts
- Combining type with images

Finding images to experiment with

There are lots of places you can find images to use on your front cover:

- Use an image from inside your book
- Use a photograph taken by yourself or someone else
- Use a piece of art or illustration created by yourself or someone else
- Purchase an image from an online image bank

If you don't have any images to try, browse through images at an online image bank for inspiration. It's a great way to get ideas and see what kinds of images appeal to you. Find your notes from your target market research and get started. Here are a few image banks to try:

- Adobe Stock (part of Creative Cloud)
- istockphoto.com
- dreamstime.com
- shutterstock.com
- 123rf.com
- morguefile.com (free photos)
- imagezoo.com (for illustrations)

Start by searching for some words or a phrase and see what comes up in the results. You'll most likely get several pages of results and can scroll through thumbnails. If one appeals to you, click on it to see a larger version of the image, together with the prices.

Right-click on a larger image and save a copy to use in your design. This image will be low resolution and have the image bank's watermark on it, but it'll be fine to use for experimenting with your cover designs. When you've settled on an image for your cover you'll purchase the high-resolution image, but for now just gather ideas.

Some of the image banks offer a Lightbox feature, where you can store thumbnails of your favorites as you continue to search.

Use as many search terms as you can think of. Try keywords from your book's title. Try phrases from your chapter titles. Try concepts. When you find an image with potential, look to see what search terms have been used for that image. You can click on those search terms to find similar images, and you can view other images by the same person.

Creating a cover design file in InDesign

It's easiest to experiment with cover designs in an InDesign file set up for that purpose. So start a new document using the dimensions of your front cover, like this:

Start a new document by clicking File>New>Document or pressing Ctrl/Cmd+N.

Naturally you should use the dimensions of your own book in the Width and Height fields.

A few pages to experiment on

Printers don't allow important info within 0.25" of the trimmed edges.

Your image will extend into the bleed area.

Placing your images on the pages

Images are always *placed* in InDesign, rather than copied and pasted, so that a link is created to the image's file on your hard drive.

To place an image, choose the Selection Tool and click File>Place (or Ctrl/Cmd+D), then browse through the Place dialog box to find the image you want to place. Select an image and click Open. Your cursor will now be loaded with the image. Click anywhere on page 1 and the image will be placed at its actual size. Move the image around the page by selecting and dragging it with the Selection Tool. Enlarge or shrink it by pressing Shift (to keep the proportions the same) and using the Free Transform Tool.

Each page in your document will be a sample cover design, so place all the images you gathered onto separate pages. Add more pages to your document (see page 329) if you need them.

If you've already placed images inside your book, some of this material will be a review. Just skim through until you get to something new.

Switch from the Selection Tool to the Free Transform Tool by pressing E. Switch back again by pressing V.

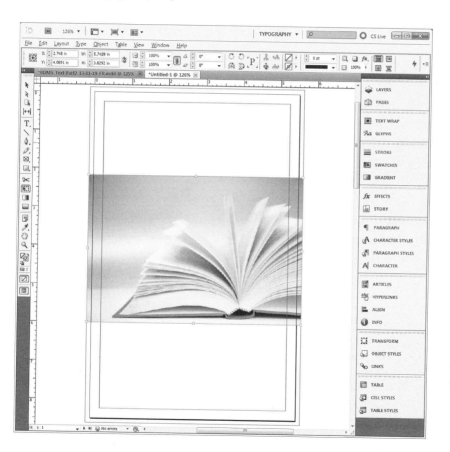

When you're browsing the Place dialog box for images to place, you can load the pointer with several images at once by holding Ctrl/Cmd and clicking several images. They'll all load onto the pointer at the same time.

Then click on a page to add the first image at actual size, or drag to add the image at the size of your choice.

To place subsequent images loaded on your pointer, go to the next location and click or drag. You'll "unload" the pointer one image at a time.

Starting with page 1, find the most pleasing placement of your image. You're just experimenting at this stage, so have fun! Try these ideas:

Flip the image horizontally or vertically by clicking Object>Transform>Flip Horizontal/Vertical, or by clicking one of the Flip icons in the Control panel.

 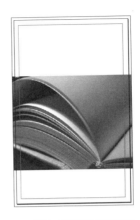 

To enlarge or shrink an image, click and drag any corner box with the Free Transform Tool (press E to switch to that tool). To keep the proportions of the image, hold down the Shift key while you're resizing it.

Free Transform Tool

To rotate an image, hover anywhere outside the image with the Free Transform Tool. You'll see a curved arrow and can rotate the image by simply clicking and dragging. Or click one of the Rotate 90° icons in the Control panel.

Experimenting with title layouts

Using the Type Tool, drag a text frame across the full width of your front cover and type in your title. It's easiest to experiment with the type using the Paragraph Style dialog box, so create a new paragraph style (see page 56) for your title and name it, say, **title1**. Now open the paragraph style and try some different typefaces and sizes for your title (see page 384).

Set up your Basic Paragraph style to the same specifications you used for the main narrative in your pages (see chapter 7). That way, when the time comes to add your back cover, you can use the same typeface for your back-cover copy.

Choosing appropriate typefaces

Open the paragraph style you created for your title by double-clicking it in the Paragraph Styles panel, and make sure the Preview box at the bottom left is checked (see left). Now any changes you make in the paragraph style will immediately show in your title. Position your page and Paragraph Styles panel so you can see your title while you're changing the paragraph style settings.

Start by centering your title (Indents and Spacing tab) and making its size bigger (Basic Character Formats tab). Still in the Basic Character Formats tab, click the Font Family drop-down menu, scroll up to the top of the list of typefaces, and select the first one. Using your down arrow key, go down through the list and see how your title looks in each typeface.

When experimenting using the Paragraph Styles dialog box, make sure the Preview box in the bottom left corner is checked. That way you can see all your changes on the fly.

In your Font Family drop-down menu, select the typeface at the top of your list. You'll see your title change to that typeface.

Then use the down arrow on your keyboard to see how your title looks in every font available to you in InDesign.

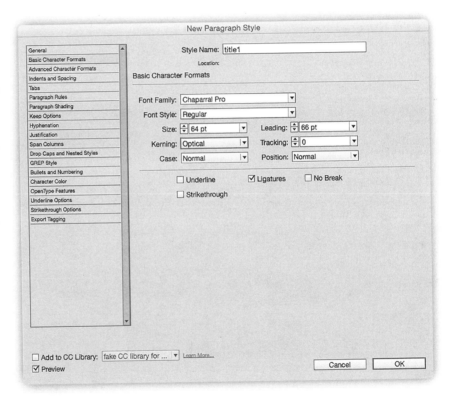

Write down the typefaces your title looks good in. As with shopping for clothes, not everything you try will be the right fit or style. Review the list of descriptive words you made in the previous chapter when thinking about your target market. Which typefaces best suit your subject matter? If you've written a business book, do the typefaces you've chosen look businesslike? If you've written a romance, does your title look romantic?

Now try your title in all caps (select All Caps from the Case drop-down menu) and go through the list of typefaces again.

Make a list of finalists. These are the typefaces you'll experiment with in your front cover designs.

Try new typefaces! In Adobe Typekit, type your book's title in the Choose Sample Text field and try any font that appeals to you before downloading it.

Book Design Made Simple
AbsaraHeadOT 29 pt

Book Design Made Simple
Chaparral Semibold 29 pt

Book Design Made Simple
Corinthian Regular 42 pt

Book Design Made Simple
Arno Regular 31 pt

BOOK DESIGN MADE SIMPLE
Myriad Regular 26 pt

Finding interesting title layouts

Take a moment to study the words in your title. If your title contains just one word, then it can go straight across the cover. Or, if your title lends itself to being broken into two or more lines, you can split the words up. Remember, if your book is sold online you'll want the title to be readable at thumbnail size. Try splitting your title into sections. Is it better or worse that way?

Part of your title could be set in a different type style or typeface, to give it more prominence. Some words can be larger and some smaller. Try setting part of your title in italics or all caps. Try all lowercase letters, a mix of upper- and lowercase, and small caps. Keep experimenting.

If the author is well known, you may want the author's name to be more prominent on the cover than the book's title. If this is the case, focus on creating an interesting type treatment for the author's name that could be used on several books.

AbsaraHeadOT 38 and 31 pt. Looks good centered on 2 lines. See how the g and l connect nicely? However, the k looks strange with the missing serif on the bottom.

Book Design
Made Simple

Chaparral Bold 36 pt and Semibold Italic 30 pt. Emphasizes first two words; looks better left-aligned, all letters lowercase.

book design
made simple

Corinthian Regular 72 pt, all lowercase, and Myriad Semiextended 15 pt, all caps. Second line centered between left edge and swoosh of g.

book design
MADE SIMPLE

Look at other books to get ideas. Every book on your bookshelf holds potential inspiration for your title. Round up some books and try the same title treatments with your title without judging in advance how it'll look. You may be surprised!

You might find it easier to split the words or phrases into separate text frames. That way you can move the frames around on the page with your Selection Tool to find the best juxtaposition of the words.

If you find a layout that's interesting but isn't working with a particular typeface, try the same layout with a different typeface. There might be a letter or word in your title that looks great in one typeface and is too difficult to read in another.

If your final title is comprised of more than one text frame, you can group them together. Select all the frames by dragging the Selection Tool, then group them together by pressing Ctrl/Cmd+G. To ungroup them, press Ctrl/Cmd+Shift+G.

Arno Regular 50 and 33 pt. Arno's k is a better choice than AbsaraHeadOT's. Taking the connecting g and l further, the first phrase is split onto two lines, and the o and d are connected. Lowercase letters connect more easily.

Myriad Regular 42 pt and Light 18 pt. (The Corinthian script was too flowery.) Myriad is used inside the book for captions, so could be a good choice for the title, although it looks a bit cold and formal.

Setting up your design document

Now that you've experimented with some suitable images and possible treatments for your title, it's time to experiment with some front cover designs using those elements.

Choose a title treatment and add it to a page in your design document. Then add any other text you need, such as the subtitle, author's name, or testimonial, by creating a text frame and typing in the words. Leave all the text black for the time being. Add an image if you intend to use one.

Using layers to organize your cover elements

It's a good idea to place your front cover elements onto layers at this stage. Using layers separates your text frames from your images and makes it easier to lock some elements in place while you move others around.

Refer to chapter 32 to set up layers for your book cover. It's useful to create three layers for your book cover: Text, Graphics, and Background. The Text layer is in *front* of all other layers and includes all your text frames. The Graphics layer is *behind* the Text layer and in *front* of the Background layer, and it includes images (later on you'll add your publishing logo and barcode to the spine and back cover). And the Background layer includes all your elements that are *behind* everything else, such as a solid background color or image.

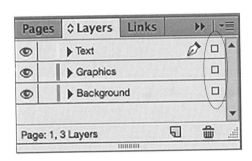

Take a moment now to create the layers you'll need, and place your text and image frames onto the appropriate layers.

Experiment with some different designs at the same time

Once you've set up a page with your front cover text and image on the appropriate layers, it's easy to duplicate that page and create some already-set-up pages to experiment with.

Simply open your Pages panel and drag the page you've set up onto the Create New Page icon at the bottom to create identical new pages. Now you can experiment with some variations in the same document.

Create New Page icon

If you have a great testimonial from a well-known person, consider adding the best part of it to the front cover for impact (see page 428 on typesetting testimonials).

Select any frame with your Selection Tool, and its frame will match the color of the layer it is on. Move it to a different layer by dragging its color square (shown at right) onto the appropriate layer.

A few design principles

You can probably recognize good or bad design when you see it, but you may not be aware of *why* one design is more successful than another.

Following are a few design principles that will help you create a more effective book cover. Keep these in mind while you're experimenting with your cover designs in chapter 59.

Keeping it simple

Keeping it simple is important for any kind of design, but it's especially important for the front cover of your book. It's tempting to try to capture every single thing about your book on the front cover—every plot twist, every character, or every concept. Don't do it!

Potential customers and readers will often be looking at a very small image of your front cover, probably a thumbnail on the Internet or in a catalog (perhaps even printed in black and white). Make sure your cover is easy to understand at a small size.

As you design your front cover, keep asking yourself which elements are *really* necessary and whether they can be simplified. Keep your type as simple as possible, without strokes or drop shadows unless absolutely necessary. Just because lots of effects are available in InDesign doesn't mean they should all be used.

Try zooming out to a mini view so you can see what elements disappear at a small size, what elements might need to be enlarged, or which ones overwhelm the rest.

TITLE TITLE

Which is easier to read, the plain word or the one with the embossing, stroke, and drop shadow?

Choose one or two typefaces at most. Simplify an image by cropping or removing it from its background. Use a limited color palette.

You'll find lots of ideas in this chapter, so be selective, and just use the ideas that make *your* book cover more compelling.

Creating a focal point

Busy covers with lots of competing elements are confusing. Everything is vying for attention, so where do you look first?

Make it easy for your audience by creating a hierarchy of elements on your cover. Your focal point will be dominant, and the surrounding elements will support the focal point without competing with it. Your focal point could be your title or a portion of it, an image or a portion of it, or the author's name. What will *your* hierarchy be?

There are many ways to draw your reader's eye to a specific element on your cover. Here are some ideas:

All elements are identical. There is no focal point.

Use a different **color** to create a focal point.

Use a different **shape** to create a focal point.

Use **white space** to create a focal point.

Use placement or **position** to create a focal point.

Use a larger **size** to create a focal point.

Using type as a visual element

Part of keeping your cover design simple is using type in a clean and uncluttered way. There are lots of ways to create visual interest with your type using size, contrast, and color. Here are some ideas:

Use size extremes (Arno Pro, 105/13 pt).

Use contrasting typefaces (Corinthian Pro/Myriad Pro).

Darker and bolder type is more dominant.

Lighter and thinner type is less dominant.

Use color and weight (Myriad Pro, 100/50% black).

When designing your title treatment, keep in mind the typefaces you've used inside your book. Perhaps the same typeface(s) can be used on the cover, too, if not for the title then for other text, such as the author's name, endorsements, or back-cover copy.

Just because the other text on your front cover isn't your focal point doesn't mean it should be boring. Here are a couple of ideas for treatment of authors' names:

FIONA RAVEN • GLENNA COLLETT

Add lots of tracking to all caps (Myriad Pro Black with 500 tracking).

FIONA **RAVEN**
GLENNA **COLLETT**

Myriad Pro Light/Bold adds contrast, and the alignment adds interest.

Using repetition and alignment to create a unified look

Repetition and alignment help to tie different elements together to create a unified look for your cover.

Repetition means repeating colors, shapes, lines, and textures:

Repeating color blocks adds symmetry and focus.

A **predictable shape** allows a focus on the words.

Overlapping creates tension, but symmetry relieves it.

In symmetrical designs, elements are aligned consistently, and colors and weights can be repeated. In asymmetrical designs, there is a visual relationship that unifies but also often creates a path for the eye to follow. Asymmetry can create interesting tensions between elements.

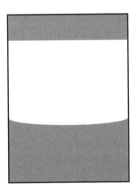

The **weight** of this cover is at the bottom.

Lines of type are **off center** but still **balanced.**

Overlaps, bleeds, and differing **shapes** create interest.

Using white or negative space

White space is the breathing space around type and images, and it doesn't have to be white. Also known as negative space, it's the areas on your cover that *don't* include information. These areas are just as important as the areas that do include information.

Let's say you have a busy background image to use on your cover. As you'll see in the example below, a busy background is difficult to set type over, and it also reduces the significance of both the image and the type. Try removing part of the image and replacing it with a color to create a clean area for type with an uneven edge. Adds interest, right?

See page 403 to learn how to hide part of your image .

A busy background image adds clutter and makes type harder to read.

Removing part of your image adds focus, clarity, and interest to your cover.

Making an image small can magnify its importance and create a focal point.

Sometimes making an image quite small makes it seem more important. It's like a little treasure. You have to look a bit closer, perhaps actually pick up the book in a bookstore. It draws people in.

One design corner you might get backed into is when all your elements are rectangular. This can easily happen when using photographs and all caps. Even the border around the cover creates a rectangle.

Try taking images out of boxes and putting them on a plain background with perhaps a drop shadow. And try changing type from all caps to upper- and lowercase. Free yourself from the rectangle!

Rectangular shapes abound in photos and all caps.

There are no rectangles here, just various shapes.

58

Creating a color palette

How do you choose suitable colors for your type and other elements? And how will you know which colors go well together?

An easy way to create a color palette for your book cover is to use the colors within an image. If you're using an image on your front cover, you can pick colors from that image. If not, find something that has a color palette you like, such as a postcard, a surface (like brick or marble), a piece of fabric, a china pattern, a scarf, or anything that can be scanned or photographed to create a digital image.

Creating a color palette from images

Color Theme Tool
(it may be behind the
Eyedropper Tool or
the Measure Tool)

You can use the Color Theme Tool to create color palettes right from any image placed in InDesign. Select the Color Theme Tool, then hover over any image or frame. You'll see a larger border appear around any frames that can be sampled for colors. Click on any image and a palette with five colors appears (see below). If you want to clear that palette and sample something else, press Esc and try again. You can sample a part of an image by dragging the Color Theme Tool over a specific area, or even sample several images at a time by dragging across all of them.

Click arrow to see all five color themes

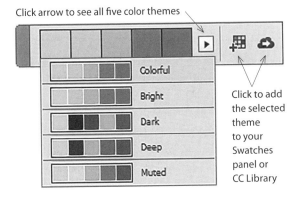

Click to add
the selected
theme
to your
Swatches
panel or
CC Library

Click on the arrow in the color palette and up to five color themes appear. Each theme is named and includes five colors.

Converting your Color Theme Tool to CMYK

Since you're creating a file for print, you'll want any colors you select to be CMYK colors (see page 257). Double-click on the Color Theme Tool in the Toolbox to open the Color Theme Options dialog box. Choose Convert to CMYK in the drop-down menu, and click OK.

Pay attention to the names of the color themes because one or more of them might correspond to the feeling you are aiming to convey. But if you planned for a bold, bright cover and are currently leaning toward more muted colors, it might be appropriate to rethink the goals you set up in chapter 55.

You only need to choose Convert to CMYK once. All subsequent color themes will be in CMYK color.

Color Theme Options	
☐ Ignore opacity and other applied effects while picking colors	OK
When applying colors: Convert to CMYK ▾	Cancel

Adding colors to your text, shapes, and images

It's easy to add any of the colors in your color theme to text, shapes, and images. Click on the theme of your choice, then on one of the colors in that theme and you'll see the eye dropper change direction; now it points to the right and has a color square next to it.

Hover over text and a small T appears, then click on the text to apply the color to it. Hover over the edge of any frame and the color square will show an outline, then click to apply a color stroke to the frame. Hover inside a frame and click to apply a color fill to the frame.

You can add any of these color themes to your Swatches panel by selecting one and clicking the Swatches icon (🔡) on the Color Theme palette. The colors are added to a theme folder in your Swatches panel. If you want to change the name of the folder, double-click it and type a new name. To experiment with or expand the theme—or any of the colors in the theme—first select the theme, then click on Add this theme to my current CC library (☁). Now continue on to the next page.

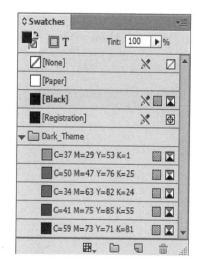

When you add a color theme to your Swatches panel, the colors are in a folder with the name of the theme you chose.

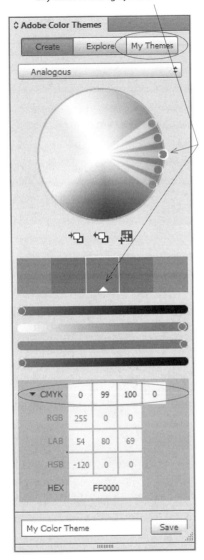

The tiny white triangles indicate your current base color. Be careful not to move this arm of the wheel unless you actually want to change your base color.

Find your CC Library by opening Adobe Color Themes and clicking on My Themes. The color themes will also be available to you in all your other Adobe applications.

Expanding your color palette

The colors in the color themes you got from your image will obviously go nicely with it. But chances are good that you'll want a wider range of suitable colors in your palette, including an accent color or one that will really stand out.

Expanding your color palette is easy using the InDesign color wheel. Click Window>Color>Adobe Color Themes to open your Adobe Color Themes panel (see left). Click CMYK in the bottom section so all the colors you choose will be CMYK.

Click the My Themes button at the top right and look for a theme you just added (see bottom of page 395). Under your theme, click on Actions>Edit This Theme. Now you'll see the color wheel with your theme displayed below. Pick one of the colors to become the one you'll base your experiments on by clicking the small triangle that appears at the bottom of the color (it says Set as Base Color when you hover over it). This color will stay the same as you try new colors to go with it. Try different settings from the drop-down menu just above the color wheel: Analogous, Triad, and so on. Each setting will show you different colors that go nicely with your base color.

If you want to make changes to your base color, drag the circles in the color wheel around. Dragging a color toward the center of the wheel makes it lighter or grayer, and dragging it toward the outside makes it darker or more intense. To fine-tune a color even further, use the sliders below the theme. If you just want to get back to your original color, start over in My Themes and choose your theme again.

To make a theme from one of your other swatch colors, type the CMYK values of the swatch in the area below the wheel.

When all the colors in the theme are exactly as you want them, click Save at the bottom right. Choose whether you want to save it as a new theme (Save a Copy) or to replace your original one (Save Changes), and your color theme will be saved in the My Themes section. To save this theme to your Swatches panel, return to My Themes, click Actions (under the theme), then click Add to Swatches.

Polishing your front cover

You've set up your InDesign document to experiment with some front cover designs and added some great colors to your Swatches panel, but your cover doesn't look remotely professional yet! Don't panic . . . book covers normally go through a stage where they look just terrible. Every book cover and its designer endures this stage in the creative process before the cover evolves into its final form.

Now you'll focus on fine-tuning and polishing the elements on your cover to make it look just right. This is when the disparate parts come together to form a cohesive whole. You'll experiment with type treatments, images, color, balance, and proportion (all the while keeping your list of descriptive words from chapter 55 in mind), and hopefully enjoy the design process!

Lots of ideas follow in this chapter, so be sure to try any you think could be suitable for *your* cover.

Fine-tuning the type on your front cover

Now that you've placed your text on the front cover and positioned it appropriately, you'll want to make more improvements. Here are a few tricks to upgrade your type.

Adding color to your type

Add color to your type in InDesign by 1) selecting it with the Type Tool, then using the Swatches panel to apply a stroke or fill, the same way you apply colors to a shape (see page 259), or 2) select a color with your Color Theme Tool and drag over your text to change its color (see page 395).

Start with your title (or the type you want to be the most prominent), and try all the colors in your color palette. Lighter colors generally display better over darker backgrounds, and vice versa. See page 391 for examples of possible type treatments for your cover.

If you find a particular color you want to use for your title, but it's too loud or quiet, make the type smaller or larger until you find the right balance of color and size. Large type with a quieter color will seem equally prominent as small type with a louder color.

book

Here are a few more tips when adding color to your type:

BOOK DESIGN

Add a solid fill and/or stroke by selecting the type and assigning fill and stroke colors (see page 259).

BOOK DESIGN

Complementary colors, such as blue and orange, can make text pop in a bad way. Try darkening or lightening them a bit.

BOOK DESIGN

Try printing your cover in b&w to check the type contrast, in case it's featured in a b&w catalog or publication.

BOOK DESIGN

If your type doesn't stand out sufficiently against your background, consider adding a drop shadow (see page 405).

BOOK DESIGN

Consider using different colors for words in your title or author's name, to give one more prominence.

book design

Feel free to let type flow outside of the edges of any background shapes, as it adds interest!

Stretching type to fit a specific space

Let's say you want your title or author's name to fit across the width of your cover or to fill a specific space. One way to stretch or shrink type is by using the Vertical and Horizontal Scales in your Character panel (below), but this can create distorted-looking type. There are several other ways to stretch or shrink your type's width and/or height using a combination of tracking and condensed or expanded typefaces.

Use the up and down arrows in the Character panel's Vertical and Horizontal Scales to stretch and shrink your type.

BOOK DESIGN

Stretch your title's width by applying tracking and a bolder typeface (Myriad Pro Black 18 pt with 300 tracking).

BOOK DESIGN

Increase your title's width and height by increasing the type size (Myriad Pro Bold 28 pt with 50 tracking).

BOOK DESIGN

Use a condensed typeface to increase the height of the title (Myriad Pro Bold Condensed 37 pt with 50 tracking).

BOOK DESIGN MADE SIMPLE

To create a consistent-looking block of text using different sizes of words, choose a typeface with several weights (from light to bold) as well as Condensed or Expanded instances. Set each line of type in a size and instance to fill the space. (Myriad Pro: BOOK=Bold SemiExtended 61/40+50Tracking, DESIGN=Condensed 87/76, MADE=Light SemiExtended 44/46+510Tracking, SIMPLE=Semibold 56/54+50Tracking.)

Kern → Kern

If your type doesn't have consistent spacing *between* the characters, you can kern them (see page 337).

Combining type and images on your cover

Finding the right combination of type and images for your cover is important. You'll want the type to be easily readable and your images interesting but not overwhelming your type.

Successfully combining type and images depends on what kind of images you're using. If an image fills your cover, you'll be looking for ways to make your type stand out on top of it. In this case, you might add a drop shadow or a color bar behind your text. Or, if your image won't fill your front cover, then you'll be looking for interesting juxtapositions between your image and type.

Using horizontal images on vertical covers

Most fiction and nonfiction books are taller than they are wide, so they lend themselves nicely to using an image with a vertical orientation that fills the cover. But suppose the image you want to use on your vertical cover has a horizontal orientation? Or it's just not the right shape?

There are a few ways of getting around this dilemma that you'll recognize from other book covers you've seen. You can add a color bar across the top and/or bottom to fill the white space or add a color background behind the image (see chapter 33). If you have the skills in Photoshop, you can make your image the right size and shape to fill your cover.

Create a color bar above and/or below the image.

Add a color background that blends with the image.

Change the image in Photoshop so that it fits the cover.

Or use a combination of these ideas to suit *your* cover.

Matching a color background to the image on your cover

Suppose you're creating a color background for your front cover, and you want the color to match a specific color in your cover image. How do you find out what that color is? That's what the Eyedropper Tool is for.

Select the Eyedropper Tool, and you'll be able to move it around with your mouse. It'll be pointing down from the right, just like in the Toolbox icon. Click the eyedropper on any color on your cover to "pick" the color and load it into the Eyedropper Tool. When it's loaded, the Tool will look half full and shift its position to the left.

Click the eyedropper on any shape you've made to fill it with the color you picked. Or, select type with the eyedropper to color the type. (To remove this color from the eyedropper, simply click again on the Eyedropper Tool in the Toolbox.)

The color you picked will appear in the Swatches panel as the current fill or stroke color (whichever is in front in the upper left corner of your Swatches panel). To add it to your swatches so you can use it again, select New Color Swatch from the Swatches fly-out menu and your new color will appear. Make sure that the Color Type is Process and the Color Mode is CMYK. Next, click Add, then Done.

The Eyedropper Tool may be behind the Measure Tool or Color Theme Tool.

Using the Eyedropper Tool is a simple way to pick just one color—it doesn't involve making a palette of colors the way the Color Theme Tool does.

If your cover has a black background, use a rich black (combination of ink colors) rather than just 100% black ink. A nice, rich black is 60% cyan and 100% black.

NOTE: Offset printers will not accept colors that contain more than 300% ink colors. In other words, a color with 100% cyan, 100% magenta, 100% yellow, and 20% black contains too much ink—it will saturate the paper beyond what it can absorb.

This is known as ink density, or total area coverage (TAC).

Unbox your images and set them free!

Removing an image from its box can change its shape from a square or rectangle to a more dynamic shape. It can also create new white space (space without information) in which to place your type.

To remove the background from your image, open it in Photoshop. Open your Layers panel by clicking Window>Layers. You'll see that your image is on a layer called Background. This layer is automatically locked, so create a new unlocked layer by following the steps below.

Drag the Background layer onto the New Layer icon to create a copy of that layer.

Now drag the Background layer onto the Trash icon to delete that layer.

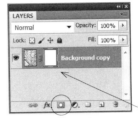

To add a layer mask to your new unlocked layer, click the Add Layer Mask icon.

A layer mask allows you to hide parts of your image without actually deleting those parts. That way, you can add them back if you change your mind later.

Click the curved arrows once to switch the background color to the foreground.

Foreground and background colors are set to black and white when you're working in your layer mask.

Pressing the \ key will give you a pink checkered background, which might help you better see what you're drawing.

Now you have a layer with your image and a layer mask. In the Layers panel, you'll see two thumbnails on your layer: one of your image on the left, and the Layer Mask Thumbnail box (currently white) on the right. Click once in the Layer Mask Thumbnail box to make sure it's selected.

Now look at the foreground and background colors at the bottom of your Toolbox (they'll be black and white when you're working in your layer mask). With black as your foreground color, select your Pencil Tool (🖉) or Brush Tool (🖌), which can be found by hovering on the Pencil Tool, and drag anywhere directly on your image. When black is selected, that part of your image becomes masked (invisible!)—and you'll see a checkered background revealed behind it. That area is now transparent.

When you draw in black, the areas you cover become hidden. You'll see black showing on the layer mask thumbnail in the Layers panel. When you draw in white, those areas are revealed again. The Pencil Tool makes a sharp edge, and the Brush Tool makes a soft edge. Select the hardness of the brush or pencil using the Brush Preset Picker just above the Toolbox. You can also select degrees of transparency (Opacity: 100% or less).

Keep in mind:

- Black hides and white reveals. Switch by clicking the curved arrows.
- To change the size of your Pencil or Brush Tool, press [to make it smaller and] to make it larger.
- To zoom in or out of your image, press Ctrl/Cmd and the plus (+) or minus (-) signs.
- If you mistakenly do the wrong thing, press Ctrl/Cmd+Z to undo it.

Original image, full size.

It's easiest to first zoom in on the edge of the image you want to isolate. Next choose the Pencil or Brush Tool and adjust the size of the Tool so it's easy to see. Then start drawing around the edge of your image. To create a smooth edge, click the Tool at your starting point, then hold the Shift key and click farther along the edge. Holding the Shift key fills in the area between clicks and creates a smooth line (see below).

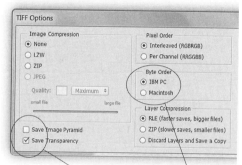

Once you've isolated the edge of your image, "erase" the rest of your background image by enlarging the Pencil Tool and drawing with black over the rest of the background.

When you're done, save your image as a PSD (or a TIF with the settings shown at the right). Finally, place your image in InDesign, and its background will be transparent.

Choose your platform here.

Be sure to check the Save Transparency box.

First zoom in to your image and trace around the edge with a small tool (use the Pencil Tool for a crisp edge or the Brush Tool for a soft edge).

Then switch to a large Pencil Tool and "erase" the whole background. You'll see the area you've hidden shown in black in the layer mask thumbnail in the Layers panel.

Move the Opacity slider to make your image more or less transparent.

Image at 100% opacity before screening to 10%, enlarging, and placing behind the main narrative to the right.

Text of different opacities require separate frames. In the two examples to the right, the screened text is in one frame and the 100% black text in another.

Screening images, shapes, and text

You may want some type or an image to be screened—in other words, to make it partially transparent.

To screen an image or text, click Window>Effects to open the Effects panel in InDesign. Select your image or text frame with the Selection Tool, and you'll see its opacity is 100% in the Effects panel. To change the opacity, simply click on 100% and move the slider to the left until the image is at the desired opacity.

Screening images

An image used in the background of your cover or pages can be screened to, say, 10 or 15% to give the effect of a watermark (like the large background image on this page). If the image is screened back enough, it's easy to read type placed on top of it, even small type like in this paragraph.

Screening shapes

It might be hard to read your title because of the background image. Adding a screened shape (like a rectangle or oval) between the title and image makes the title easier to read. In the example below, the rectangle is screened from solid white to 65% opacity.

Screening text

Making type partially transparent can produce interesting effects on your book cover, as shown below.

Making type stand out using drop shadows or outlines

A sure sign that a book is self-published is extensive use of default drop shadows and strokes, so don't use them on your cover unless they're absolutely necessary to make your type more visible against a background image. Before resorting to a drop shadow or stroke, try making your type bigger, bolder, or brighter first.

One circumstance where a drop shadow and/or stroke will help your title to pop out of the background is when you have a light-colored title against a darker, busy background. Below you'll see how a drop shadow can create more contrast without being obvious.

In the Effects panel, click *fx* and select Drop Shadow from the fly-out menu.

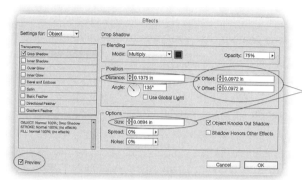

Reducing these numbers brings the drop shadow closer to your text.

The default Drop Shadow settings are applied here. See that the K in BOOK is not properly visible because the shadow is too far below the text. To optimize your drop shadow, check the Preview box at the bottom left of the Effects panel, then experiment with your settings.

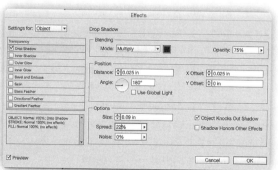
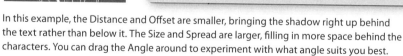

In this example, the Distance and Offset are smaller, bringing the shadow right up behind the text rather than below it. The Size and Spread are larger, filling in more space behind the characters. You can drag the Angle around to experiment with what angle suits you best.

Try adding a stroke around the type (see page 272) using a dark background color.

Finishing your front cover
Getting proofs printed

When you have one (or a few) front cover designs coming together, it's often helpful to get prints made. Simply export your InDesign file to PDF (see chapter 71) and email or upload the PDF to your local copy store. Ask them to print the cover(s) on glossy cardstock (80 lb or thicker) on a high-quality color laser printer. Then trim the cover(s) to size on a paper trimmer using the crop marks.

These prints come in handy. Stand them up on a table or shelf and live with them for a while. Take them to your local bookstore and stand them on a bookshelf with other books in your genre. How do they compare? Get feedback from people whose opinions you value, but keep in mind you won't please everyone, nor will you follow every suggestion given.

You'll undoubtedly make a few adjustments after seeing printed proofs, perhaps fine-tuning colors or adjusting sizes of type and images.

When you're satisfied with your front cover, you'll want to save it in a folder together with its fonts and images using the Package feature.

Packaging your front cover

To package your front cover, first save it with a current name (perhaps including today's date in the file name). Then follow the instructions in chapter 45 to package your file. The only difference in packaging your front cover is that your images may be in RGB color and will therefore show an error message. No need to worry about that now.

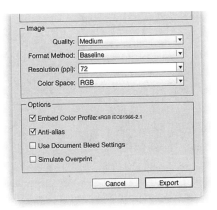

If you're using your front cover for an ebook, your images can stay in RGB color. Save your cover as a JPG for uploading to ebook vendors by clicking File>Export then choosing JPEG from the Save as type (PC) or Format (Mac) drop-down menu and click Save. Next you'll see the Export JPEG dialog box (right). Use the settings shown and click Export. The resulting JPG is suitable for uploading to ebook vendors.

The settings shown to the right will produce a JPG file at 72 ppi and the same dimensions as the trim size of your book (for example, 5.5″ × 8.5″ or 396 × 612 pixels).

Choosing your book's binding

There are many types of book bindings available. Which is best suited for *your* book? (If you're publishing an ebook and not a print edition, then skip to the next chapter, as ebooks only require a digital front cover.)

Types of book bindings

Trade paperbacks

Trade books are what you see in a bookstore. They are aimed at the general public. Bookstores are filled with trade paperbacks of all shapes and sizes in every category. Is *your* book a trade paperback? Most likely, the answer is yes, but if not, you have other options.

Trade paperback with flaps

Some trade paperbacks have flaps on their covers, much like the flaps on dust jackets. The cover on a paperback with flaps is a little sturdier because of the double layer of cover stock when it's folded over. You might choose this binding if your front and back covers are filled with large, significant images that you don't want overprinted with type, or you might have a great deal of important information that simply must be on the cover somewhere. On the other hand, you might just want your book to stand out a little from the rest.

Hardcover with dust jacket

Traditionally, most books started out as hardcover books and then, if they proved popular, came out in paperback form. These days, the vast majority of books start life as paperbacks and stay that way. But a hard cover still makes a book seem more important than a soft cover does.

If you decide to use a hard cover, you'll need to make design decisions about the cover itself as well as the dust jacket that protects it. Hard covers and dust jackets cost more than paperbacks to produce.

Perfect binding is a method of binding both hardcover and softcover books whereby the pages are glued along the spine edge, and then the cover is glued to the spine.

Smyth-sewn binding is a stronger (and more expensive) method of binding whereby the signatures are sewn together along the spine edge, and the pages are held to the spine with some cloth and the endsheets. Books lie open flatter with sewn binding, and libraries prefer it because of its durability.

Most hardcovers are wrapped with colored paper or cloth, foil-stamped on the spine with the book title and author's name, then wrapped with a dust jacket. Children's books and picture books are often hardcovers wrapped with printed paper, and the dust jacket is optional.

The dust jacket includes information and images that would appear on a paperback cover, and you will use the jacket flaps as well. The front flap usually gives information about the content of the book, sometimes continuing onto the back flap. The back flap often has the author's photo and bio, and credits for the jacket design and artwork. This leaves the back of the jacket for your marketing blurbs and reviews.

Less common binding styles to consider

There are plenty of other kinds of bindings that might fit *your* book better than the more common hard and soft covers. Here are some ideas:

- **Saddle stitch** Used for very short books that consist of only one signature (see pages 321–322). The signature is stapled two or three times at the fold.
- **Spiral** Like a spiral notebook, with metal or plastic-coated wires.
- **GBC binding** Also called Cerlox®, it holds the pages together with a cylindrical plastic comb. It requires rectangular holes to be punched near the inside edges of your pages. You can choose from many colors and sizes, and the binding can be printed on with your spine information. Consider using this for cookbooks or technical books.
- **Wire-O® binding** Similar to spiral, but the wires are parallel to each other and in pairs. Used sometimes for technical or reference material.
- **Concealed Wire-O** Like Wire-O, but the front-cover material continues across to the back (as in a hardcover book) and conceals the wires so the spine can be printed on.

In most of the bindings listed above, the inside margin on your pages must be wide enough to allow for the holes that need to be punched for the binding (usually 0.5"). Ask your printer for their requirements.

Your book will lie open flat with all of these types of binding.

Hard and soft covers and their parts

Paperback (with flaps)

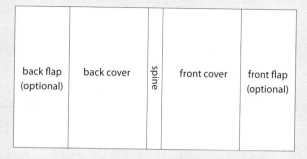

| back flap (optional) | back cover | spine | front cover | front flap (optional) |

Casebound hardcover

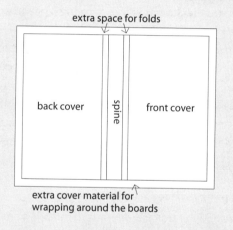

extra space for folds

back cover | spine | front cover

extra cover material for wrapping around the boards

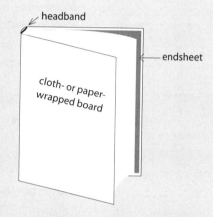

headband

endsheet

cloth- or paper-wrapped board

Dust jacket

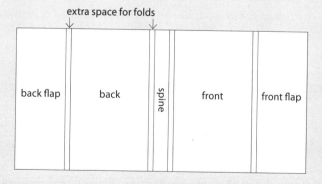

extra space for folds

| back flap | back | spine | front | front flap |

Inside covers

Printing on the inside covers will add to the cost of printing, and most print-on-demand and digital printers don't offer this option.

However, if your printer supports this option, you may choose to use the extra space on the inside covers for:

- **Advertising** Showcasing other books you've written or adding testimonials.
- **Maps and diagrams** If your readers are going to have to refer repeatedly to references such as maps, charts, diagrams, or lists, consider putting them on the inside cover.
- **Decorative** The inside cover can be printed with a color wash, to add impact to the overall book design.
- **Mimicking flaps on a dust jacket** If you're creating a paperback edition from a hardcover edition and want the cover to look similar to the dust jacket, then the material from the flaps can be printed on the inside cover.

Note that most printers do not allow anything to be printed in the area where the cover will be glued to the spine of the book, because the ink interferes with the adherence of the glue in the binding process.

Endsheets (for hardcover editions only)

To set up a template for your endsheets, see page 443.

Endsheets (also known as endpapers) are glued to the inside of hardcover books and are partially responsible for holding the cover and pages together. All hardcover books have endsheets. Think of the them as a 2-page spread, one at the front of your book and one at the back. They can be printed (using either the same material for the front and back or different material), or you can simply use plain colored paper to lend a little color to the inside of the book.

Once you've decided which type of binding is appropriate for your book, your next step is to download or create a template in InDesign for your whole book cover. The following two chapters will help you do that.

Using a printer's cover template

If you're printing your book with a POD printer such as CreateSpace or IngramSpark, you can generate a template for your book cover on their website. Just fill in the specs for your book (trim size, page count, and so on), and request the template. Either you'll download it or it'll be sent to your email address, depending on the printer.

Cover templates come in a variety of formats, but they fall into two categories: an InDesign file or a file that can be placed into an InDesign file (such as PDF, PNG, and EPS). Choose the format you feel most comfortable working with based on the processes explained below.

POD printers' templates are often set up on a large sheet of paper, with specific placement of the book cover on that sheet.

Using an InDesign cover template

If you choose "InDesign CS3 and newer" for your template, you'll get an InDesign file that is already set up on the correct sheet size, and it'll include guides to show you where to place all the elements on your cover.

Open the template in InDesign and save it with a new file name. Note that there are two layers in the file, Guides (a locked layer) and Layer 1. Click the eye icons at the left of each layer to show and hide them so you can see what they include. Usually the bottom layer has colored areas showing you where to place your images and text, and the top layer has non-printing guides, written specs, and possibly a barcode.

The typical layers included in a printer's cover template.

Next you'll copy and paste the front cover you've already created into layers that are *between* the two existing layers. So go ahead and create new layers between the two existing layers with the same names you used in your front cover InDesign file (see page 388). Then open your front cover InDesign file and select everything on one layer (lock the other layers to make that easier). Copy everything on the layer by clicking Edit>Copy, then paste it into the new layer on your new template by selecting that layer and clicking Edit>Paste. Finally, drag the text and images into the appropriate place on your template.

The keyboard shortcut for Copy is Ctrl/Cmd+C.

The keyboard shortcut for Paste is Ctrl/Cmd+V.

Using a PDF, PNG, or EPS cover template

If you choose a file format other than InDesign for your cover template, you'll incorporate that file into your existing InDesign front-cover file by placing it onto a separate layer. Here are the steps:

Click in this column
to hide a layer.

Click in this column
to lock a layer.

Two new layers at the top
for guides and template.

For a more detailed
explanation on adding
guides, see page 421.

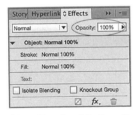

Move Opacity slider to 50%.

1 Open the file by double-clicking it and look for the Document Size or Sheet Size (usually 17″ × 11″ or 15″ × 12″ or something similar).

2 Open your front-cover InDesign file and change the width and height of your document (click File>Document Setup) to match the Document Size or Sheet Size in your template.

3 Create two new layers *above* your existing layers (see page 388) and call them Template and Guides.

4 Select the Template layer and place your template on it by clicking File>Place (or pressing Ctrl/Cmd+D), selecting the file, and clicking Open. Line up the edges of the template with the edges of your document (not the bleed). Don't resize the template.

5 Select the Guides layer and add vertical guides to the left and right edges of your cover (line them up on the trim marks), and to the left and right edges of your spine (line them up with the fold marks), by dragging guides from the ruler at the left. (If your rulers aren't showing, click View>Show Rulers or press Ctrl/Cmd+R.) Add horizontal guides to the top and bottom edges of your cover (line them up on the trim marks), by dragging guides down from the ruler at the top.

6 Now make the template transparent so you can see your cover through it. Open your Effects panel by clicking Window>Effects. Select your template using the Selection Tool, then move the Opacity slider in the Effects panel to 50% so your template is transparent.

7 Lock the Template and Guides layers by clicking in the Lock Layer box (see above left), then drag to select all your front cover elements and move them into position, lining them up with the template and guides.

8 Finally, hide the Template layer by clicking the eye icon (see above left). Now you'll be able to build your spine and back cover using the guides, and any time you need to refer to your template, simply show the Template layer (click the eye icon again), and change the opacity back to 100%.

Creating your own cover template

If you haven't decided yet where you'll be printing your book, you can still create a cover template based on your trim size and type of binding. Estimate the spine width for the time being, and adjust it at the last minute when you've chosen a printer and learned the thickness of their paper.

Here are the steps you'll take:

1 Calculate your cover's approximate dimensions
2 Set up your template in InDesign
3 Add guides to show fold and spine allowances (if needed)

You'll notice that the whole book cover—front, spine, and back—is printed on one sheet of paper, with the back on the left and the front on the right. If you're designing a dust jacket, it will also include the back flap on the left and the front flap on the right.

1 Calculate your cover's approximate dimensions

To calculate the size of your cover template, you'll need the trim size of your pages (for example, 5.5″ × 8.5″, 6″ × 9″, etc.), and for now you'll just estimate the width of the spine as a starting point. You'll request the exact dimensions of the cover from your printer later on, after you've chosen a printer and established your exact page count. But for now, it's easy to get started using an approximate spine width.

On the following pages are examples of different types of book covers, showing their dimensions. Find the appropriate cover and binding for *your* book, and use the example shown to calculate the dimensions for your cover template.

You'll see that the size of the bleed is not included in the calculations, as you'll add the bleed to the *outside* of your cover template using the bleed feature in InDesign.

The spine width will be finalized at the last minute, when your page count is final and when you know the thickness of the paper your printer will be using.

Softcover

When a softcover book is bound, the cover is wrapped around the *book block* (the block of printed pages) and glued down the spine, then the bleed is trimmed off the outside edges. The final spine width provided by your printer allows for the fold at the edges of the spine.

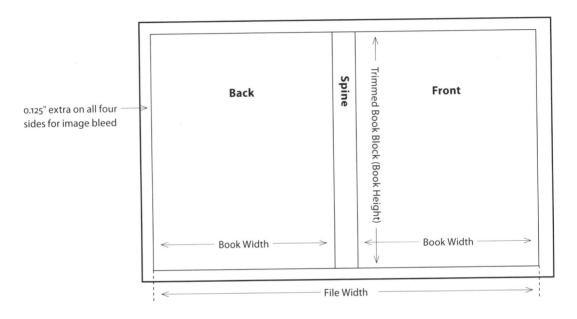

File Width Formula: Book Width × 2, plus Spine Width
File Height Formula: Book Height

Let's say your trim size is 5.5″ × 8.5″ and you have approximately 200 pages. Your book width is 5.5″, your book height is 8.5″, and you can estimate your spine width for the time being at, say, 0.5″. Therefore your file width is 11.5˝.

$$5.5 \times 2 = 11 + 0.5 = 11.5''$$

Softcover with flaps

When a softcover book with flaps is bound, first the bleed is trimmed off the left and right edges and the flaps folded in. Then the cover is wrapped around the book block and glued down the spine, and the bleed is trimmed off the top and bottom. The final spine width provided by your printer allows for the fold at the edges of the spine; however, you'll need to add a small amount to the width to allow for the flaps to fold into the book.

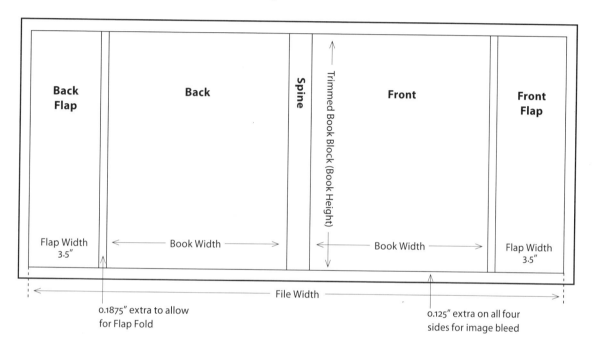

Width Formula: Flap Width × 2, plus Flap Fold × 2, plus Book Width × 2, plus Spine Width
Height Formula: Book Height

Let's say your trim size is 5.5″ × 8.5″ and you have approximately 200 pages. Your book width is 5.5″, your book height is 8.5″, say your flap width is the standard 3.5″, and say your flap fold is 0.1875″. You can estimate your spine width for the time being at, say, 0.5″. Therefore your file width is 18.875″.

$$(3.5 \times 2) + (0.1875 \times 2) + (5.5 \times 2) = 18.375 + 0.5 = 18.875″$$

Printed hardcover wrap

When a hardcover book is bound, the cover is glued to the *book boards* (the three cardboard pieces—front, spine, and back—that form the hardcover), and the large bleed wraps around to the inside of the boards. The spine width is larger than for softcover books to allow for the width of the boards, and extra allowance is given for the spine fold.

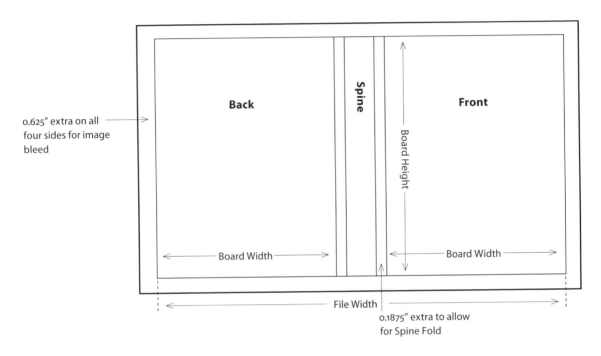

0.625" extra on all four sides for image bleed

Board Height

Back

Spine

Front

Board Width

Board Width

File Width

0.1875" extra to allow for Spine Fold

Width Formula: Board Width × 2, plus Spine Fold × 2, plus Spine Width
Height Formula: Board Height

The Board Width is usually about 0.1875" less than your trim size, and the Board Height is usually about 0.25" more than your trim size. So calculate those two numbers first. Let's say your trim size is 5.5" × 8.5" and you have approximately 200 pages. Your board width is, say, 5.3125", your board height is, say, 8.75". You can estimate your spine folds at 0.1875" each and the spine width for the time being at, say, 0.75". Therefore your file width is 11.75".

$$(5.3125 \times 2) + (0.1875 \times 2) = 11 + 0.75 = 11.75''$$

Dust jacket

The dust jacket (DJ) will be trimmed on all four sides after it's printed, then wrapped around a hardcover book. The spine width is larger than for softcover books to allow for the width of the hardcover boards, and extra allowance is given for the flaps to fold around the boards.

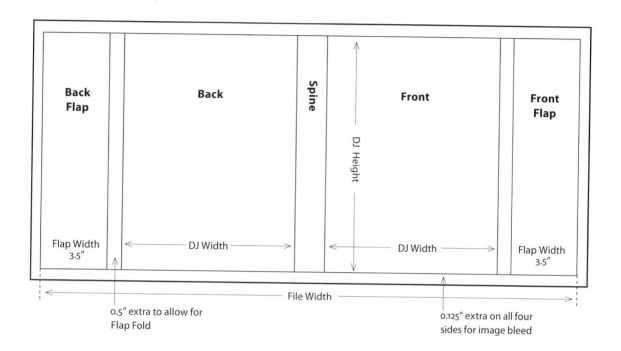

Width Formula: Flap Width × 2, plus Flap Fold × 2, plus DJ Width × 2, plus Spine Width

Height Formula: DJ Height

The DJ Width is usually about 0.1875″ more than your trim size, and the DJ Height is usually about 0.25″ more than your trim size. So calculate those two numbers first. Let's say your trim size is 5.5″ × 8.5″ and you have approximately 200 pages. Your DJ width is, say, 5.6875″ and your DJ height is, say, 8.75″. You can estimate your flap folds at 0.5″ each and the spine width for the time being at, say, 0.5″. Therefore your file width is 19.875″.

$$(3.5 \times 2) + (0.5 \times 2) + (5.6875 \times 2) = 19.375 + 0.5 = 19.875″$$

2 Set up your template in InDesign

There are two ways to set up your template: by creating a new InDesign cover template, or by changing your existing front cover InDesign file to include the cover template. If you've already designed your front cover in InDesign, it will be easier to change your existing document.

Creating a new InDesign document for your cover template

Start a new document in InDesign by selecting File>New>Document (Ctrl+N). Fill in the boxes using the calculations you made earlier in this chapter, then click OK. (In the example below, the dust jacket calculations from page 417 were used.)

Fill in the Width and Height you calculated earlier in this chapter.

The Number of columns is 2, and the Gutter between the two columns is your estimated spine width.

If your book cover includes flaps, add left and right margins to act as guides for the flaps at 3.5". Otherwise, leave all the margins at zero. Click the "link" button to enter different numbers in the boxes.

If you don't see the Bleed and Slug options at the bottom, press the triangle here.

Fill in the amount of bleed for your book cover here. All four numbers are the same. Use 0.125" for all covers except a printed hardcover, which has a bleed of 0.625".

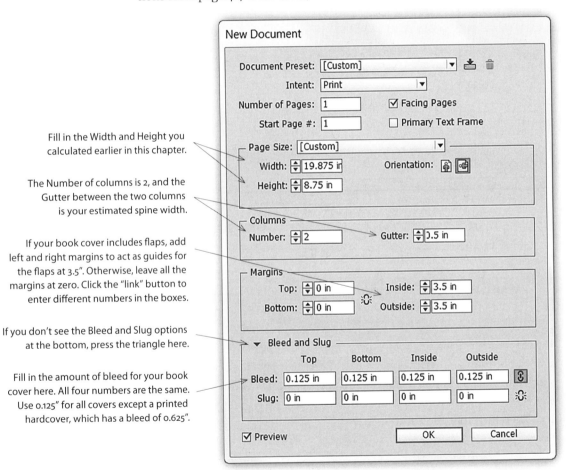

The cover template you've created will look similar to the template for your type of cover shown earlier in this chapter. (The example below is from the dust jacket template shown on page 417). Regardless of which template you've created, you'll see that the gutter between the two columns in the center forms the spine of your book. And, if you've created a template for a cover or dust jacket with flaps, the left and right margins show the fold of the flaps.

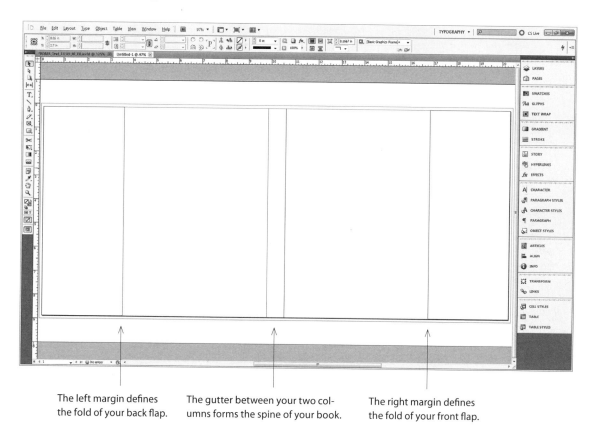

The left margin defines the fold of your back flap.

The gutter between your two columns forms the spine of your book.

The right margin defines the fold of your front flap.

If you've created a softcover template without flaps, then you're done! However, for any other cover template you'll want to add guides (see page 421) to show where the fold allowances lie, so you don't accidentally put any important information there.

If you want to copy and paste an existing front-cover design into your new template, follow the instructions on page 411.

Changing your existing front-cover InDesign file into a template

To change your existing InDesign file into a full cover template, you'll change your document dimensions in two places: in Document Setup and in Layout>Margins and Columns. Here are the steps:

1 Make sure you're in Normal view by selecting the Selection Tool and pressing W. That way you can see the margins and columns.
2 Select File>Document Setup and change the Width and Height to the numbers you calculated for your template. Add your bleed. Click OK.
3 Select Layout>Margins and Columns. Change the Number of columns to 2 and add your spine width to Gutter. Click OK.

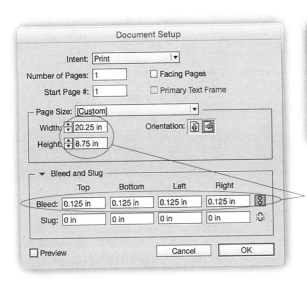

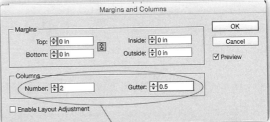

Change the Number of columns to 2, and add the spine width you calculated (or estimated) to Gutter.

Fill in the Width and Height figures you calculated earlier in this chapter, then add the amount of bleed (0.125" for any cover except a printed hardcover, which has a bleed of 0.625").

4 Now select and drag your front cover design into the appropriate position on the right side of your template (remember the front cover is on the right and the back cover is on the left).
5 And finally, save your whole cover with a new name.

If you're creating a cover with flaps or a spine width allowance, you'll want to add some guides to show where those allowances are and avoid putting any important information there (see next page).

3 Add guides to show fold and spine allowances (if needed)

Adding guides to the fold and spine allowances is a handy reminder of which parts of your cover won't be readily visible when your book is bound.

Guides are easy to set and won't show either on your printed document or when you view your document in Preview mode. Here's how to set them:

If your book-cover template is for a softcover, you won't have any fold or spine allowances and so won't need to add guides for them.

1 To add a vertical guide, click anywhere in the ruler on the left side, and drag to the right. Release the mouse at the place you want the guide to be on your template.

Press Ctrl/Cmd while dragging, and the guide will extend across the pasteboard, too.

2 To add a horizontal guide, click anywhere in the ruler across the top, and drag a new guide down.

You may want to add a guide a specific distance from something, such as a guide to show a fold allowance 0.5″ from the fold of a dust-jacket flap. To do this, set the ruler to zero at the fold by dragging from the cross-hairs where the rulers meet. Then drag a guide to 0.5″ away from the fold to show the fold allowance.

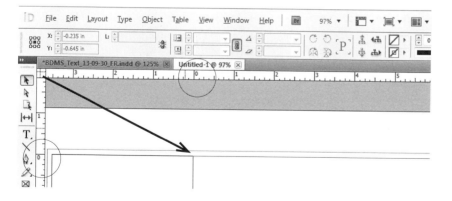

Set your ruler to zero in the place you want to measure *from*. Then drag a guide to the correct distance from it.

Later, you can return your zero point to its original position by double-clicking on the intersection of the rulers at the top left of your screen.

Planning your back cover

Front covers grab and back covers sell . . . this is where you make your sale! Plan what you need to include on your back cover, and keep it simple. When deciding what to include on your back cover:

- Ask yourself what the main benefits are to your target readers. Leave out everything else.
- Don't clutter your back cover with too much information and a busy background.
- Presenting less information in an easy-to-read type size is better than cramming in lots of information with a small type size.

Remember, your back cover copy can be just as powerful a marketing tool as your front cover. Be clear about the benefits of buying your book, and you'll deliver an irresistible message.

Use this chapter to decide what you'll include on your back cover, then write your copy and compile your testimonials and images. You'll add them to your cover template and typeset them in chapter 64.

Assemble your back-cover copy in Word. Then you'll be able to place your Word document into your cover template in InDesign.

Tagline

Grab your reader's attention by placing a catchy tagline at the top of your back cover. Don't just repeat your book's title on the back cover. Your tagline can be a short phrase or a whole sentence, or it can pose a question. Just make sure it's to the point and will draw your reader in.

Summary

Don't give away the entire plot or all the contents; just offer an enticing taste of what's inside. If your book is nonfiction, tell your readers what a great benefit your book will be to them. It'll be easy to use, or fast to use, or it'll keep your reader up to date. It'll simplify your reader's life or make him/her an authority on the subject. Write advertising text that blends with a summary of your book. Not many bookstore browsers are going to read the whole thing and wish for more, so one or two paragraphs should be enough. And remember that this is not the same style of writing as inside the book; this is ad copy.

Testimonials, endorsements, reviews, blurbs

Gather comments from other authors, people in your field, or celebrities, if you happen to know any. Always print an attribution after the reviewer's name. If he or she is an author, give the name of their most relevant book. This is the major way to reward them for writing your review.

Someone may want to give you a testimonial but be unsure about what to write. In this case, write a good testimonial and ask permission to use their name with it.

On the back cover, use your best testimonials (best description or author), and just use the phrase or sentence of each testimonial with the most impact. Make the testimonials as short as possible while retaining the key words and intent. Keep it honest, too. If a reviewer says, "This book is the best example of garbage I've seen this year," don't edit it down to "This book is the best I've seen this year." Ask the reviewer's permission to edit their copy if necessary so that it fits nicely on the page. (The full testimonials can be printed on the first page or two inside the book.)

If you don't have any testimonials yet, consider printing some advance review copies to give to potential reviewers.

What if you get a bad review? You don't have to put it on your cover, and who would? But take the reviewer's words seriously, and see whether there is a way to improve your book. Thank the reviewer for his or her candid views and suggestions.

Author biography

Just a short bio will do, including only relevant information (why you are an expert on the book's subject). You can include a more complete bio on the last page inside the book if you want to.

Author photo

Everyone likes to see what the author looks like. In most cases a professional photo works best, but don't rule out snapshots taken by friends, as a candid shot can be very charming. Narrow the choice down to a few images, then poll your friends and family about which one they like best. Make sure that *you* are the main feature in the photo; unnecessary extras can be distracting. If your book is about lion taming, it's fine to show a lion nearby, but probably not with your head inside its mouth! Be sure to include a credit for the photographer under the picture or on the copyright page.

For a fiction work, the author bio can be lighthearted and vague, or it can list education, career, and family details, especially if they are relevant to the book's topic. For nonfiction, and especially a how-to book, the author's credentials are essential. Keep the biography short (one paragraph) and to the point.

Publishing information and bookstore categories

QR code

Your publishing information is usually placed at the bottom of your back cover. This includes a barcode with ISBN and price (see chapter 70), your publishing name and logo (optional), your website URL (if you have one), and a QR code (optional, see below).

List one or two catagories so that bookstore staff will know where to shelve your book. The categories are usually shown at the top left corner of your back cover but can instead be placed at the bottom with your publishing information. Find your category at bisg.org.

Create a QR (Quick Response) code

A QR code is programmed with a website URL address and, when scanned with a mobile device, opens the specified website in a browser.

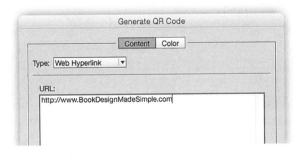

To create a QR code in InDesign, click Object>Generate QR Code with your Selection Tool. Choose Web Hyperlink from the Type drop-down menu, then enter the URL of your home page (or Buy the Book page) on your website, then click OK. The QR code will load onto your pointer. Click anywhere on your page or pasteboard to place the QR code, and it can be placed at any size since it is a vector image (based on math rather than pixels).

Designing your back cover

There are as many ways to design a back cover as there are books out there. So start by keeping it simple, and embellish later when you see how much space you have available.

The steps you'll take are:

1 Typesetting your back cover copy
2 Typesetting your bio and adding your photo
3 Adding your barcode and publishing information
4 Fine-tuning your back cover

Keep in mind there are no hard and fast rules for designing back covers. If a different kind of design suits your book, feel free to deviate from the guidelines in this chapter.

1 Typesetting your back-cover copy

Start by placing your back-cover copy onto the Text layer on your back cover. Using your Selection Tool, click File>Place, browse for the Word document containing your back-cover copy, and click Open. When your pointer is loaded with the text, drag a frame to fill your back cover to flow the text in.

The keyboard shortcut for Place is Ctrl/Cmd+D.

Drag the edges of the text frame so they are approximately 0.5″ in from the edges of the cover. (This leaves an ample area between the text and the edges of the back cover, and you can decrease that space later if needed.)

Next, create and apply paragraph styles for your tagline, summary, testimonials, and testimonial attributions, following the guidelines on pages 426–429. Make sure the text fits nicely into the top two-thirds of the back cover. If you discover you have too much copy and your back cover looks crowded, simply edit it to fit.

Organize your existing paragraph styles

If you need a refresher on creating paragraph styles, see chapter 10 and/or the box on page 61.

Before creating new paragraph styles for your back cover, take a moment to organize your paragraph styles. You probably have some unused ones left over from your front-cover designs. Remove unused paragraph styles by clicking the fly-out menu on the Paragraph Styles panel then choosing Select All Unused. Click on the trash can icon at the bottom right, and you'll see the Delete Paragraph Style dialog box (shown below). Choose the option shown, then click OK.

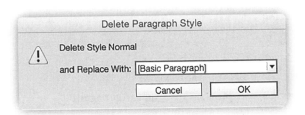

Now open your Basic Paragraph style by double-clicking it, and select Basic Character Formats on the left. Make sure the typeface chosen for Font Family is the same typeface used in the main narrative for your pages. That way your back-cover copy will be set in the same typeface and your cover will complement your pages.

Creating and applying your back-cover copy styles

On pages 427–428 are sample paragraph styles for your tagline, summary, and testimonials. These are very general paragraph styles to get you started, and you'll need to tweak them to suit the amount of back-cover material and style of book *you* have. For now, just create the styles and apply them to your text. When you're finished, your Paragraph Styles panel should look like the one shown to the right.

To sort your paragraph styles alphabetically, click the fly-out menu and choose Sort by Name.

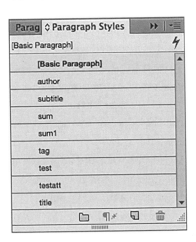

☐ **Tagline [tag]**
General:

Parent = [Basic Paragraph]
Style Name = **tag**
Based On = [Basic Paragraph]

Changes from the [Basic Paragraph] style:
Basic Character Formats:

Font Style = Semibold Italic
Size = 18 pt

Indents and Spacing:

Alignment = Center
Space After = 14 pt *or* 0.1944 in

Design your own book with confidence! ← Here's what your tagline looks like using the Tagline [**tag**] style above. Later you can change it to suit *your* back cover by changing its typeface, size, color, and/or alignment.

Do you want to create your book cover and/or pages yourself? Well, now you can! Follow this simple step-by-step guide to design and typeset your own book using Adobe InDesign.

Learn the basics of book design from experts. We'll help you through every stage of your book's design, from getting started in InDesign to uploading your digital files to your printer.

☐ **Summary, First Paragraph [sum1]**
General:

Parent = [Basic Paragraph]
Style Name = **sum1**
Based On = [Basic Paragraph]

Changes from the [Basic Paragraph] style:
None

☐ **Summary [sum]**
General:

Parent = **sum1**
Style Name = **sum**
Based On = **sum1**

Changes from the [Basic Paragraph] style:
Indents and Spacing:

First Line Indent = 0.2 in

Apply the **sum1** style
to your first summary
paragraph and **sum** to
subsequent paragraphs.
These paragraphs cur-
rently match the main
narrative in your pages.

Do you want to create your book cover and/or pages yourself? Well, now you can! Follow this simple step-by-step guide to design and typeset your own book using Adobe InDesign.

Learn the basics of book design from experts. We'll help you through every stage of your book's design, from getting started in InDesign to uploading your digital files to your printer.

☐ **Testimonials [test]**

Parent = [Basic Paragraph]
Style Name = **test**
Based On = [Basic Paragraph]

Changes from the [Basic Paragraph] style:
Basic Character Formats:

Size = 10 pt
Leading = 12 pt

Indents and Spacing:

Alignment = Center

☐ **Testimonial Attributions [testatt]**
General:

Parent = **test**
Style Name = **testatt**
Based On = **test**

Changes from the Testimonials style:
Basic Character Formats:

Size = 8 pt
Leading = 10 pt

Indents and Spacing:

Space Before = 0.0625 in
Space After = 0.125 in

Apply the **test** style to
your testimonials and
testatt for the attributions. Later you'll make
sure the testimonials with
more than one line split
in appropriate places, and
you'll add small caps and
italics to the attributions.

A testimonial goes here, saying how wonderful the book is!
—Attribution, author of *Another Book*

A second testimonial goes here, with lots of kudos about the book . . . really a spectacular endorsement.
—Testimonial Name, CEO of Great Company

A third testimonial goes here.
—Testimonial Attribution, book designer

Now that you've set up your back-cover copy with paragraph styles, it should fill the top two-thirds of your book cover, leaving room for your bio, photo, publishing info, and barcode below.

2 Typesetting your bio and adding your photo

Place your bio in a new text frame below the text frame containing your back-cover copy. It's handy to keep your bio in a separate frame so it can be moved and sized independently from the back-cover copy. Create the Bio [**bio**] paragraph style shown below and apply it to your bio.

If your book cover is a dust jacket or soft-cover with flaps, your bio will go on your back flap (see page 436).

☐ **Bio [bio]**

Changes from the [Basic Paragraph] style:
Basic Character Formats:

Parent = [Basic Paragraph]
Style Name = **bio**
Based On = [Basic Paragraph]

Size = 10 pt
Leading = 12 pt

Next, place your photo (see page 288) on your Text layer, and apply a text wrap to it (see page 296). Your photo is placed on the same layer as your text rather than the Graphics layer so that the text wrap affects the text (text wrap doesn't affect text on a layer above it).

Fiona Raven and Glenna Collett are book designers who share a keen interest in all things relating to book design. The question arose, "Why isn't there a book that explains step-by-step how to create a book in InDesign?" We have shelves full of books that explain part of the process—books about design, typography, InDesign, image optimization, publishing, and so on—but not a single book that walks you through the whole process of creating a book from start to finish in simple terms.

Apply the **bio** style to your bio, then place your photo and make it a suitable size using the Free Transform Tool. Then apply a text wrap (see page 296) to your photo and move it next to your bio.

3 Adding your barcode and publishing information

If you already have your barcode (see chapter 70), place it at the bottom of your back cover on the Graphics layer. With the frame selected, open your Swatches panel and select [Paper] for the fill color (see page 259). Most printers allow light-colored backgrounds for barcodes; however, some POD printers require a white background, so start with that.

If you don't have a barcode yet (and this is most likely the case), create a placeholder by drawing a 2″ wide × 1.25″ high white rectangle using your Rectangle Tool (see chapter 33), and add your barcode to it later.

Always place a barcode at actual size, and don't resize it. If you need a slightly bigger box behind it, use the Selection Tool to enlarge the frame without changing the size of the barcode.

Possible placement of category for bookstores

If your barcode doesn't come with a human-readable price, you must add one yourself.

Adding your other publishing information is optional and depends on what you have available:

- **Publishing name** Create a new text frame on the Text layer, type your publishing name, and create a new paragraph style for it. Or, if it's an established brand, typeset the name using the colors and typeface of your brand, or place an image of your brand name there.

- **Publishing logo** If you have a logo for your publishing company, place it at the bottom of your back cover on the Graphics layer.

- **Website URL** If you have a website, type the URL in a new text frame on the Text layer, and create a new paragraph style for it.

- **Category** If you want to let bookstores know where to shelve your book, create a new text frame on the Text layer, type your category, and create a new paragraph style for it. Put it at the top left of your back cover or at the top left corner of your barcode box (see above).

The Book Industry Study Group lists book subject categories at bisg.org.

4 Fine-tuning your back cover

Now that you have all your information laid out on your back cover, you'll need to make it all fit nicely and add some color.

Look at the examples below to get some ideas for your back cover. Put what you feel is most important at the top. If you'd prefer to have your testimonials above your tagline and back-cover copy, just cut and paste them at the top.

If you're designing a dust jacket or softcover with flaps, your bio and author photo will go on the back flap rather than the back cover (see page 436).

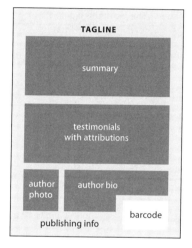
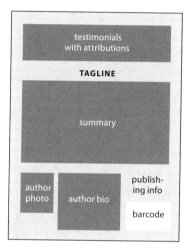
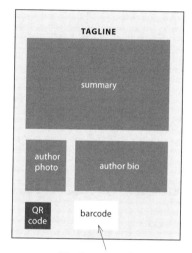

Distributors and bookstores usually require that barcodes be placed in compliance with Book Industry Study Group standards (a minimum of 0.25" and a maximum of 0.75" from the bottom edge of the back cover).

Experiment with your paragraph styles to make your type larger or smaller to fit the space. If your type is too small to read comfortably, consider rewording some of your material to make it more concise. Think about your potential readers . . . what will appeal most to them? Make sure you are speaking to them directly. Make it clear and easy to read.

You'll need to give credit for the cover design and images, including the author photo. Credits usually go on the copyright page (see page 226), with two exceptions: if your cover is separate from the book (i.e., a dust jacket), then the credits go on the back flap (see page 436), and if you're designing the cover but not typesetting the pages, you should add the credits to the back cover.

See pages 432–433 for ideas on embellishing your back cover.

Simple back cover

Tagline set in all caps to fit the width of the text block

Summary is longer as there are no testimonials.

The red of the tagline, bullet paragraph separators, and title on the front cover are all taken from the red of the publishing logo.

Publishing name/logo and website URL

From *Mastering Massive Complexity* by Don Johnson

Gradient color background

Tagline set in yellow and fits on one line in width of the text block

Summary set in white

Testimonials set in yellow with attributions in turquoise

Bio set in white with author's name set in yellow

No publishing info or website URL

Gradient background fades from dark blue at the top to light blue at the bottom to match front cover. See page 262 to learn to make a gradient.

From *All The Way Home* by David Berner

Box around testimonials

Tagline set in green italics in typeface used on front cover

Summary set in black, with book title set in pink used on front cover

Testimonials set in black, attribution names set in green small caps

Website URL set large in green

From *How to Help Others Without Losing Yourself* by Debbie Holmes

Green is brought around spine from front cover and repeated on both sides of back cover to add color

Green box around testimonials with inverse round corners and a Thick-Thin 3 pt stroke

Color bars top and bottom

Tagline set in white in top color bar

Headings for bulleted lists set in red in same typeface used on front cover

Bio does not include a photo

Publishing info in bottom color bar, including publisher's contact info in black and website URL in white

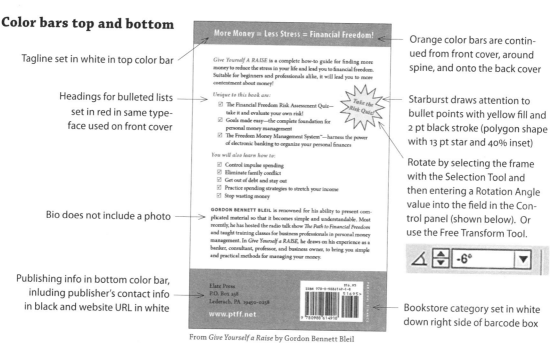

From *Give Yourself a Raise* by Gordon Bennett Bleil

Orange color bars are continued from front cover, around spine, and onto the back cover

Starburst draws attention to bullet points with yellow fill and 2 pt black stroke (polygon shape with 13 pt star and 40% inset)

Rotate by selecting the frame with the Selection Tool and then entering a Rotation Angle value into the field in the Control panel (shown below). Or use the Free Transform Tool.

Bookstore category set in white down right side of barcode box

Typesetting tips for your back cover

Here are some ideas for making the type on your back cover look great:

- If you've used a different typeface for type on your front cover, or for the titles and headings in your pages, consider using that typeface for your tagline, author's name, and other special type on your back cover.
- It's best to use black ink for your summary, but consider using another color for your tagline, testimonial attribution names, author's name, website URL, and so on. Choose a color that ties in with your front cover or publishing logo.
- When typesetting testimonials and attributions, you don't need to include the quotation marks around the testimonials. Try center justifying the testimonials and centering the attributions (shown below), or left aligning the testimonials and right aligning the attributions.

A testimonial goes here, saying how wonderful the book is!
—FIONA RAVEN, coauthor of *Book Design Made Simple*

Try placing an em dash before the attribution. Try setting the attribution author's name in small caps, bold, and/or a different color, to make it stand out. If there is a book title in the attribution, be sure to set it in italics.
- You might choose to dispense with your publishing name and logo on the back cover and simply feature your website URL. Try making the URL larger, and set it in a color taken from your front cover (shown below). If you have several words in your URL, capitalize the first letter in each word to make it easier to read at a glance. Adding a QR code to your back cover will simplify steering viewers directly to your website, or to the "Buy the Book" page on your website.

www.BookDesignMadeSimple.com

Embellishing your back cover

Just having type filling the space can be a bit uninspiring. Consider adding a few other embellishments, as long as they don't make the back cover too crowded or hard to read.

Keep in mind the colors, typefaces, and graphic elements you've used on your front cover and in your pages. Can you use the same colors on your back cover?

You can add:

- A background color for your back cover that complements your front cover. Choose a pale color that type will show nicely against. Or, if your front cover is dark, consider a dark background color with light-colored boxes between the background and your type (put those shapes on your Graphics layer)
- Color bars across the top and/or bottom of the back cover, or down both sides to bring those colors around from the front cover (like the examples on page 433)
- A color box between your text and background images, to make the text easier to read (see example to the right, from page 404)
- A box around text to separate it visually from other text (see top example on page 433)
- Paragraph separators or paragraph rules between text to separate different sections, especially if you used paragraph separators in your pages (see top example of bullets on page 432)
- A bulleted list to simplify your summary using special bullet points to add color and interest, such as arrows, checkboxes, or even just colored dots (see bottom example on page 433)

A color box between text and background images helps the text to stand out.

If your book doesn't have a lot of back-cover copy, you can really use colored shapes and paragraph separators to your advantage, to add color and interest to your back cover and to help fill space. If you have a lot of back cover copy, then separate the sections of text visually by using different sizes of type, colored backgrounds, and/or paragraph separators.

The most important issue is that your back cover draws your reader in by being uncluttered and inviting to read.

Back cover and flaps for dust jacket or softcover with flaps

Dust jackets and softcovers with flaps have a slightly different back-cover layout because they include flaps.

The author's photo and bio goes on the back flap (on the left in your InDesign file). For a dust jacket (where the cover can be separated from the rest of the book) be sure to add your design and image credits, and especially the country where your book was printed, at the bottom of the back flap. Put "Printed in [Country]". This is required by customs if your book is shipped across a border.

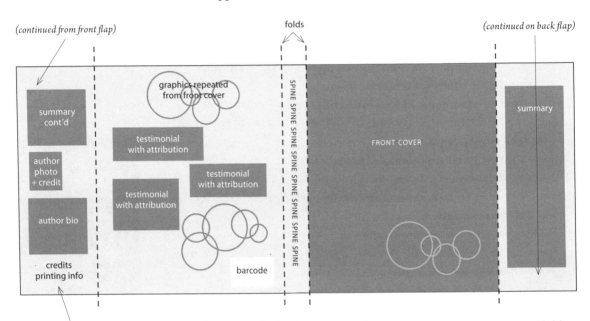

(continued from front flap)   folds   *(continued on back flap)*

graphics repeated from front cover

summary cont'd

author photo + credit

author bio

credits printing info

testimonial with attribution

testimonial with attribution

testimonial with attribution

barcode

SPINE SPINE SPINE SPINE SPINE SPINE SPINE SPINE

FRONT COVER

summary

Jacket design by Jane Doe
Cover photo by John Smith
Author photo by Moe Curly
Printed in the USA

With flaps and a back cover, you have a lot more cover space available to you. Use the front flap for a straightforward summary or synopsis of the book—no direct marketing. If you need more space, continue it at the top of the back flap, and add "*(continued . . .)*" at the bottom of the front flap and top of the back flap as shown above.

On the back cover, put your testimonials with attributions. You might also choose to include your marketing summary. Look at other dust jackets in your genre to get ideas of what will be best for *your* back cover. And see pages 431–435 for ideas on embellishing your back cover and flaps using typefaces, colors, and graphic elements from your cover and pages.

Designing your spine

The spine may be the first part of your book that a reader sees, and it also connects the front and the back covers. Try to keep both of these factors in mind as you decide how to present your book to the world.

Consider the following as you think about your spine:

- If your front cover has an overall background color, do you want to use that same color on the spine?
- What solid color would appeal to your target audience and also match the color on the rest of the cover? (For POD printing, it's not recommended that a color be placed *just* on the spine, as often the binding is slightly off, and this will make binding flaws very obvious.)
- If your front cover has an image, do you want it to spill over onto the spine and perhaps onto the back cover too? If you do so, will the spine type be readable? (If not, consider a color box behind the type.)
- Is there a small image you could place at the top, middle, or bottom of the spine to entice a reader to pick your book off the shelf?
- If you use the same typeface as for the title on the front cover, will it be legible from a distance? If your title is long, you may need to use a sans serif (even a condensed one) to make your title fit and be easy to read.
- If you're producing a series of books, plan ahead. You'll want all of them to have a similar spine design so they'll look like a set. Try the same placement and type treatment for the title and author's name, but vary the colors of the background and/or type. If you plan to number the series, add a number to the top, middle, or bottom of the spine.

The spine is an important part of the cover that'll help to sell your book because unless you're lucky enough to have your book facing out on a bookstore shelf or table, the spine will be the first thing a customer sees. So make the most of this valuable marketing opportunity!

Books are displayed lying face up on a table, so the front cover and spine must look good together. The type on the spine should be right side up when a book is in this position.

Test the longest and shortest titles in your series to see how well they fit in the space. If both look fine, then your medium-length titles will work, too.

As a corollary to this, the words in your book's title should have immediate impact. Not even a great design will make up for a weak title.

Choosing elements to include on your spine

Here is a list of things you can choose to add to your spine. You'll probably want your book title and author's name as a minimum, but there are other options too:

A spine measuring 0.125″ or less is too narrow to have type on it. The printer cannot guarantee that the type would not slide over onto the front or back cover in the binding process.

☑ book title
☑ author's name (or just surname if you prefer)
❑ subtitle
❑ publishing name
❑ publishing logo
❑ small image
❑ series number
❑ graphics (rules, bullets, and so on) used elsewhere on your cover or pages

Adding a background to the spine

Before adding any elements to your spine, choose a background image or color. Consider wrapping your front cover image onto the spine (and possibly ¼–½″ onto the back cover as well) if there is enough image available. If the image creates a busy background and makes your type too hard to read, you can add a white or color box between the type and the background image. Screen the box back to 20–30% (see page 404) or however much is needed to make the type easy to read.

It's more common to carry an image or color onto the spine from the front cover than from the back cover. That way, when the book is lying on a table with the front cover up, the front cover and spine appear seamless.

If you've used a solid color on the front or back cover, it could be extended onto the spine. If your books will be printed digitally, keep in mind that your books will be bound one at a time, and the binding machine will not be adjusted specifically for *your* book. This means that the cover may shift slightly side to side or up or down during the binding process. So avoid putting a separate color *just* on the spine, as the spine could shift in the binding process. If you do want a separate color on the spine, make it narrower than the spine width (use the allowable width for text, as explained on page 439). You'll notice on *this* book there is a color bar down the spine, narrower than the actual spine width, and that's specifically for digital printing, in case the spine isn't perfectly lined up during the binding process.

Adding guides for spine-text clearance

Most printers require a minimum clearance of 0.0625″ (¹⁄₁₆″) between anything on the spine and the edges of the spine. Here's how to add two guides as a reminder to keep all your spine elements inside the clearance space.

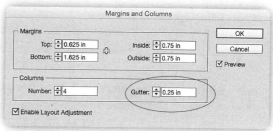

Click Layout>Margins & Columns and in the Columns section see what your spine width is set at (the Gutter number). Subtract 0.125″ from that number, put the resulting number in the Gutter box, and click OK. Drag guides from the left ruler (see page 421) onto your two new column guides, then go back into Margins & Columns and change the Gutter number back to your proper spine width.

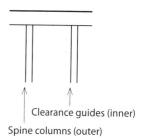

Clearance guides (inner)

Spine columns (outer)

Adding type sideways down the spine

Here's an easy way to add your title sideways down the spine. Select Basic Paragraph style in your Paragraph Styles panel, and create a new text frame by dragging the Type Tool on your Text layer. Type your title in the text frame, then select the title and create a new paragraph style (see page 61) called Spine Title [**sptitle**].

Switch to the Selection Tool, select the text frame, and click the Rotate 90° Clockwise icon in the Control panel. After your text frame rotates, drag it onto the spine, and line up the edges of the text frame with the sides of the spine. With the frame still selected, click Object>Text Frame Options, then under Vertical Justification change the Align drop-down menu to Center and click OK.

Rotate 90°
Clockwise icon

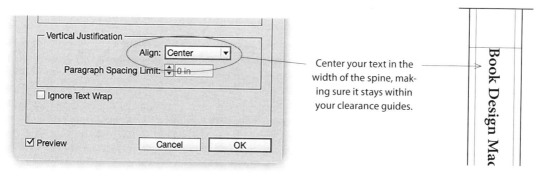

Center your text in the width of the spine, making sure it stays within your clearance guides.

You may notice that some of your type doesn't look centered on the spine. You can shift the type left or right (actually up or down) using Baseline Shift, found under the Advanced Character Formats tab in your paragraph style.

Fitting everything onto the spine

Create separate text frames and paragraph styles for the other text on your spine, and place any images you intend to include. Then change the size of your type and images to fit on the spine.

Sometimes a book title is too long, or there's more than one author, making it difficult to fit everything in. Rather than crowding it all onto one line, try stacking names or the title on two lines. Study other book spines for options. Your main goal is to make the most important information clear and readable from a distance.

Most of the time, spine type reads down from the top. If the spine is wide enough, though, you can place some of the elements horizontally.

Below are some ideas on how to fit everything onto the spine.

Don't even think about hyphenating the title to get this effect! If the words don't fit, set them vertically.

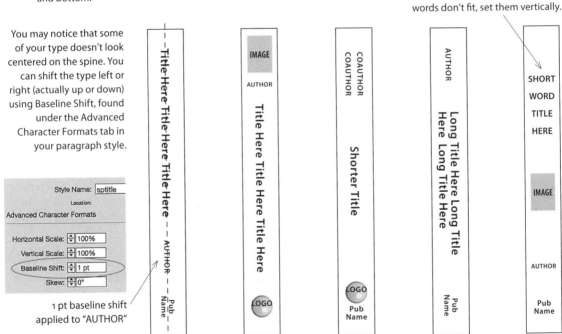

1 pt baseline shift applied to "AUTHOR"

Designing extras for hardcovers

If you've designed a dust jacket for your hardcover book, then you'll need to create a digital file for the foil stamping on the hardcover's spine, as well as choose colors for the foil stamping, headbands, and hardcover wrap (the paper or cloth that covers it). You'll also decide whether to create custom endsheets or simply use white paper.

Creating a digital file for the spine imprint

Hardcover books are stamped with foil on the spine. Create an InDesign file for your spine by clicking File>New>Document. Fill out the dialog box as shown to the right, then click OK.

Open your dust jacket file, select the text and images you want on your hardcover spine, and copy them (click Edit>Copy or press Ctrl/Cmd+C). Now go back to your new document, and Paste in Place those elements into your spine (click Edit>Paste in Place or press Ctrl/Cmd+Shift+Alt/Opt+V). Save your new file.

Your new digital file for foil stamping can only contain 100% black ink, with no shades of gray. So open your Swatches panel and select all of the colors except the defaults in square brackets. Then click the Trash icon to delete them all, and the Delete Swatch dialog box will appear as shown to the right. Replace all the swatches you're deleting with default [Black].

If you have a logo or image on the spine that cannot be translated into one solid color, you may need to leave it off the hardcover spine or substitute a more suitable image.

Put the spine width from your dust jacket in the Width box and the height of your dust jacket in the Height box (and you may need to set your margins to zero).

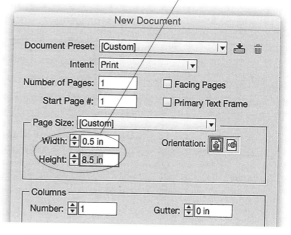

Choosing colors for your hardcover

You'll need to choose colors for the foil stamping on the spine, your hardcover wrap (the paper or cloth that covers the hardcover), the headbands, and a ribbon (if you decide to include one). You can request samples of these from your printer. All of these color choices are included in the cost of printing your hardcover book. There is usually an extra charge for using a cloth hardcover wrap (instead of paper) and always for adding a ribbon.

Hardcover wrap

You'll probably choose a colored paper wrap, but cloth is available for an extra cost if you're so inclined. Look through the color samples from your printer, and choose one to complement your dust jacket. You might choose a color that you've used in your cover design, a neutral color (such as black, gray, taupe, or white), or an accent color, like bright red or yellow, to make a statement.

Foil stamping

Gold and silver are the most common choices for foil stamping, but there are several colors available as well, such as red, green, blue, yellow, and black. Choose a color that complements your hardcover wrap.

headband   endsheet

cloth- or paper-
wrapped board

Headbands

The headband (see diagram at left) adds a decorative touch to the book binding. It is the small, ribbon-like cloth band attached to the top and bottom of the hardcover spine. Choose your headband color to complement your hardcover wrap and/or dust jacket.

Ribbon(s)

Ribbons are used as place markers, and you can choose to add one or two. They come in a variety of widths (usually ¼″ or ½″ wide) and colors. Choose from your printer's samples.

Paper color for the pages

You'll have a choice of white- or cream-colored paper for your pages and can probably choose from thicker (60 lb) or thinner (50 lb) paper.

Endsheets: white, colored, or printed?

All hardcover books automatically come with white endsheets at no extra cost. Or, for a small extra cost you can choose to have endsheets made from colored paper (and choose from a number of standard colors).

If your printer doesn't have a suitable color in their colored papers, you could choose to have the endsheets printed with a color wash (a solid color of your choice, printed on the endsheets). This will cost a bit more than colored-paper endsheets, but you'll get the exact color you want. You can choose from a CMYK color or a spot color (such as a metallic or neon color, or a bright color that can't be duplicated using CMYK colors).

A more expensive option is to design printed endsheets. The cost will depend on the number of ink colors (one color is cheaper than four) and whether you create different endsheets for the front and back of the book or use the same one for both. Keep in mind that the flaps of your dust jacket will obscure part of the endsheets, which might influence your decision.

Create an InDesign file for printed endsheets by clicking File>New>Document. Add two columns with no gutter so you can see where the endsheet will fold (and keep any crucial parts of your design away from the fold). Note there is a bleed of 0.125″ on all four sides. Fill out the dialog box as shown to the right, then click OK.

Create an endsheet on page 1 of your document. If you choose to have different endsheets at the front and back of your book, then put the front endsheet on page 1 and the back endsheet on page 2. Consider placing a guide (see page 421) where the flap of your dust jacket will overlap the endsheet, as that area will be covered.

Be aware that endsheets are always made from uncoated paper so that glue will be absorbed into them. After all, the endsheets are glued to both the hardcover and the pages to hold the book together. Uncoated paper absorbs more ink, so colors will look less intense than they will on coated paper.

In the Width box, put the width of your page times 2. So if your book is 5.5″ wide, your endsheets will be 11″ wide.

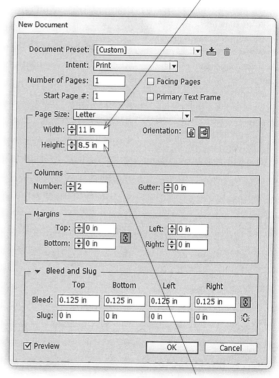

In the Height box, put the height of your page.

67

Printing color cover proofs

You'll want to get color proofs of your cover printed *before* your book goes to press to make sure the colors are perfect for your book and that they print as expected. You certainly don't want any surprises after you've uploaded your book to your printer. An easy way to check your colors is to send a PDF to your local copy store and ask them to print your cover.

To create a PDF, click File>Export, and check that the name of your PDF is okay (InDesign will use same name and file folder as your cover document, except with the file extension .pdf). Choose Adobe PDF (Print) from the Save as type (PC) or Format (Mac) drop-down menu. Click Save to get the Export Adobe PDF dialog box. Choose High Quality Print from the Adobe PDF Preset drop-down menu at the top, then select Marks and Bleeds from the menu on the left, and fill out that section as shown below. All the other sections can remain the same. Then click Export to generate your high-resolution PDF.

Send the PDF to your copy store by email, use FTP transfer, upload it to their website, or hand-deliver a memory stick. For softcovers, ask them to print your cover on 11″ × 17″ glossy cardstock (coated one side, or C1S). For dust jackets, ask them to print on 28 lb paper (or their equivalent). If the dust jacket is too wide to fit on one sheet of paper, ask them to tile it (print it on two pieces of paper), with the spine showing on both pieces. Later you'll be able to trim and fold it using the crop marks. Now take the proof to your local bookstore, wrap it around a similar-sized book, and set it on the shelf to see how it fits in with other books.

Congratulations, you've finished your cover!

> If you're not sure about a color, try a few options in the same InDesign file. In your Pages panel, drag your cover page icon onto the Create New Page icon at the bottom to duplicate your cover, then try some variations of colors on the new page. Duplicate as many pages as you need to experiment with different colors.

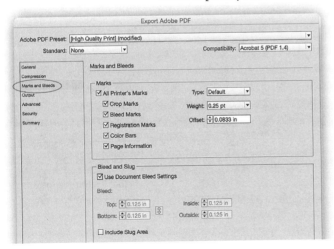

Part IX: Preparing to Publish

445

68

Obtaining and assigning ISBNs

One of the things you'll need to do as a publisher is obtain a block of International Standard Book Numbers (ISBNs) for your books. Some printers, print-on-demand publishers, and ebook vendors will offer to provide you with an ISBN, but it's better to get your own. Part of the ISBN includes a "publisher number," which is assigned to a specific publisher. Therefore, if you allow another company to provide the ISBN, then that company will be listed as the publisher of your book. ISBNs are easy to obtain online, and using your own numbers means that you'll retain control over your books.

Pages 448–449 offer more details to help you decide how many ISBNs you'll need.

ISBNs are assigned by the ISBN agency in your country. They usually come in blocks of 10, 100, or 1,000, and you'll need a separate ISBN for each edition of your book. If you're publishing one book, be sure to get more than one ISBN as you'll probably produce more than one edition (for example, a softcover edition and a Kindle edition). You might even have other editions, such as hardcover, EPUB, and PDF.

Getting ISBNs in the United States

ISBN suppliers are listed on pages 227.

Go to the U.S. ISBN Agency website and click on the "buy your ISBNs today!" button to get to their purchase page. ISBNs are available one at a time, or in blocks of 10, 100, or 1,000. It's best not to buy just one, as you'll need a unique number for each edition.

Once you've purchased a block of numbers, you can assign the ISBNs to your books as they're published.

Getting ISBNs in Canada

ISBNs are free to Canadian publishers and are issued in 10 days. Go to the Library and Archives Canada ISBN website, where you'll see the steps to register explained. Once approved, you'll receive a user ID and password by email, together with instructions for using your online account. You'll then be able to assign a unique ISBN from your block to each edition of your book through your online account.

Getting your own ISBNs is easy to do online, and allows you to retain control of your books after they're published. You might choose to get your books printed somewhere else down the road or produce an updated version or second edition. When you have your own block of ISBNs, you'll be in control of your books' destiny.

Getting ISBNs outside North America

Go to the International ISBN Agency website and click the "Find an agency" button. Select your country from the drop-down menu and you'll see information there on how to obtain your ISBNs.

What do the numbers in the ISBN stand for?

In North America, most retail products are marked with a UPC symbol. The corresponding barcode symbol in use outside North America is the European Article Number (EAN). Every EAN begins with a two- or three-digit prefix, which indicates the country of origin. EANs for companies registered in France, for example, might begin with the prefix 34; Australia's prefix is 93. Since the book industry produces so many products, it has been designated as a country unto itself and has been assigned its own EAN prefix. That prefix is 978, and it signifies Bookland, that wonderful, fictitious country where all books come from.

The publisher number is a unique seven-digit number assigned to your publishing company. All the books you publish will have the same country prefix, country indicator, and publisher number. The only digits that will change from book to book are the title number and check digit.

You'll assign a unique title number to each edition of each book you publish (see page 448).

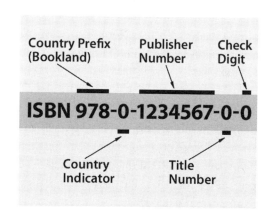

Assigning ISBNs to print books

When you've obtained your block of ISBNs, you'll need to assign a unique ISBN to each edition of every book you publish. Let's say your first book is a novel called *Raven* and it's a hardcover book. That means your first ISBN number will be assigned like this:

ISBN 978-0-1234567-0-0 / BookTitle1 / Hardcover Edition

The second-last number is 0, the first digit in your block of ISBNs. This number is always assigned to the first edition (in this case the hardcover edition) of your first book. The last number is automatically calculated by an algorithm, and it's called the "check digit." (Sometimes the check digit is an X, so don't worry if you get an X as the check digit in one of your ISBNs.)

Let's say you also release a softcover edition of your book. You'll assign the next ISBN in your block of numbers to your softcover edition:

ISBN 978-0-1234567-1-7 / BookTitle1 / Softcover Edition

The second-last number is 1, the next digit in your block of ISBNs. And the last number is the check digit. So far so good, right?

Assigning ISBNs to ebooks

There are three main formats for ebooks: MOBI (for Kindle), EPUB (for other ereaders, such as Nook, Kobo, iBooks), and PDF. And this is where assigning ISBNs gets a bit trickier, as it depends on how you intend to *sell* your ebooks.

Selling ebooks yourself through different ebook retailers

If you'll be selling your ebooks yourself through different ebook retailers, you'll need to assign one ISBN for each ebook format. For example, if you sell your MOBI format at Amazon's Kindle Direct Publishing and your EPUB format at Barnes and Noble, you'll assign one ISBN for each of those formats, like this:

ISBN 978-0-1234567-2-4 / BookTitle1 / Digital Edition (Kindle)
ISBN 978-0-1234567-3-1 / BookTitle1 / Digital Edition (EPUB)

Selling ebooks through an ebook service

Several companies will act as a sales channel for all your digital editions. BookBaby, Smashwords, and Vook are examples of these services. If you're using one sales channel for all your digital editions, then you'll need to assign one ISBN for that sales channel, like this:

ISBN 978-0-1234567-2-4 / BookTitle1 / Digital Editions (BookBaby)
or
ISBN 978-0-1234567-2-4 / BookTitle1 / Digital Editions (Smashwords)

Can your ebook be published without an ISBN?

Yes. If you are only publishing a Kindle edition through Amazon's Kindle Direct Publishing, you can use their internal ASIN tracking number to track your sales instead of an ISBN. Or, if you are only selling ebooks from your own website, you can choose not to assign ISBNs to them.

Keep in mind that publishing ebook editions using your own ISBNs means that you'll be listed as the publisher in the appropriate Books in Print database, and that may help readers search for your ebook online.

How do I tell whether my updated book is a reprint or a second edition requiring a new ISBN?

If you are ordering another print run of your book with no substantial changes (just fixing a few typos, for example), then you don't need to assign a new ISBN. If you've changed the cover but not the text, you can continue to use the same ISBN.

If you've changed the content of your book or added new material (another chapter, preface, appendix, or other content, for example), then you'll need to assign a new ISBN. A new edition is considered a different product and therefore gets its own ISBN.

69

Setting your book's retail price

Determining your book's retail price can be nerve-wracking. If it's too expensive, your book may be priced out of the market. If it's not expensive enough, you won't even recover your costs. How do other publishers decide? Consider three things: cost per book to print, pre- and post-printing expenses, and the price of similar books in the marketplace.

One way to calculate your book's retail price is to take your printing cost per book and multiply it by five. That may seem like a lot, but consider this: if you sell to a distributor or online retailer, they usually take 65% off your retail price, and you pay the shipping; and if you sell directly to a bookstore, they often take 50% off your retail price, and you pay the shipping. You need to have enough left over to cover your pre- and post-printing costs, and then some.

You are not just paying for printing books. Your pre-printing costs can include editing, proofreading, book design and typesetting, images, indexing, and your ISBN number and barcode. These are all expenses you'll have paid before your book goes to press.

After your book is printed, you could have any or all of the following expenses: packaging, delivery (gas), postage, advertising, long distance telephone charges, bank charges, website design and maintenance, web hosting, and book marketing. Don't forget you'll also be giving away free books to stores and distributors as samples to generate sales, as well as paying for the return of any books damaged in shipping or unsold in stores.

What are books like yours selling for in the marketplace? Your book's price should be in the same ballpark. If your book is thicker, printed in color, has more images, or is unique in subject, people will pay more for it.

Before you decide on a retail price for your book, consider carefully all of the costs to produce it, and anticipate your future costs as well. Then compare prices of similar books in bookstores, and you'll be on track to setting the right price for your book.

Obtaining a barcode

Barcodes are scannable codes that allow booksellers to automatically capture an ISBN (and retail price, if encoded). The Bookland EAN is the barcode used by the book industry. It's actually two barcodes side by side. The larger barcode to the left is the encoded ISBN, and the smaller barcode to the right is the encoded price.

encoded ISBN →

$12.95 ← human-readable price
ISBN 978-0-9896511-0-3 ← ISBN
51295 > ← 5-digit price add-on
← encoded price

You might find later on that your book distributor, if you use one for printed books, requires the price to be encoded. So if you are certain of your price, you might as well include it with the barcode.

Before obtaining a barcode, you'll need to decide whether to encode your retail price. If you choose to encode your price, you'll decide what the five digits will be in the five-digit price add-on. The first digit is the currency indicator. Five is the designation for U.S. dollars, and six is the designation for Canadian dollars. An add-on of 51095 encodes the price $10.95 in USD. A book priced at $3.00 in USD would have the add-on 50300. Books priced at $99.99 or higher use the add-on 59999. If you choose not to encode your retail price, the add-on is 90000. This indicates there is no data encoded.

A free barcode is included on any cover template from POD printers such as CreateSpace and IngramSpark. Place the cover template on your book cover a second time, then using your Selection Tool, drag the frame sides in to fit around the barcode (this will hide the rest of the template). Move the barcode into position, but take care not to enlarge or shrink it, as doing so may affect its scanning readability. For tips on placing a barcode on your back cover, see page 430.

If you order a barcode from an encoding service, choose EPS or PDF format. The minimum EAN size allowed for book covers is 80% of the barcode's original size, and 2350 resolution is standard. See www .BookDesignMadeSimple .com/Resources for links.

71

Packaging for your printer

Preparing your InDesign file for the printer involves five important steps:

1 Finalizing your InDesign file
2 Checking for errors
3 Packaging your InDesign file
4 Generating a printer-ready PDF
5 Uploading the PDF to your printer

1 Finalizing your InDesign file

Finalizing your InDesign file involves getting rid of extraneous colors, styles, master pages, and fonts. Here's how:

❑ Open your Swatches panel and from the fly-out menu click Select All Unused. If any swatches are highlighted, delete them by clicking the trash icon. If there are any RGB or spot colors in the Swatches panel, convert them to CMYK by double-clicking the color then changing Color Type to Process.

❑ Open your Paragraph Styles panel and from the fly-out menu click Select All Unused. If any paragraph styles are highlighted, delete them by clicking the trash icon.

❑ Open your Character Styles panel and from the fly-out menu click Select All Unused. If any character styles are highlighted, delete them by clicking the trash icon.

❑ Check at the bottom of the Pages panel to make sure the total number of pages is correct. You should have an even number of pages. If not, add a blank page after the last page.

❑ Go to Type>Find Font and look at the list. Make sure that all the fonts you used are listed and that there are no warnings or question marks next to any of them. If you're using Typekit, all the fonts you've used should be listed. If any are missing or have a warning, select the font, then find it using the Replace With drop-down menus. If the font isn't listed there, you'll need to install it. If there are fonts listed that you didn't mean to use (they might have been imported with your manuscript), click on each one and enter the name of the correct font in the Replace With box below. Go to Find First, then click Change or Change All, and the substitutions will be made. Repeat for each unwanted font.

❑ In the Layers panel, click the eye icon next to any layers you don't want to print so that they become invisible.

2 Checking for errors

By the time you've finished with the steps listed above, it's unlikely that you will still have anything to fix. But take a look at the bottom of your screen and you might see a red dot and some number of errors next to it. Double-click on this error list to open the Preflight dialog box. It will show you the details of each problem and where it appears, so simply click on the page number shown to jump directly to the trouble spot. You might see any one of the following:

❑ **Missing font** You have already taken care of any font troubles in step 1, so there should be no warnings, but if there are, go through that step again.

❑ **Missing link** If any images have come unlinked, select each one, click the Relink button, and link it up again (see page 317).

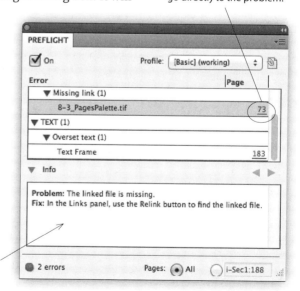

If you discover that the unwanted or missing font is used in one of your paragraph or character styles, click here and the style setting will change when you click Change All.

Click on the page number to go directly to the problem.

The highlighted error is explained in the Info box.

❑ **Overset text** The text frame has words that don't fit in the frame. Stretch the text frame down to see the words, then either find a way to fit them on the page, or delete them. When you are finished there should no longer be a red "⊞" icon (out port) at the bottom right side of the text frame. Remember to restore the text frame to the right size.

❑ **Other errors** Each is explained in the Info box. Click on the listed page number to go to the problem and correct it.

3 Packaging your InDesign file

Don't forget to go through the packaging process with both your pages and your book cover (the process will be the same for both).

Now that your entire book is organized, everything is gathered together, and all errors are corrected, you will package it all one last time. Packaging a file creates a folder that contains the InDesign file, all fonts (except those used in Typekit), all links, and a customized report.

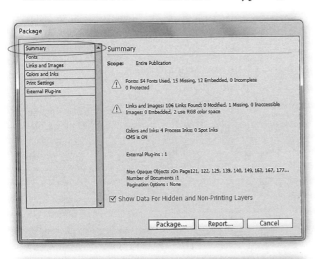

Summary

Save your InDesign file using today's date, then click File>Package. The first section of the resulting dialog box is Summary. If you see a warning symbol, go to the relevant section in the dialog box and find out what the problem is. In this example, there are problems with the fonts and the links.

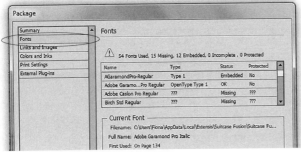

Fonts

In this example, fonts are missing. Click on Cancel, then install the missing fonts, or substitute another font by going to Type>Find Font, selecting the problem font, and replacing it with another one.

Links and Images

This is the final test of all of your graphics and photos. As you can see, the book in the example has images that are improperly linked or are missing (see the Status column). Select a missing link, then click the Relink button. You'll be able to find the problem link and relink or update it. Don't worry about RGB images showing as problems. You'll convert them to CMYK when you create a PDF.

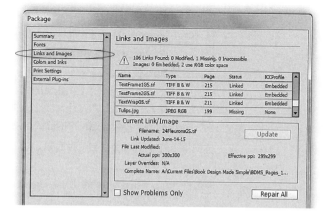

Colors and Inks

In this box you should only see the four CMYK colors: cyan, magenta, yellow, and black. If any other colors are listed, such as spot colors, you'll need to convert them to CMYK in your Swatches panel (see page 452), and do the same for any images coming from another application, such as Photoshop or Illustrator.

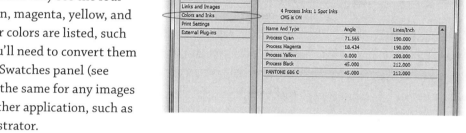

Print Settings

These specifications relate to the printer at the top of the list. This is probably the one you've been using to check your layouts. This information is irrelevant to the final printing of the book, so just ignore it.

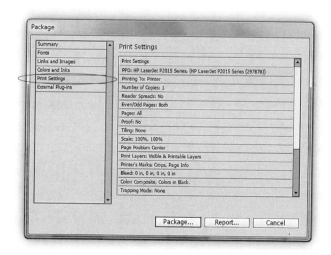

External Plug-ins

Most likely, this box will be blank. If you purchased a plug-in, though, it should be listed.

The final steps

Now click on Package and the next dialog box is Printing Instructions. You may ignore this page and click Continue to get the Package Publication (PC) or Create Package Folder (Mac) dialog box.

Browse for a suitable place to save your new folder, and type a name for the folder in the Folder Name field at the bottom (PC) or Save As field at the top (Mac). Check the boxes shown below. Here is a quick explanation of what these features do:

- **Copy Fonts** InDesign creates a subfolder called Document Fonts and copies all the fonts used in your document into this folder, except for Typekit fonts, Chinese, Japanese, and Korean (CJK) fonts, and any fonts that do not include copying in their license. If you've used any fonts that aren't included (besides Typekit fonts), add them to the packaged folder yourself. No need to worry about Typekit fonts.
- **Linked Graphics** InDesign creates a subfolder called Links and copies all the graphics used in your document into this folder. You want InDesign to copy linked graphics and to make sure the graphics are the updated versions, so check the second and third boxes.
- **Hyphenation** The prepress or printer's computer might have a dictionary program that's different from yours, and it might make the

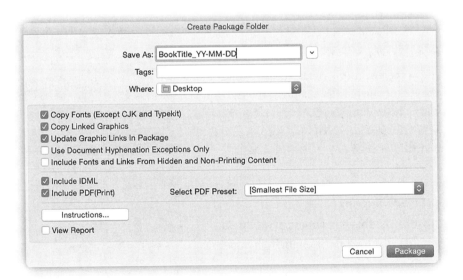

hyphenation in your book change, causing lines of type to move. You don't want this to happen, so check this box if you're going to send your InDesign file (rather than a PDF) to a service provider before printing.

- **Hidden and Non-Printing Content** If you have graphics and fonts on your pasteboard or on a layer that is not visible, and you want those graphics and fonts to be included in your package, then check Include Fonts and Links From Hidden and Non-Printing Content. If you don't want them included, leave it unchecked.
- **Include IDML** IDML is a file extension for an InDesign file format that can be opened by earlier versions than Creative Cloud. It's good to have an IDML file of your book, in case you ever want to open it in an earlier version.
- **Include PDF (Print), Select PDF Preset** This automatically creates a PDF of your InDesign file, which can be handy to have. Choose Smallest File Size for the Preset; that way you can easily email your PDF if needed.
- **View Report** If you check this box, you'll see the complete packaging report in a text editor program immediately after packaging. You can review the report later, so there's no need to check this box.

Click Package to continue. If you've included fonts in your book that aren't from Typekit, you'll see a warning screen like this one (right) explaining how you may use the fonts. Any reputable printer will be happy to explain their font rights and policies to you.

Click OK, and in a few moments your entire book will be grouped into the folder that you named. Now close the InDesign file you were just working on, and open the new file in the packaged folder. Check your Links panel once again to make sure all your images are linked, and click Type>Find Font to make sure your fonts are used properly, and that everything still looks the way it did a moment ago in your original file. From now on this is the file you'll be using.

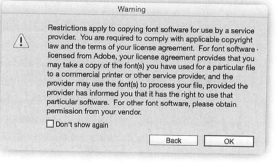

> Warning
>
> ⚠ Restrictions apply to copying font software for use by a service provider. You are required to comply with applicable copyright law and the terms of your license agreement. For font software licensed from Adobe, your license agreement provides that you may take a copy of the font(s) you have used for a particular file to a commercial printer or other service provider, and the provider may use the font(s) to process your file, provided the provider has informed you that it has the right to use that particular software. For other font software, please obtain permission from your vendor.
>
> ☐ Don't show again
>
> [Back] [OK]

The font legal issues are irrelevant if you're going to send a PDF to the printer instead of sending your InDesign file with fonts. But if necessary, review page 132 for more about fonts and their legal use.

4 Generating a printer-ready PDF

If you haven't done this already, you should now obtain your printer's instructions for making a PDF they can work with. Often you can get this information from your printer's website, but if not, contact your customer representative. The instructions may be available in a PDF you can download, or they may simply instruct you to use an Adobe PDF Preset.

Whichever method you use, you'll be generating a high-resolution PDF using the InDesign file you most recently packaged.

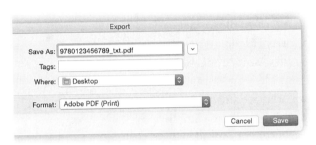

Click File>Export (or press Ctrl/Cmd+E) to open the Export dialog box. Browse to the same packaged folder your InDesign file is saved in (the one you just created). In the Save as type (PC) or Format (Mac) drop-down menu, choose Adobe PDF (Print). In the File name (PC) or Save As (Mac) field, type a name for your file. Your printer may have specific instructions on how to name your book files. CreateSpace and IngramSpark require your book's ISBN plus "txt" for pages and "cvr" for covers, like this:

9780123456700_txt.pdf (for your pages)
9780123456700_cvr.pdf (for your cover)

Then click Save, and you'll see the Export Adobe PDF dialog box. The settings you choose in this dialog box will depend on whether you are using an Adobe PDF Preset or custom settings.

Using a PDF preset

Look in the Adobe PDF Preset drop-down menu at the top of the Export Adobe PDF dialog box (see next page). You'll see there are several choices. Find the one that your printer has specified. Do not change any of the default settings. Be sure you are saving the file as single pages and not spreads. Click Export, and you are done! Your PDF should automatically open in Acrobat; however, not all of the presets have the View PDF after Exporting box checked, and if not, you may need to open Acrobat and then open your file.

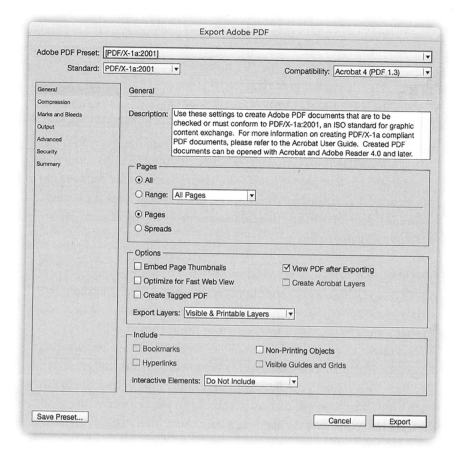

This Export Adobe PDF dialog box shows a typical preset used by printers.

Generating a custom PDF

If your printer has given you specific custom PDF settings, don't panic. This won't be difficult. There are two ways that printers can give you their settings for PDFs: by providing instructions to create a custom preset, or by providing a .joboptions file.

1 **Instructions to create a custom preset** Simply follow the printer's instructions, dialog box by dialog box, and copy every setting precisely. If you run into trouble, the customer rep is there to help. When you've created all the settings, save the printer's settings as a custom preset. Click Save Preset at the bottom left of the Export Adobe PDF dialog box, and name the preset for the printing company, such

as CreateSpace or IngramSpark. Next time you make a PDF for that printer, you can simply select the preset from the drop-down menu at the top and click Export.

2 **Providing a .joboptions file** This is a small file that your printer can provide to you, containing their custom preset. To load this file into your preset list, click File>Adobe PDF Presets>Define, and you'll see the Adobe PDF Presets dialog box. Click the Load button on the right side, and you'll be able to browse for the .joboptions file your printer provided. Select the file, then click Open. Now you'll see the preset in the Adobe PDF Preset drop-down menu at the top of your Export Adobe PDF dialog box.

Checking your PDF

Check this PDF over very carefully. Don't be surprised if you suddenly spot mistakes that you never noticed, even though you've looked through the book and checked the cover dozens of times before!

You might find it helpful to view your pages PDF as 2-page spreads. With your PDF open in Acrobat, go to View>Page Display and click on Two Page View, Show Gaps Between Pages, and Show Cover Page in Two Page View. The pages will display in spreads so you can make sure that each 2-page spread has the same number of text lines, the folios are in the right place, etc.

You can even get the PDF printed at your local copy store if you prefer to proof a hard copy. Have it printed double-sided and trimmed to size, then bound with velo, cerlox, or spiral binding.

Take your time, and make sure that every single thing is right before you upload the PDF to your printer.

Uploading to your printer

Every printer has a slightly different process for file delivery. When you're ready to upload your PDFs, contact your printer to find out the procedure. There are a few different ways of uploading to a printer:

1 **Uploading to their website** POD printers such as CreateSpace and IngramSpark will have you log in to your account on their website, then upload the PDFs in the appropriate place within your account. Usually you'll upload the pages PDF first and then you'll upload the cover PDF, and both will run through a file checker. You'll wait for 24 hours to get an email confirmation that the files are ready to go. You can order a printed proof at this time too (the first printed copy of your book!).

2 **Uploading via FTP** Your printer may provide instructions together with an FTP address, username, and password. You'll be able to upload your two PDFs to their FTP site. Once the files are uploaded, confirm with the printer by email that you've uploaded the files, and let them know what your file names are.

3 **Uploading to a printer's production site** Some printers use specific software, such as Insite or MyBooks, to exchange files, proof files, and track your book's production. Your printer will provide you with a login and password, together with instructions for using the site.

Sometimes printers ask you to send the packaged files for your book cover: the InDesign file, linked images, fonts (if you used any outside of Typekit), and high-resolution PDF. This is requested just in case they need to adjust your book's spine width to accommodate a change in paper stocks.

The easiest way to provide your packaged files is to create a .zip file, which compresses all the files and folders into a single file.

Creating a .zip file in Windows

To create a .zip file in Windows, open Windows Explorer. Find the folder containing the files you want to place into your .zip file. Click once on the folder to select it. Right-click your mouse, go to Send to, and click Compressed (zipped) folder. A new .zip icon or file will appear, and you can type in a name for it. Drag any files onto the .zip file that you want to include in it, and the Add dialog box will appear. Click Add to add the file(s), then click OK. To view the contents of the .zip file, simply double-click it to display its contents in Explorer.

Creating a .zip file on a Macintosh

To create a .zip file on a Macintosh, select the packaged folder, then click File>Compress. The resulting file name will end with .zip.

Reviewing printer's proofs

When your printer sends the proofs, check them carefully. Here's what to look for:

- Pages in the right order, all right side up
- See-through issues—hold the pages up so they are backlit and check to see whether the lines of type that are visible through the paper line up with the ones on the other side of the page
- Spots, marks, or streaks on the pages
- Spelling issues on the cover—one last careful check
- Cover colors—they should be very close to what you expect
- Book spine on center
- Dust jacket spine centered and flap copy properly placed

Avoid making any changes to the words in your book at this point. Changes will be expensive.

Congratulations! You're a published author!

Ebook editions: EPUB and MOBI

In this book we are not going to describe how to create an ebook from your InDesign file because the methods are improving and changing all the time, and the topic is big enough to fill another book. This chapter will explain what to expect from an ebook edition and how to prepare your file for conversion.

In this chapter you will learn:

- What EPUB and MOBI files are and why you need both
- What you will lose in an ebook edition
- What you will gain in an ebook edition
- When an ebook edition would be impractical
- How your book is protected against excessive downloads
- How to prepare your InDesign files for conversion

We recommend sending your well-prepared InDesign file to an ebook conversion service.

What are EPUB and MOBI files?

Basically, an EPUB file is an ebook file that can be read on all ebook readers (except the Kindle), and by Adobe Digital Editions on a computer or mobile device. A MOBI file can be read on a Kindle device or the Kindle ebook reader for a computer or mobile device. InDesign exports only to EPUB, and the EPUB file must be further converted to create a MOBI file. In order to make downloading as easy as possible for your potential readers, you need to offer both formats.

Adobe Digital Editions is available for download, free of charge, at www.adobe.com/products/digitaleditions. It is not an ebook reader but simulates the ebook reading experience pretty well.

What you will lose in an ebook edition

Some of the features that you designed with great care are going to disappear in your ebook. Similar to a website, the way an ebook looks depends on the device that's being used to view it. Some ebook readers have color screens, and some don't. Some have built-in proprietary designs that take over all books and simply display them all the same. The only thing that's guaranteed to remain in the ebook is the words. Once you come to terms with this idea, you'll feel better about losing the features in the list below.

Of course you can leave all of these features in your print book. But you might need or want to go back and make a new version for EPUB. Remember to give it a different file name.

- **Folios and running heads** In an ebook, your folios and running heads become irrelevant because the sizes of the screen and the text determine the page breaks.
- **The back cover** Sadly, this is not needed in an ebook. All that great information that you gathered for the back cover can go on your book's website and on the online bookstore's description instead. You can use it for your ebook's and website's metadata descriptions, too.
- **Extra word spaces and linespaces** Remember that we advised you not to use multiple linespaces or word spaces when typesetting? This is the reason. Ebook coding cannot recognize multiple word or linespaces and will use only one, no matter how many you have on your page. If you need to, go back and find (Ctrl/Cmd+F) all the multiple word spaces and change them to en, em, or other fixed spaces. Also, add Space Before and Space After in your paragraph styles.
- **Tabs** Believe it or not, EPUB does not recognize tabs. Go back and convert your tabbed lists to tables or put them in multicolumn text frames. For numbered lists, use the Bullets and Numbering area of the Paragraph Styles panel to change your numbered list styles. Bulleted lists, if styled as described in this book, will be fine the way they are.
- **All your careful typesetting** In your ebook you will see widows and orphans everywhere! But try not to fret because someone else will see different widows—it all depends on their device and the size of the text on their screen. If there is some type that simply must sit just so on a page, alert your conversion service. They will isolate that section and treat it like a piece of art, placing it where you want it. (See an example on page 468.)

If you need to change your list styles, carefully review each list afterward to see how it turned out. You might need to delete some numbers or make other changes.

What you will gain in an ebook edition

In some cases, ebooks can give the reader a better experience than a print book. One reason is that they can see color versions of your illustrations (if they have a color device). For some people, being able to greatly enlarge the type makes ebooks the only viable way to read a book at all. Other readers simply like the fact that they can loads dozens of books onto their device at once. Also, because ebooks usually cost less, people buy more of them. And don't forget that reading ebooks saves trees, too.

Specifically, here's what you'll gain in your ebook edition:

- **Color** If your book is printed in black only and you have illustrations, save RGB color versions of the illustrations and use them here. Even without illustrations, your book can be made more appealing with color in your headings, chapter openers, sidebar backgrounds, and so on. You can go back now and create a new RGB color version of your book by making a few changes in your paragraph styles. (Aren't paragraph styles wonderful?)

- **Hyperlinks** InDesign automatically creates links to websites (from URLs in the text) or email addresses (if they are spelled out in the text) when the file is converted to EPUB. If the device is able, it will jump to the link on the Internet while the reader is still on the book page; this is indisputably very handy. Also you can add links to websites, to other pages in your book, or to your glossary, and even have pop-up footnotes or definitions for your key terms. (Some reader devices support this, but others don't.) And finally, your automatic table of contents (see chapter 28) links to the pages listed there.

Review how to convert from one color mode to another in chapter 46.

ı of the Paragraph Styles
ƷB colors.
ıdd <u>hyperlinks</u>. Set the l
) and
n sei

hyperlink A reference that the reader can directly follow either by clicking or by hovering or that is ɗ tɑl followed automatically.

a pop-up

When an ebook would be impractical

There are several factors that might make your book a poor fit for ebook conversion:

- **Complicated layout** The more complex the layout of your book is, the more difficult it will be to convert. If you have tables, sidebars, pullout quotes, large illustrations, and other complicating items in your print book, you might find that the cost of conversion is not worth it. You might also find that it's not possible to place all the images and sidebars exactly where you'd like to see them.

- **Many illustrations** A heavily illustrated book might result in a file that's too large to be practical for downloading. Also, you might be

Creating hyperlinks

A hyperlink has two parts: a destination (a website or a phrase in the text) and a source (the text or image you want to jump from to get to the destination). To make a hyperlink in InDesign, you must create the destination first and then link to it from the text. Destinations can be used multiple times, but each source can link to only one destination.

Destination

Open the Hyperlinks panel by going to Window> Interactive>Hyperlinks. Select New Hyperlink Destination from the fly-out menu. Choose Text Anchor (specific words somewhere in your text), or URL (web address) destination type. Choosing a Page destination is impractical in an ebook because, of course, you don't know what ebook page any of your text will be on.

- **To make a Text Anchor destination,** highlight the destination word(s) (the anchor) in your text, open New Hyperlink Destination, choose Text Anchor from the Type list, then name the anchor carefully, keeping in mind other destinations that might have similar names. Keep a record of your anchors—the text itself, the anchor names, and where they are located.
- **To make an Internet destination,** open New Hyperlink Destination, choose URL from the Type list, and type (or paste) the address in the URL field. You may also give the URL a name in the Name field. If you have used this URL as a destination before, the name will appear in the drop-down list at the top of the panel.

Source

Highlight the source in the text—the words or image you want to jump from to get to the destination. Open the Hyperlinks panel and go to New Hyperlink in the fly-out menu. Specify the kind of destination in the Link To list: Text Anchor or URL (or files or email). Then choose the name of the specific destination from the drop-down list. Make sure you are linking to the correct document, too.

If you've made a hyperlink character style, you can apply that style in the lower part of the dialog box.

Click OK and your hyperlink is in place. To delete your link, highlight the source, then click on the trash can on the main page of the Hyperlinks panel.

To find out about some of the other hyperlink functions, complete an InDesign tutorial.

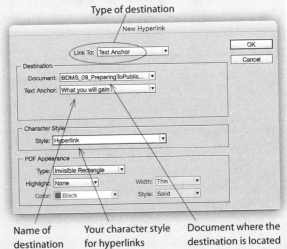

Type of destination

Name of destination

Your character style for hyperlinks

Document where the destination is located

disappointed by the size and look of the images, especially in a black-only ereader or a tiny phone.

- **How-to books** In some cases, the reader needs to have a physical book to view while working step-by-step through a complicated process, such as designing a book. If you think the user should be able to flip back and forth between pages and perhaps write in the margins, you very well might want to avoid an ebook version. (As we write this, we are pondering whether an ebook would be a useful option for potential readers of *Book Design Made Simple*.)

To sum this up, ebooks work best for material that is linear in nature—beginning to middle to end—like a novel. The more additional features the book has, the less likely it is to work well as an ebook. But consult with your conversion service to see whether they can handle your material, and ask to see samples of similar ebooks that they have made.

Protection from excessive downloads

Your ebook file is not automatically DRM (Digital Rights Management) protected. This protection is added by your vendor, if you choose to use one. For example, when your MOBI file is uploaded to your Amazon Kindle Direct Publishing account, Amazon will add DRM protection and sell your ebook to the public in their AZW format. This format restricts the number of downloads by the same user to six different devices.

How to prepare your InDesign files for conversion

If you have carefully followed the instructions in *Book Design Made Simple,* your files should be almost ready for conversion now. Did you remember to:

- create a paragraph style for every single paragraph in your book?
- create a character style for every single character in your book (except those that are [None])?
- use em, en, and other set spaces in place of multiple word spaces?
- use Space Before and Space After in place of multiple linespaces?

- avoid using tabs? EPUB does not recognize tabs. (This might affect your numbered lists but probably not your tables.)
- generate an automatic table of contents (if you have one)?

If you've answered "yes" to all of the above, good for you! You now simply need to consider a few more things—we mentioned these earlier:

- You may use color illustrations in place of your grayscales ones. Most images start out in RGB mode, but if you need to convert from CMYK, return to chapter 46 to review how to do that. If necessary, go back to page 317 to learn how to replace the old images with new ones by relinking.
- You may make color headings, chapter openings, and sidebar backgrounds if you like. To do this, change your paragraph and character styles. Go to the Character Color area of the Paragraph Styles and/or Character Styles panels and specify RGB colors in the Character Color area and/or the Paragraph Shading area.
- You may add hyperlinks. See the sidebar on page 466 for instructions. Make a new character style for the link sources. Often they are set in a different color (usually R0_G0_B255).
- You should tell your conversion people about anything that you need to cement in place on a page. For instance, you might have some display type that needs to be positioned just so, like this:

Haunted House
THIS Way →

They will save it as an object and anchor it to the page just where it belongs.

There may be other ways that you can redesign certain elements that would conform better to ebook requirements—consult with your conversion provider. Good, direct communication with your provider is very important. For the simplest books, one of the less expensive services might be all you need, but for those with higher levels of complexity, we recommend using a conversion provider with personal service and a good reputation.

See our website at www.BookDesign MadeSimple.com for recommended providers.

References

Glossary

The page on which each term is defined or first mentioned is listed in parentheses.

2-up (*14*)   With both pages of a 2-page spread visible at once.

anchored object (*350*)   A graphic or photo that is locked in place in a line of text. In this book we refer to these as *inline objects*.

autoflow (*48*)   An InDesign feature that allows text to flow from one page to all of the rest of the book pages automatically. To use autoflow, with the Selection Tool, click on the **out port** on the current last page of text, and you'll see the loaded text icon. Go to the next page, press the Shift key, and click the left mouse button in the upper left corner of that page. The remainder of your text will automatically flow onto the rest of the pages of the book.

back matter (*23*)   All the material that comes after the last page of regular text in a book. Also called *end matter*.

banding (*263*)   In a gradient, the appearance of bands of color.

bitmap (*303*)   A format for art files that are only black and white with no grays or color. Can be abbreviated .bmp in filename extensions but is also supported by **TIFF** format.

bleed (*275*)   Anything that runs off the edge of the page when printed. In your InDesign document, this material should overlap the edge of the page by 0.125″.

book block (*414*)   After the pages are printed on large sheets of paper and folded into **signatures**, the signatures are assembled into a book ready for binding. The set of signatures for one book is called a book block. Another name for this is **F&Gs** (folded and gathered).

bottom margin (*124*)   White space at the bottom of the page. Optimally, this space should be quite large, allowing plenty of room for the reader's thumb to hold the book without blocking any of the text.

bounding box (*298*)   The rectangular **frame** that surrounds a graphic object or image. The box has eight handles for editing its shape and size. Also referred to as a **frame**.

caption (*27*)   Text commentary related to an illustration, photo, or chart. A caption is usually placed just above, below, or to the side of the illustration.

cardstock (*444*)   Thick paper that is used for softcover book covers.

casebound (*409*)   *See* **hardcover**.

chapter title (*27*)   The name given to a section of a book.

character (*80*)   Unicode is an international system that organizes and names every symbol in each of the world's writing systems. Each symbol (e.g., T, a, &, ġ, ÷) is called a character. *See also* **glyph**.

character style (*80*)   A collection of attributes applied to a type character.

CMYK (*257*)   Cyan, magenta, yellow, and black, the four ink colors that make up a regular "full-color" printing job. *See also* **RGB**.

coated (*444*)   A paper surface with a smooth material applied to it. Not the same as a protective coating.

concealed Wire-O® (*408*)   A **Wire-O®** binding in which the wires are concealed by the cover material so that the spine can be printed.

Control panel (*18*)   The panel across the top of the InDesign workspace. It displays most of the type or object settings that are currently in use.

crash (*171*)   When two characters touch each other it's called a type crash. Usually the characters should be separated; use **kerning** (for two characters) or **tracking** (for a series of characters), or add leading for crashes between two lines.

crossover (*293*)   A single shape or image that spans both pages of a spread.

digital press (*22*)   High-quality laser press that uses toner rather than ink to apply type and images to paper.

dingbat (*220*)   Nonalphabetic type symbol , such as ■, ③, ✗, or ➜. Dingbats are often made up into their own font (e.g., Wingdings or ITC Zapf Dingbats). *See also* **ornament**.

discretionary hyphen (*359*)   A hyphen inserted manually (Type>Insert Special Character>Hyphens and Dashes>Discretionary Hyphen) that remains invisible unless needed to break a word. Also called a soft hyphen.

dot leader (*233*)   A tab function that creates a horizontal line of dots from the cursor to the next tab stop. Commonly used in tables of contents, charts, or lists, to connect information visually for the reader.

dots per inch (dpi)   In printing, the number of dots of ink in a one-inch line that make it possible to print **grayscale** or **CMYK**; also called lines per inch. In digital printing, dpi is the output resolution of the printer—as opposed to the input resolution, or **ppi**, of an image. "150 dpi" is actually 150 × 150 (22,500) dots in a square inch.

drop cap (*40*)   A large initial uppercase letter with its baseline aligning with the base of the second, third, or lower line of the paragraph. *See also* **initial cap**.

em   A horizontal measurement that is equal to the size of the type. An em in 11-point type is 11 points; in 24-point type it is 24 points.

em dash (*340*)   A dash that is approximately equal to the width of an **em**.

em space (*185*)   White space that is equal to the width of an **em**.

en   A horizontal measurement equal to one half of an **em**. An **en** in 11-point type is 5.5 points; in 24-point type it is 12 points.

en dash (*340*)   A dash that is approximately equal to the length of an en. En dashes are used primarily between two numbers (e.g., 12–27).

en space (*185*)   White space equal to the width of an **en**.

endnotes (*25*)   Numbered notes that are gathered at the end of the book or chapter instead of being set as footnotes.

endsheets (*410*)   The paper pasted to the inside of the front and back covers of a **hardcover** book. The sheets serve to hide the turned-in parts of the cover material and to attach the pages to the cover. Also called *endpapers*.

epigraph (*24*)   A quotation that appears at the start of a book.

EPS (*303*)   Encapsulated Postscript format that can contain vector and bitmap graphics produced in Illustrator or Photoshop.

F&Gs   Stands for folded and gathered. *See* **book block**.

fly-out panel (*17*)   A menu that appears when a topic is selected in the set of panels on the right side of the InDesign workspace.

figures (numbers, digits) (*42*)   Arabic numerals.

folio (*26*)   Page number.

font (*131*)   The electronic mechanism that delivers a **typeface**. Each typeface may consist of several different fonts, such as italic, bold, bold condensed, etc. *See also* **typeface**.

footnote (*348*)   Explanatory note that appears at the bottom of a page.

frame (*47*)   Every object in an InDesign document is contained in a frame. Even if you do not draw a frame, InDesign will make a box around type or graphics. *See also* **bounding box, text frame**.

front matter (*23*)   All the material before page 1 in a book.

GBC (*408*)   This type of binding holds the pages together with a cylindrical plastic comb, requiring rectangular holes to be punched near the inside edges of the pages. The spine can be printed on. The name comes from the company that introduced the technique: General Binding Corporation.

GIF (*408*)   Graphics Interchange Format (pronounced "jiff"). This file format is used mainly for solid-colored graphics on the Internet. The files are compressed to the smallest possible size. Usually not compatible with book printing unless used very small.

glyph (*337*)   A specific design of a type character. For instance, the Q character has a different glyph in each typeface: Q, Q, Q, etc. *See also* **character**.

gradient (*262*)   A smooth transition between two or a series of colors or tints, such as black to white, or orange to purple to blue.

grayscale (*303*)   The term for what used to be called "black and white," as in photos. Grayscale includes all shades of gray as well as black and white and so is a more accurate description.

GREP (*51*)   A type of search used in the Find/Change function that looks for patterns rather than specific words or characters. The term comes from an application designed in the early 1970s for a Unix computer system and stands for Global/Regular Expression/Print.

gutter (*126*)   The space between columns. Also, the inside margin where facing pages meet.

H&J (*39*)   Hyphenation and justification.

hanging indent (*65*)   An indent with the first line sticking out to the left more than the lines that follow it. The glossary you are reading is set using hanging indents.

hard page break   *See* **page break**.

hard return (*50*)   A line return that forces a new paragraph; also called an end-of-paragraph return. Place the cursor where you want the break, then press Enter/Return. *See also* **soft return**.

hardcover (*407*)   A book binding with a cloth- or paper-covered board on the front and back. Also known as *casebound*.

headband (*409*)   A decorative cloth band fastened under the spine at the top and bottom of a hardcover book.

heading (*26*)   Title of a section of text.

hyphen (*39*)   A short dash used to break a word between lines or parts, or between digits in a phone number. Do not confuse with an **en dash** or **em dash**.

ICC color profile (*307*)   The International Color Consortium develops international color standards (profiles) that are vendor-neutral. This makes the color data for a book both understandable to and portable among printers.

imposition (*321*)   The arrangement of pages on a printing sheet so that they will be in the correct order when folded.

in port (*49*)   A small box that appears near the upper left corner of a text frame in InDesign, visible when the text frame is selected with the Selection tool.

initial cap (*165*)   A large letter set at the beginning of a section. An initial cap aligns at base with the first line of regular text. *See also* **drop cap**.

ink density (*401*)   The total amount of ink that is on the printing press in any one spot. This is measured by adding up the percentages (tints) of the C+M+Y+K inks in that spot. Also called **total area coverage**, or TAC.

inside margin (*124*) The margin next to the inside edge, where facing pages meet. Also known as the gutter margin.

JPEG (.jpg) (*305*) Joint Photographic Experts Group photo file format commonly used by digital cameras and on the web. These files can be used for printing, although **PSD** is a surer bet.

justification (*40*) This refers to the way text lines align with each other. The most common examples are *left* (aligning at left but not on the right—also known as **ragged right**), *center, right* (aligning at right but not on the left), *left justify* (aligning both left and right, but the last line of a paragraph can be short), and *full justify* (aligning both left and right, including the last line of the paragraph). In InDesign, letter and word spacing preferences related to text alignment can be specified (File>Preferences>Justification on a PC, or InDesign>Preferences on a Mac). *See also* **justified**.

justified (*37*) The common name for type that is left justified. *See also* **justification**.

kerning (*337*) Adding or subtracting space between any two type characters. *See also* **tracking**.

keyboard shortcut (*67*) A combination of keys that can be used instead of selecting a menu item. See page 477 for a list of common shortcuts.

leading (*36*) (rhymes with "heading") Space between lines of type, measured in points from the base of one line to the base of the next. The term comes from the days of metal type, when thin bars of lead were placed between lines of type for spacing.

letter spacing (*358*) The space between letters in the same word. You can set values for this in the Justification area of the Paragraph or Paragraph Styles panel. Letter spacing is also affected by **kerning** and **tracking**.

ligature (*36*) Two letters tied together in the same character for better appearance. The most commonly seen are *ff, fi, fl, ffl,* and *Th.*

line art (*310*) Black and white images with no grays. Also called a **bitmap**.

lines per inch *See* **dots per inch (dpi)**. *Compare with* **ppi (pixels per inch)**.

lining figures (*42*) Arabic numerals that are the same size as the uppercase letters of the same font. *See also* **oldstyle figures**.

master page (*119*) A special page in an InDesign document on which all the standard margins and elements that will appear on the actual book pages are set up. A book can have one or many master pages.

normal view (*16*) A view that shows margins, columns, and text and object frames in the InDesign document. Toggle back and forth between normal view and preview (which shows no margins, columns, or frames) by pressing W when nothing else is selected.

offset press (*22*) A press that uses plastic plates and rollers to print ink on paper. Most efficient for 1,000 or more copies.

oldstyle figures (*42*) Arabic numerals that are the same size as the lowercase letters in a font. *See also* **lining figures**.

opening quote (*27*) A quotation that appears at the start of a part or chapter. Usually followed by a **quote attribution**.

OpenType (*42*) A type font format that is interchangeable between Windows and Macintosh systems. OpenType fonts have several useful features, such as built-in small caps, oldstyle numerals, ligatures, and easily built fractions. OpenType faces with "Pro" in the name include European letters with accents; those with "Std" in the name do not. In the InDesign Control panel, each typeface in the list at the upper left has an icon next to its name. A two-color italic "O" is the OpenType icon.

ornament (*105*)   A decorative symbol used most commonly as a paragraph separator. Ornaments may be included as part of a font character set, or they may be gathered into a font of their own.

orphan (*224*)   1) A single word on a line by itself at the end of a paragraph; 2) the first line of a paragraph, positioned at the bottom of a page. Both kinds of orphans should be avoided whenever possible. *See also* **widow**.

out port (*49*)   The small box at the bottom right corner of a page frame, indicating that there is more text. When the out port has a red "+" in it, the text has nowhere to go and should be flowed, or threaded, to the next page. *See also* **overset text**.

outside margin (*124*)   The margin next to the outer edge of a page.

overset text (*454*)   Text that does not fit in a text frame or table cell. Change the shape of the text frame or table cell to accommodate the overset text, or use the **out port** to thread the text to another page or text frame.

page break (*330*)   This forces everything that follows onto the next page. Place the cursor where you want the break, then press Enter/Return on your numeric keypad, or choose Type>Insert Break Character>Page Break.

paragraph separator (*26*)   A graphic, **dingbat**, **ornament**, **rule**, or series of asterisks between paragraphs, indicating the passage of time or a change of topic.

paragraph shading (*211*)   A color or shade that appears behind the type in a paragraph. Shading can be applied in the Paragraph Styles panel or Control panel.

paragraph style (*56*)   A collection of type style, size, spacing, and color attributes assigned to a paragraph.

pasteboard (*14*)   In the InDesign workspace, the area outside of the pages. Use this area for experimenting and for storing objects or type.

Nothing that is on the pasteboard will appear in the book.

PDF (Portable Document Format) (*301*)   A file format that preserves the layout, type, and images just the way you created them in InDesign or another program. Your work is "cemented" in place and can be shared with anyone who has the freely distributed Acrobat Reader. To make a PDF, go to File>Export and choose Adobe PDF.

pica (*33*)   A traditional typsetting measurement unit equal to one-sixth of an inch; 1 pica = 12 points. *See also* **point**.

PNG (*315*)   Portable Network Graphics image file format, best used on the web (RGB color).

point (*33*)   A typesetting unit equal to one 72nd of an inch. 12 points = 1 pica. Abbreviated as pt. *See also* **pica**.

PostScript Type 1 (*132*)   One of the two type "flavors" of OpenType. In the upper left of the Control panel, PostScript font names are shown next to a red lowercase "a" icon. *See also* **OpenType** and **TrueType**.

ppi (pixels per inch) (*306*)   For most book printing, 300 is the optimal ppi for photos, and 800–1200 ppi is recommended for line (bitmapped) art. *Compare with* **dots per inch (dpi)**.

preflight (*453*)   Checking an InDesign document for errors prior to going to press. The Preflight panel is a live checker showing errors at the bottom of the screen.

prepress (*302*)   The work that the printer does to an InDesign, PDF, or Photoshop file to get it ready to go on press.

print-on-demand (POD) (*21*)   A method of digital printing that makes it possible to print one book at a time, as it is needed.

pt (*33*)   Abbreviation for **point**.

quotation (*27*)   Words attributable to a writer or speaker other than the author; usually followed by an attribution (*see* **quote attribution**).

quote attribution (*27*)   The writer or speaker of the words in the quotation.

ragged right (*37*)   Type **justification** with all lines aligning on the left but not on the right (such as in *this* glossary).

recto (*24*)   Right-hand page.

resample (*303*)   An action in Photoshop that rearranges the pixels of an image in order to change its **resolution** while maintaining its physical size.

resolution (*306*)   *In digital images,* the amount of detail the image holds, measured in **pixels per inch (ppi)**—this is the input resolution. 72 ppi is standard for a computer, phone, or camera screen. 300 ppi is standard for printing. *In printing,* the number of ink **dots per inch (dpi)** that the offset or digital printer can produce—this is the output resolution.

RGB (*257*)   Red, green, and blue, the three colors used by digital cameras, scanners, and computer monitors to display "full color." RGB is not used in printing on a press. *See also* **CMYK**.

rule (*57*)   A straight line in any style (dashed, dotted, etc.) that is drawn or typeset.

run-in subhead (*26*)   A heading that appears at the start of a paragraph, with text following it on the same line.

running head or foot (*26*)   Information about the book, placed above or below the text block. It can be used for navigation of the book, or it can simply show the book author and title.

saddle stitch (*408*)   A binding for books consisting of only one **signature**. Two or three staples hold the pages together at the fold.

sheet-fed press   A printing press that prints ink on single sheets of paper. *See also* **offset press** and **web press**.

shortcut (*67*)   A keyboard shortcut can be created and used to apply character or paragraph styles to text. See a list of commonly used shortcuts on page 477.

short-run printing   Printing in small quantities (usually 50–999).

sidebar (*70*)   Supplemental material that is designed differently and placed apart from the rest of the text on the page.

signature (*322*)   Group of book pages that are printed on the same sheet and folded so that they form a booklet. Signatures are then gathered together and bound. The number of pages in a signature varies according to the dimensions of both the paper and the book pages. Common numbers of pages in a signature are 16 and 32 (for sheet-fed presses), and 24 and 48 (for web presses).

small caps (*81*)   Capital letters that are approximately the same height as the lowercase letters in a font. Commonly used for acronyms and terms such as A.M., P.M., B.C., and A.D.

Smyth-sewn (*408*)   A type of binding that involves sewing signatures together before putting the cover on.

soft hyphen (*359*)   *See* **discretionary hyphen**.

soft return (*147*)   A line return that forces a new line but keeps it within the same paragraph. Place the cursor where you want the break, then press Shift+Enter/Return. *See also* **hard return**.

softcover (*407*)   Commonly called a paperback, but softcovers can also be made of a plastic material.

spiral (*408*)   A type of binding that uses one continuous metal wire (plastic coated or not), curled into a spiral, to hold the pages together. Also called *coil*.

stamping (*442*)   The process of using ink or metal foil to apply lettering or other designs to a cloth-bound hardcover book. With blind stamping (also called *blind embossing*), the design is pressed into the cover with no ink or foil.

story (*97*)   All the text that is connected by the same series of text **threads**.

swatch (258)   A small sample of a color. The Swatches panel in InDesign lists all the named colors in the document.

tabular figures (42)   Numerals, either **lining** or **oldstyle**, that are spaced evenly so that they can be aligned in columns.

text block (46)   The area on a page in which the main body of text is placed. The text block does not include the **running head**, **running foot**, or **folio**, or any material in a side column.

text frame (16)   A box in which type is placed.

text wrap (296)   The means for allowing type to run around the edges of a graphic shape or image rather than flowing in front of or behind it.

thread (49)   In InDesign, a link from one text frame to the next. Text threads can be made visible by going to View>Extras>Show Text Threads, then selecting any text frame with the Selection tool.

TIFF (.tif) (303)   Tagged Image File Format. A flexible image format that supports all color modes. Easily imported into InDesign, it is a popular file format used in printed books.

tint (259)   Less than 100% of a color. For example, a light gray is actually 10% black.

top margin (124)   The margin at the top of a page; also known as the head margin.

total area coverage (401)   *See* **ink density**.

tracking (36)   Adding or subtracting space between groups of letters. Not the same as **kerning**.

trade paperback (407)   A paperback produced for the general public, as opposed to a textbook, an academic book, or other specialized book.

trim size (20)   The size of the pages of a book, measured in inches, horizontal × vertical, after the book has been trimmed down to its final size.

TrueType (132)   One of the two typeface "flavors" of OpenType. In the upper left area of the Control panel, TrueType fonts have a blue double "T" icon next to them. *See also* **PostScript Type 1** and **OpenType**.

turnover line (205)   A line in a list entry or a heading that continues after the first line. Also called *turned line* or simply *turn*.

typeface (5)   A group of related styles of type. Garamond and Minion are two examples of typefaces; each has many instances, such as italic, bold, semibold, etc. *See also* **font**.

uncoated (443)   Paper that has not been treated with any substance to make it smoother.

vector image (303)   A drawing in which shapes are described with mathematical expressions called vectors. Vector images generally have a flatter appearance than photographs. They can be printed at any size without loss of quality. Anything drawn in Adobe Illustrator is a vector image.

verso (24)   Left-hand page.

web press (22)   A very large printing press that prints from rolls of paper and is used to print great quantities of books. *See also* **digital press, sheet-fed press,** and **offset press**.

weight (192)   Thickness.

widow (38)   The last line of a paragraph that is positioned at the top of a page. Widows are forbidden in bookmaking. *See also* **orphan**.

Wire-O® (408)   A type of binding that is similar to **spiral** but sturdier. The wires are paired and parallel to each other. *See also* **concealed Wire-O**.

word spacing (40)   The amount of space between words, controlled in the Justification section of the Paragraph or Paragraph Styles panel.

Keyboard shortcuts

InDesign provides many, many keyboard shortcuts. Below are some of the ones you'll use most often.

File functions

New . . . . Ctrl/Cmd+N
Open . . . . Ctrl/Cmd+O
Close . . . . Ctrl/Cmd+W
Quit/Exit . . . . Ctrl/Cmd+Q
Print . . . . .Ctrl/Cmd+P
Export (to PDF) . . . . .Ctrl/Cmd+E
Save . . . . .Ctrl/Cmd+S
Save As . . . . Ctrl/Cmd+Shift+S

Navigation

Page view—Normal to Preview, Preview
    to Normal . . . . W
Zoom in . . . . .Ctrl/Cmd+=
Zoom out . . . . Ctrl/Cmd+- (hyphen)
Fit page view to window . . . . Ctrl/Cmd+0 (zero)
Actual size . . . . Ctrl/Cmd+1
Jump to page . . . . . . .Ctrl/Cmd+J, then page number

Type and objects

Switch to Selection Tool. V
Switch to Type Tool. . . . . T
Undo . . . . .Ctrl/Cmd+Z
Redo . . . . Ctrl/Cmd+Shift+Z

Find/Change . . . . .Ctrl/Cmd+F
Show Tabs panel . . . . Ctrl/Cmd+Shift+T
Select all . . . . .Ctrl/Cmd+A
Group . . . . Ctrl/Cmd+G
Ungroup . . . . .Ctrl/Cmd+Shift+G
Em space. Ctrl/Cmd+Shift+M
Em dash . . . . Alt/Opt+Shift+- (hyphen)
En space . . . . .Ctrl/Cmd+Shift+N
En dash. .Alt/Opt+- (hyphen)
Forced line break. . . . . .Shift+Enter/Return
Nonbreaking space . . . . .Ctrl/Cmd+Alt/Opt+X
Copy . . . . .Ctrl/Cmd+C
Cut . . . . .Ctrl/Cmd+X
Paste . . . . .Ctrl/Cmd+V
Paste in Place . . . . Ctrl/Cmd+Alt/Opt+Shift+V
Place (image or text). . . . . Ctrl/Cmd+D
Bring to the front . . . . .Ctrl/Cmd+Shift+]
Send to the back . . . . .Ctrl/Cmd+Shift+[
Bring forward . . . . Ctrl/Cmd+]
Send backward . . . . Ctrl/Cmd+[
Text frame options . . . . .Ctrl/Cmd+B
Select frame on master . . . . . . Ctrl/Cmd+Shift+click
Quick scroll to a new typeface
    in the Control panel. . . . . .Type first letter
                     of typeface name

The self-publishing process

Note that several activities can be going on simultaneously. The items in gray boxes are discussed in this book, with chapter references noted in parentheses.

1
- Begin your market research (chapters 5 and 55).
- Write the book.

2
- Work with an editor until your copy is finished.
- Ask for permission to borrow material (chapters 28 and 41).

3
- Plan your pages for design (chapter 6).
- Lease Adobe Creative Cloud package (chapter 3).

4
- Design and lay out your main text (chapters 1–54).
- Design your front and back matter (chapters 28 and 29).
- Obtain your ISBN, CIP, and/or LCCN (chapters 28 and 68).

5
- Send your pages out for proofreading (chapter 53).
- Obtain your permissions (see step 2).
- Create your book's website (with blog) and social media.

6
- Design your cover (and dust jacket) (chapters 55–67).
- Choose a price and obtain your barcode (chapters 64 and 70).
- Order advance review copies.

7	Typeset your proof-reader's corrections (chapter 53).	Send your chapters out to an indexer (chapter 54).	Send out advance review copies.
8	Add testimonials to book cover (chapters 63 and 64).	Finish cover and jacket (chapter 67).	Complete your copyright page (chapter 28).
9	Add your index (chapter 54).	Prepare final PDFs and send to printer (chapter 71).	Prepare your file for an ebook edition (chapter 73).
10	Review printer's proofs (chapter 72).	Update your website and start selling.	Make arrangements with distributors or online vendors.
11	Receive printed books.	Notify www.BookDesignMadeSimple.com of publication. Send PDFs of your pages and cover for inclusion on the website.	
12	Congratulations, you're a published author! Way to go!		

Bibliography

Adobe® InDesign CS3 User Guide for Windows and Macintosh. San Jose, CA: Adobe Systems Incorporated, 2007.

Adobe® Photoshop CS3 User Guide for Windows and Macintosh. San Jose, CA: Adobe Systems Incorporated, 2007.

Birdsall, Derek. *Notes on Book Design*. New Haven: Yale University Press, 2004.

Bringhurst, Robert. *The Elements of Typographic Style*. Vancouver: Hartley & Marks, 2004.

The Chicago Manual of Style: 16th Edition. Chicago: University of Chicago Press, 2010.

Craig, James, and William Bevington. *Designing with Type*. New York: Watson-Guptill Publications, 1999.

Eckersley, Richard, et al. *Glossary of Typesetting Terms*. Chicago: University of Chicago Press, 1994.

Felici, James. *The Complete Manual of Typography*. Berkeley: Peachpit Press, 2003.

Haslam, Andrew. *Book Design: A Comprehensive Guide*. New York: Abrams, 2006.

Hendel, Richard. *On Book Design*. New Haven: Yale University Press, 1998.

Holleley, Douglas. *Digital Book Design and Publishing*. New York: Clarellen and Cary Graphic Arts Press, 2001.

Kelby, Scott. *Photoshop 7 Down & Dirty Tricks*. New Riders Publishing, 2002.

Lee, Marshall. *Bookmaking: The Illustrated Guide to Design & Production*. New York: R.R. Bowker, 1965.

Lupton, Ellen. *Indie Publishing*. New York: Princeton Architectural Press, 2008.

Lupton, Ellen. *Thinking with Type*. New York: Princeton Architectural Press, 2004.

McClelland, Deke. *Adobe Photoshop CS5 One-on-One*. Sebastopol, CA: Deke Press/O'Reilly Media, Inc., 2010.

Mitchell, Michael, and Susan Wightman. *Book Typography: A Designer's Manual*. Somerset, UK: Butler & Tanner Ltd., 2005.

Rafaeli, Ari. *Book Typography*. New Castle, DE: Oak Knoll Press, 2005.

Ross, Marilyn, and Sue Collier. *The Complete Guide to Self-Publishing: Everything You Need to Know to Write, Publish, Promote and Sell Your Own Book*, 5th ed. Cleveland: Writers Digest Books, 2010.

Spiekermann, Erik, and E.M. Ginger. *Stop Stealing Sheep & Find Out How Type Works*. Berkeley: Adobe Press, 2003.

Williams, Robin. *The Non-Designer's Type Book*. Berkeley: Peachpit Press, 1998.

Wilson, Adrian. *The Design of Books*. San Francisco: Chronicle Books, 1993.

Index

uploading files to printer, 461–462

printer's proofs, reviewing, 462

print-on-demand printers, trim sizes for, 21

Printorium, trim sizes for, 21

proofreading corrections, 366–367

symbols for, 366–367

proofs with front cover, printing, 406

Proportional Lining figures, 42

Proportional Oldstyle figures, 42

PSD format, optimizing images in, 305

public domain images, permissions for, 284

publisher numbers

explanation of, 447

in ISBNs, 446

publishing information

adding, 430

on back cover, 424

on copyright page, 225, 226

punctuation

boldface for, 341

italics for, 341

roman punctuation, using, 341

typesetting punctuation, 339–341

Puritan Capital, trim sizes for, 21

Q

QR (Quick Response) codes, 424

quality of printing methods, 22

Query drop-down box

beginning/end of paragraph, removing spaces from, 52

end-of-paragraph returns, removing, 51

quotation marks, changing, 53

question marks, typesetting for, 341

quotation marks, 45, 53

with chapter opening quotes, 195

with extracts, 195

as first character in chapter, 153

quotations. *See also* extracts; opening quotes

attributions, 27

pages, 24

Typographer's Quotes, 45, 53

R

ragged right text, 39

Rectangle Frame Tool, 267

rectangles

corner options, adding, 273

creating, 266

Rectangle Tool, 266–267

corner options to rectangles, adding, 273

recto pages, 23

blank recto pictures, 361

folios, adding, 111

increasing page count by starting pages on, 323

part openers on, 175

running heads, adding, 112

starting chapters on, 107

reference numbers, 81, 85, 93, 337, 348

references, designing, 253–254

relinking optimized images, 317

repeat elements

for chapter openings, 143–144

in part openers, 175

on title page, 223

repetition in front cover design, 392

Replika, trim sizes for, 21

reports on packaging files, viewing, 457

resolution issues with PPI, resolving, 306–307

restoring to earlier version, 86

reversing mistakes, 86

reverting to last save, 86

reviews on back cover, 423

RGB colors, 257

camera/scanner images in, 307

Illustrator, converting to CMYK in, 311

optimizing images and, 303

Photoshop, converting to CMYK in, 308

ribbons for hardcovers, 442

RIFF format, 303

rivers, avoiding, 360

roman numerals for front matter pages, 24

roman type for punctuation, 341

rotated ornament, characteristic chapter openings with, 169–170

rotated text, 433

roughing in

back matter, 109

front matter, 95

rounded corners, modern sidebar with, 214–217

.rtf files, importing, 44

rule of three, 144–145

in part openers, 175

on title page, 223

Ruler Units to inches, changing, 33

rules. *See* paragraph rules

run-in style headings, 185

run-in subheads, 26, 80

creating character style for, 84

running heads/feet, 26, 27

alignment for, 219–220

A-Master, adding to, 112

author's name, 219

baseline grids, adjusting for, 139–140

book title in, 219

examples of, 137
for folios, 221
increasing to add page count, 324
margins and, 125
for running heads/feet, 221
setting, 135
Type Tester, Typekit, 10
Type Tool, 16, 18
Typographer's Quotes, 45
typographic elements, 26–27
and paragraph styles, 57

U

underline options, 42
undoing
margin changes, 127
mistakes, 86
unnumbered/unordered lists, designing, 201–203
URLs. *See* website URLs
U.S. Copyright Office address, 227
U.S. ISBN Agency, 446

V

verso pages, 23
folios, adding, 111
running heads, adding, 112
starting chapters on, 107
View Tool, 16

Vook, 449

W

website URLs
adding, 430
on back cover, 424
on copyright page, 225, 226
enlarging, 434
QR (Quick Response) codes for, 424
white space
benefits of, 123
for chapter openings, 145
in front cover design, 393
Hyphenation Zone limiting, 39
paragraph styles controlling, 57
in part openers, 175
rivers, avoiding, 360
on title page, 223
widows, 38
defined, 224
layout and, 358
Wikimedia Commons images, 283
Windows OS
OpenType fonts with, 132
working with InDesign in, 4
.zip files, creating, 462
WingDings, 106
Wire-O bindings, 408
Word

bold character style, applying, 90
character styles imported from Word, applying, 88–89
converting to InDesign, 2–3
images from document, extracting, 287
indexes into Word document, 370–371
paragraph styles imported from, 100
placing manuscript from, 44–49
tables to InDesign, importing. 342–344
word breaks, fine-tuning, 359–360
word spacing, 358
in ebooks, 464
justification settings and, 40
wrapping text. *See* text wrap
Wrap To list, 299

Z

.zip files
Macintosh, creating on, 462
Windows, creating in, 462
Zoom Tool, 13, 16

About the authors

Fiona Raven, of Vancouver, Canada, has designed hundreds of books for small presses, independent publishers, and self-publishing authors since 1995. Her clients come from places as far-flung as Saudi Arabia, Japan, and Tonga. Fiona is a self-taught book designer, having learned her craft from reading and examining countless books on typography, design, layout, and software. Every now and then she still gets a hankering to create a book the old-fashioned way—by printing on handmade papers, illustrating with woodcuts or watercolors, and creating a binding by hand.

Glenna Collett has been a book designer in the Boston area for over forty years. She created her first book by hand using metal type, a letterpress, silkscreen illustrations, and a sewn binding. Since then, she has designed more than 100 textbooks for large publishers and dozens of self-published books for individual authors. Glenna also teaches self-publishing workshops, and now that she is a self-published author herself, she brings a deeper understanding of the issues her students may face.

Visit us at

www.BookDesignMadeSimple.com

for updates and more typesetting tips and tricks.